Civil-Military Relations and Shared Responsibility

Civil-Military Relations

AND

Shared Responsibility

A Four-Nation Study

DALE R. HERSPRING

The Johns Hopkins University Press

Baltimore

Printed in the United States of America on acid-free paper
9 8 7 6 5 4 3 2 1

The Johns Hopkins University Press
2715 North Charles Street
Baltimore, Maryland 21218-4363
www.press.jhu.edu

Library of Congress Cataloging-in-Publication Data

Herspring, Dale R. (Dale Roy)
Civil-military relations and shared responsibility : a four-nation study / Dale R. Herspring.
p. cm.
Includes bibliographic references and index.
ISBN 978-1-4214-0928-3 (hbk. : alk. paper) — ISBN 978-1-4214-0929-0 (electronic) — ISBN 1-4214-0928-3 (hbk. : alk. paper) — ISBN 1-4214-0929-1 (electronic)
1. Civil-military relations—Case studies. 2. Civil-military relations—North America. 3. Civil-military relations—Europe. I. Title.
JF195.H47 2013
322'.5—dc23 2012036884

A catalog record for this book is available from the British Library.

Special discounts are available for bulk purchases of this book. For more information, please contact Special Sales at 410-516-6936 or specialsales@press.jhu.edu.

The Johns Hopkins University Press uses environmentally friendly book materials, including recycled text paper that is composed of at least 30 percent post-consumer waste, whenever possible.

To
Lt. Col. and Mrs. Douglas Gillander, RCAF (ret)

In appreciation for their 32 years of dedicated service to an often ungrateful government

Contents

Preface

Of all the books and articles I have written, this is indeed one of the most difficult. Attempting to compare four different polities, each with its own history and culture at times seemed like an overwhelming undertaking. Yet, it seemed to me that it was time to try to test at least one proposition on more than one country. I was lucky that I had already done extensive academic work on civil-military relations and had many years of related professional experience in the State Department and the Pentagon. At State and the Pentagon, I saw the process from both sides. I also had many opportunities to deal with the Soviet, and later Russian, militaries face to face. So, I felt confident in looking at these two polities.

But I needed more than just two. I finally decided on Germany and Canada. I explain in the introduction why I chose these countries, but once having made the decision, I discovered how difficult it is to try to understand civil-military relations in polities such as Germany and Canada after only six to eight months of research. With that in mind, I am fully aware that a Canadian or German expert may find some of my statements or conclusions overly simplistic. I apologize in advance. My purpose was not so much to appear as an expert on the internal military-political politics of either country. Rather, it was to draw attention to some general similarities (and differences), recognizing that one could easily quibble over some of my conclusions and interpretations. Recognizing the idiosyncratic nature of civil-military relations in every polity, one of my goals was to see whether we could make some generalizations, or what some call nomothetic observations.

Another purpose I had in writing this book was to encourage others to undertake similar studies. One challenge is that such analyses often require the knowledge of two or more languages. It also requires knowledge of the countries' history and a sense of their cultures. Unfortunately, given the attitude toward languages, history, and culture by many in my discipline, I suspect this study may be unique. I hope it is not. I encourage those who have language competency and an interest in history to apply this model to other countries, and in the process, confirm or correct some of my conclusions.

If there is one thing that became clear to me early on, it was the invaluable role that readers can play. I was especially lucky to have Marybeth Ulrich read the entire manuscript for the Johns Hopkins University Press. She made invaluable comments, and, most important, did not shy away from making it clear when she believed my comments or assertions were not valid. I tried to incorporate all of her comments, although I suspect she will still disagree with many of my findings.

I sought out others who knew something about the Canadian and German Armies firsthand. Canada was difficult in one sense: of all the four countries discussed here, in Canada the viewpoints of those with a military background and those who were civilians are least compatible. I was able to get some retired Canadian Forces officers to read the Canadian chapters of the manuscript and make corrections, and one of the country's leading civilian specialists, Peter Krasuak, made useful comments. Patrick Armstrong had some helpful observations on the Canadian civil-military process. Given the often bitter differences between the two sides in Canada, I doubt if I have either done justice to the situation or made either side happy.

The same was true of the Bundeswehr. Col. Larry Kelly, USMC (ret), who has lived in Germany and worked with the German military for many years, took the time to comment on the manuscript, as did Professor Donald Abenheim of the Naval Post Graduate School. Their insights as well as the comments by Brigadier General Dieter Farwick (ret) were invaluable, although I may not have always followed their advice. I was fortunate to have several retired Russian officers look over the chapters on Russia.

In addition to the above, I owe several others a big note of thanks. My former colleague Amanda Murdie was supportive throughout this process—working overtime keeping me sane when the combination of Russian, German, and Canadian spelling was close to driving me nuts. Then, too, there was my editor at the Johns Hopkins University Press, Suzanne Flinchbaugh. I owe her a debt of gratitude for her encouragement and willingness to suggest changes when the text did not seem to make sense or she thought of a better, more succinct way of making a point. I would also like to thank Helen Myers for an outstanding job of editing, forcing me to avoid verbosity while pushing me to be clear in dealing with a number of complex issues.

Finally, there is my biggest supporter, one who read and reread parts of the book in an unselfish display of love and devotion to her husband, my wife, Maureen. Her patience in putting up with many, many hours while I was in my study working on this book is appreciated more than she will ever realize. As Hawaiians say when they want to express their deep appreciation for a service rendered, Mahalo nui loa.

Civil-Military Relations and Shared Responsibility

CHAPTER 1

A Conceptual Framework for Shared Responsibility

> Military Service stands by itself; it has some of the qualities of a priesthood, a professional civil servant; of a great bureaucratized business organization and an academic order. . . . It has something of each of these in it but it corresponds to none.
>
> WALTER MILLS

The primary focus of the study of civil-military relations in established, mature, stable polities should not be political control, for political control in such systems is usually a given: officers in all four armies discussed in this book—Germany, Canada, Russia, and the U.S.—took an oath recognizing civilian supremacy. A more useful approach to understanding this special relationship is to focus on the process and not assume a battle between two dichotomous, potentially hostile entities. The uniformed military can be of considerable use to civilian elites in dealing with security issues, provided its views are respected, and senior military officers can provide honest advice without fear of career or personal reprisals. In such a relationship, civilian authorities respect the military and are interested in hearing what senior officers have to say about national security affairs. However, everyone concerned understands that civilian authorities make the final decisions.

In this book, I argue that conflict in the relationship between the civilian and the military is normal, positive, and healthy, provided it is regulated.[1] Give-and-take is at the heart of civil-military relations. Conflict is ubiquitous: it is the engine that drives the national security decision-making process, provided there is mutual respect. Focus, thus, should be on the nature of interactions between the military and its civilian masters. The key to healthy relations is to create and maintain a good working relationship between the two sides, one that is constructive and in which both sides respect each other.

The Nature of Conflict

The relationship between officers and civilian politicians is marked by conflict, in part because every military budget is finite. In the countries discussed here, it is up to the executive, usually in the form of a department of the treasury, to recommend how much of the country's funds to spend and on what. Admirals always think they need more expensive ships, and Marine generals want more and better equipment and weapons. The air force would spend most of the budget on new, faster stealth aircraft or more advanced missiles. And since it bears the brunt of fighting in areas like Iraq, Afghanistan, and Chechnya, the army believes the majority of the budget should be spent on conventional forces.

Deciding which countries have a realistic chance of building a constructive working relationship between the civil and the military is subjective. This framework of mutual respect is of no value in the study of countries in which the military is in charge of the political process; it only applies where the military is subordinate to civilian control, and yet the civilian leaders are interested in working with the military.

Soldiers and Civilians

If conflict is inevitable, how should it be managed? One suggestion comes from Sam Huntington in his seminal work *The Soldier and the State* (1957),[2] in which he argues that strategy and military operations should be separated from policy.[3] Politicians should determine the country's policy and goals, while the military professionals implement their orders. The two factions live in separate worlds. A senior military officer may advise but not become involved in policy making. It is the task of a military professional to learn the mechanics of war and to train the troops so they can carry out missions assigned by the civilian leadership. As Huntington put it, the primary task for the professional military officer is "the direct operation and control of a human organization whose primary function is the application of violence."[4] Because the nature of war has become so technically complex, military specialists are needed in the application of these new deadly forms of violence. Only military leaders know how much force to use and when and how to apply it. If civilians become involved—as is their right—they may undermine the entire operation, since they may not understand either the weapons systems or how to best utilize them in carrying out the mission.[5]

Some scholars agree with Huntington in his attempt to draw a clear line between the tasks carried out by civilians and military officers. For example, Michael Desch maintains, "The best indicator of the strength of civilian control is who prevails when civilian and military preferences diverge."[6] This suggests that it is possible to distinguish between civilian and military preferences in the decision-making process and that the respective individuals should remain within their areas of professional competence. Similarly, Kemp and Hudlin argue, "civilians decide on the ends of policy, and the military is responsible for the means." Furthermore, "the civilians decide where the line between ends and means is drawn."[7] While no one in uniform would question the second statement, this writer argues that the first is an oversimplification.

There are several problems with Huntington's paradigm. It simplifies the nature of the relationship between the military and civilians. Each country discussed here has dealt with serious civil-military problems, but the demarcation between senior military officers and the civilian leadership was seldom as rigid as Huntington's paradigm suggests. The attempt to find the "magic" line over which the military may not cross is illusionary: when the military gets out of line, as happened with General Douglas MacArthur in Korea, it is obvious. In most other cases the boundary shifts depending on the issue and the individuals involved.

I would go farther and suggest that military influence, while important, is not the critical factor in the civil-military relationship.[8] If there is too much emphasis on military influence, in other words on political control, one runs the risk of overlooking the interactive nature of the relationship. It is the interaction between civilian and military leaders that helps define "healthy conflict."[9]

Too often, observers have focused on which side prevailed in the decision-making process: the military or the civilians. This view overlooks the interactive nature of the process. In a shared relationship, neither side "wins." For example, it was long assumed that the military leadership was more in favor of the use of force than civilians. But research by Peter Feaver and Christopher Gelpi has shown that is not the case. Speaking about the George W. Bush administration, they note:

> Within the administration, the strongest proponents of going to war with Iraq were the civilians, especially those who had never served in the military; Vice President Dick Cheney, Deputy Secretary of Defense Paul Wolfowitz, and Chairman of the Defense Policy Board Richard Perle; they argued that the creative uses of special forces and limited strikes could topple the Hussein regime and eliminate Iraq's weapons of mass destruction (WMD).[10]

In many instances, we may never know who cast the deciding vote for policy *x* or *y*.

Assuming the military was excluded or ignored in the decision risks underestimating the complexity of the decision-making process. Not only is it wrong to contrast civilian and military leaders, it is inaccurate to assume that all military officers think or act alike. The different services are often at odds regarding the purchase of weapons systems; one military officer may oppose the use of force in a given situation while another may favor it. The same contradictions apply to civilian leaders.

In most cases political-military decision making is not a zero-sum game. As Gibson and Snider maintained, when it comes to most issues, the two sides will be involved in an "area of overlap and tension." They noted that in the American case, "To our understanding, such decisions are most often made (particularly within the multilevel 'interagency') in a more informal, collegial manner during which the positions of both senior civilian and military leaders are fully vetted and debated."[11] To effectively utilize military power it is necessary to relate issues such as natural resources, demography, political objectives, and the definition of war, including strategy, to the military tools available to achieve foreign policy goals. While civilians are in charge, both sides should learn from each other, and when positions are put forth, both sides need to be prepared to compromise. When civilian officials are wrong, someone from the military must point out the policy's problems. Indeed, if the military is forbidden to speak or is ignored by political authorities, civilians run the risk of ordering the military to do something for which it is not prepared. Deborah Avant emphasized the positive impact of military input when she observed, "A military that uses its expertise to influence policy may be a good thing if it creates policy more likely to achieve a country's goals in the international system."[12] But in the end, it is the civilians who make the final decisions.

Interaction between the military and the civil authorities, however, is not the same in the countries and time periods considered in this book, and is closer and more symbiotic in some instances than it is in others. The American military is more active in the political-military decision process than the Russian armed forces, but even in postcommunist Russia, military officers have been involved in political-military decisions, for example, in Chechnya.

While there have been many studies of civil-military relations in one country, few scholars have analyzed this relationship in a comparative context. One exception is the classic study by Samuel Huntington and Zbigniew Brzezinski, *Political Power, US/USSR* (1964).[13] While both authors were experts in their fields, the book lacked a common framework other than to compare the different structures in both countries. The most ambitious comparative study was written by Michael Desch,[14] who analyzes four countries—France, Germany, Japan, and Russia. He maintains that "militaries with primarily external missions were more amenable to civilian control than militaries with internal missions."[15] Desch points to the oft-neglected importance of external threats, but he does not help us understand situations in the absence of an external threat such as symbiotic or hostile relationships. Desch's analysis seems to be for a broader audience.[16] Peter Feaver applied the rational actor approach to analyzing civil-military relations.[17] In focusing on the United States, he looks at rewards and punishments to determine how and why military officers obey their civilian leaders. However, officers sometimes obey simply out of a sense of duty. Feaver's framework also has limited utility for comparative analyses, as the culture surrounding rewards and punishments may be different depending on the polity concerned.

Rebecca Schiff's useful study marks a step forward because it goes beyond the "institutional or purely rational choice models," instead focusing on the impact of culture on civil-military relations.[18] It highlights the idea of partnership between elites. As she put it, "In fact, the partnering of political elites, the military and the citizenry is the hallmark of concordance theory as well as the institutional and culture perspective the theory offers to the field."[19] She is one of the few theorists willing to take on the much-maligned concept of culture and is to be commended for doing so.

In this study, I focus on a special term: "a shared relationship." It was coined by Douglas Bland, who, with the Canadian situation in mind, suggested that one way of getting around dichotomizing the military and civilian relationship is to look upon political-military decision making as a "shared responsibility." According to Bland, one of the key prerequisites for any model is that it should be capable of analyzing the civil-military relationship in a variety of polities:

> Civil control of the military is managed and maintained through the sharing of responsibility for control between civilian leaders and military officers. Specifically, civil authorities are responsible and accountable for some aspects of control, and military leaders are responsible and accountable for others. Although

> some responsibilities for control may merge, they are not fused. The relationship and arrangement of responsibilities are conditioned by a national evolved regime of "principles, norms, rules and decision-making procedures around which actor expectations converge" in matters of civil-military relations.[20]

Bland noted that this approach is based on two assumptions. First, "the sole legitimate source for the direction and actions of the military is derived from civilians outside the military/defense establishment." Second, "civil control is a dynamic process susceptible to changing ideas, values, circumstances, issues and personalities and to the stresses of crisis and war."[21] Both sides agree to these "rules of the game." As Bland put it, what is involved is "*civilian direction* of the military," not domination.[22] Military officers understand that they are accountable not only to their superior officers, but to the civilian leadership. By and large, misdeeds by uniformed personnel will be handled by the military (e.g., the navy will relieve the captain of a ship if it runs aground), but should an officer fail to carry out a task assigned by the civilian leadership, civilian heads can hold him accountable. In essence, this means that civilians have the right to make mistakes. Military officers do not.

From a theoretical standpoint, shared responsibility is an ideal type, and whether there is shared responsibility is the key question. The answer in this study is situational and also subjective in that the author, after looking at the evolution and nature of civil-military relations in a given period, will have to state why he believes this was or was not a situation of shared responsibility. In this sense, this study cannot be quantified. In attempting to determine whether a system of shared responsibility exists from either the civilian or the armed forces' point of view, the key causal factors from the military's side will be examined.

One might argue that a study of the factors that contribute to the military's willingness (or unwillingness) to participate in shared responsibility might turn out to be "promilitary." The purpose of this book, however, is to provide a conceptual framework to better understand the dynamics of civil-military relations from both sides, but especially from the perspective of those in uniform. The goal is to provide civilians with an understanding of the conditions that are most likely to lead to shared responsibility.

Military Culture

While the idea of culture has long been out of vogue, it remains a useful tool that will provide a basis for comparing the degree to which the civilian and military in each of these countries enjoys or does not enjoy a relationship of shared responsibility.

In their study of military culture, Dorn, Ulmer, Collins, and Jacobs defined culture as "the prevailing values, philosophies, customs, traditions, and structure, that over time, have created shared individual expectations within an institution about appropriate attitudes, personal beliefs and behavior."[23] In another study, Nick Jans and David Schmidtchen noted that "organizations that endure—have distinct and stable personalities that govern most of their behavior, even though they may comprise many, ever-changing individuals."[24] Culture is learned behavior, and in the armed forces, members are socialized to learn how to "act properly" inside the confines of the various services. Military culture is, to a large degree, a result of the organization's effort to prepare its members for its end goal, often referred to as "to kill and break things." The military's organizational culture, by definition, is structured to enable it to fight wars. In fighting a war, military service is unique because the soldier, in carrying out the mission, may be required to lay down his or her life. In this sense, military culture is different from culture in all other organizations.[25]

From the military standpoint, military culture is critical. As Sarkesian and Connor put it, "The military profession stands and falls according to its ability to maintain and reinforce military culture."[26] Military culture sets the soldier or sailor apart from the civilian world. Efforts to compare the military to a business organization or a social group fail because the military's task is different, in that the soldier or sailor stand a higher chance of losing his or her life than in other professions.

Military culture determines how military personnel interact with each other, how they carry out their missions, how they see the outside civilian world, and, perhaps most important in terms of civil-military relations, what kind of behavior they expect from civilians and how they will act in dealing with them. Some of the norms of behavior that are an integral part of military culture exist in all regular armed forces (e.g., saluting, uniforms, chain of command). Others are unique to a particular country (e.g., brutality in the Russian military, bilingualism in the Canadian military). This is to be expected, as some countries share some aspects of political culture but not others, and these four military cultures are reflections of these four civilian societies.[27]

Military culture also refers to virtues such as honor, devotion to duty, service to the nation, and subordinating oneself to those in command—all the way up to the senior civilian official in charge, be he or she president, prime minister, or some other title. However, civilian authorities may modify military culture, at times strengthening the military, as, for example, with the addition of females and African Americans to the American armed forces.

Recognition of the norms of military culture is not a panacea for creating shared responsibility, for the possibility exists that a senior military officer may push matters too far, as General MacArthur did. However, if the norms of military culture are respected, military leaders will be more likely to speak openly and provide their views on issues critical to the political leadership. Conflict between civilian and military may also decrease if the military officers feel they have had their say, even if the political leadership decides on another course of action. The political leadership has the option of treating the military however it wishes, and by and large the latter will obey. However, civilian respect for military norms will maximize communications and result in healthy conflict that will optimize political/military inputs to policy decisions.

Operationalizing Military Culture

Although the concept of military culture is difficult to quantify or define, it is nevertheless useful in helping us understand civil-military relations. In examining military culture, this book will focus on civilian respect for the military and its unique culture. The following indicators of a shared responsibility are based on a wide variety of U.S., Canadian, German, and Russian sources.[28] They are present to varying degrees in all four militaries, although some indicators are more important in one country than in another.

1. *Executive Leadership and Respect for Military Culture.* From the standpoint of a relationship of shared responsibility, this is the most important factor. All militaries are hierarchical. The private looks to the sergeant for direction, the sergeant to the captain, the captain to the colonel, and the colonel to the general. The general at the highest level looks to the civilian leadership. Not only do military officers accept civilian leadership, they expect it. A failure to provide such leadership leads to uncertainty and confusion in the armed forces and difficulty working with the senior civilian leadership. The generals may go off on their own, and lacking central direction, lose the order that is so critical to their effectiveness.

Richard Betts commented that military leaders are expected to play a role in civil-military decision making. How much of a role they play depends on the president/prime minister or the secretary/minister of defense. He noted that when the military is ignored, it becomes "alienated from their administrative superiors." Furthermore, "Military leaders become alienated from their civilian superiors in direct proportion to the decline in their direction, influence and their perception of the gap between their rightful and actual authority."[29] In a polity in which the military is ignored, for whatever reason, the creation of shared responsibility is impossible.

The late American political scientist Richard Neutstadt once observed, "The power of presidential politics is the power to persuade."[30] A president, chancellor, or prime minister, a minister of defense or a secretary of defense will have a better chance of getting senior military officers to accept policies enthusiastically if the generals and admirals believe they are part of the process.

The greater the degree orders are unclear or senior officers are disrespected, the less the chance for shared responsibility.

2. *The Military and Shared Responsibility.* Military officers in all four countries take an oath to obey their civilian superiors. But there are many ways to carry out an order, and a shared responsibility is a two-way street. Generals and admirals must be willing to be involved in a relationship of shared responsibility as well as understand the civil-military process and the limits of their role in it.

The more military officers refuse to deal openly with their civilian superiors, the less the chance for shared responsibility.

3. *Military Symbols.* The military is conservative. It looks to the past for the symbols it lives by—whether medals, the names of bases and barracks, traditions, or procedures. Those who have commanded in major battles, or whose sacrifice was "above and beyond the call of duty" are revered by those in uniform. Military bases, streets on military installations, or even ships are named after them, passing on traditions of bravery, honor, and steadfastness to those who come after. For example, the name of General George S. Patton is ubiquitous on American army bases as is the name of Ulrich de Maiziere in Germany, the name of Georgiy Zhukov in Russia, and the name of General Rick Hillier in Canada.

Failure on the part of civilian leaders to respect military symbols and traditions will lessen the chances for shared responsibility.

4. *The Need for a Military.* For a successful shared relationship, the civilian elite must believe a military is necessary, and that it plays an important role in the national security decision-making process.

Failure on the part of the civilian elite to believe in the necessity for a viable, strong military force will lessen the chances for shared responsibility.

5. *Promotion Process.* The military does not normally object to civilian

involvement in promotion at the highest level, for example, the chairman of the Joint Chiefs of Staff, or chief of the general staff, and perhaps even the heads of the services. The idea of a civilian official, whether from the executive or legislative, determining who gets promoted at lower levels is a violation of military culture, will alienate the serving military, and make those who get promoted look like creatures of the administration and not representatives of the services.

Interference by civilian authorities in the promotion process will lessen the chances for shared responsibility.

6. *Civilianization.* The military believes that it has a specific culture that enables soldiers to carry out their difficult tasks. It strongly objects to those that hold that soldiers are just like civilians, because some jobs may appear similar. An electrician in the navy works on different equipment under different conditions than does a civilian electrician. The same could be said for doctors, chaplains, and public relations officers, not to mention the lack of a civilian counterpart to an infantryman or a tanker. The military will fight hard to avoid having the military civilianized.

Efforts to push civilianization will be opposed by the military and lessen the chances for shared responsibility.

7. *Change.* Change is difficult to accept in any part of military life. Military personnel are some of the most conservative members of society, and they are opposed to anything they believe will undermine combat readiness or unit cohesion. This includes such issues as the integration of blacks and women in the U.S. military or the integration of francophones in Canadian military, or women and former East German military personnel in the German military. Civilians will always be in charge of the process, but the key factor insofar as a shared relationship is the involvement of the military in the process as well as the swiftness and magnitude of change.

Efforts to bring about radical change in the military may undermine any opportunity for shared responsibility.

8. *Dissent.* One of the more sensitive aspects of civil-military relations is the expression of dissent by senior military officers. All of the civilian leaders in the polities discussed here agree that the military has a right to dissent privately. Indeed, it is a critical component of a shared relationship. But what about public expressions of dissension? Here the situation is culturally dependent. Some American scholars have suggested that dissension should be prohibited, even by retired military officers, much less by serving officers.[31]

Authorities in other countries would prohibit dissenting opinions by serving officers but permit officers who object to policy to resign if they feel they cannot carry orders out in good conscience.

The less hospitable the civilian leadership is to the articulation of dissent by retired officers or the resignation/retirement by others, especially if civil-military relations are restrained, the more difficult it may be to maintain a shared relationship.

Implementing the Conceptual Framework

In my book on civil-military relations in the U.S.,[32] I sought to determine whether a relationship of shared responsibility between uniformed military officers and their civilian superiors offers a useful tool for understanding civil-military relations. In the case of the U.S., the study suggested that the key factor was presidential leadership style. If the president wanted to work with the military and the generals were prepared to work with him, the relationship was symbiotic. An additional comparison of U.S. and Russian civil-military relations suggested that this framework could be a useful tool for understanding the Russian situation.[33] But what is the utility of this conceptual framework for understanding civil-military relations in other polities? This framework only applies to polities in which the military demonstrates its acceptance of civilian superiority in the political process. In most cases that means taking an oath, as did members of all four of the militaries discussed in this book. Further, the military must have demonstrated over time that it accepts civilian supremacy, even when it disagrees with the decisions taken by civilian leaders. The U.K., Australia, Italy, China, or France are other states where one would expect this framework of shared responsibility to be useful. The same is true of very small countries such as Sweden and Ireland, in which the military's primary duty has been peacekeeping. However, there are states where it would be difficult to apply this model, for example, Pakistan, Egypt after Mubarek, Argentina at various points in its history, and Germany and Japan prior to and during World War II.

Likewise, the civilian leadership must be interested in working with their military colleagues to build a shared responsibility. For example, President Lyndon Johnson of the U.S., Defense Minister Paul Hellyer of Canada, Russian Defense Minister Anatolii Serdyukov, and German Defense Minister Rudolf Scharping all had little interest in working with senior military officers to develop a shared relationship.

Basic Premises

This book proceeds from the assumption that a shared relationship between civilians and military officers in national security decision making provides a useful framework for viewing civil-military relations for a number of reasons.

First, the U.S. was selected because it was the foundation upon which this model was originally tested. A superpower and a country that has seen stability in civil-military relations for many years, sometimes personal relations between the U.S. president and the military have been good, and sometimes not. But the structural relationship has remained intact. Furthermore, the U.S. is a country in which the military has played a vital role in foreign policy; the president needs the military if he hopes to carry out an effective foreign policy.

Second, Germany provides a very different situation. The Wehrmacht was destroyed in the ashes of World War II, and Germany was left without an army. In the mid-1950s the long struggle to build the Bundeswehr began. This situation provides an opportunity to analyze the search for tradition as well as to observe the military as it went through a lengthy period of adaptation, when it was presented with the need for radical change as its role changed from that of territorial army to an expeditionary force. There was also a lengthy battle over the role for the Bundeswehr in the political system and in the political process. While Russians, Americans, and even Canadians in uniform had their role models, in Germany for many years it was unclear who the soldier should emulate. It was a matter of not just rebuilding the military, but of reintegrating the armed forces into German society. The definition of military culture itself was open to question.

Third, Canada provides yet another type of civil-military relations.[34] In the post–World War II period, civilian leaders such as Trudeau tended to ignore the military, which only played a minor role in foreign policy. Its primary role was peacekeeping, and it was not until the 1990s that it began to play an important part in foreign policy as a combat military force.

Fourth, Russia is unique because it is a former superpower in which the military played an important role during the attempted coup. When the country broke up, however, the military came close to collapse. Civilian leadership ignored the military while the latter struggled to survive. In 2000, a new leader, Vladimir Putin, took over, and attempted to rebuild the military. In 2007, when he learned that 40 percent of the military budget was being siphoned off, he changed defense ministers, appointing a man who undertook a radical restructuring of the Russian military.

Time Periods

Given the profound differences in civil-military relations in these four polities, drawing one time line to fit all of four countries is not useful. For the U.S., I decided to begin in 1960, the beginning of the Vietnam War. One of the most heated periods in civil-military relations in the U.S., it serves as a useful contrast to later administrations. For Russia, I chose to begin with the collapse of the USSR in 1991, which left the Russian military with a new and hostile world of civil-military relations. The military went from being one of strongest institutions in the country, which received whatever it wanted, to a pauper working for a president who had little interest in it.

For Germany, I decided to begin with the creation of the Bundeswehr in 1955, when the military began to be a force in German politics. Its creation led to clashes between the military brass and the civilians over topics such as tradition and historical legitimacy. For Canada, I began with 1965, when major post–World War II changes were introduced to an unhappy and resistant officer corps.

In contrast to most works on civil-military relations dealing with these four countries, this book is not about creating democratic civil-military relationships.[35] First, few would consider today's Russia "democratic" by Western standards. Second, this book is not about creating a normative relationship. Rather, its focus is on creating a shared relationship in either democratic states like the U.S., or polities like the Russian Federation. A country may be nondemocratic and still have civil-military relations marked by a shared relationship; in Russia there was a time when that was the case.[36]

This study is divided into eight chapters, two chapters on each country, and an introduction and conclusion. The relevance of shared responsibility for each country is analyzed. In the conclusion, I examine the value of this concept for analyzing civil-military relations in the four countries. Is this model too culturally bound to be useful in looking at civil-military relations in polities other than the U.S. and Canada? Or does it represent a new and useful way to look at civil-military relations? I examine each issue to determine its universal application.

Sources

Ideally, a study of this nature would include questionnaires administered to senior officers in all four militaries. As this approach was not feasible, I examined a plethora of secondary material on all four countries, primary material from my own extensive files on the U.S. and Russian militaries, and secondary sources available for Canada and Germany. I was also fortunate in meeting and discussing this book with several experts, some of whom served in either a civilian or military capacity in one of these armed forces. Hopefully, these sources are sufficient to provide an adequate picture of civil-military relations and the possibility of achieving a special relationship in the countries discussed herein.

PART I / United States

A great politician is not of necessity a great military leader.

GENERAL GEORGE S. PATTON

CHAPTER 2

From John F. Kennedy through Jimmy Carter

> There is no question of resisting civilian authority. However, it is very proper for the military commander to point out to civilian authorities the military risks of military decisions.
>
> ADMIRAL GEORGE ANDERSON

During John F. Kennedy's presidency, the U.S. military became involved in three major actions—the Bay of Pigs, the Cuban Missile Crisis, and Vietnam. Kennedy attempted to move toward a relationship of shared responsibility with the military, but for several reasons he did not achieve it. The main reason was Secretary of Defense Robert McNamara's refusal to work with the armed forces. Kennedy's successor, Lyndon Johnson, decided early on that despite the problems he faced in Vietnam, there was nothing to be gained by working with the military. The seven years of the Johnson administration were one of the most negative periods in the history of recent U.S. civil-military relations.[1] Richard Nixon made a major call for improved civil-military relations, but he too refused to create shared responsibility; at times, he acted as if he did not trust the military. Jimmy Carter, himself a Naval Academy graduate, also showed little interest in a relationship of shared responsibility.

John F. Kennedy (1961–1963)

Kennedy's leadership style was laid-back compared with his predecessors. He was open to military input, but not formal input, as noted by General Maxwell Taylor: "The President would have little of my feeble effort at regimentation and found it far more stimulating to acquire information from the give-and-take of impromptu discussion."[2] Kennedy's approach often frustrated the military because it "produced few clear and properly considered recommendations."[3] Participants were often unsure of their responsibilities, and decisions were unclear and ambiguous. But Kennedy did recognize the importance of strong conventional forces. To deal with the problems of the day, he believed the U.S. must have "military capabilities across the spectrum,"[4] an idea the military supported.

KENNEDY SELECTS ROBERT MCNAMARA

Of all the decisions that Kennedy took in office, none would impact civil-military relations more negatively than his appointment of Robert McNamara, a former executive with Ford Motor Company, as secretary of defense. Indeed, from the military's standpoint, McNamara would turn out to be one of the two worst appointments to secretary of defense since the end of World War II. McNamara had no interest in creating shared responsibility, and he had little respect for the military or its culture. Rather, he was determined to control the Pentagon. As Lawrence Freedman explained, "The military appeared as amateurs in his presence, fumbling for answers to questions that had never been asked before, expected to explain their programs without recourse to the normal slogans or a sense of what the political marketplace would bear."[5] In short, McNamara discounted their knowledge and looked down on them.

To make matters worse, McNamara arrived in Washington accompanied by his so-called "Whiz Kids," the majority of whom came from places like the Rand Corporation, where they had relied on such analytical frameworks as systems analysis to understand and address defense issues. McNamara made his point of view clear from the start: "I am sure that no significant military problem will be wholly susceptible to purely quantitative analysis. But every piece of the total problem that can be quantitatively analyzed removes one piece of uncertainty from our process of making a choice."[6] This approach even led to a new budgeting system. However, McNamara showed little concern for military culture. For example, military forces were divided into strategic offensive and defensive forces and general-purpose forces. Hence, the services were mixed together: the Polaris missile systems and the air force's missiles and bombers came under one heading, as would the army and the Marine Corps—a guaranteed recipe for interservice rivalry.

From the standpoint of the Joint Chiefs, when it came to designing and building weapons systems as well as determining their mix, it appeared as if their jobs were being taken over by amateurs. The Whiz Kids proceeded from the assumption that "military people were border line literate at best and communicated by animal noises."[7] The generals reciprocated the attitude. To quote General LeMay, "The Kennedy Administration came in and right from the start we got the back of the hand. Get out of our way. We think nothing of you and your opinions. We don't like you as people. We have no respect for you. Don't bother us." The problem was not limited to the Whiz Kids. McNamara himself was often impossible to deal with. "We [the Joint Chiefs] started off trying to talk to him. It was like talking to a brick wall. We got nowhere. Finally it was just a waste of time and effort. We could state opinions when we had a chance. That was all."[8] The problem was so serious that Maxwell Taylor found it necessary to urge Kennedy to rely primarily on the Joint Chiefs for military advice, and not on the Whiz Kids.[9]

THE BAY OF PIGS

When Kennedy took over he inherited a policy of his predecessor, Dwight Eisenhower: to overthrow the Castro regime. The plans called for American assistance to individuals who would be infiltrated into Cuba. Planners assumed that the Cuban masses would then rise up, thereby enabling the U.S. to recognize a provisional government and then send in a pacification force.[10]

The CIA was in charge of the operation, which created serious problems because of the basic differences between their organizational culture and that of the military. In the military, when someone supervises an operation, he or she takes control of it, runs it, and accepts responsibility for it. If the mission is under civilian control and the military officer is not in the chain of command, he or she stays out of the way and permits the person in charge to run the operation. In this case, the CIA was in charge, so the military's only task was to provide assistance as requested. The Joint Chiefs of Staff (JCS) never received written information on the operation. On more than one occasion, the JCS asked the CIA for documentation but were turned down.[11] For the CIA it was as a CIA operation, and, therefore, there was no reason to release highly sensitive information to the military. They might leak it. Even though the Joint Chiefs had a senior officer assigned to follow events closely, he was often kept in the dark by the CIA.

The Joint Chiefs were formally informed of plans to overthrow Castro on January 11, 1961. Two weeks later, Kennedy presided over a meeting on Cuba attended by several senior officers. Kennedy asked the military to take a look at the CIA's optimistic plans for overthrowing Castro. The president also reiterated Eisenhower's ban on U.S. participation in the operation.

Then, on January 31, CIA operatives again briefed the JCS representative. The Joint Chiefs discussed the problem and came to the conclusion that an uprising by the Cuban people was key to the success of such an operation. Without that support, they cautioned, Cuban forces would probably drive the invading volunteers into the sea. The JCS document sent to the president said, "despite the shortcomings pointed out in the assessment, the Joint Chiefs consider that timely execution of this plan has a fair chance of ultimate success."[12] Unfortunately, the civilian leadership did not understand that in military language the term "fair" meant only a 30 percent chance of success; certainly, no one asked the Joint Chiefs what "fair" meant. Here was a critical piece of information that, in a shared relationship, might have been made clear.

At a key meeting in the White House on March 11, the CIA argued that there was no alternative to using the brigade of Cuban volunteers to topple Castro. Kennedy feared he would run serious domestic political risks if he decided to cancel the invasion idea: he would be condemned by the Cuban exiles and blasted by the Republicans. He had to do something.

The Joint Chiefs made a grave error when they decided to support the invasion, even if it only had a "fair" chance of success. General Lyman Lemmitzer, chairman of the Joint Chiefs, later commented, "Probably no JCS paper of this period proved more controversial, and surely none did greater damage to the JCS's reputation."[13] The Joint Chiefs were on record in favor of the invasion, and worse, they later supported the CIA's assurance to the president that there was no doubt that the Cuban populace would rise up.

The CIA was in charge of operational matters, and the Joint Chiefs were excluded from the process, other than to offer comments. The CIA refused repeated requests by several of the Joint Chiefs to set up a military briefing for the president, so he would understand just how big a risk he was taking. On August 16, 1961, Kennedy formally approved the plan.

In fact, the operation had begun the previous day with a strike by three World War II B-26s. Then Kennedy cancelled the next air strike, aimed at knocking out the rest of Castro's air force. The new plan called for air strikes only to be used after the invading brigade had captured the airstrip at the Bay of Pigs; the Joint Chiefs were completely left out of this disastrous decision:

> In Fort Meyer, near the Pentagon, Generals Wheeler and Gray rang General Lemnitzer's doorbell about 2 a.m.
>
> The Chairman of the Joint Chiefs, sleepy and in his bathrobe, inquired, "How did things go?"
>
> "They cancelled the air strike!"
>
> Lemnitzer couldn't believe it. It sounded so unbelievable that he called the JCS situation room to confirm it. "Pulling out the rug like this was absolutely reprehensible, almost criminal."[14]

In retrospect, it was clear that the invasion was severely handicapped by the secretive way in which the CIA handled matters. The military was never shown the invasion plan, and as a consequence, the navy was unable to make contingency plans necessary to rescue the Cuban brigade if something went wrong. "Not surprisingly, in common with other orthodox military men, the alarmed Admiral concluded that the whole Cuban project should have functioned directly under his own centralized control rather than that of the CIA in Washington."[15] He was right: the navy and the Marine Corps understood the problems of amphibious warfare and the CIA did not.

The Joint Chiefs were just as upset with the president as they were with the CIA. These senior officers accepted the president's authority, but they were disturbed by his interference in operational and tactical matters. On the day of the invasion, for example, the president seemed "stunned" and confused, lacking a clear idea of what to do. Admiral Burke, the senior military officer on the scene, was "pressing for every yard of ground he could get in the direction of more participation by American forces in at least limiting the damage. Kennedy kept saying no. He went so far as to demand that navy ships stay over the horizon so they could not be seen from Cuba."[16]

The Bay of Pigs fiasco worsened the Joint Chiefs' relationship with the president, and this mistrust went both ways. To Kennedy, the Joint Chiefs had "disappointed him,"[17] and after this experience he began to question their professional competence. The problem was a clash of cultures. The president expected the military to speak up if and when they had misgivings. They had waited to be asked. As General Taylor noted, "there is a time when you can't advise by innuendos and suggestions. You have to look him in the eye and say, 'I think it's a lousy idea Mr. President. The chances of our succeeding are about one in ten.' And nobody said that."[18] In the aftermath of the Bay of Pigs incident, the president met with the Joint Chiefs at the Pentagon and made it clear that in the future he expected them to speak up. The issue was the absence of joint responsibility: had the military been willing to speak up with rational arguments, Kennedy might well have listened.

THE CUBAN MISSILE CRISIS

In the aftermath of the Bay of Pigs, American intelligence was fully aware that the Russians were supplying Castro with weapons. However, by 1962, as American intelligence officials began to pay increased attention to Cuba, the volume of weapons increased significantly. According to General Taylor, between July and September 1962, about "seventy shiploads of war material had arrived in Cuban ports." These ships brought in a wide variety of weapons: artillery, tanks, MIG fighters, Komar missile boats, and surface-to-air missiles.

The impending crisis was confirmed on October 14, 1962, when a U-2 plane took photographs showing that the Soviets were deploying missiles capable of carrying nuclear warheads. On October 15, an extremely upset president was shown the pictures. The question was, what to do? The Joint Chiefs were strongly opposed to a limited air strike. According to McNamara, "[They are thinking not of] twenty or fifty sorties or a hundred sorties, but probably several hundred sorties." Such an assault on Cuba the defense secretary acknowledged, almost certainly, "will lead to a Soviet military response of some type someplace in the world. It may well be worth the price."[19]

Kennedy was convinced that the Joint Chiefs wanted war. Indeed, Robert Kennedy referred to LeMay when he spoke of "the many times I heard the military take positions, which, if wrong, had the advantage that no one would be around at the end to know."[20] The relationship between the civilians and those in uniform became tense. LeMay asked to brief the president but was told by Robert Kennedy that would not be possible. LeMay later observed, "What a dumb shit."[21]

Such outbursts by the Joint Chiefs had a negative impact on Kennedy, who had gone through a period in which the Joint Chiefs said almost nothing; now he was faced with an aggressive, fire-eating general who understood nothing of the political aspects of the proposed action. He had a single solution to the problem: bomb Cuba regardless of the implications for U.S. security. Eventually, the president decided on a naval quarantine around Cuba.

One of the most interesting events for civil-military relations during the Cuban Missile Crisis took place between Admiral George Anderson, the chief of naval operations, and McNamara. The latter was concerned that the navy might be too provocative in dealing with the Russians, so he went down to the Navy Flag Plot, storming into the place "like a madman" and began chewing out one officer after another until Anderson appeared.[22]

> The encounter started badly. McNamara spotted a marker showing an American ship off by itself on the vast ocean, far away from the interception area. "What's it doing there?" he asked. Anderson did not answer directly, because—as he later explained—too many others were listening. Eventually, he drew McNamara aside and explained that the lone ship was sitting on top of a Soviet

> submarine. McNamara asked about the first interception: "exactly what would the Navy do?" Anderson replied there was no need to discuss the issue; the Navy had known all there was to know about running a blockade since the days of John Paul Jones. But, McNamara was not about to be put off. "We must discuss it."[23]

McNamara explained that the president wanted to be sure that the United States did not humiliate the Russians. The secretary of defense then proceeded with an unprecedented move, and went over the details of the intercepts with the chief of naval operations. "No Secretary of Defense had ever spoken that way to a member of the Joint Chiefs of Staff." The incident ended with Anderson commenting to McNamara, " 'Now Mr. Secretary, if you and your deputy will go back to your offices, the Navy will run the blockade.' Making no reply, McNamara walked out," noting to his deputy, "That's the end of Anderson." (In 1963, Anderson was appointed ambassador to Portugal.)[24] Several years later, Anderson, commenting on the incident, said that McNamara's intervention reminded him of the Bay of Pigs, when civilian interference violated military culture. "I endeavored to do everything possible to ensure that the navy kept the president fully informed of every aspect of the naval blockade, while precluding interference into military operations by civilian authorities, who had a tendency to bypass the normal military chain of command."[25] McNamara's grilling of Anderson was not appropriate in the admiral's opinion. (It would be reminiscent of Hellyer's treatment of the Canadian navy.) While it is hard to imagine a general like LeMay or an admiral like Anderson working smoothly in a relationship of shared responsibility, it was clear that McNamara was not interested in dealing with the missile crisis in cooperation with the military.

Lyndon Johnson (1963–1969)

Of all of America's post–World War II presidents, no one had a more negative role in American civil-military relations than Lyndon Johnson. Like Canada's Trudeau, he made no secret of his contempt for the military, believing that many of them were "arrogant," that they were contemptuous of new ideas, and mean and thoughtless in dealing with their subordinates. As one writer put it, "Johnson could be merciless when he talked about the generals."[26] As time passed, Johnson's lack of respect for the Joint Chief's was reciprocated. The relationship became so bad that there was never any thought of shared responsibility on either side. For the first and only time since 1940, the Joint Chiefs came very close to resigning.

VIETNAM

In spite of his lack of interest in foreign policy, Johnson's time in office was dominated by the war in Vietnam. Johnson's goal was to limit the role played by the war in American politics, but as time went on, it grew bigger until it virtually consumed his presidency. In the meantime, he handed over conduct of the war to Secretary of Defense McNamara.

McNamara's attitude toward dealing with the military resembled that of Canada's Hellyer or Russia's Serdyukov. Rather than asking the Joint Chiefs for their suggestions for a strategy in Vietnam, he forced his own ideas on them. McNamara's approach for dealing with Vietnam was aimed at "not imposing his will on the enemy, but to communicate with him."[27] Another component of his approach to war was his penchant for quantification. In his mind, the military had to be monitored, just as workers had to be monitored at the Ford Motor Company. The best way to accomplish this goal became the infamous body counts. If the numbers went up, the military was doing its job. If they went down, it would be clear that he had to take action. The problem was that numbers were inevitably exaggerated as they worked their way up the chain of command. However, from McNamara's standpoint, these statistics gave him something solid he could take to the president to show the U.S. was winning in Vietnam. The military opposed McNamara's mathematical approach, and constantly criticized him. " 'This guy McNamara,' they said, 'he tries to quantify everything.' " But McNamara defended quantification, arguing that it was necessary "when you are fighting a war of attrition."[28]

In order to operationalize McNamara's goal of taking territory away from the enemy, the U.S. commander in Vietnam, General William Westmoreland, employed a "search and destroy" strategy. According to Westmoreland, this "was nothing more than the infantry's traditional attack mission: locate the enemy, try to bring him to battle, and either destroy him or force him to surrender."[29] There would be heavy bombing, artillery, and heliborne machine-gun attacks. The problem was that the Americans were fighting a new type of war: instead of destroying the enemy, by the time massive Americans forces arrived, the enemy was gone. Still, McNamara dictated this course.

Not only did he interfere in the war, he involved his hated Whiz Kids in planning military operations. Every time Westmoreland requested more troops, McNamara turned for advice to his civilian analysts, who knew little or nothing about military matters. Deputy Assistant Secretary for Systems Analysis Alain Enthoven commented in 1965, "I don't know anything about it [the situation in Vietnam]. If I barged into a situation where I knew nothing, I would be attacked. I was under attack already from many fronts. I was vulnerable."[30]

As far as the Joint Chiefs were concerned, McNamara also employed a policy of graduated response. To them this idea was nonsense. They felt so strongly that Admiral Moorer later commented, "We could have polished those clowns off in six months."[31] General Andrew Goodpaster was also critical of the strategy. He protested to McNamara in the fall of 1964, " 'Sir, you are trying to program the enemy and that is one thing that we must never try to do. We can't do his thinking for him.' Goodpaster's words fell on deaf ears."[32]

The military continued to be frustrated with McNamara. On January 18, 1964, the infuriated Joint Chiefs again sent a plan to McNamara calling for a series of escalatory steps against North Vietnam, but nothing came of it. General Wallace Greene, the Commandant of the Marine Corps, "believed that the time had come to 'either pull out of South Vietnam or stay there and win'; He told his colleagues that the Marine Corps' position was that victory ought to 'be pursued with the full concerted power of U.S. resources.' "[33]

It was one thing for the generals and admirals to disagree with the administration's policy, but it was something else to be excluded from military decision making. For example, after assuring the Joint Chiefs that they would be kept carefully and completely informed of any changes in strategy, on March 13, 1964, the secretary sent a draft presidential memorandum to the White House calling for "tit for tat graduated military pressure."[34] With the exception of General Taylor, who was chairman, the other Joint Chiefs knew nothing about the memo and were angry when they learned of it.

President Johnson met with the Joint Chiefs on March 4, and was taken aback when Generals Greene and LeMay told him it was time to "either get in or get out." Faced with an election in November, the president was not about to agree to a major escalation. When they finally had an opportunity to see the March 2 memo McNamara had sent to the president, all of the Joint Chiefs except for Taylor, blasted it for its use of "half measures."[35] They were furious, and McDonald, Greene, and LeMay complained to General Chester Clifton, the president's military aide, arguing that their views had been misrepresented. The Joint Chiefs did not accept the idea of limited war, a concept that Johnson believed in for both practical and political reasons. Johnson feared that the approach the Joint Chiefs favored would quickly escalate into a major war, perhaps involving Russia and China. In response, Johnson extended LeMay in his position but did little else.

At this point, McNamara decided to cut off all lines of communication between the Joint Chiefs and the president, giving McNamara a stranglehold on policy advice to Johnson. "All military requests for appointments or decisions" were to "come though the McNamara channel."[36] It became clear to the Joint Chiefs that Johnson would never listen to them, because to him, Vietnam was not a battle to win; rather it was an irritant to be kept quiet if at all possible.

On November 1, 1964, the Viet-Cong attacked the American air base at Bien Hoa. The Joint Chiefs immediately asked permission to launch a strike against the North, but the president said, "no." In effect, the Bien Hoa attack started what amounted to an elaborate dance between the president and the Joint Chiefs. "The response to Bien Hoa typified what would become a pattern in the relationship between the JCS and Lyndon Johnson's administration. The Joint Chiefs tried to use the attack to gain approval for additional actions on the list they had developed less than a week earlier. To keep the Joint Chiefs 'on board,' President Johnson and his closest advisors appeared sympathetic to the JCS recommendation and held out the promise of future actions."[37] The problem continued. The Joint Chiefs would make a recommendation, but McNamara would refuse to forward it to the president. He continued to tell the Joint Chiefs that their advice was unwelcome and, if given, would not be taken seriously.

THE JOINT CHIEFS CONSIDER RESIGNING

The Joint Chiefs were well aware that Johnson was not interested in their opinions. For example, Hugh Sidney noted, "one high general late at night in a Washington men's club told a disturbed group around him that the NSC session seemed more an occasion for issuing orders to the military, or at least for informing them of decisions that had been made, than a deliberative affair where alternative actions were weighed and diverse voices listened to."[38]

The situation between the president and the Joint Chiefs continued to deteriorate. When the president decided not to call up the reserves for fear of the domestic response in the U.S., General Johnson, who had a reputation for honesty and integrity, was "almost desperate." He purportedly put on his best dress uniform and informed his driver he was going to see the president. "On his way into Washington, Johnson reached up and unpinned the stars from his shoulders, holding them lightly in his hands. When the car arrived at the

White House gates, he ordered the driver to stop. He stared down at his stars, shook his head, and pinned them back on." Many years later he reportedly regretted his decision. "I should have gone to see the President. . . . I should have taken off my stars. I should have resigned. It was the worst, most immoral decision I ever made."[39]

Tension between the Joint Chiefs and Johnson and McNamara continued to rise as shown in the following report of a meeting between Johnson and the Joint Chiefs:

> LBJ turned away for a moment, then whirled on the assembled senior military leadership and attacked them in the most vile and despicable terms, cursing them personally, ridiculing their advice, using the crudest and filthiest language. They were . . . subjected to the worst side of a "venal and vindictive man." Dean Acheson had spoken of Lyndon Johnson's "swinish bullying boorishness which made his last three years unbearable," and the nation's military leadership was getting an undiluted demonstration of these appalling qualities. . . . Still screaming and cursing, LBJ told the Joint Chiefs of Staff that "he was not going to let some military idiots talk him into World War III and ordered them to "get the Hell out of my office!"[40]

Almost as damaging to the relationship was McNamara's public rebuke of the generals, which is reminiscent of Yeltsin's public criticism of General Igor Rodionov. He openly suggested that the generals did not know what they were doing.

> Halfway through his testimony, McNamara looked up and paused, purposely emphasizing his next statement: "There can be no question that the bombing campaign has and is hurting North Vietnam's war-making capability." There was silence in the hearing room, a palpable sense of tension. "A selective, carefully targeted bombing campaign, such as we are presently conducting," he reiterated, "can be directed toward reasonable and realizable goals. This discriminating use of air power can and does render the infiltration of men and supplies more difficult and more costly." His words were almost a shout. While Johnson's policy might be debatable, he was saying, its impact wasn't; it was working. The North Vietnamese were buckling. America was winning the war in Vietnam.[41]

The Joint Chiefs were stunned by McNamara's devastating testimony, which dismissed their crucial contention that the war could be won only by shutting off supplies to the North. Civil-military relations had not been so seriously undermined since World War II.

General Wheeler, the chairman, suggested on November 25, 1967, that the Joint Chiefs consider resigning en masse. After the Joint Chiefs had reviewed McNamara's testimony, Admiral Moorer said he wasn't surprised, and General McConnell said he would follow the majority. "[General] Johnson was the most outspoken proponent of resigning, saying that the military was being blamed for a conflict over which it had very little control."[42]

The next day, General Wheeler had second thoughts. He called a meeting at 0830 and retained the previous day's rules, no aides, no notes, and a pledge of absolute secrecy. Wheeler argued that what the Joint Chiefs were considering was mutiny. Johnson disagreed, arguing that "no one was really paying any attention to their recommendations." They eventually decided not to resign, but civil-military relations in the U.S. had reached a new low point. Their future meetings with McNamara "were ruled by an icy cordiality that conformed strictly with the requirements of courtesy, but no more."[43]

The Joint Chiefs feelings toward McNamara bordered on insubordination. "Not only was Harold Johnson ridiculing the civilian part of the Pentagon as the 'Department of Deceit,' Wheeler constantly modified the secretary's full name into a more suitable description of the JCS feelings, calling him Robert 'Very Strange' McNamara, which brought smiles to the frustrated and overworked JCS Staff."[44] Eventually, President Johnson realized that McNamara's inability to work with the Joint Chiefs had deteriorated to the point that it was time to appoint a new secretary. More importantly, Johnson had lost confidence in McNamara; he asked Clark Clifford to take over as secretary of defense on March 1, 1968.

The Joint Chiefs felt considerable relief at the retirement of "Very Strange McNamara" and his Whiz Kids. In contrast to McNamara, Clifford asked for the Joint Chiefs' opinions, treated them with respect, and appeared to value their views, even if he did not agree with them. After five years of the Vietnam War, Johnson was feeling besieged. He then announced, "I shall not seek, and I will not accept, the nomination of my party for another term as your President."[45]

Johnson's departure was music to the ears of the Joint Chiefs. They had reached the point where they believed that just about anyone would be an improvement over Johnson. In some ways, Richard Nixon was an improvement: he seemed to listen to them. But in other ways, he would turn out to be just as duplicitous as Johnson.

Richard Nixon (1969–1974)

Nixon distrusted the federal government and that included the country's senior military officers. This meant that, with a few exceptions, they seldom became involved in policy making; instead their role was to implement policy. The most a senior officer could hope to do was to try to persuade Nixon to slightly modify or delay implementing a decision he had already made.

A result of this procedure was that it put the White House in the center of the decision-making process. The White House staff was expanded from 292 under Johnson to 583 by the end of Nixon's first term.[46] In addition, the Nixon White House created six special committees that operated out of the National Security Council (NSC). Chaired by the president's national security assistant, these committees comprised "the Vietnam Special Studies Group, the Washington Special Actions Group (to deal with international crisis), the Defense Programs Review Committee, the Verification Panel (to deal with strategic arms talks), the 40 Committee (to deal with covert actions), and the Senior Review Group (to deal with all other policy issues)."[47] Often, key officials had no idea what was going on. For example, Secretary of State William Rogers "was not even informed in advance of the administration's most innovative foreign policy initiative—the opening to China, which Nixon visited in February 1972."[48]

The Joint Chiefs were in a difficult position. They were trained to follow the chain of command. This meant that they resisted the idea of being told something but withholding it from their superior, especially if they believed that the senior officer would oppose the order. To make matters worse, the Nixon White House made extensive use of back channels—thereby leaving the Joint Chiefs unaware of what was being discussed. Nixon also was more than prepared to blame the Joint Chiefs for policy failures, even when they were following his direct orders. General William Westmoreland, who was serving as army chief of staff at the time, offered an excellent description of how the Nixon White House with Henry Kissinger, Nixon's special assistant, conducted foreign policy:

> As President Nixon came into office, new personalities and a new modus operandi entered into the conduct of White House affairs and the war in Viet-Nam. For the first time all policy in connection with the war was centered in a person other than the President, the President's adviser on national security affairs, the erstwhile Harvard Professor whom I had known for a number of years,

> Henry Kissinger. No longer did initiative come from the American command in Saigon; it came from the White House and Dr. Kissinger.[49]

Kissinger understood the low morale of the military in the aftermath of the Johnson administration, and he decided to try to reinvigorate it "even if it meant using more hawkish officers . . . as a lever against those who advocated a faster disengagement."[50] Another influential officer in the Nixon White House, Lt. Col. Alexander Haig, was Kissinger's military assistant. He was soon promoted to colonel, then to brigadier general, major general, and then skipped lieutenant general, going straight to four stars. The Joint Chiefs were furious at seeing a relatively junior officer with minimal management experience promoted to the same military rank they wore, and to discover that he often knew more than they did about critical security policies and was in a more influential position than all of them put together.

Much to Kissinger's chagrin, Melvin Laird was appointed secretary of defense. From the beginning, Kissinger believed Laird was out to get him, while Laird objected to Kissinger's effort to assume total control over security policy, especially on Vietnam. Kissinger believed that Laird was a dove, afraid to use American military power. Kissinger would do his best to use the (in his mind, hardline) Joint Chiefs to circumvent Laird, to get the military to do something without ever letting Laird know what was going on. As far as the military was concerned, Laird was like a breath of fresh air.

> In the history of the JCS, the Laird introduction of January 22, 1969, stands out as the primary example of just how a civilian leader can both dampen military distrust and gain military allegiance for controversial foreign policy initiatives that run counter to traditional military beliefs. . . . Indeed, the Laird meeting proves the point: of all the secretaries who have served in the Pentagon, Laird remains among the most respected not because he agreed with military programs and policies (he often didn't), but because he was willing to compromise on JCS positions and accord the chiefs the respect they thought they deserved.[51]

Not all of the country's senior officers were prepared to go along with Kissinger. For example, when Admiral Elmo Zumwalt was asked by Kissinger to set up a back-channel communications system, he answered that he preferred to receive all White House orders via the secretary of defense. According to Zumwalt, he ignored Kissinger and instead informed Admiral Thomas Moorer, the chairman of the Joint Chiefs, of whatever Kissinger happened to tell him. When the latter became chief of naval operations, he passed such information to Laird, or his executive assistant.[52]

ENDING THE WAR IN VIETNAM

When he ran for president, Nixon claimed that he had a "secret plan" for ending the war in Vietnam. The Joint Chiefs were encouraged: perhaps they finally had a president who would permit them to unload on the North Vietnamese. In fact, Nixon did not have a "plan." In setting up his Vietnam policy, Nixon decided that a key to getting the North to pay attention to him was to convince them that he really was crazy enough to bomb them into the Stone Age. As Haldeman reported him stating, "I want the North Vietnamese to believe I've reached the point where I might do *anything* to stop the war. We'll just slip the word to them that, 'For God's sake, you know Nixon is obsessed with Communism. We can't restrain him when he's angry—and he has his hand on the nuclear button,' and Ho Chi Minh himself will be in Paris in two days begging for peace."[53]

The generals were uneasy with Nixon. Was he just posturing? Would he continue to send American GIs into combat in Vietnam without the support of the American people? Working with Laird was certainly better than working with Kissinger, and he was respectful to them, putting the decision-making process in their hands. For example, he told them that it was up to them what kind of weapons their services purchased in the future. However, he also told them that if they wanted new weapons, the U.S. would have to get out of Vietnam. As one author put it, "The payoff for Laird was immediate: he had gained the JCS's support of the program for an early withdrawal from Vietnam without threatening the new spirit of cooperation between the JCS and himself."[54]

The Joint Chiefs continued to push for a more aggressive policy toward North Vietnam in the belief that it would help end the war quickly. One target was Cambodia. The North Vietnamese had chased Cambodians out of the Cambodian region opposite South Vietnam. It had become a military base for the North Vietnamese where they stockpiled weapons, ammunition, and other supplies. The urge to bomb or occupy the area was almost irresistible. It would not kill Cambodians, and it could create logistical chaos for the North Vietnamese. Furthermore, it might be done secretly.

On March 18, 1969, B-52 bombers struck Cambodia. According to Nixon, the raid was a success. "We received reports that our bombs touched off multiple secondary explosions, which meant that they had hit ammunition dumps or fuel depots."[55] There was a problem, however. The secrecy of the operation haunted the Joint Chiefs. No one except those directly involved knew that the bombings had taken place. The secrecy forced the Joint Chiefs to keep two books: one was for the normal operation of its bombings and one was for the bombings in Cambodia. "In the Pentagon only the secretary of defense, the JCS, a handful on the Joint State and the service DCSOPS [Deputy Chiefs of Staff, for Operations] were privy to the secret arrangements."[56]

This put the Joint Chiefs in a hopeless situation. They had to lie publicly about what they considered a "legitimate wartime operation." Consequently, "General McConnell, the Chief of Staff of the Air Force, began grumbling about the operation, labeling the effort to conceal the bombing 'stupid' and the other chiefs present chimed in."[57]

MORE CONSPIRACIES

Another issue that confronted the Joint Chiefs was how to respond to the President's directive in 1969 that they should consider modalities for a possible withdrawal of American forces from Vietnam. Once again the White House tried to deal with them directly, thereby cutting the "soft" Laird out of the action. At a White House reception, Kissinger reportedly told General Earle Wheeler that neither he nor the president believed that Laird could be trusted. "Within days, the president himself reiterated Kissinger's point, saying that he hoped Wheeler would be 'frank' in his appraisal of Laird's views." This kind of behavior put Wheeler in an impossible position. He worked for Laird, even though Nixon was the commander in chief. A month later Kissinger again approached Wheeler,

> Nixon wanted a "more open policy" on Vietnam, a policy that, he explained, the Secretary of Defense "doesn't seem to agree with." Kissinger intimated that Wheeler's report "in this matter" was "certainly appreciated," and that a means had to be found to "communicate the president's concern directly to the men in the field"—a euphemism. He meant that White House officials wanted to run the war without passing orders through Laird. Indeed, Wheeler soon realized that the White House was not only intent on bypassing Laird in the chain of command, it wanted to obtain information on Laird's programs at the Pentagon.

The situation worsened to the point that Kissinger reportedly ordered Haig to wiretap the phone of Colonel Robert Pursley, Laird's military assistant.[58] The

White House prodded the Joint Chiefs to use aggressive military tactics in Vietnam, while their direct boss, Laird, let them know that if they pushed too hard for the use of greater force in Vietnam, their budget would suffer.

Nixon was determined to get American troops out of Vietnam. He had made several concessions to the North, but Hanoi had ignored him. The new chairman of the Joint Chiefs, Admiral Thomas Moorer, was willing to play along with the White House. Accordingly, he had the Joint Chiefs draw up plans for opening a new offensive against the North without telling Laird. The White House decided, however, to bide its time.

Cambodia remained a serious problem. The North Vietnamese had rebuilt their base and were now bringing down new supplies from the North. On April 24, 1970, Nixon met with Admiral Moorer and others, while excluding Laird. The issue was what to do about two areas in Cambodia that were being used as sanctuaries: especially a fishhook-shaped portion of the Cambodian border. Nixon ended up calling for plans to invade the area based on recommendations from the Joint Chiefs, not the Department of Defense.[59] In short, Nixon ignored his civilian advisors in what turned out to be a major escalation of the war.

The U.S. invaded, and destroyed tons of North Vietnamese weapons, munitions, and supplies, but they were unable to find the elusive North Vietnamese headquarters, their real target. By the end of June they left Cambodia with most of their mission completed.

ADMIRAL MOORER BECOMES CHAIRMAN

On July 1, 1970, General Wheeler retired as chairman of the Joint Chiefs of Staff. His successor, Admiral Moorer, had been acting chair for some time. Considered by the White House to be the perfect candidate, Moorer was hawkish on Vietnam and outspoken to a fault, for instance calling an officer who disagreed with him "a dirty bastard," or "an unshaved peacenik."[60] He operated more secretively than his predecessor—just the kind of officer the Nixon White House preferred; he made little effort to inform his fellow chiefs of what was happening at the White House. He was fully aware of the existence of the back channel communications system in the Pentagon's basement that was under twenty-four-hour guard and reported directly to Kissinger, thereby bypassing Laird.

One of the more bizarre affairs in American civil-military affairs was the case of Yeoman Charles Radford. Radford was a young sailor assigned to the White House JCS Liaison Office, and from this position he was sending secret documents to the JCS without the president's knowledge. When the issue came to light, Nixon refused to have Radford court martialed. Since Radford was sending material to Moorer, disciplining Radford would force Nixon to fire his favorite admiral. As far as civil-military relations were concerned, while it did not excuse the JCS from "spying" on the President, it demonstrated that the Nixon White House was so secretive that the Joint Chiefs believed they had no alternative but to go to such lengths to learn what was going on in areas of their direct competence.

One of the most important aspects of the Radford Affair was the increased respect Kissinger developed for Moorer—he wasn't the country bumpkin that Kissinger had thought. He was able to play the game of conspiratorial politics as well as others. He would have to be taken seriously in the future.

Meanwhile, the North Vietnamese were planning a major offensive against the South. On March 30, 1972, General Vo Nguyen Giap sent his armored columns across the seventeenth parallel. As soon as the skies cleared, B-52 bombers began pounding the North's forces. In early May, Nixon authorized the mining of northern harbors, including previously untouchable Haiphong Harbor. In spite of Laird's opposition, Moorer was prepared to stand up to him as he strongly supported the president's decision to apply greater pressure on the North. Once again, Nixon was impressed with Moorer: he did not ask questions, he supported the president, and if anything, he was a bigger hawk than Nixon.

As far as the military operation, called Operation Linebacker, was concerned, its purpose was nothing less than to pulverize North Vietnam. Nixon hoped that if it hurt North Vietnam enough, it would force Hanoi to pull back its troops and make concessions at the Paris talks that were to decide Vietnam's future. The situation did not improve, so Moorer took the unheard of and insubordinate step of telling the president that the JCS was so concerned that the Joint Chiefs believed that mining Haiphong Harbor (despite the presence of Russian and other foreign flag vessels) was vital. The Joint Chiefs "were ready to walk out of the door unless Nixon did it." Moorer did so, in spite of his immediate boss's opposition. Indeed, Moorer ignored Laird's efforts to interrupt him. He commented later, "Hell, someone had to say something. Here we'd been talking for so long. If we hadn't done something, we'd still have men in prison there."[61] In essence, Nixon handed over operational command to Moorer without setting any parameters as to what he steps he could take. In essence, the Chairman of the Joint Chiefs was in charge of U.S. policy regarding North Vietnam. When the campaign ended on October 22, 2,346 U.S. aircraft strikes had delivered 17,876 bombs totaling approximately 150,000 pounds.[62] North Vietnamese dead may have exceeded 100,000.

Nixon's relationship with the military was hardly a case of shared responsibility. He used the military for his own ends, especially once he found that Admiral Moorer was willing to play his game. He had no inhibition about lying to the generals and admirals when it suited him, and was prepared to fire them if they disagreed with him, regardless of how outrageous or even illegal his orders might have been.

On December 18, the U.S. began one of the most punishing air operations of the war. By December 26, Hanoi expressed its desire to resume negotiations, and on December 30, the U.S. ended the bombings. North Vietnam lay in ruins. By January 13, 1973, the North had agreed to a basic document. Hostilities resumed, and two years later Saigon fell. A major chapter in U.S. civil-military relations closed.[63]

Jimmy Carter (1977–1981)

The situation facing the military when Jimmy Carter assumed the presidency was difficult at best. It was attempting to rebuild itself from the many problems it inherited from the Vietnam War. Equipment was worn out, morale was at rock-bottom, and medical problems including the use of drugs were rampant. However, the Joint Chiefs doubted that Jimmy Carter would be willing to deal with these issues. True, he was a graduate of the U.S. Naval Academy—the first president to come from the school by the Severn—but during his presidential campaign he had emphasized domestic programs. He was aware that the U.S. economy would not permit him to spend money on both domestic and military programs. When faced with such a choice he chose to cut military programs. In fact, his presidency would be a disaster from the military's standpoint. He not only denied the military the additional money it requested, he cut its budget.

Bureaucratically, the Joint Chiefs found it difficult to deal with Carter. He did not believe in structure—the kind of bureaucratic process called for in military culture. One never knew who was responsible for what; one never knew what the president wanted. This was a recipe for bureaucratic confusion if not chaos.

Carter had been a nuclear submariner and an engineer, and he took from that background a tendency to micromanage. As one analyst put it, "his desire to get involved in details, evaluate a range of alternatives, but ultimately to make his own judgment caused him to utilize a variation of multiple advocacy with undesirable consequences. His policy lacked direction and consistency."[64] This approach was guaranteed to lead to conflict with the generals.

THE MILITARY BUDGET

The end of the Nixon administration was one of budgetary retrenchment. Defense spending decreased, and Washington changed its strategy from having a military capable of fighting two-and-a-half wars simultaneously to one able to fight one and a half. The downward trend began to change during the next administration of Gerald Ford, who became president when Nixon resigned. It recognized "that during the previous ten years American defense spending had declined by about 7 per cent, while that of the Soviet Union had continued to increase by about 3 or 4 per cent each year."[65]

The U.S. military was badly in need of repair and modernization. For example, the number of general-purpose ships (excluding aircraft carriers and strategic nuclear submarines) had fallen from 840 in 1968 to only 450 in 1975.[66] The rest of the armed forces were in similar condition. Something had to be done—immediately. The Ford administration agreed to increase spending by 6 percent a year in real terms and to expand the navy to 540 ships by the 1980s. Ford was also in favor of upgrading the country's air and ground assets.

The Joint Chiefs' first meeting with Carter proved a disaster. The Joint Chiefs went through their normal briefing modules, with graphs, slides, and explanations. Their goal was to convince Carter that the Soviets were ten feet tall and that an expansion of the military budget was in order. Otherwise, they suggested that the red flag of mother Russia might soon be flying over the White House. After the Joint Chiefs answered some of Carter's questions, the president dropped a bombshell. "By the way," he asked, "how long would it take to reduce the numbers of nuclear weapons currently in our arsenal?" General George Brown, the Chairman, was confused. He broke in and asked about different categories. Carter replied, "No, no. I guess I want to ask what you think it would take to cut the missiles, how we could cut the number of missiles?" Brown still did not understand the president's point. Finally, Carter said "What would it take to get down to a few hundred?"[67] While one could argue that they should have been aware of his campaign promises, the Joint Chiefs had either not paid attention to them or did not believe he was serious. They were stunned. He had not even asked them for their opinion. So much for shared responsibility in decision making.

The next shoe that Carter dropped came in the form of a presidential memorandum sent to General John Vessey, the commander of U.S. Forces in Korea. It was a draft plan for a major withdrawal of U.S. troops from the Korean Peninsula. The memorandum was dated January 27, 1977, a date that indicated that it could not have been sent to the Pentagon for comments. Once again the Joint Chiefs were ignored.

On May 12, 1977, Carter signed the directive that announced the withdrawal of American troops from South Korea. Not only was State opposed to the withdrawal, the staff of the NSC as well as the U.S. ambassadors to China and Japan opposed this action. Army commanders were shocked. They had asked for an increase in troops, and instead, the president was cutting them. Eventually, Carter decided not to implement this directive. However, it was not because of concern expressed by the Joint Chiefs but reaction to the intense public outcry against such an action combined with intelligence reports indicating that the North was building up its forces.[68]

Carter then took on the air force and its desire to field the B-1 bomber. During the election campaign, Carter said it was "a gross waste of money in the Pentagon" and that the B-1 was too expensive.[69] This put Secretary Brown in a difficult position. Carter was his boss. However, he had spent enough time around the military to know that he could not run the Pentagon without its cooperation. Then on June 30, Carter cancelled the B-1. "Within twenty-four hours of Carter's decision, the JCS issued a strong protest to the president through channels."[70] On February 22, 1978, the House voted 234 to 182 to eliminate $500 million from the first two production models of the B-1.[71] However, Carter paid a heavy price for this victory. His cancellation of the B-1 turned the JCS and especially the air force against him.

Carter's problem with the air force went deeper. Air force officers began "shirking," to use Peter Feaver's term,[72] looking for ways to circumvent Carter, including making deals with members of Congress behind the president's back. A retired air force officer claimed that "Carter's decision on the B-1 was a disaster for him. . . . It really made him a lame duck with us [on the air force staff] long before his other decisions made him a lame duck with the American people."[73]

The navy was also upset with Carter. The navy's primary modernization goal was the construction of a 90,000-ton Nimitz-class aircraft carrier. This ship was critical if the navy hoped to reach the 600-ship level. Admiral James Holloway, chief of naval operations, led the fight for the carrier. He succeeded in getting the House Armed Services Committee to include $2.1 billion for it in the budget. Then Carter, unexpectedly and without discussing it with the navy, vetoed the bill.

Carter soon violated military culture again. When Admiral Holloway retired, by tradition, he was supposed to have a private meeting with the president. Carter refused. Holloway's successor, Thomas Hayward, attempted to calm the storm by ordering senior naval officers to remain silent. However, navy officers were extremely angry. "These orders evoked such anger in the Navy that Hayward's positive memo to flag officers one week later was an exercise in ambiguity that avoided clear support for the president. In truth, the Navy's base clearly supported an override of the president's veto with nothing less at stake than naval superiority . . . not mere equivalence with the Soviet fleet."[74] By the time of his reelection bid in 1980, Carter had succeeded in alienating all three services. He was having a hard time escaping the Republican charge that he "was soft on defense," because, in a sense, he was.

Carter continued his battle to shrink the military budget. The generals constantly told him that his proposed budget was far too small to deal with the many problems facing the military. The Joint Chiefs were getting restless. On March 1, General Jones told the House Budget Committee the military would need "substantial" increases above and beyond those proposed by Carter. At the time, Congress was getting numerous reports suggesting that the military was in a mess. Congressman Jack Edwards, the ranking minority member on the House Defense Appropriations Subcommittee, remarked that "only 56 percent of the Air Force's hottest fighter, the F-15 Eagle, were ready for combat at any one time last year, and only 53 percent of the Navy's F-14 Tomcat fighters were ready. The percentages for forward-deployed aircraft, such as F-15s based in Europe, were not much better. . . . About 70 percent of the planes should be ready to go at any given time."[75]

Carter refused to back down. He asked the chairman of the Armed Forces Committee, Senator John Stennis, to remove $6.2 billion in hardware purchases from the bill. He also asked Stennis to say "no to taking capital ships out of mothballs, no to stepping up F-18 production, no to extra submarines and frigates and, of course, no to resurrecting the B-1 bomber" in order to save $3.1 billion.[76]

The Joint Chiefs responded on May 30. They made it clear that they were not satisfied with the President's proposed budget. The army chief of staff bluntly stated, "Right now, we have a hollow Army." And he continued, "I don't believe the current budget responds to the Army's needs for the 1980s." When General Robert Barrow, the Commandant of the Marine Corps, was asked if the budget was adequate, he answered, "In a word, no." General Lew Allen, the chief of staff of the air force, commented, "increased defense spending is required to meet the increased danger." Admiral James Watkins, who was substituting for Admiral Hayward, responded that if "Carter's five-year program for the navy were followed... [We] would come close" to meeting the danger, but he added that he was skeptical about that happening. Even General David Jones, who had just been reappointed Chairman of the Joint Chiefs, commented, "I would vote against the defense part of the compromise budget resolution now before Congress." The level of opposition was so strong and so unified that it led one author to note, "In the 33 years since the Defense Department was created, individual chiefs on rare occasions have publicly differed with the decisions. But seldom, if ever, in the memory of Pentagon observers, have the Joint Chiefs collectively split with the President on the military budget, as they did in an understated way today."[77]

Carter was particularly angry with army General Edward Meyer, in fact, he was so mad, that, according to one writer, Brown called Meyer into his office and "demanded an apology." However, remembering Harold Johnson's experience as army chief of staff, he said he was prepared to be fired or to resign, but that he would not retract his statement. "You know, we have a responsibility to Congress, too, we don't just serve at the behest of the Secretary of Defense," he said. Brown backed down and the statement stood.[78]

Ironically, Carter did what few presidents were able to do, and that was to unify the armed forces against him. However, with election time approaching, Carter backed down. He reversed himself on military pay, and by August he was ready to approve Congressionally mandated pay raises. On November 1, Congress passed an 11.7 percent pay raise with better benefits and bonuses. Indeed, Carter gave so much on the military budget that, as one observer commented, he approved what was at that point, the "biggest peacetime modernization program ever funded."[79] This budgetary increase was also influenced by the Soviet invasion of Afghanistan.

The creation of a joint relationship between Carter and the generals was an impossibility. The president was not interested in working with the Joint Chiefs, and for their part, once they understood that he was not interested in working with them, they tried to work around him.

THE IRANIAN RESCUE ATTEMPT

If there was one instance in which Carter showed respect for the country's senior military officers it was in the effort to rescue the 70 members of the

American Embassy who had been seized by a group of students in Teheran. Carter and his aides discussed a variety of options, but the president asked the Pentagon to undertake contingency planning on two tracks: first, the Pentagon was to devise a rescue plan "in the event it was needed": and second, it was directed to devise options for a punitive military strike, "in the event the hostages were harmed."[80]

It soon became clear that diplomatic efforts to free the hostages would not work. Teheran had no intention of letting them go. So attention focused on the rescue idea. In this context it is important to keep in mind that putting together the rescue team was very difficult. For example, the helicopters selected were from the navy, but navy pilots were not qualified for such a job, so Marine pilots were selected. Unfortunately, they too were lacking in the requisite kind of flying experience.

In the planning this mission, Carter's Naval Academy background came through. As military culture dictated, he told the planners to do their best to avoid collateral damage, but emphasized that the planning was their job. In a meeting on April 16 in the White House, Carter turned to General Jones and said, "David, this is a military operation and you're going to run it." As the colonel in charge of the mission commented, "It was clean, simple and direct. A precedent had been set that night in the White House. I hope future American presidents, if faced with a similar situation, will follow."[81]

The president stayed out of operational matters, and demonstrated something that went to the heart of military culture—individual responsibility. As Beckworth quoted Carter saying, "I want you, before you leave for Iran, to assemble all of your force and when you think it's appropriate give them a message from me. Tell them that in the event this operation fails, for whatever reason, the fault will not be theirs, it will be mine."[82] What a difference from Johnson or Nixon.

The mission failed. Several of the helicopters had problems and had to land or turn back, leaving the team with fewer helicopters than needed to carry out the plan. The team prepared to turn back when one of the helicopters collided with one of the C-130s. Several members of the group were killed, and "The rescue mission, which had been developed in elaborate detail and rehearsed over a period of months, collapsed in ignominious failure and human tragedy within its first hours."[83]

Carter offered to call the families of the men killed and wounded, but Secretary Brown convinced him to let the army do the job. After the Delta Team had returned to their base, Carter paid them a visit. Not only were members of the Delta Team present, but the marine pilots, drivers, and the Farsi-speaking translators were also there. According to Beckworth, Carter

> spoke softly and sincerely.
>
> No matter what happened, he appreciated what these men had done for their country. Then he expressed his concern for the hostages, who, you could see, still commanded his full attention. We needed to consider, he stated, to help him find a way to get them released.
>
> After this short message, he told me he wanted to meet and speak to each person individually. The President then walked through the formation, shaking each man's hand. He spoke to most for a minute, and to some longer.

He ended by telling Colonel Beckworth, "I am very proud of these men."[84] It was the high point of Carter's relationship with the military.

CHAPTER 3

From Ronald Reagan through Barack Obama

> A lot of people believed that the military is eager to go out and shoot somebody, or that it should be; that's what they expect from the military. The modern military is not like that at all. In my experience, the civilians in the government were more eager to go shoot somebody than was the military.
>
> ADMIRAL WILLIAM CROWE JR.

Despite continued policy differences and a sometimes rocky relationship, civil-military relations saw the emergence of shared responsibility in a number of cases, in particular under Ronald Reagan, George W. Bush, and Barack Obama. Differences of opinion under these administrations were worked out in a congenial, if sometimes energetic fashion.

Ronald Reagan (1981–1989)

When Reagan came into office he did so on a promise to restore military morale by offering the armed forces the respect they had enjoyed in the past. In addition, he made it clear from the beginning that he would provide the armed forces with the needed money to rebuild and modernize their forces. Given the devastating impact of the Vietnam War on military equipment and installations, and Carter's attempts to starve them, such talk was welcome.

When it came to dealing with Reagan, the Joint Chiefs were of two minds. On the one hand, he was publicly supportive of them. On the other, working with him could be difficult. His lack of precision created havoc in the Pentagon. But in contrast to some past presidents, Reagan listened to the Joint Chiefs. Overall, the Joint Chiefs were particularly appreciative of his willingness to pour millions of dollars into rebuilding the military.

Reagan's secretary of defense, Caspar Weinberger, was also very promilitary and prepared to spend whatever was necessary to reequip the armed forces with modern weapons. Weinberger, however, often thought he understood military matters as well as or better than the generals. At his first meeting with them on January 15, 1981, after shaking hands with the Joint Chiefs, he surprised them by explaining the Reagan administration's defense policies. Just before the meeting was adjourned, Weinberger made a suggestion. "Since we are required to remedy our vulnerability in the strategic area . . . I suggest we resolve the MX basing debate and vulnerability of the rest of our ICBM force here and now." The Joint Chiefs and their deputies were stunned. One does not normally solve an incredibly complex question such as a basing mode for the MX in a few minutes. Weinberger suggested that the United States should put MX missiles on "ships." "The room became dead silent. The Air Force's Lew Allen turned to face Jones, his hand over his mouth, his eyebrows up, questioning. . . . No one seemed more surprised than CNO Hayward, who looked straight at Weinberger in apparent disbelief, his jaw slack." Weinberger broke the silence by asking if anyone at the table supported his great idea. The room remained silent. All eyes focused on General Jones. In what must go down as one of the more courageous acts of Jones's career, he "looked straight at Weinberger and said, 'Well, I think that is the kind of idea that *Reader's Digest* would like.' " Everyone was stunned. "Weinberger stared at Jones, his anger apparent. 'That happens to be where I get my medical advice,' he said and got up and stomped out of the room."[1] Senior Canadian, German, and Russian military officers are not the only ones who have had to deal with defense ministers who often know little about military matters.

The lesson was simple: humor the secretary when he makes military suggestions. At the same time praise him for the vast sums he is bringing into the Department of Defense. This was not an especially positive beginning to the creation of a period of shared responsibility. The secretary and the president were convinced that the U.S. lagged behind the Soviet Union, and that spelled serious problems for the West. To quote Reagan:

> Pentagon leaders told me appalling stories of how the Soviets were gaining on us militarily, both in nuclear and conventional forces; they were spending fifty per cent more each year on weapons than we were; meanwhile in our armed forces, the paychecks are so small that some married enlisted men and women were eligible for welfare benefits; many military personnel were so ashamed of being in the service that as soon as they left their posts, they put on civilian clothes.[2]

INCREASING THE BUDGET

Colin Powell put it best when he observed, "This was Christmas in February. This was tennis without a net. The Joint Chiefs began submitting wish lists. The requests initially totaled approximately a 9 percent real increase in defense spending."[3] It was hard for the Joint Chiefs to believe it: for the first time since World War II, they could lobby for spending increases without facing opposition from either the White House or Congress. And the military went on a spending spree. During the first two years of the Reagan administration, the services' requests were "packed with everything you can think of."[4]

While the military was overjoyed to have an administration that was willing to provide them with all the equipment, weapons, and other items needed, the Joint Chiefs were concerned with the seemingly irrational way material was purchased. It went against military culture, which calls for careful planning. For example, General Jones would have been much happier to have had a smaller but predictable increase in the defense budget over a longer period of time. There was no conceptual framework for the military buildup. When Weinberger decided the military needed something, he ordered it. He did not worry about its impact on the military budget.

Jones's concern was valid. By fiscal 1983, the military budget had increased 25 percent above inflation. Within five years, the Pentagon's budget would double. Almost all of the money was being spent on weapons, with little attention being paid to training, operations, and maintenance. By 1984, something had to be done. There was no way the government could pay for both the military buildup and the weapons that had been ordered but not yet paid for.

By the end of the Reagan administration, the Pentagon believed that the president had been only partially helpful. They were happy to have the MX, the B-1, the Trident, and the new carriers. However, a Marine general outlined the problem from the Joint Chiefs' standpoint:

> "If you could tell me tomorrow what the Corps would get over the next three to five years, and leave me alone, I could restructure inside and get you a better program," said Lt. General Charles H. Pitman, chief of Marine aviation. "If you don't do that, I've got to fight for everything. If we could go to a three-to-five year [budget] program that meant something, then these contractors could quit sending their guys over to see me. Somebody has to take charge—set goals and decisions."[5]

Ironically, the military's financial problems were worse when Reagan left than when he arrived. As one source put it, "We're in for creeping embarrassment, just like the 1970s. It's already happening. The Army is smaller than when Reagan came in, the Navy has had to retire ships and the Air Force has fewer wings." To make matters worse, military preparedness had declined.[6] The administration's decision to hand over responsibility for budgetary items to the Joint Chiefs was not the basis for joint responsibility. It should have been a two-way street.

SENDING MARINES TO LEBANON

Lebanon was an instance in which the military did not want to go to war. The generals and admirals, supported by Weinberger, did everything they could to dissuade President Reagan from sending Marines to Lebanon. It was to no avail. As was appropriate, he decided their presence was in the U.S. national interest.

General Vessey spoke at length with the president about the many problems the Marines would face, from rules of engagement to the danger of getting caught in the middle of a PLO/Israeli crossfire. Reagan said he would not let it happen. "But even more important, Reagan promised the JCS that the Marines would be in Beirut only as long as it took to carry out its mission—in any event, no longer than thirty days."[7]

The Marines landed in Lebanon and oversaw the departure of the PLO, an event that took seven days. The Joint Chiefs began to relax and began pushing the White House to withdraw the Marines. The president agreed, and on September 10 they began to redeploy to their ships. Then on September 14, Lebanon's president was assassinated. The Israelis quickly became involved, and on September 16 and 17, seven hundred Palestinian refugees were massacred by Lebanese Christian militiamen while the Israelis looked on.[8]

While the Joint Chiefs objected, the President asked that the Marines be sent back into Lebanon. After considerable back and forth between Weinberger and Secretary of State George Schultz, it became clear that the president had made his decision—the Marines would be going ashore again. The Marines went ashore on September 29, 1982.

The Marines had not been trained for such an operation, and their location at the airport was a military disaster. They were surrounded on three sides by high ground inhabited by potential enemies. Then there was the disaster of October 23, which Larry Speakes, the White House press spokesman, called "perhaps the worst day of the entire Reagan administration."[9] On that day a truck loaded with five thousand pounds of explosives managed to get past the guarded gate and blew up in the building that housed the Marine battalion's headquarters and barracks. A total of 241 Marines, sailors, and soldiers were killed.[10] The president was determined to retaliate, given that the Marines were still in Beirut.

Gradually everyone, including the president, began to realize that having the Marines in Lebanon served no useful purpose. In February he ordered them to leave, and if there was any criticism of it, it was that "Our troops left in a rush amid ridicule from the French and utter despair from the Lebanese."[11] The Marines were now gone. The Joint Chiefs had opposed it from the beginning,[12] but in contrast to many other presidents, Reagan listened to them but made the final decision, just as he should under a policy of joint responsibility.

OPERATION URGENT FURY

The small Caribbean island of Grenada was important to Washington for two reasons. First, there were a number of American students studying at a medical college on the island, and second, the Cubans were building an unusually long runway on the island, which Washington feared would be used for large planes supporting the Cubans' efforts at subversion in Africa.

On October 19, 1983, the island's prime minister, Maurice Bishop, was murdered, "with the assistance of General Hudson Austin, Commander in Chief of the Armed Forces,"[13] The airport was immediately closed and a twenty-four-hour curfew imposed. Austin warned that anyone caught out during curfew would be shot—and that included the American students. Weinberger asked the JCS what troops would be available if the president decided to use force. The Joint Chiefs immediately identified some Marines along with army battalions and airborne forces from Ft. Bragg and Ft. Campbell. The JCS plan called for a quick seizure of the airfield at Point Salinas and the airport at Pearls. The other key targets were the two campuses of the medical school, the governor general, and any political prisoners on the island. But intelligence was lacking. As McFarlane put it, CIA Director "Bill Casey didn't have much he could tell us. A couple of Navy Seal teams had been sent in to reconnoiter but had not reported back. The best estimate, Casey said, was that there were a couple of hundred Cubans on the island, chiefly airport workers, who probably had some military training as members of the Cuban reserve."[14] In other words, an operation would be carried out in the dark.

President Reagan met twice with the Joint Chiefs on October 24. During the morning meeting he asked each Chief for his views on the operation. All of them agreed that there was no option but the use of force, and they "assured the president that the operation would succeed." That evening the Joint Chiefs explained the operation to Congressional leaders. General John Vessey, who had been briefing the members of Congress then turned to the president and said,

> As soon as I send the message to the Pentagon to go ahead, I'm going home to go to bed. We've given this mission to an operational commander. He has the forces that he believes he needs. He knows that he has the full support of the Secretary of Defense and of you . . . and the Joint Chiefs of Staff. If he needs more help, then he'll call for it, but otherwise, there's nothing you or I can do until these troops have landed unless you decide to call it off between then and now. I'm going home to bed and in the morning . . . wait for the first reports to come in. The President replied, "I'm going to do the same thing."[15]

The Joint Chiefs couldn't ask for stronger support. In contrast to the Lebanon operation, Reagan left the details to his military commanders.

From the military standpoint, the operation was a reminder of the attempt to free the American hostages in Teheran. The services made little effort to work together. Perhaps the best-known operational problem involved communications. An army officer was "so frustrated by difficulties in communicating with navy ships that he used his AT&T calling card on an ordinary pay telephone to call his office at Fort Bragg, North Carolina, to relay his plea for fire support to higher headquarters and finally down to the navy ships a few miles away from him."[16] An equally shocking case of the failure of interservice cooperation comes from General Norman Schwarzkopf, who was at that time serving as a deputy to Admiral Joseph Metcalf, the operational commander. According to Schwarzkopf there were army Rangers aboard his ship whom he needed to get ashore quickly to help rescue the students. The two star general approached the Marine colonel in charge of Marine helicopters and asked if he would take the rangers ashore.

> "I'm not going to do that." "What do you mean, I asked?" "We don't fly Army soldiers in Marine Helicopters." I looked at him incredulously. "Colonel, you don't understand. We've got a mission, and that mission is to rescue those students *now*. Your Marines are way up in Greenville securing that area, and your helicopters are right here. The way to get the job done is to put Army troops in those helicopters." "If we have to do it, I want to use my Marines. They'll rescue the hostages," he maintained stubbornly. "How long will that take?" He

looked me straight in the eye and said, "At least twenty-four hours." "Listen to me very carefully, Colonel. This is a direct order from me, a major general, to you, a colonel, to do something that Admiral Metcalf wants done. If you disobey that order, I'll see to it that you are court-martialed." He agreed to do it.[17]

While he assumed personal responsibility for the operation, Reagan left operational matters to the generals. The military itself recognized that it failed to properly carry out the mission. They had not learned the lesson of Teheran.

CORRECTING THE PROBLEMS OF COOPERATION

With service rivalry remaining a problem, something had to be done. By 1985, Senator Sam Nunn began drafting a major reorganization plan to be called the Goldwater-Nichols Defense Reorganization. The problem for Admiral William Crowe, the chairman of the Joint Chiefs, was that not only were the Joint Chiefs less than enthusiastic about this reorganization, his boss Secretary of Defense Weinberger was totally opposed. Weinberger feared that strengthening the chairman's authority would weaken him. Crowe said that he tried his best to dampen the Chief's opposition. Whether they liked it or not, Goldwater-Nichols was coming.

The new legislation was signed into law on October 1, 1986. The chairman became the president's primary advisor on military matters, which meant that he could provide his guidance directly to the secretary of defense and the commander in chief. No longer would he be obligated to provide an opinion based on the lowest common denominator among the Joint Chiefs. Other changes included placing sixteen hundred Joint Staff personnel under the chairman, and the addition of a deputy chairman, whose authority over the other Joint Chiefs would ensure critical continuity when the chair was away on a trip or tied up by another issue.

To address the tendency of some services, like the navy, to play down the importance of joint assignments, the act placed greater emphasis on "jointness." By requiring officers to have a joint assignment before making general or flag rank, the act forced the services to pay more attention to such assignments. Requiring such interservice assignments for flag rank also meant that the services would be forced to send their best officers to joint assignments.

Both the chairman and combatant commanders emerged from the legislative process in much stronger positions. In addition, the word "purple" (to refer to a joint assignment) was now something that would enhance an officer's career, which, in turn, would improve unified command in time of war.

In some ways, Reagan was a boon to shared responsibility. He listened to the generals on Grenada, for example, and he showered money and public acclaim on them. However, there was little fiscal rationality in the way he and his secretary of defense provided resources. Military culture calls for careful planning in the allocation of resources, so in that regard, he violated it. However, when compared to presidents during the past 35 years, Reagan provided a breath of fresh air.

George H. W. Bush (1989–1993)

George H. W. Bush played a greater role than Reagan in issues related to national security. He did not micromanage the process, but he expected to be consulted. He was lucky to have Brent Scowcroft, a retired air force general, as his national security advisor. As one writer noted, "Scowcroft spent more time with Bush than any other official in the administration, and reports indicate that he freely expressed his views to the president, but made it clear to Bush when he was doing so."[18]

Bush also differed from some of his predecessors in that he believed in collegiality and made the process work. He differed philosophically from Reagan; he was not driven by ideology, but gathered the facts and then acted in a pragmatic fashion. With the exception of his secretary of defense, Richard Cheney, all of his advisors reflected his views. He also welcomed different points of view, even when they disagreed with him. In contrast to Johnson and Nixon, he did a much better job of "keeping his cabinet officers involved in the policy process."[19] He was also able to communicate to his subordinates exactly what he wanted them to do.

Cheney knew very little about the military. He was exempted from the draft. When he arrived at the Pentagon, like many individuals in a similar position, he decided that the first thing he had to do was to show the military he was in charge. This led to his criticism of General Larry Welch. Welch had spent considerable time trying to work out a basing system for the MX missile—one of Washington's seemingly intractable problems. After informing Scowcroft, Welch went to the Hill to discuss possible basing plans with members of Congress. On March 23, *Washington Post* correspondent George Wilson called Welch to task about his activities on the Hill. Welch "confirmed that he had been 'pulsing the system.' "[20]

Cheney was furious when he saw the story. At a press conference the next day, he claimed that Welch's "freelancing" was not speaking for Defense. When asked if he accepted such behavior, Cheney replied, "No, I am not happy with it, frankly." For his part, Welch was stunned. He spoke with Cheney and told him that he was not a "freelancer." Cheney then said that the case was "closed." Most importantly, Cheney had made his point. He was in charge—at the expense of the chief of staff of the air force.

INVADING PANAMA

Manuel Noriega, a brutish and crude Panamanian army officer, became president of Panama in 1981 when the country's president, Omar Torrijos, was killed in a plane crash. Noriega quickly "moved to tighten his grip on the army and reassert its position in Panamanian society."[21] By early 1989, he had stepped up harassment of American GIs. In February, Panamanian Defense Force (PDF) thugs beat up a navy civilian employee at a police station. Between January 19, 1989, and the end of February, "SOUTHCOM had logged about sixty incidents of harassment by the PDF, bringing to more than one thousand the number of incidents recorded since early 1988."[22]

Noriega then nullified an election he lost. Bush became concerned. The U.S. could not just sit by and do nothing. In response Bush began to build up U.S. forces in Panama. This prompted Admiral Crowe, the chairman of the Joint Chiefs of Staff, to wonder if the president intended to rely on "military solutions . . . often the first resort rather than the last."[23]

General Maxwell Thurman was about to end his 36-year career and retire from the army when General Carl Vuono called during the first weekend of July and asked him to go to SOUTHCOM. Thurman had a widespread reputation of being married to the service. He was a bachelor "who would call a staff meeting on Christmas Eve night, expecting every officer to be prepared for whatever briefings he might require."[24] Known as a hard-charging workaholic and highly aggressive officer, many considered Thurman to be the perfect choice. He flew to Washington the next day, spoke with Vuono, and agreed to take the post.

By August, Noriega had installed his own government. Bush reacted by stating that "Panama is, of this date, without any legitimate government"; he added, "The United States will not recognize any government installed by General Noriega." It was beginning to look like the president intended to resolve the matter by military means. When Crowe returned from an NSC meeting in September, he told his subordinates, "I am absolutely 100 percent convinced that the only way the situation is going to be resolved in Panama is with military force. You guys better be ready. . . . I can't tell you when it is going to happen, and I can't tell you what the trigger is going to be, but I'm convinced that's the only way it's going to be resolved."[25]

On December 16, four American servicemen were driving in downtown Panama City when they were stopped at a PDF roadblock. When the PDF guards started waving their AK-47 assault rifles in the faces of the car's occupants, the driver panicked and drove off. The PDF guards fired, and one of the bullets hit Marine Lieutenant Robert Paz. Another round hit a Marine officer's ankle. The wounded Marines were taken to the military hospital where Paz died.

The U.S. military in Panama immediately put all troops on alert. By the next morning, SOUTHCOM went to "the highest state of alert, and moved their forces in Panama to their ready positions under Operations Plan 90-2. Soldiers manned defensive positions at Fort Clayton and Fort Amador."[26] Then Thurman, who was in Washington, immediately went to the Pentagon's Situation Room together with the new chairman of the Joint Chiefs, Colin Powell. Powell commented, " 'Noriega has gone over the line' . . . [and] took the position that the killing was an outrage and an affront to the country."[27]

Powell met with his assistants again the next morning at 0500 to hear from Thurman, who had flown back to Panama. Powell recommended that the U.S. hit Noriega with everything it had. Cheney agreed. Powell then called a meeting of the Joint Chiefs where he informed them of his recommended course of action.

Powell met with the president and presented the plan. Bush's primary concern was to be sure that the operation would not "backfire as had the attempted rescue of U.S. hostages in Iran during the Carter administration. He also wanted to preclude the interservice problems that arose in 1983 during the intervention in Grenada."[28] Bush asked why not just "snatch" Noriega, thereby avoiding a full-scale invasion. Powell responded by noting "that the massive use of force was in fact *less risky* than a smaller effort. This was the prudent course, he told Bush." He maintained that the choice was simple: pay now or pay later. "You go down there to take Noriega out and you haven't accomplished that much because he would be replaced by another corrupt PDF thug."[29] Powell warned the president that "there will be a few dozen casualties if we go. . . . If we don't go, there will be a dozen over the next few weeks and we'll still have Noriega."[30] Powell, Cheney, and Scowcroft agreed that the time for talking was over: it was time for action. As Powell tells it, Bush then "gripped the arms of his chair and rose. 'Okay, let's do it,' he said: 'the Hell with it.' "[31]

The operation was almost a model of joint responsibility. As soon as the president made it clear that he intended to use force, Cheney got involved, but, according to Powell, the chain of command remained clear. "The President talked to Cheney, Cheney talked to me; and I talked to Max Thurman, who talked to Carl Stiner. Thurman and Stiner were the pros on the scene, and our job in Washington was to let the plan unfold without getting in their way."[32]

There appears to have been only one case of micromanagement by a civilian, in this case Cheney. The *New York Times* had a reporter in the theater while the invasion was under way. He complained that he was trapped and the *New York Times* called Scowcroft asking for the military to rescue him. The request was passed on to Powell who checked with Thurman who said the reporters were in no danger, so Powell declined the request. Scowcroft called again, and Powell again said the journalists were not in any danger. "Only a few minutes passed before Cheney called. There was no discussion. Do it, he said. No more arguments." Powell then called Thurman and Stiner, stating, "Get those reporters out, and I'll try to keep Washington off your backs in the future." The Eighty-second Airborne rescued the journalists, but as Powell noted in the memoirs, three soldiers were wounded, one seriously, and a Spanish photographer was killed. Most important, however, was the manner in which Powell reviewed the issue with Cheney afterward. As Powell commented:

> I told Cheney that I did not want to pass along any more such orders. "If the press has to cover a war," I said, "there's no way we can eliminate the risks of war." Cheney called Scowcroft and asked him not to issue any more orders from the sidelines. This was a new, tough age for the military, fighting a war as it was being covered.[33]

From the standpoint of civil-military relations, the most important aspect of the Panamanian invasion was that it showed Bush's willingness to listen to the military while retaining overall command of the operation.

THE PERSIAN GULF WAR

The Persian Gulf War was a new, different kind of war. As Michael Gordon and Bernard Trainor commented, "It was the dawn of a new era in which high technology supplanted the bayonet, a war in which one side had a clear picture of events while the other floundered deaf, dumb and blind."[34]

On July 17, 1990, Saddam Hussein publicly threatened both Kuwait and the United Arab Emirates, claiming that they were "shoving a 'poisoned dagger' into Iraq's back by exceeding production quotas set by OPEC."[35] He claimed that this was leading to a decline in the price of oil, Iraq's primary export. That would inevitably hurt Baghdad's economy. Saddam was clearly playing a game. On July 25, he summoned the U.S. ambassador with only one hour's notice. He criticized a statement that Cheney had made the previous week that the U.S. would "stick by its friends in the Gulf." He argued that Cheney's statement was directed against Iraq.[36]

General Norman Schwarzkopf, Centcom (the Central Command, which included Iraq) visited Washington, and Powell asked him to brief Cheney and the Joint Chiefs on the situation. According to Powell, "I arrived at the tank about the same time as Dick Cheney. The Joint Chiefs rose, and we took our places. Cheney had me lead off. I quickly turned the floor over to Schwarzkopf whose robust six-foot-three-inch frame and forceful personality filled the room. . . . 'What do you think they'll do?' Cheney asked. 'I think they're going to attack,' Norm said."[37] From the American standpoint, the problem was that there were only 10,000 military personnel in the Gulf—and most of them were navy.

On August 1, Iraqi forces invaded Kuwait. It was a major military move involving hundreds of main battle tanks racing toward Kuwait's capital. Powell called Schwarzkopf and told him "You were right. They've crossed the border."[38] Bush was furious, and like most other presidents, wanted the U.S. to retaliate immediately. However, it would take some time before the U.S. and its allies were prepared to move militarily.

On August 2, the NSC met. Powell, Schwarzkopf, Cheney and the deputy secretary of defense, Paul Wolfowitz, and Secretary of State James Baker attended. Schwarzkopf told Bush that he couldn't do much to stop Saddam, but there was an option to punish him and demonstrate U.S. resolve. It was important to keep in mind that if Saddam moved toward the Saudi oil fields, the Saudis only had an army of about 70,000 to stop him. He then proposed a two-tier response. The first tier included single retaliatory strikes that would have to be carried out by the navy because there were no air force planes in the area. The second tier response would take months to prepare and involve 100,000 to 200,000 personnel from all of the services.

The president repeated something he had said previously. "We just can't accept what's happening in Kuwait just because it's too hard to do anything about it."[39] Given Bush's desire to do something as soon as possible, Cheney called a meeting of his senior military and civilian aides. Cheney was upset when he realized how few realistic options were available to the U.S. Powell tried to explain the problems: Kuwait is 6,000 miles away and the Iraqis now occupied the country. The U.S. was faced with the difficult task of removing them while at the same time ensuring that Saddam was not able to take the Saudi oil fields. As far as air strikes were concerned, Powell turned to Cheney and stated, " 'We don't have any ground forces and an air strike would be pissing in the wind and might provoke what we don't want—an assault on Saudi Arabia.' It was one of the tensest exchanges the two ever had."[40] Cheney was not about to permit Powell to steal the show, so he asked the services to come up with their own proposals.

At a subsequent meeting, Cheney asked Powell to list the units available for movement to the Gulf. Powell then returned to a theme he had articulated in the past.

> I detected a chill in the room. The question was premature, and it should not have come from me. I had overstepped. I was not the National Security Advisor now; I was only supposed to give *military* advice. Nevertheless, I had wrestled with the politics and economics of crisis for almost two years in the White House, in this very room. . . . More to the point, as a middle-level career officer, I had been appalled at the docility of the Joint Chiefs of Staff, fighting the war in Vietnam without ever pressing the political leaders to lay out clear objectives for them. Before we start talking about how many divisions, carriers, and fighter wings we need, I said we have to ask, to achieve what end? But the question was not answered before the meeting broke up.[41]

The point Powell was trying to make was that if the U.S. was determined to evict Saddam, it had to make a major commitment. It could not be done on the cheap.

Then the president dropped a bombshell. Reporters were pushing Bush on what he intended to do to Saddam. "His face hardened, he began jabbing the air with his finger. '*This will not stand*, this will not stand,' he said, 'this aggression against Kuwait.' "[42] In a word, the president had fundamentally changed U.S. policy. Now it was not just a case of protecting Saudi Arabia, the task now was to liberate Kuwait. The U.S. was moving ever closer to a military solution. On August 6, Cheney telephoned Powell to tell him that Saudi Arabia had agreed to the stationing of American troops. Furthermore, he told him that the president had agreed to inserting an American force and asked him to issue the necessary orders to send U.S. troops to Saudi Arabia.

Another meeting was held with the president on August 15. By the first of December, Powell told the president the U.S. would have around 180,00 troops in Saudi Arabia. He also told the president that what the military needed "is for you to tell us before that mission is accomplished what you want us to do next—so if we have things in the military supply pipeline, do we stop the pipeline or keep it going, or whatever?"[43] Powell continued to play a major role, especially in his relationship with Schwarzkopf. On August 23, he called Schwarzkopf and asked him to stop by Washington on his way back to the U.S. and provide a briefing on "your offensive—campaign—air and ground both." Schwarzkopf was furious. He said he had already briefed the president on a defensive plan and then asked:

> I'm following orders to put a defensive plan in place, and all of a sudden you guys in Washington are asking me to prepare an offense using that defensive force. Something is wrong here. I can give you my conceptual analysis, but that's all it is, apart from the phase-one air attack, it's nothing I'd recommend, nothing we've actually planned on, nothing I'd act on. I'm afraid somebody who doesn't understand what is going on will turn around and say, "execute this offensive."[44]

Powell responded by noting that Schwarzkopf did not realize the amount of pressure on him from civilian authorities. " 'Norman! Trust me. You've got to trust me.' Powell exclaimed. 'Do you think I'd ever let that happen? My problem is that I've got all these hawks in the National Security Council who keep saying that we ought to kick Saddam out of Kuwait now. I've got to have something to keep them under control.' "[45]

The critical question of offense versus defense continued to overlay the discussions. However, as both Cheney and Powell realized, it was already September and a decision would have to be made by the president in October on whether or not to continue to bring in the troops and supplies needed for an offensive campaign. They met with Bush on September 24 and began by noting that the U.S. had two options: to go on the offensive or to continue to rely on sanctions. Powell told the president that the U.S. should prepare "for a full-scale air, land and sea campaign," adding, "If you decide to go that route in October, we'll be ready to launch sometime in January."[46]

The president then asked for a briefing on what an offensive operation entailed. Powell immediately called Schwarzkopf on the phone and asked him to send a team to Washington to brief the president. Schwarzkopf was less than delighted to be asked to brief the president on an offensive campaign at this point. As he put it on the phone, " 'Goddamn it, I told you over and over again, we can't get there from here.' But Powell insisted. The White House 'is on my back,' he explained. 'They want to see what we can do.' "[47]

On October 6, one of Schwarzkopf's subordinates presented the plan to Schwarzkopf. It called for a straight-ahead attack into Kuwait at night all the way to the Kuwaiti capital and then on to Basra in Iraq.

> "Do you think this will work?" he asked Pervis.
>
> "It's very high risk," Pervis replied. "It may work."
>
> "What would it take to guarantee success?"
>
> "Another corps," Pervis answered promptly. Two or more divisions made up a corps. The Army's XVIII Airborne Corps currently in Saudi Arabia comprised four divisions, but only two were armed with heavy tanks.
>
> Schwarzkopf nodded, "I agree."

Schwarzkopf's only comment to the team he sent to Washington was, "We don't bullshit the President."[48]

On October 11, Schwarzkopf's team met with the president. Like the Joint Chiefs, Bush and others were concerned about the ground phase. As Scowcroft put it, why did you decide to go "right up the middle." "Why don't you go around?" Powell tried to point out that the problem was logistics. "To 'go around,' Schwarzkopf would need an additional corps."[49]

On October 24, Cheney was called to the White House where Bush informed him that he was leaning toward the offensive option. Cheney made some comments while Powell was in Saudi Arabia, suggesting that the president had selected the offensive option. When Powell heard these reports he asked one of his aides, "What's going on?" Once he figured out that Bush was serious, he told one of his aides, "Goddammit, I'll never travel again. I haven't seen the president on this."[50]

Cheney was unhappy with Schwarzkopf's plan, and as a result he had enlisted some officers on the Joint Staff to come up with a plan and had them brief Bush. Cheney's plan called for the U.S. to send a couple of divisions to occupy the western part of Iraq and pose a direct threat to Baghdad. If the Iraqis moved forces to counter the Americans they would be sitting ducks for American air power. The generals wanted no part of Cheney's plan. Schwarzkopf sent in scathing criticism, and Powell added his opinion, making it clear that he was not happy with it either.

At a NSC meeting on October 31, Powell stated the problem clearly and bluntly. " 'Now, if you, Mr. President, decide to build up—go for an offensive option—this is what we need.' He then unveiled the Schwarzkopf request to double the force." The president then formally approved the idea of sending an additional 200,000 troops to Saudi Arabia, as long as the Saudis granted permission. Ultimately, Schwarzkopf received more troops than he requested. Once he had reached a decision, Bush believed it was the military's job to fight the war and they should have whatever they needed and then some. As he put it, "If that's what you need, we'll do it."[51]

Looking at the preparation and carrying out of the Persian Gulf War, the operation was a smooth one, primarily because of the shared relationship between the military and civilian leaders. That was true not only in the conduct of operations, but in deciding when and where to end the war. Bush was careful to consult his generals before making a final decision. Throughout this operation, civilians made the final decisions, but listened to the generals and took their advice seriously. It was a clear case of shared responsibility.

William J. Clinton (1993–2001)

Clinton's relations with the military were anything but smooth. He was the first president since the end of World War II who had not served in the military and as a result had little understanding of military culture. He often took actions that worked against its principles, evident in his unstructured and often chaotic leadership style. Many military officers believed that Clinton did not respect them or their ideas. They opposed what they saw as his tendency to use the military as a laboratory for social engineering. One well-known presidential scholar called Clinton's approach to politics, "Ad-hocracy in action."[52] This author maintained that Clinton had little interest in the decision-making process. He often equivocated and then made a decision on the spur of the moment. In such cases, only later would he inform the bureaucracy, and that included the Joint Chiefs, of the solution he had selected. One example will serve to illustrate the problem. When Robert Patterson, a former military aide to Clinton, arrived at the White House, he asked for a "wiring diagram," a chain-of-command chart that would show who was in charge of the various issues, something that is available in just about every civilian and military organization in the U.S. In response, he was told, "There isn't one."[53] In short, instead of stepping in at critical points as had Bush and Carter, Clinton often refused to make a decision.

If his personal leadership style was not enough of a problem, the generals and admirals had serious questions about him personally. First, there was the draft. Clinton had done his best to manipulate the system to avoid being drafted. At one point in his life, he even sounded like Trudeau noting that he "loathed the military."[54] His salute to the military was in their eyes a disgrace. "The tips of the fingers would furtively touch his slightly bowed head, as if he was being caught at something he wasn't supposed to do."[55] One of his military aides had to take him aside and teach him how to salute.

Coming into office, Clinton further irritated the military by announcing that he was going to freeze military pay despite studies showing that pay had fallen 20 percent behind the private sector (almost 80 percent of the military made less than $30,000 per year), and that 20,000 enlisted personnel were eligible for food stamps.[56] To many, Clinton seemed motivated more to save money than to develop an effective fighting force. As one Marine lieutenant colonel complained, the Clinton administration was "just making cuts, without examining what future missions would be."[57]

Illustrative of the administration's lack of regard for the military was a White House aide's now famous snub of then Lt. Gen. Barry McCaffrey. General McCaffrey, who had most recently served in the Persian Gulf War, encountered the aide in a White House hallway. He said, "Good Morning," only to have the aide reply, "I don't talk to the military."[58] Although the president personally apologized to McCaffrey and took him jogging with him, word of what had happened quickly went around the Pentagon. The damage had been done.

HOMOSEXUALS IN THE MILITARY

During a November 11, 1991, press interview, Clinton renewed his campaign pledge to allow homosexuals to serve openly in the military. Ironically, this issue had not been a major topic in the election, and he could have avoided it. But Clinton was determined to carry out his campaign pledge, and perhaps he overestimated his own power and authority. Powell warned him, "Lifting the ban is going to be a tough issue for you, and it's a culture shock for the armed forces. The chiefs and the CNIC's don't want it lifted. Most military people don't want it lifted. I believe a majority in Congress are against lifting the ban too."[59] A few days later, Clinton announced his intention to lift the ban.

That announcement had the effect of uniting the military against him to a degree that insiders could not believe. The Joint Chiefs primary concern was that they feared the president would permit "gay culture."[60] They worried that Clinton would not back them when they wrote regulations that the gays opposed. Shortly thereafter Clinton decided that this was a fight he could not win, something the Joint Chiefs, who had enlisted their allies on the Hill and in the media, also understood. Indeed, the latter seemed to be saying, "Keeping this promise will cost you the military. Fight us now and you'll lose—and it won't be pretty."[61] In the end, the two sides reached a compromise: Stop asking and stop pursuing. Gays and lesbians could serve in the military, but they would have to keep their sexual orientation to themselves. From the standpoint of civil-military relations, the rank and file of the military were furious at him for trying to foist this policy on them. Clinton and the military would fight other battles in the social sphere, most notably on the role women were to play in the armed forces, and the military would resist. But in the case of women, the Joint Chiefs went along, if reluctantly. The military was not interested in a shared responsibility when it came to the role of gays in the military. The generals were opposed and prepared to hold this position regardless of what Clinton wanted to do.

SOMALIA

In Somalia, Clinton was faced with a major problem inherited from the Bush administration. The latter had sent food supplies to help the thousands in Somalia who were dying of starvation in 1992. Clinton supported this action.[62] Accordingly, on December 2, 1992, Bush dispatched advance troops to Somalia as part of a 21-nation force with Clinton's agreement.[63] By the end of the year, 146,000 tons of food had been delivered.

As far as most observers were concerned, the 35,000 American troops were deployed to carry out this mission. Problems continued. Shortly after Clinton became president, talk of sending more Americans to Somalia to help rebuild the country became increasingly pervasive. It was not long, however, before Mohammed Adid, the key warlord in the area, struck back and changed matters. On June 5, his forces killed or wounded 73 Pakistanis. The next day, the UN passed a resolution "calling for the arrest and punishment of those 'responsible' for the peacekeepers' deaths." In fact, according to one source, no one in Washington paid much attention to the resolution.[64]

Both Powell and Secretary of Defense Les Aspin wanted the U.S. to withdraw. However, on October 3, the worst possible scenario became reality.[65] Working together, the Rangers and the Delta Force launched a heliborne attack in an effort to capture Adid and his senior colleagues. As soon as the helicopters arrived at their destination, one was shot down by a rocket-propelled grenade (RPG). The operation immediately shifted from finding Adid to saving the crew of the downed helicopter. "By the time the battle was over and relief columns were finally able to fight their way through to rescue the trapped units, eighteen Americans had died, at least seventy-four were wounded, and two helicopters had been shot down."[66] When Clinton learned what had taken place, his response was "how did this happen?"

Clinton was angry. He wanted to know why the U.S. had permitted itself to be pushed around by people he referred to as "two-bit pricks." In addition, he asked why he had not been informed of the problems inherent in U.S. policy toward Somalia and why that policy had shifted without his "*informal approval.*" "He believed that people who were supposed to protect him had not. He had been a little careless, more than a bit disengaged, in fact, but that did not mean he entirely accepted responsibility for what has happened."[67] He claimed that he would have never approved the mission had he known that it was to be carried out during daytime.[68] This was typical of the way Clinton responded to foreign affairs crises that went against the U.S.: he knew nothing about it, he would have never approved it, and it was his advisors, including the Joint Chiefs, who let him down. The military response was predictable. David Hackworth, a retired colonel and one of America's most decorated soldiers, vented his bitterness over the president's refusal to accept responsibility when he claimed, "Clinton was dangerously out of touch with foreign policy issues."[69]

Since the president was not responsible, someone else was. It was not long before Clinton found a scapegoat—it was Secretary of Defense Les Aspin, who had turned down a request to send additional tanks to Somalia. In addition, many in Washington felt that Aspin was doing a poor job of running the Pentagon. When he was called to testify on the Hill, he could not articulate a clear U.S. policy toward Somalia because the U.S. did not have one. On December 13, Aspin was told that the president had lost trust in him and thought it was time for a change. Aspin tried to fight the decision but was formally dismissed on December 15.

HAITI

In contrast to the other incidents where force was used during Clinton's time in office, Haiti was an exception. After some initial complaints about being "cut out of the action," Clinton worked closely with his generals, listening to their advice and using it when he felt it appropriate. By and large, it was a case of shared responsibility.

The poorest country in the Western Hemisphere, Haiti was ruled by a military junta. Initially, Clinton hoped to rely primarily on sanctions in an effort to apply pressure on the junta to change its policies.[70] During the election campaign, Clinton had criticized Bush's Haitian policy as too restrictive, implying that he would be more forthcoming in dealing with that country's problems. As one observer put it, Clinton's comments "implied a welcome to Haitians fleeing poverty and misery, as well as, in some cases, political persecution."[71] The result was an avalanche of boats—most of which were not seaworthy—on their way to Florida. Florida's governor objected, and Clinton soon realized that he had a serious political problem on his hands.

By the summer of 1994, there were suggestions that the U.S. was considering an invasion of Haiti. Domestic pressure on Clinton was growing stronger by the day. On July 3 and 4 alone, the U.S. Coast Guard intercepted over 6,000 boat people trying to make their way to the U.S.[72] By September the invasion plan was complete. For his part, Clinton again blamed his staff for getting him into this mess: "I can't believe they got me into this. . . . How did it happen: We should have waited until after the elections."[73]

General Raoul Cedras, the leader of the Haitian junta, met with American negotiators, but refused to budge until his associates warned him that C-130s carrying the 82nd Airborne had begun to leave Fort Bragg. Cedras then capitulated, and a date was set for him to leave. It was a bloodless and successful operation, even if Clinton did not want to accept responsibility for it.

BOSNIA

Bosnia was a bloody affair. There were three distinct ethnic groups—Muslim Bosnians, Croatian Bosnians, and Serbian Bosnians, all of whom had lived in the area for centuries. Now, however, the Serbs were determined to take control of the province by forcing the Muslims, in particular, to leave or to be exterminated. Diplomatic efforts were made by the U.S. and U.K. to break the region into cantons: Muslim, Serbian, and Croat. Clinton rejected this approach and instead asked General Powell what the U.S. could do to stop the killing. Powell replied that the U.S. options ranged from limited strikes around Sarajevo to a heavy bombardment of Serb targets throughout the region.

It was at this time that one of the more memorable events in U.S. civil-military relations took place. Powell was explaining the importance of thinking matters through, when Madeleine Albright, then the U.S. Ambassador to the UN, "asked [him] in frustration. 'What's the use of having this superb military that you're always talking about if we can't use it?' "[74] Powell almost had an "aneurysm." Soldiers were not toys to be moved from place to place; they were human beings and should only be utilized when absolutely necessary, once again revealing the gap dividing military officers from civilians.

On April 29, Clinton met for two hours with the Joint Chiefs and senior civilians in the Oval Office. The group reviewed all the options, including lifting the arms embargo on the Muslims, thereby permitting them to obtain the weapons they needed to defend themselves. Clinton expressed his concern about getting sucked further into Bosnia, the mission creep that so worried the Joint Chiefs.

In July, the Bosnian Serbs intensified their siege of the city of Sarajevo. Clinton was in the Far East but saw pictures on TV that shocked him. He asked for options, including military ones. While Washington debated its options, the Serbian machine continued to roll on. Attention was soon focused on the small mining town of Srebrenica. Its population had been swollen by Muslim refugees. On July 11, 1995, the town fell to the Serbs. As David Halberstam described the situation, "Now having taken charge of the village, the Serbs started to rid the area of all Muslims. The Serbs might not be good fighters, but they did pogroms very well indeed. They were familiar with the drill, and the entire process had a macabre efficiency." According to one report, 7,000 Muslim men were executed.[75]

On August 28, 1995, the Bosnian Serbs attacked. Sarajevo was the straw that broke the camel's back. August 31 was "the busiest day of military action in NATO history, with planes ranging across all of northern and Western Bosnia."[76] On September 11, Clinton attended a meeting in the White House to discuss the issue. He asked if the bombing campaign had reached a point of diminishing returns or was it worth continuing? When he was told that there were still targets remaining, he said what he should have said previously, "Okay. . . . But I am frustrated that the air campaign is not better coordinated with the diplomatic effort." Finally, on September 14, the Bosnian Serbs agreed to cease offensive operations and to remove all heavy weapons from the area within a week. In addition, they agreed to open a road to Sarajevo and to reopen the airport within 24 hours.

GENERAL WESLEY CLARK

The way the new Secretary of Defense William Cohen dealt with General Clark provides interesting insights on civil-military relations during the latter part of the Clinton administration. Cohen appointed Clark SACEUR (Supreme Allied Commander, Europe). However, over time Cohen became concerned about him: Clark was too ambitious. Indeed, he owed his appointment as SACEUR to a number of civilian officials outside of the Department of Defense. He would follow every route available to get what he wanted. It should be noted that at this time, there was an "us" and "them" perception in Washington. The civilians did not trust the military and vice-versa. Thus, Clark's first loyalty should have been to the secretary of defense, and Cohen warned him that he was too close to civilians outside of the department of defense. As Clark noted, some asked, "Was he really one of theirs? Was he too political, too likely to grandstand? Did his ambition reach too far?"[77] Clark claimed that he was given minimal guidance from Cohen in spite of his repeated requests. The situation deteriorated to the point where Cohen and General Hugh Shelton, the chairman of the Joint Chiefs of Staff, ordered Clark to provide them with copies of his itinerary prior to coming to Washington.

KOSOVO

Kosovo was the final military action under Clinton. Although primarily populated by Albanians, Kosovo contained some of the Serb's most sacred and treasured pieces of historical real estate. Hatred between the two groups was bitter and long-standing. While the Serbs governed the region, the Albanians wanted autonomy at a minimum, and independence if possible. The Albanian Kosovo Liberation Army (KLA) began a guerilla war.

Clark's relations with the Pentagon continued to deteriorate. The commander of U.S. troops in Bosnia recommended that the U.S. continue to maintain 10,000 troops in the region. The next day, the American military representative in NATO disavowed his recommendation. Clark was clearly on a collusion course with the Pentagon.

Clark's political situation deteriorated even further when he returned to Washington for consultations. General Shelton was not available, so he met with a senior official in the State Department. The Pentagon quickly assumed that Clark was working behind its back—with the civilian side of the house. Clinton did not seem interested in the subject: he paid no attention to the deep divide between the civilians and the military over Kosovo. This was even more evident at a conference at Rambouillet in France. The assumption was that all of NATO's senior military officers, including Clark, would be attending. In February, Clark was told that "the Secretary of Defense doesn't want you there."[78] Then Cohen called and said he could go, but could only talk about the military annex to the document that was being discussed.

In Kosovo, the Serbian response to increased KLA activity was an even more brutal crackdown on the Albanians in Kosovo. Violence escalated, and the Albanians were given more than their share of martyrs. The Joint Chiefs remained determined to limit U.S. military involvement. There were simply too many missions and potential missions around the world to risk tying up

U.S. forces in Kosovo. Toward that end, the Joint Chiefs agreed to a bombing plan in the hope that it would bring Serbian leader Slobodan Milosevic to his knees. The current plan was not succeeding. He remained as defiant as ever. The political pressure forcing pilots to attack only certain targets was so strong that there were constant complaints from those flying the air war.[79]

By the third week of the air war, a consensus began to form in Washington: ground troops might be necessary. However, trying to get specific guidance was next to impossible. There was no decision-making structure, and the president had not decided what to do. On April 23, the Fiftieth Anniversary NATO Summit was held in Washington, an especially important event for the future of the Alliance. The Allies agreed that they would do whatever was necessary to win the war in Kosovo. Fortunately, Belgrade's decision on June 3, 1999, to capitulate made a ground invasion unnecessary.

Clark's saga continued. When he arrived at a reception for senior officials, he started toward Clinton and his senior advisors to pay his respects, but "the body language was uninviting. I turned away and halted about twenty feet behind and off to the side of the group." According to Clark, as he traveled back to Brussels, some journalists misinterpreted his words to suggest that NATO was not winning the war. The next evening Shelton called him, "The Secretary of Defense asked me to give you some verbatim guidance, so here it is: 'Get your f______g face off the TV. No more briefings, period. That's it.' I just wanted to give it to you like he said. Do you have any questions?" According to Clark, Clinton reportedly saw a transcript of what he said and saw nothing wrong with it.[80]

It is difficult to classify the Clinton administration. There were times when shared responsibility was the name of the game—in Haiti, Bosnia, and Kosovo. Then there was at least one incident—the role of gays in the military—when the two sides parted company. The major problem seems to have been Clinton's primary focus on domestic problems. He did not appear strongly interested in foreign policy, so he was often not aware of the latest developments in that area. However, when it came to resolving issues, he worked closely with the military.

George W. Bush (2001–2009)

The Bush administration began quietly. There was talk of the need for military transformation, greater reliance on high technology and less on mass, a line the military had heard previously. Bush praised them and their culture. When it came to leadership, Bush's style was similar to that of many CEOs in major corporations. He was not interested in details, and instead relied on his advisors—including the military. Bush would present or discuss a problem and leave it to senior officials to tell him what procedure to follow. Bush also expected quick decisions on national security questions. To quote Bob Woodward, "Bush's leadership style bordered on the hurried. He wanted actions, solutions."[81] The major difference from previous presidents was the very active role that he permitted his vice president, Richard Cheney, to play. Bush allowed him to become deeply involved in almost all of the country's national security decisions, especially after 9/11. The other major figure in Bush's national security cabinet was Donald Rumsfeld, a pugnacious, arrogant, bright, brusque individual who had little respect for the military. Like a number of other civilians who had the defense portfolio, he was convinced that he and his civilian advisors understood military tactics, operational art, and strategy far better than those who had worn the uniform for 30-plus years.

Rumsfeld's style in dealing with the Joint Chiefs quickly became apparent. General Hugh Shelton, the chairman of the Joint Chiefs of Staff at the time, discovered that Rumsfeld expected to play a central role in all significant military decisions. He even went to the point of suggesting to Shelton that—in violation of the Goldwater-Nichols Act—he go through him before speaking to the president. Shelton refused. In short, while the Joint Chiefs appreciated Bush, they had little respect for his secretary of defense, a man who "relegated Shelton and his staff to the status of 'second-rate citizens.' "[82] As another senior officer put it, "The fact is, [Rumsfeld] is disenfranchising people."[83]

Shelton's term as Chairman expired in September. Rumsfeld replaced him with a more compliant and pliable, albeit very gentlemanly air force officer, Richard Myers. Myers, was a fighter pilot and a specialist in space weapons. His selection made it clear "that the administration wanted obedience, not officers who might make waves."[84] Myers might disagree with Rumsfeld, and sometimes those differences were significant. However, rather than fighting for the military's point of view, Myers worked hard to find a way to accommodate Rumsfeld. In contrast to Shelton, Myers agreed to go through Rumsfeld when he had views or information that should be brought to the president's attention.[85]

AFGHANISTAN

The attack on the World Trade Center in New York City and on the Pentagon on September 11, 2001, transformed the Pentagon's world: "Osama bin Laden abruptly ended Rumsfeld's campaign to reign in the armed forces."[86]

Focus was no longer singularly on modernizing the military; now the most important task was striking back at the terrorists, regardless of where they were.

Bush wanted to know how the U.S. could retaliate—and he meant *now*, not in a couple of weeks or months. The problem, however, was that while the Pentagon had plans for military engagements all over the world, no one had ever thought to draw up a plan for military operations in Afghanistan. Consequently, Rumsfeld's response to Bush was "Very Little Effectively." Feeling the heat, Rumsfeld turned to General Tommy Franks, the commander of CENTCOM. He told Franks "You don't have months." He and the president wanted something done in weeks or days. The problem, Franks tried to point out, was that Afghanistan was on the other side of the globe, even farther away than Kuwait. Furthermore, "Al Qaeda was a guerilla organization whose members lived in caves, rode mules and drove large sport-utility vehicles." Rumsfeld responded, "Try again."[87]

On September 18, Bush again reiterated his desire to retaliate as soon as possible. "This is a new world," Bush noted. "General Shelton should go back to the generals for new targets. Start the clock. This is an opportunity. I want a plan—costs, time. I need options on the table. I want Afghan options by Camp David. I want decisions quick!"[88] The meeting at Camp David was held three days later. Shelton had three options: first, strike with cruise missiles; second, use cruise missiles with manned bombers; third, employ cruise missiles, plus bombers and the special forces, and perhaps regular forces, and Marines.

The following Monday, Bush informed the group that he had decided on option three. But given the magnitude of the problems involved in military logistics, the Pentagon was having problems coming up with a plan. At a meeting on September 24, an angry Rumsfeld "beat up on Franks incessantly," but to no avail.[89]

On October 2, Rumsfeld sent the service chiefs, the combatant commanders, and the under secretaries a fifteen-page top-secret order titled, "Campaign against Terrorism: Strategic Guidance for the Department of Defense." Rumsfeld laid down the law. The department should anticipate "multiple military operations in multiple theaters."[90]

On October 7, the Pentagon was ready with a plan, and Bush signed the papers to begin hostilities in Afghanistan. On October 19, the bombing campaign was supplemented by the arrival of a 12-member contingent of army special operations forces, deployed in the north. If the Afghan operation taught Rumsfeld anything, it was that the U.S. required a more flexible, robust, and lethal force to deal with similar contingencies around the world.

TRANSFORMATION

Rumsfeld was convinced that the U.S. military, and especially the U.S. Army was living in the last century. It was time to modernize it by making greater use of technology, thereby decreasing the need for reliance on large numbers of troops. As he put it on February 1, 2002, transformation was, "the military buzzword for a change from heavy, slow-moving forces to lighter, more agile units, employing the latest information technology, to wage computerized warfare."[91]

One of Rumsfeld's worst performances was his treatment of General Eric Shinseki, the army's chief of staff. Shinseki realized early on that the army needed to modernize if it was going to be relevant in the days of smaller armies and greater reliance on high tech, and he had begun his own policy of transformation. The problem, however, was that the army had more missions than it could carry out with the forces it had.

The dispute between Shinseki and Rumsfeld went public when Shinseki was asked in his testimony before the Senate Armed Services Committee how many troops would be needed for the invasion of Iraq. He responded by stating "something on the order of several hundred thousand soldiers is probably a figure that would be required."[92] Wolfowitz and Rumsfeld were furious, and both publicly criticized the quiet, soft-spoken Shinseki. Rumsfeld fired the secretary of the army, who supported him. It was an unusual display of civilian pique over a general giving his honest opinion to a Congressional Committee—as he was required to do by law.

INVADING IRAQ

Rumsfeld's interference in military matters was most obvious and his impact most tragic, during the invasion of Iraq.

Throughout the period from 9/11 until U.S. troops invaded Iraq, Rumsfeld, Wolfowitz, and the vice president were the cheerleaders calling for the use of U.S. military power against the Iraqi dictator. They cited all sorts of reasons, most significantly Saddam Hussein's purported possession of weapons of mass destruction. They did their best to sideline Secretary of State Colin Powell, who was less enthusiastic about the use of American military power against Saddam.

Rumsfeld began his effort to control the invasion by incessantly beating down General Tommy Franks, who agreed with Shinseki that several hundred thousand troops would be needed. Over and over, Franks would be asked to come up with a plan, and every time he did, Rumsfeld would maintain that he was calling for the use of too many troops. Franks would go back with a lower number only to have Rumsfeld dismiss it as too high. Rumsfeld dismissed the importance of Phase IV, that part of military operations that comes after the war fighting is over—"post-hostilities" operations. He was convinced that American troops with their high-tech weapons would move through Iraq with ease. He had spoken with a shadowy Iraqi exile leader, Ahmed Chalabi, and was convinced that the Americans would be greeted like liberators and be able to return home in a few weeks or months.

The war did not turn out as Rumsfeld anticipated. Instead, the U.S. military became bogged down and was soon faced with a guerilla war. To make matters worse, Rumsfeld created two lines of authority: one military and one civilian, a clear violation of military culture. The contrast between the two individuals in command could not have been greater. General Ricardo Sanchez was on the military side, while Paul Bremer, a former foreign service officer and former ambassador to The Netherlands, was on the civilian side. Neither could abide the other, and orders were often cleared through only one channel. What is more, Rumsfeld gave Bremer permission to issue the two worst orders enforced during the entire episode—the disbandment of both the Bath Party and the Iraqi army. The latter in particular, put hundreds of thousands of soldiers out of work, eliminated forces to enforce law and order, and provided the insurgents with many willing candidates.

Rumsfeld also dictated policy in Iraq. He repeatedly ignored Colin Powell and the State Department and interfered with such critical matters as the Time Phased Force and Deployment Data (TPFDD). "The TPFDD for Iraq was an unbelievably complex master plan governing which units would go where, when, and with what equipment, on which planes or ships, so that everything would be coordinated and ready at the time of attack."[93] Sequencing is key; tanks cannot arrive before their crews, nor can infantry units arrive before their tanks. But Rumsfeld had nothing but disdain for the TPFDD. It was just another example of the military's refusal to modernize, so he pulled out units he thought should not be in Iraq and refused to allow others called for by the plan to mobilize. As a result, some reservists ended up getting only five- to six-days notice while others got the news thirty days prior to mobilization. According to a participant, Rumsfeld was "looking line-by-line at the deployments proposed in the TPFDD and saying, 'Can't we do this without some company?' " or, "shouldn't we get rid of this unit?" Making detailed, last-minute adjustments to the TPFDD was in the army's view, pulling cogs out of a machine at random. "The generals would protest, saying, Sir, these changes will ripple back to every railhead and every company."[94] But Rumsfeld was running the show. By the end of December, Rumsfeld had authorized sending 200,000 troops to the Gulf, but his constant interference was becoming a major problem. Army officials would decide to activate a reserve unit, only to discover that Rumsfeld had vetoed it. This was the first time in U.S. military history that a secretary of defense had micromanaged matters to this extent. Neither the Germans nor the Russians had to put up with this level of micromanagement in a combat situation; the closest comparison was probably Trudeau's interference with Canadian forces in NATO.

Military officers were becoming increasingly frustrated at what they saw as a march to war. In mid-October combatant commanders were notified that an order would shortly be issued stating that a war with Iraq would be part of the war on terror. Senior officers were incensed. "How the hell did a war on Iraq become part of the war on terrorism?" demanded one officer on the Joint Staff, summarizing the "reaction of four of those commander's staffers." Another argued, "There is no link between Saddam Hussein and 9/11. . . . Don't mix the two. This is going to work hell with the Allies. What is going on?"[95]

Rumsfeld was undaunted by the criticism, even after it became obvious that his plan for Iraq did not work. The U.S. was soon faced with a civil war. His standard response was to refer to the American experience, noting, "Just as it took time and patience, trial and error, and years of hard work before the founders got it right, so too it will take time, and patience, and trial and error, and hard work for the Iraqi people to overcome the challenge they face."[96]

Rumsfeld and his associates continued to alienate the uniformed military. It was not long before he and NSC advisor Condoleezza Rice ran into problems over the future of Iraq as she began to articulate her preferred policy of "Take, Clear, Build." Several retired generals also began to attack Rumsfeld, arguing that the mess in Iraq was largely his fault and that it was time for him to leave. In March 2006, Major General Paul Eaton, wrote an op-ed in the *New York Times*, which maintained that Rumsfeld was "not competent to lead our armed forces."[97] This was soon followed by criticism from LTG Gregg Newbold, Major General Charles Swannack, Major General John Batiste, and Major General John Riggs. Rumsfeld brushed such criticism aside. However, it was becoming clear that he had to go, and he finally submitted his resignation to Bush on November 6, one day before the off-year election. Building a shared relationship was not in Rumsfeld's vocabulary.

ROBERT GATES

As a replacement for Rumsfeld, Bush selected Robert Gates. Gates spent most of his life in the Washington bureaucracy and in contrast to Rumsfeld understood the system. It was understanding he would need, because he had to devise a new strategy to win the war in Iraq as well as to find a way to reopen communications between the defense secretary and the uniformed military.

Gates made it clear from the beginning that he intended to work closely with the Hill, that he would take the counsel of the military professionals under his command, and that he understood the need for teamwork in working with other parts of the government in constructing policy.[98]

The key question facing the Bush administration was whether the addition of thousands of more U.S. troops (the "surge") could turn things around in Iraq. Bush met with several experts, including retired army General Jack Keane, who argued that more troops were needed to ensure security in Iraq. Bush was determined to take hold of U.S. policy, and he was convinced that a surge offered the only way to begin to turn things around in Iraq. An early hint that Bush was leaning in that direction was the announcement that he was appointing General David Petraeus as commander of U.S. forces in Iraq. Bush admitted that the U.S. had made mistakes in Iraq and, in a TV address on January 2007, announced that the United States would introduce an additional 20,500 (later increased to 30,000) troops. He said the plan to secure Baghdad has "failed for two principal reasons: there were not enough Iraqi and American troops available to secure neighborhoods that had been cleared of terrorists," and he said that de-Baathification had gone too far.[99]

Gates also reversed the procedure for briefing the president on an issue like Iraq. Instead of speaking on behalf of the generals or bringing along generals who would meekly support his position, Gates encouraged the generals to give Bush their honest opinions. And they did.[100] For example, General Petraeus and Admiral William Fallon openly disagreed on U.S. strategy for Iraq in a meeting with Bush.[101] Gates also went out of his way to rebuild the Pentagon's relations with Congress and did something Rumsfeld avoided: he told the truth about the situation in Iraq. On August 2, 2007, for example, he stated openly, "I think the developments on the political side are somewhat discouraging at the national level."[102]

It was not long before Petraeus's new strategy began to work. Casualties on both the U.S. and Iraqi side went down. U.S. military deaths decreased from 101 in June to 39 in October.[103] Anbar Province, previously an insurgent stronghold, turned on al Qaeda and began to work with the Marines to subdue insurgents in the province.

Barack Obama (2009–)

One of Obama's first decisions was to keep Robert Gates as defense secretary. He listened to Congress. For example, after discussing the appointment of General Peter Pace as chairman of the Joint Chiefs of Staff with key members of Congress, and realizing the problems involved in his appointment as chairman, Gates decided against the appointment.

Gates also made it clear that he believed in the military concept of accountability. He began by criticizing Pentagon planning for postwar Iraq, and then fired two generals as well as the secretary of the army over the shabby conditions at Walter Reed Army Hospital. He fired the secretary of the air force as well as its chief of staff because of their failure to secure "sensitive military components" involved in the protection of nuclear weapons.[104] Gates also pushed through a rethinking of U.S. military strategy in favor of one focused on counterinsurgency, promoted General David Petraeus who favored it, and saw to it that several colonels whose support for it had killed their promotion chances in the past were given the opportunity to pin on their first star. He also forced a reluctant air force to deploy more airborne surveillance systems in Afghanistan, and he ordered the military to focus on procuring weapons that would be of immediate use in Afghanistan and Iraq.[105] Despite strong Congressional opposition, he trimmed the budget for the army's Future Combat Systems and he cut the budget for missile defense programs. Most notably, he led a successful fight to limit the number of the air force's F-22s.[106] He also succeeded in getting Congress to expand the size of the army and Marines and in one very important case, he oversaw the ousting of one military commander (in Afghanistan) in favor of another.

In contrast to Rumsfeld, Gates and his boss, President Obama, have shown considerable respect for the military—a key component of military culture. One of the first signs was the president's appointment of Admiral Mike Mullen as chairman of the Joint Chiefs. One of Mullen's first actions was to reassert the role of the chairman as the primary military advisor to the president. He did that with Gate's blessing, and in sharp contrast to the Rumsfeld period, Mullen publicly disagreed with Gates on occasion.[107] If nothing else, this demonstrated that both Gates and Obama trusted Mullen enough to permit him to speak his mind on sensitive issues. Furthermore, Gates and Obama have constantly lauded the role of the military and in contrast to Rumsfeld, have played up the role of Mullen and Secretary of State Hillary Clinton.

Even more important from the standpoint of shared responsibility, Mullen and the commander of forces in Afghanistan, David Petraeus, dealt directly with the president on what to do next in Afghanistan. Indeed, the interaction between the president, the defense secretary, and the military as discussed in *Obama's Wars* could be seen as a model of shared responsibility.[108] They were allowed to express their own views, even if neither Gates nor Mullen agreed with them. It was clear to all that the president was the final authority. Even more important, on an issue as sensitive as the "Don't Ask, Don't Tell" controversy, the debate over whether homosexuals should serve openly, the chief of staff of the army, the commandant of the Marine Corps, and the chief of staff of the air force felt confident enough of their relationship with Obama to openly disagree with him on this issue.[109] Equally important, when the president ordered them to allow gays to serve openly, they fully implemented the policy.

From the standpoint of the military and military culture, they could hardly ask for more. Shared responsibility was a reality. Assuming a desire on the part of both sides to work together, one can only hope that the process continues.

PART II / Germany

Soldiers need trust in the political leadership if they are to render obedience based on a realization of the essential nature of their service.

MG Jörg Bahnemann

CHAPTER 4

From Konrad Adenauer through Willy Brandt

> A military without tradition is like trees without roots.
>
> EBERHARD BIRK

Unlike the case in the United States, Russia, and Canada, civil-military relations in the Federal Republic of Germany started from scratch. There wasn't a German army (Bundeswehr) prior to 1955. When the Germans created it, they not only had to build a structure, find qualified personnel, and obtain weapons, they had to break with Germany's military past, especially that of the Wehrmacht and National Socialism.[1] It was critical that the new military demonstrate to the West as well as the German people that it was a new military: different from the Wehrmacht as well as the German Democratic Republic's (GDR's) National People's Army (NVA). It had to be an army whose attitudes were compatible with and supportive of a democratic political system. From a symbolic standpoint, it meant the creation of new symbols—uniforms, traditions, and heroic figures. Given the lack of support by the West German populace for the newly created Bundeswehr (German armed forces), as well as the fear of German militarism on the part of its neighbors, the leaders of the Federal Republic of Germany (FRG) were also faced with the task of gaining public support.

Military Tradition

According to Donald Abenheim, military tradition is "the sum of attitudes, customs, and symbols of military life that succeeding generations have preserved and adapted in armies over time."[2] Tradition refers to the symbols from the past that are unique to the military's history and values that govern many aspects of military life; it is a subset of military culture. For most in the developed world, the concept of tradition is simple. I would suggest that few in the American or Russian militaries think about it. It appears on patriotic holidays or at solemn military events, but a careful analysis of where this or that military figure stands on the Pantheon of military historical figures is normally left to the training of cadets and midshipmen and to military historians.

However, for German civil-military relations, the creation of tradition has been a difficult, protracted problem. Tradition means providing values for a very unique organization. To quote General Hans von Seekt, the spiritual father of the Reichswehr,[3] "Whoever refuses to recognize the uniqueness of the military psyche will fail to understand the deeper meaning of these externals and dismiss them as theatricalities."[4]

In creating tradition, the primary problem was the German officer corps' tendency to see itself as a "warrior caste," as part of the German society of the premodern estates, a group of men with their own code of honor, system of law, and beliefs, "which had little in common with those of men in industry, science, commerce, and parliamentary politics."[5] Germany did not have the luxury of slowly developing new, more democratic military symbols. By the early 1950s, Germany faced an immediate need to create something new: a military tradition that was compatible with the FRG's democratic values in a country that had a catastrophic experience with the first republic and its flawed democracy. As a Bundeswehr publication noted, "The cultivation of tradition is the process of selecting events from history to highlight certain values."[6] But which values to highlight? To be sure these values had to be in accord with the country's constitution, the *Grundgesetz* or Basic Law. But determining what part of the past was compatible with the new system and which was not would be a Herculean task that would occupy Germany's political and military leaders for the next 40 plus years.

In a sense, the Federal Republic's political leadership faced an impossible situation. Even simple matters like the World War II Wehrmacht helmet, or the field-gray uniforms, or mention of legendary German generals or admirals brought back memories of a bitter and destructive past. Initially, the Germans reached a compromise "between two extremes; the maintenance of tradition under Hans von Seeckt on the one hand, and the popular revulsion against the military in postwar Germany on the other."[7] The task was not to abandon older fundamental values. General Adolf Heusinger, who was a leader in the Military Section of the Office Blank, the office that would become the basis for the future Ministry of Defense, commented, "We should determine which part of military tradition has been overtaken and should therefore be eliminated, in order that *the good old part is transmitted to the troops*."[8] This task was easier said than done.

Military culture is vital if the army is to function effectively. The Germany military sociologist Bernard Flekenstein illustrated the problem when he noted:

> For some time now, the debate in the Federal Republic of Germany on the nature of the military vocation has been dominated by two major approaches: the civilian-oriented approach, which analyzes the military vocation as an element of a large bureaucratic-technical organization and ascribes to it civilian occupational concepts, and the military-oriented approach, which differentiates between the functions of military and civilian occupations. The advocates of the civilian-oriented approach view the soldier as an employee like any other, whereas those favoring the military-oriented position, emphasize the unique features of a soldier's profession.[9]

One strong opponent of military values commented, "it is primarily and only about making the *military* norms democratic. *Democracy has a higher value than military efficiency.*"[10] Those on this side of the debate believe military culture is inherently nondemocratic and want no part of it. It should give way to democratic civilian culture.

INNERE FÜHRUNG

To help integrate the Bundeswehr, into a pluralist state and society, its founders came up with several ideas. The first and best known is *Innere Führung*, an expression that is difficult to translate into English. A translation of "inner command," "moral leadership," and "moral education, barely conveys the meaning of this term in German."[11] The central concept of Innere Führung is as much freedom in military service as is possible within the confines of command and obedience.[12] The concept attempts to combine the ability to follow one's conscience with the chance to fight for freedom. Every soldier has human value, as delineated in Article I of the Basic Law. Class or group membership is not important, rather everyone should be viewed as an individual. No longer can the military demand unquestioned obedience. Instead, the military is part of the civilian legal system. In that context, the Germans created what is called "conscience obedience." "Conscious obedience presumes a connection to political-moral basic values."[13] There is and presumably always will be a conflict between the ideas of subordination, uniformity, and obedience and the idea of Innere Fürhrung.[14] However, the Bundeswehr is clear on the issue of "carrying out orders." "Orders may not be obeyed if that would result in committing a criminal act. And orders should not be carried out if they are against human rights or are aimed at non-duty purposes."[15]

Despite the seeming contradictory nature of the ideas of tactical and operational efficiency and Innere Führung, the small group of former German officers who came up with the idea in the early fifties were convinced that it was possible to have a soldier who was both free and obedient. As one of the best-known German military reformers, General Ulrich de Maiziere, put it, "Innere Führung assures the Bundeswehr's readiness for action [while remaining] within the framework of our system of rights."[16] Those who supported the ideas of Innere Führung in the 1950s and 1960s became known as the reformers. Those who tended to adhere to the privileges and ideals of the military past were known as the traditionalists. These two groups would battle each other from the 1950s until the 1970s.

Another term that plays a major role in the concept of Innere Führung is the primacy of politics. This idea is aimed at ensuring that the military never again becomes insular as was the case of the Reichswehr. In the Bundeswehr, there is no such thing as a "military solution" to a problem; the only option is a political solution that makes use of military means. The idea that the armed forces can avoid being involved in politics as their forefathers often did was unacceptable. The military is under the control of the country's parliament and executive branch—a further action aimed at ensuring that the military would never again be misused or allow itself to be misused.[17] This approach also places greater pressure on military leaders. Since they cannot simply order soldiers to do their bidding as in the past, it is the officers' job to concern themselves with the needs of subordinates, while setting an example for them.

Innere Führung is an evolving term. The principles enumerated in 1953 have been adapted to various phrases in the evolution of the Bundeswehr until the present. The purpose is always to harmonize the tension between the individual as a citizen and his right to liberty with the requirements of the armed forces for obedience and order.[18]

Given the pressure to quickly create the Bundeswehr, compromises were made. The government of Konrad Adenauer did not want to alienate those upon whom they were relying, which in this case were primarily veterans of the Wehrmacht. There were those, especially on the left, who objected strongly to anything that brought back memories of the militarism and misapplied soldierly ideals that had ended in total war and total defeat. The result would be a rather confused policy in terms of military traditions, especially symbols and ceremonies. There were vague comments about the importance of the constitution, but the government hesitated to adopt specific language.[19]

An historical overview of the evolution of post–World War II civil-military relations illustrates these concepts.

Konrad Adenauer, Christian Democratic Union, CDU (1949–1963)

Konrad Adenauer became chancellor on September 15, 1949. Theodor Blank was his primary advisor on military matters in the cabinet. Adenauer intended to tie the Federal Republic of Germany to the Western alliance, and when it became clear that the new NATO Alliance both wanted and needed a West German contribution, Adenauer backed efforts to build a German army, albeit one governed by democratic principles. In that sense, both Blank and Adenauer agreed. On October 16, 1956, the colorful Franz Jozef Strauß took over as the country's first defense minister when Blank's health failed.[20] While he understood the need for a democratically oriented military, he sided with the generals in believing that the military values of the past were important: the Bundeswehr could not simply ignore the past fifty odd years. Nor could it get away with coddling soldiers in training. It was critical that a new West German army reflected the military values that would be needed should the Bundeswehr go into nuclear combat.

CREATING THE BUNDESWEHR

The attitude toward the military by much of the West German population in the aftermath of World War II was best expressed in the German term *Ohne mich* ("without me"). The war's devastation and the tremendous loss of life convinced many Germans that the one thing they were sure of was that they did not want to live through another war. Thousands worked hard in the peace movement and in civil society to prevent rearmament and the creation of a national German army.

Amid various incognito preparations, some sponsored by the British and some by the U.S., a small group of former officers met secretly in the Abbey Himmerod in the Eifel in October 1950. The result was a document entitled, "Memorandum on the Formation of a German Contingent for the Defense of Western Europe within the Framework of an International Fighting Force." The drafters of the document were in a difficult situation. The country did not yet have a constitution, so the document put the matter off by suggesting that the chancellor could make use of the emergency provisions of the Basic Law, while the actual military legislation would be drafted later.

The drafters were well aware of the military's problems under Hitler, but they had no idea how the military should or could be subordinated to civilian authorities in practice. Despite its tentative nature, the Himmerod Declaration marked a step forward. "For the first time in the prehistory of the Bundeswehr, the concept appeared that advocated reform—later described as the 'citizen in uniform,' a term that signified a willingness to refashion the public image and the self-image of the Bundeswehr."[21] The idea was to recognize that when the citizen became a member of the West German military, he or she did not lose identity as a citizen.

At the end of October, Adenauer appointed Blank to be the head of an office directly subordinate to the chancellor. The office's task was to outline steps to be taken to create a new German military contingent in a European army. Blank was joined by former Wehrmacht generals and colonels as advisors. The so-called "Amt Blank" marked a major step forward in the effort to change the nature of civil-military relations. Under the prewar administration, military planning was totally controlled by the military, but now civilians and military officers were working together, in spite of differences of opinion, to create a new more open, democratic, and civilian-run military. This was nothing less than a reordering of the role of the soldier in Germany. They were, in essence, sharing responsibility in working to develop a new German army.

Amt Blank soon began to put some of the democratic ideas expressed above into action. It stated that soldiers would be allowed to vote and, unlike in the past, they would have the right to a private life and to be involved in civilian activities. They could also run for elective office—from serving in a local civic organization to becoming a member of the Bundestag. However, training was a problem. It began with a recognition of the importance of drill in the training of a soldier; without it, training would be impossible. However, it had to be modified to rid the organization of blind obedience. Primary focus would be on constructing unit cohesion in a more cooperative method (versus drill and abuses heaped on recruits), thereby getting soldiers to work together in solving problems. Members of Amt Blank went out of their way to protect the average soldier from being abused by superiors. They also worked to make the process fully transparent by bringing parliament into the foundation of the new army. Much to the chagrin of many former soldiers, Amt Blank decided not to permit the wearing of medals awarded in World War I or II if they had any Nazi symbols on them. The same was true of many other practices reminiscent of the Reichswehr and Wehrmacht.

THE BATTLE OVER TRADITION

Of all the German soldier-intellectuals who struggled with the issue of tradition, none was more eloquent than General Wolf Graf von Baudissin, a member of Amt Blank and the person primarily concerned with developing the inner structure of the new military. In a speech in December 1951, Baudissin argued that just as it would be absurd to try to resurrect the past, it would be wrong to "throw overboard all things from before."[22] This was a point that General Adolf Heusinger (who had served in the OKH—Army High Command during World War II) picked up on in his role as future chief of staff. He worried that a lack of tradition would create problems when the new recruits joined the Bundeswehr. There had to be some way to utilize the past to legitimize actions in the new Bundeswehr. After all, the new military would have no alternative but to rely heavily on members of the Wehrmacht. As Adenauer commented, "Do you believe anyone is going to find an 18-year-old admiral or general for us?"[23] So the traditions the military adopted would have to be acceptable to the new German democracy as well as meaningful for those who had served in the Wehrmacht.

THE BUNDESWEHR DEPLOYS ITS FIRST TROOPS

On June 7, 1955, Theodor Blank became the Federal Republic's first defense minister. It was his job to create a Bundeswehr, one fully supportive of the new democratic Germany. A month later, the Bundestag passed military amendments to the Basic Law to create the Bundeswehr. In August 15, 152,366 volunteers reported (of those 40,613 were former Wehrmacht officers, 87,089 former noncommissioned officers in the Wehrmacht, and 24,664 served as regular Wehrmacht soldiers).[24] All officer applicants were interviewed to determine their acceptability in a new democratic armed forces. Most former members of the SS were excluded.[25] It was up to the applicants to convince the boards that they supported the new German democracy. On November 17, the 200th birthday of the Prussian military reformer Gerhard von Scharnhorst, a date selected for its symbolic importance, the first 101 volunteers were sworn in. It was a motley crew. The uniforms were a slate grey color based on Anglo-Saxon combat dress of the late war era. These new soldiers faced the monumental task of building a new army—that included rebuilding bases, recruiting new personnel, and creating new values and a new military tradition. By January 1956, another 1,000 volunteers had joined, but by July 1, 1956, the total number of those in uniform had only increased to 10,000.[26]

Questions about a military tradition continued to haunt the Bundeswehr. For example, in 1956 the Social Democratic (SPD) representative Carlo Schmid attempted to fix this problem by trying to convince other members of parliament to focus on outstanding military personalities, regardless of when they had served. As he put it, "Every state needs a tradition. One cannot build a state on principles. One needs role models. That is the sense of tradition. An army also needs role models. Not everything from the past is tradition in a creative sense."[27] He was not restricting himself to the Wehrmacht. There were other military figures from the past, for example, the Prussian reformers who could serve as role models. From a practical standpoint, in many cases reliance on the Wehrmacht or Reichswehr for symbols and tradition made more sense because the events and personalities were recent enough that those joining the Bundeswehr could relate to them.

Traditional values concern more than heroic figures. They involve uniforms, military customs and ceremonies, music, marching style, and other forms of garrison and combat behavior. Baudissin believed that Germany had to make a clear break with the past. These were not the critical components of the past, and changing them would help convince both the Germans and others that this was a new and different Germany. The new uniform for the army and air force bore no resemblance to the past. If anything, it was similar to the American army. The helmet, for example, was American as was generally the case in those NATO nations that received surplus U.S. arms as part of U.S. security assistance in the Cold War.

A new school was established by the Bundeswehr, a School for Innere Führung, originally in Cologne, but moved to Koblenz in 1957.[28] Together with the Ministry of Defense, this became the main center for dealing with the creation of tradition for the Bundeswehr. It prepared material for the troops (especially through the journal *Information für die Truppe*) and conducted classes (usually for several weeks at a time) for officers at various levels. Its particular focus was on leadership, and it worked to break down the old military attitude of separating military matters from politics, harking back to the famous Prussian military theorist, Karl von Clausewitz, who believed that every military act is a political act. A soldier cannot divorce his actions from politics.

Baudissin gave a number of speeches on tradition, insisting that the Bundeswehr had to make a clean break with the past.[29] He maintained that traditional values were critical, values such as "a desire for peace, humanity, a chivalrous attitude, loyalty, and above all, a sense of moral responsibility for one's fellow man."[30] In the process, he mentioned a number of officers from the

Prussian army. He also singled out those who had refused the blind obedience of the Hitler period, and in a major speech suggested that those who had been "conspirators of conscience" should be honored. A soldier must decide if an order is morally right or not. If the situation puts him in an impossible position, then he should model himself after the brave men who conspired to kill Hitler on July 20, 1944.

To set down in law the new status soldiers were to enjoy in the Bundeswehr, a Soldier's Law was passed. "It set down as never before the duties and rights of the West German soldier."[31] This was something unheard of in German military history. At the same time, the Bundestag passed a law authorizing conscription. Not only did the Bundeswehr need soldiers, there was a belief that the draft would help keep the military in touch with the civilian population. Accordingly, the first draftees reported to the army and the air force on April 1, 1957, and to the navy in January 1958.

The constitution also took other steps to ensure the rights of soldiers. First, it permitted conscientious objection; and second, it forbade the creation of a military justice system. Of particular significance for the military leadership was the creation of a network of civilian positions that were responsible for tasks that in the past had been assigned to military officers. If that were not enough, it gave the German parliament considerable power vis-à-vis the military. For example, it appointed a parliamentary ombudsman (military commissioner) to make certain that Innere Führung was enforced at the unit level. Hence a soldier who felt that he was wronged could appeal his case directly to a key member of the Bundestag, who could then investigate the matter. It also gave the defense committee of the Bundestag investigatory powers. The defense committee also prepared all major legislation dealing with the armed forces. In addition, it was decided that the budget must be approved by parliament annually and it must show the numerical strength of the armed forces and the main features of its structure.[32] According to Abenheim, years later both generals Ulrich de Maiziere and Baudissin argued that this law was extremely important for Germany. From the nineteenth century and the time of Bismarck, the army had been able to avoid parliamentary control, especially the power of the purse and ministerial responsibility. The old military was "a state within a state." However, this practice came to a halt with the new defense legislation and the creation of entities in parliament to enforce these checks and balances, breaking with the traditions of the past and fostering the development of the Bundeswehr's own tradition.[33] The constitution not only permitted a soldier to vote, it allowed him to remain politically active while serving, and it made it possible for him to be a member of a political party. One even had the right to be elected to political office, something unheard of in the American or Canadian systems.

The senior officer's authority was also limited. In the beginning, the country's top military officer was merely an advisor to the defense minister and the government. Rather than a military commander, he was a *Generalinspektur* ("chief of staff"). During peacetime, command authority rested with the defense minister. During wartime it shifted to the chancellor, further elucidating the primacy of civilian control. There was a civilian official (under secretary), who may have had little or no military experience, between the chief of staff and the defense minister. When the latter was gone, power shifted to the civilian, not to the senior military officer.

BACK TO TRADITION

In March 1957, Admiral Friedrich Ruge, the chief of staff of the navy, issued a letter on the question of tradition. He maintained that tradition was a term that included the military values that had endured throughout the ages. He stressed the importance of such symbols and added that things, persons, and names could serve as symbols for the navy. He warned that they should be selected with care. The problems with his letter were that it was only aimed at the navy, and he failed to provide specific guidance on what kind of symbols would be acceptable.

This was followed in October by a paper written by Col. Hans Meier-Welcker, an early member of the Blank office and first head of the military history research staff. He argued that it was critical to strike a balance between the preservation of tradition and the interests and concerns of the civilian public. From Meier-Welcker's standpoint this would not be an easy task, but it was critical for educating soldiers. He assigned unit commanders the task of deciding which units or figures from the past could be honored in his unit. As far as Waffen-SS units were concerned, Meier-Welcker rejected them out of hand, but he left the door open to former members of these units to have a lineage and honor relationship with units under certain circumstances. The critical point was that this was to be carried out at the local level, thereby keeping the military high command out of the process. This meant that lacking a decree from the national government, local officers were free, within limits, to set up whatever unofficial relationship they and their local civilian population, that is, whatever the veteran's organization, deemed appropriate.

Faced with confusion and some criticism, there was considerable pressure to have the Ministry of Defense issue a decree within the institution of Innere Führung. As a result, General Heusinger, the inspector general, issued an order on July 20, 1959, the fifteenth anniversary of the plot against Hitler. While maintaining that unit events were a positive event in Germany's life, it also contained language that sought to excuse those who served in the Wehrmacht but were unaware of Hitler's actions while carrying out orders at the front.

By the early 1960s, it was becoming common practice for the military to name bases after military heroes (including some from World War II), and it was just as common for military units to invite former soldiers who had served in their unit or similar units during World War II to their festivities. In 1961, at the suggestion of Defense Minister Strauß, the chief of staff of the Luftwaffe, Lieutenant General Josef Kammhuber, gave three squadrons the following names: Manfred von Richthofen, Oswald Boelcke, and Max Immelmann. All three individuals had been heroes during World War I. During the ceremony, Strauß provided support commenting, "The best and most modern weapons are useless if the people who use them are not convinced of the importance of their task."[34]

TRAINING AND TRADITION

It was not long before problems began to appear with the way German soldiers were trained. In January 1962, for example, a recruit died while training at the airborne base in Nagold. According to one account, "During a 15 kilometers march in unusual heat, the 19-year-old recruit Gerd Trimborn collapsed. However, his trainers then forced him to go on. The trainer's motto was 'Paratroopers are diamonds and diamonds have to be polished.'"[35] The recruit died on August 1 from kidney and liver failure, caused by his collapse in the heat.

The military maintained that it was an accident—a normal part of training. Even when "'there was reference to serious offenses against the principle of Innere Führung and disgraceful treatment of a subordinate and mishandling of soldiers,' the army chief of staff, Lieutenant General Alfred Zerbel, justified the action with these words. 'The hard demands come from the requirements that soldiers must expect in modern combat.'"[36] This continued to be the army's view even a year after the "scandal." Detlef Bald cites Chief of Staff Friedrich Foertsch's comment: "Only training, perseverance and commitment to the mission according to past measures will make it possible for these technical soldiers to perform heroic actions."[37] Eventually, one of the trainers was sentenced to eight months incarceration and thrown out of the Bundeswehr, although he was later reinstated. There were also unofficial reports that some paratroop companies celebrated the 1941 invasion of Crete.[38] The bottom line was that at least in the early 1960s the military was committed to its own interpretation of the past. Training measures partly taken from the Wehrmacht—the hard, tough, demanding actions common to a hard training course—were used to meet the demands of modern combat.

Prompting critical comments by senior army officers, the incident at Nagold, among others, led to the publication of a book sharply critical of those who complained about training procedures. Entitled *Rettet die Bundeswehr* ("Save the Bundeswehr"), the author, the conservative journalist Hans Georg Studnitz, pointed out that the public knew little about the army. He noted that there were only two officers and four NCOs to train 191 soldiers: they had too much to do and too little time to do it. The Bundeswehr, Studnitz complained, had become an army without a pathos. "The soldier is denied the glory of the past."[39] As he put it, "The Bundeswehr has become an army without glory: the most lacking in glory of the twentieth century."[40] This went to the heart of military tradition.

Studnitz zeroed in on a Brigadier General Schmückle, a supporter of Innere Führung and spokesman for Strauß, maintaining that he would not accept "that orders are holy and discipline is blind."[41] Studnitz argued Innere Führung was the main reason for many of the problems facing the Bundeswehr. He maintained that German history had been destroyed in the Bundeswehr. How could a military survive without the military pathos, even if some parts of it were unacceptable? The military handbook on Innere Führung does not have a single mention of the word "Fatherland." The only rational solution to the many problems facing the Bundeswehr was to bring back the history and traditions of the Reichswehr and the Wehrmacht. The book was a hit among professional military officers, because it highlighted their distaste at having to give up so many of their symbols and traditions.

On July 20, 1963, General Johann Adolf Graf von Kielmansegg, who at that time was NATO's commander of land forces in central Europe, received an invitation from a group of former resistance fighters (*Zentralverband deutscher Widerstand kämpfer)* to give a speech. Kielmansegg commented that for most soldiers in the Third Reich, resistance was not an option, either in peace or in war. He also rejected the idea that the model should be the soldiers who plotted to kill Hitler. According to Kielmansegg, this was such a rare and extreme event that it could not be used as an example for soldiers to emulate. Imagine, he complained, if every time a soldier who received an order he did not like simply refused to carry it out. That would be the end of the Bundeswehr.[42]

When Adenauer left the scene, military tradition was still a topic of debate, with the CDU/CSU (Christian Democratic Union / Christian Social Union of Bavaria) government favoring the generals, while the left wing of the SPD (Social Democratic Party) constantly complained about the "militaristic" nature of military tradition. Money at this point was not the problem it would become in the 1990s. The threat was clear—the danger of a Soviet-led invasion of Western Europe—and despite some residual opposition, Germany had to be prepared for the worst. The government accepted the ambiguous nature of tradition. As long as they behaved themselves, the politicians allowed the military officers to quietly make use of the past, provided they stayed away from Nazi symbols and the SS or soldiers close to Hitler. In Strauß, the generals believed they had a friend at the top who would work with them and who would attempt to protect them from the left.

Ludwig Erhard, CDU (1963–1966)

Ludwig Erhard took over the chancellorship on October 16, 1963. He was primarily interested in economic matters, as befitted a man behind the idea of a market economy. That meant that at a time when there were stresses in the civil-military relationship serious enough to require the chancellor's personal attention, he was nowhere to be found. To make matters worse, his defense minister Kai-Uwe von Hassel was unable to deal effectively with the many problems in civil-military relations. It would not be a period of shared responsibility.

The parliamentary commissioner Hellmuth Heye, a retired vice admiral, issued a report condemning the methods the military used to train its troops. In his opinion, while the generals paid Innere Führung lip service, in reality, it was ignored by the professional military in favor of some of the methods previously used in the Wehrmacht. Heye also warned that the Bundeswehr was becoming isolated from the rest of society. As the report stated, the officers "are isolated, on their own, really a state within a state. Then they are dangerous for us."[43] Heye's comments were welcomed neither by the military nor by many members of the Bundestag. With the lack of support from the defense minister, he resigned as parliamentary commissioner. Nevertheless, his past as a distinguished naval leader meant that what he said carried weight. Von Hassel tried to walk a middle line, maintaining that the situation in the

Bundeswehr was not as bad as Heye portrayed, but also that it was not as good as others claimed.[44]

THE 1965 TRADITION DECREE

Defining the term military tradition continued to be a major problem. Traditionalists continued to argue that it meant all of German history as long as the event or individual was not related to the Waffen-SS or a war crime. Reformers, however, argued against any mention of the Reichswehr or Wehrmacht. To deal with this situation, the government issued an order that attempted to make clear what was included and what was excluded.

However, it was a compromise. It distanced itself from the Wehrmacht by clearly stating that "the traditions of former units could not be passed on to Bundeswehr units.[45] That meant that a Bundeswehr unit that was the geographical or branch successor to a Wehrmacht unit—that is, the same tank regiment or air force squadron—could not make reference to its heritage in any way. However, the unit could invite members of those units to visit their "old unit" on special holidays and to participate in the festivities. As far as naming units and barracks for those who proceeded them, the decree stated that such individuals could be honored provided the unit in question received permission from the Ministry of Defense. However, they would have to be "personalities whose attitude and achievements were exemplary." The key in inviting such individuals was that "it must remain clear that the Bundeswehr distinguishes itself in its political position, its mission, and its structure from the armed forces of earlier periods."[46]

Despite the ministry's best efforts, the decree was unenforceable and satisfied no one. How was a unit commander to determine if a former member of the Wehrmacht was a person who was "exemplary?" For example, an article in *Die Zeit* responded to those who felt that World War II General Heinz Guderian was a model of military efficiency. The unsigned article argued that while he was a capable military officer, he was also involved in the execution of the officers of the 20 July movement, and that he constantly supported Hitler's irrational military actions.[47] There were also mechanical problems. Calling up a general for permission to invite someone to a unit meeting would not work, because the general might not want to make such a decision: it could cost him his job and career. So unit commanders themselves made the call. While some might err on the side of caution, others would reach back to pull up some heroic figure that from their standpoint met all the criteria, but who might be found objectionable by reformers.

While officers were involved in the drafting of such regulations, active duty military deeply resented efforts by civilian ministry officials to tell them who to admire and who to dismiss as not worthy. Some found the decree too vague, while others welcomed the freedom of action it gave them. In reality, the decree changed nothing. Unit commanders had been making those decisions in the past, only now their role was reflected in an official order. There were also expressions of frustration with Defense Minister von Hassel's effort to limit their use of the military's past. The decree called on officers and NCOs to use examples during the course of their historical instruction. But what if an officer chose General X as a speaker or invitee, only to have some senior official blast him for his choice. It could have a very negative impact on his career. Abenheim quotes an officer critical of the process:

> "What good are Scharnhorst and Gneisenau," one officer asked. "If, in looking back . . . we soldiers of the Bundeswehr prefer to choose the Wehrmacht from 1933 to 1945, one needs . . . nothing more than that." "Why is the Bundeswehr so willing to make an example of the deed and attitude of the men of the Twentieth of July, while at the same time it renounces the tradition of the simple soldier at the front?" Another officer observed: "The publication of this decree strikes me as a really risk-free deed by the ministry. Since there is nothing in the decree, no one can attack it. The ministry is then in fine shape, but we have to go before our troops with this empty pathos. The risk is thrown in our hands." Finally, as yet another officer asked, "What really is a valid heritage—the decree doesn't give any information."[48]

Opposition inside the Bundeswehr to the government's confused policy regarding tradition continued. Soldiers believed symbols were a critical part of military culture and played a crucial role in matters like unit cohesion and morale. Why was Bonn so concerned about the issue? If bringing in someone from the Waffen-SS or the Wehrmacht would help raise unit cohesion, why worry about who it was, assuming, of course, he was not a war criminal? Von Hassel was forthcoming in one sense, and that was his agreement to the naming of a number of bases after military heroes, including former members of the Wehrmacht.

As in the past, a large percentage of officers and NCOs at this time had served in the Wehrmacht; Bonn could hardly have built an army without them. They were not Nazis; they were professional military NCOs, many of whom had fought on the Russian front. They knew war firsthand, and they understood how to lead men into battle.

Recognizing the extent of military opposition to the Tradition Decree, Lieutenant General Ulrich de Maiziere, the new army chief of staff, gave a speech on the topic. He began by noting that this was the first decree of its kind in German history. He also observed that history was not the same as tradition. Tradition or the use of historical symbols required the individual to make a choice from historical events, always picking the one that matched the values of the Bundeswehr. In the current situation, he said that units should concern themselves with all of the veterans in their vicinity, not just those from their unit. As an example of tradition, he mentioned the new Leopard tank, commenting that it was a valid form of tradition because it had a symbolic connection with the Panther and Tiger tanks of World War II.

CRISIS OF THE GENERALS

Just prior to Kiesinger's takeover as head of the first Grand Coalition on December 1, 1966, a major battle between senior officers and civilians in the MoD broke out. It was a battle in which Erhard showed little interest; he continued to be more concerned with the economy. It was the antithesis of shared responsibility.

On August 12, 1966, General Werner Panitzki resigned his position as the air force's chief of staff. While some saw his resignation resulting from the constant crashing of the air force's ill-fated Starfighters, there was a deeper problem—drawing the line between the military and civilian authority in the defense department. Faced with the problems with the Starfighters, Panitzki decided to take matters into his hands. He set up a specialized working group of air force officers to try to deal with the issue. He excluded civilians, believing this was a technical air force problem. The civilians saw the issue differently. From the beginning, the defense ministry had been based on the idea of close military-civilian cooperation. When the civilians complained, it became clear that the air force would not be able to study this issue on its own. When it became obvious that von Hassel would not support him, Panitzki gave a public interview complaining about the minister's actions. He saw it as a clear violation of military culture—what do civilians know about military weapons systems?

General Heinz Trettner, chief of staff, had long been concerned about structural problems in the ministry. As would be the problem in Canada, many in uniform believed that too many civilian hands were involved in the process, as Klaus Hornung noted:

> Almost all functions were in the hands of bureaucrats: personnel, organization, finances, infrastructure, technology and the welfare of troops. In essence, the soldiers remained responsible for the establishment/organization, training and education of a unit. The military hierarchy ended with the corps. . . . We lack a military hierarchy, no discipline of authority for the inspector.[49]

The incident with Panitzki brought matters to a head. If the civilians were going to insert themselves into something as technical as an investigation into the Starfighter, there was little chance that the armed forces would ever be able to present a purely military point of view to the defense minister or chancellor. How could the chief of staff exercise his responsibility for hundreds of thousands of troops, and ensure that the minister or parliament understood the military nature of the problem if everything had to filtered through the civilian side of the ministry?

As far as Trettner was concerned, the civilian leadership refused "to recognize the uniqueness of the military occupation. Thus, for example, the military career oriented itself on the model of the civilian civil servants and officials. The similarity between military order and bureaucratic directives, let the army . . . appear like some kind of 'external police.'"[50] To Trettner, the military's purpose was to be an instrument in the hands of the civilian leadership. Now, however, its ability to carry out military missions was being undermined. During the summer of 1966, conflicts with the civilian leadership intensified. There were battles inside the ministry over the organization of the military personnel section as well as civilian involvement in the press and information section. It appeared to the military that civilians were riding roughshod over one aspect of military culture after another.

Then came the problem with the labor unions. When Germany first enacted its military legislation, it ensured that German soldiers would have the right to join a labor union, and the *Bundeswehrverband* ("military organization") was created in 1956 for that purpose. A public employees union closely identified with the SPD, the *Öffentliche Dienste, Transport, und Verkehr* ("public service, transport, and traffic," ÖTV) protested that it was being squeezed out. It demanded the right to distribute its own information to men in uniform. The idea of opening up a military base to traditional unions was unacceptable to many officers. What happens if there is a war and they decide to strike? Or if they decide they don't want to go on maneuvers?

The key actor was Under Secretary Karl Gumbel, a career civil servant who stood between Trettner and the defense minister. Trettner resented that when the minister was gone, he had to take orders from a civilian who knew little about the military. To make matters worse, for some time, Gumbel had been trying to limit the military's authority.[51] Unbeknownst to Trettner, he issued an order, "Union Decree of 1 August 1966," that gave the ÖTV access to military bases, an action that infuriated many military officers. The idea of introducing such a change without telling the senior military officer was a clear violation of military culture and a sign of disrespect for Trettner. From his perspective it was also an indication that the civilian leadership had lost confidence in him. How could he face other officers when the most senior political leadership had made this major change without informing him? Added to his fury over the union decree was the negative situation with the "crashing" Starfighters. There was no way he could continue as the chief of staff of the Bundeswehr. On August 13, 1966, he resigned.

In his resignation letter he reiterated his concerns about the way the civilian leadership was treating the military. He couldn't get his ideas and commentary to von Hassel because, like Robert McNamara in the U.S., Gumbel would intercept the ones he didn't like. The simple matter was that he believed he was unable to carry out his leadership tasks. It was not so much the outcome that, he said, infuriated him, since the MoD had no choice in the matter. A court injunction ordered the admission of unions to military installations.[52] The way the process was handled was insulting.

After Trettner's resignation, von Hassel discovered that the problems Trettner had experienced with Gumbel were replicated throughout the ministry. Tension between the military and the civilians was widespread. A few days later, Major General Günther Pape, the commanding officer of *Wehrbreich* III (military district III), resigned. Both men were disgusted with the civilian leadership. According to one writer, even though the SPD was not in direct control of the military, it was exerting its influence on military issues, much the to the chagrin of the country's senior officers.[53]

Civilian and public reaction went against the military. Some commentators worried that this could be the precursor to a "much feared revolt of the military against the primacy of politics."[54] Then there was the German youth. These were the late 1960s, and the unhappiness with American involvement in Vietnam fueled not only anti-Americanism, but coupled with dissatisfaction with the situation in the Bundesrepublik, led to an anti-Bundeswehr response. For many on the left, the Bundeswehr was what was wrong with Germany. This in turn resulted in a major rise in the number of draftees who sought alternative civilian service. Officers and NCOs faced problems in dealing with conscripts. They were rebellious, performed poorly, and often objected to carrying out orders. This attitude, coupled with a number of resignations, led some to question the value of the Bundeswehr, and that led to increasing tension between left and right. It went so far that it was called a "crisis of the generals."[55]

Both Panitzki and Trettner were invited to appear before the Bundestag's defense committee. According to one source,

> Their testimony, given in the presence of their former commander, revealed considerable differences of opinion between the civilian and military leaders of the Bundeswehr. It brought to light the fact that cooperation between military and civilian departments was often far from ideal and that continued efforts were necessary to create an effective team. Last, and perhaps most important, the generals' testimony raised the question of just how much and what type of civilian control was necessary and practical in the Bundeswehr.[56]

Relations between civilians and soldiers had reached rock bottom. Many German officers and NCOs were beginning to believe that Studnitz was right. The military was being asked to do too much with far too few resources. Violations of what the military considered its right to its own cultural symbols and traditions just made matters worse.

All of this was occurring in the face what many believed was "official indifference and public scorn for the necessities of defense."[57] Tradition? There was no tradition. Everything good and glorious from the past had been eliminated in favor of men who tried to kill the country's head of state. Most upsetting, however, were Studnitz' comments on the views held by foreign officers; if true, they marked a serious problem for the military. Many of them did not believe that the Bundeswehr was up to world standards, according to Studnitz. German officers, he claimed, agreed.

> If we ask a combat experienced battalion commander or a company commander of the Bundeswehr whether his current unit would function in an emergency situation and show itself to be as good as those companies of the Wehrmacht on Don and Volchov, by Salerno and Netruno, in Normandy and in the Ardennes—whoever he asks if he could expect his unit to have the same amount of unity, comradeship, discipline, fire power and ability to act in an emergency as was normal for an average company even in the last two years of the war—he will either dodge the question or his answer will be a clear no.[58]

American observers agreed, fearing that the Bundeswehr's problems with discipline and morale had damaged the troops "cutting edge."[59]

This concern over the army's political orientation arose again in an article in *Der Spiegel*[60] in which public opinion polls of soldiers claimed there was a right-wing tendency among NCOs, even to the point of some joining the right-wing National Party of Germany (NPD). The reasons given were a dissatisfaction with the civilian leadership, the insecurity of the country's alliance system, and the lack of clarity in issuing orders.[61] From the military point of view, the civilian leadership was violating just about every cannon of military culture. The military was bitter over its treatment by the MoD. The generals felt that the armed forces were being treated badly and that it was time to even the score. Erhard's lack of interest in the military and refusal to come to grips with the problems besetting the generals and civilians was unfortunate. Instead of forthrightly addressing these issues, he dropped the dispute between the two sides right in the lap of the new government. When Erhard left office, civil-military relations were in a "mess." Shared responsibility was nowhere to be found on either side. The civilians did not seem interested in working together with the military to solve the problems, and the generals were united against the civilians.

Kurt Georg Kiesinger, CDU/CSU/SPD (Coalition) (1966–1969)

Kiesinger took over as chancellor of the first postwar coalition government on December 1, 1966. Willy Brandt served as his deputy and as foreign minister, while Gerhard Schroeder, a CDU member, became defense minister. With the SPD in the government, the CDU's control over the MoD was over. The new government had its hands full given the "civil war" that was raging between the uniformed military and civilians.

The first general to go public was Brigadier General Heinz Karst. Karst was in charge of education and training in the Bundeswehr. He wrote a series of "training comments"; the one which drew the most attention appeared in July 1968. In it, he argued, "we military superiors are compelled more than before to render an account of where we stand in state and society."[62] Karst attacked the trends he saw in German society, maintaining that officers should uphold the authority of their position. He argued against the "lassitude" of peacetime training, especially at a time when Germany's long haired draftees were arriving at recruit centers. He was not a strict conservative like Studnitz, and he was committed to Innere Führung; but he believed that more stress should be placed on the possibility of combat.

On March 19, 1969, the vice chief of staff of the army, Major General Hans Hellmuth Grashey, spoke to senior officers at the Command and Staff College in Hamburg. His speech was not supposed to be public, but it ended up in *Der Spiegel,* giving it high visibility. In essence, his talk was nothing less than an attack on military reform.

Grashey blasted the reform process, arguing that it undermined military efficiency. He attacked what he called the "bloated civilian administration in the Ministry of Defense." He also attacked the parliamentary commissioner, maintaining that giving the average soldier the opportunity to go to the commissioner anytime he objected to an order seriously undermined the authority of the officer. What really disturbed his listeners, both in the lecture hall and beyond, was his comment that the military reform program of the early 1950s was nothing more than a mask.[63] Turning his attention to Innere Führung, he rhetorically asked, "What is so new about it?" Looking at the current period, he commented, "But, now one can finally take the mask from one's face and say, 'Well yes, it has always been there.' " In his mind, the armed forces felt themselves under attack from the left and the right. All they wanted was to be left alone to do their jobs. The constant talk about issues such as Innere Führung at a time when discipline was a major problem in the barracks made the situation worse. Talk of this kind from an officer who had been part of the Amt Blank was shocking to many. His comments also suggested that the only reason the military had agreed to the idea of Innere Führung was to get the SPD to support the creation of the new armed forces.[64] The left wing of the SPD was especially infuriated. "The primacy of politics was in danger."[65]

Grashey received support for his position from an unexpected source. Chancellor Kurt Kiesinger, in comments to the Bundeswehr Association, said that, while he believed that Innere Führung had some salutary effects on young men, he called it an "old cliché" in need of revision. "Often certain terms get worn out over time and lose some of the life they once had." As Abenheim noted, this was a signal to the opponents of Innere Führung that they could "open fire" on the process.[66] Forget a joint relationship: both sides appeared to be blasting the other.

At this point General de Maiziere, the chief of staff, who would turn out to be one of the most outstanding of Germany's postwar generals, turned to his service chiefs in an effort to bring them into the process. De Maiziere asked each service chief to write an essay on the military's role. He was determined to smooth over matters and hoped these essays would help. The responses of the navy and the air force were short and noncontroversial. However, the army's response was something else. In June, General Albert Schnez put six of his brigadier generals to work to come up with a paper that addressed the problems. It was marked "secret" and sent to de Maiziere. As is often the case with such studies, it was quickly leaked to the media.

The reformers objected to this study. To begin with, it argued that the soldier's task was not only to deter war, but if necessary, to fight and win. It gave lip service to Innere Führung, but it also suggested that perhaps that concept should be subordinated to the need to produce a fighting soldier. Much to the chagrin of the reformers, the study emphasized that "being a soldier is an assignment *sui generis*, and not a 'profession like any other.' "[67] So much for the idea that a soldier was a civilian, a citizen in uniform; that the differences between military culture and civilian culture were minimal. A critic blasted this point of view, noting that in place of democratization, the military wanted to see "discipline."[68] The paper took a direct shot at the country's most senior officer, General de Maiziere: "The weight of military decisions cannot be endangered by opportunistic behavior but can be endangered by the increasing political serfdom of military leaders."[69]

Because of its concern with war-fighting ability, the study demanded that military authority over military matters be strengthened. The paper suggested that the power of the parliamentary commissioner should be weakened, and the ability of young men to refuse military service should be restricted. The study also raised again the issue of tradition. The soldiers did not have one. With an eye toward the Reichswehr and the Wehrmacht, the study called for a more balanced view of the German soldier's historical contributions. According to Abenheim, the critical part of the letter was its concluding passage. "Every attempt to cure symptoms promises as little effective success as the removal of individual deficiencies. Only a reform that has the goal of going after the illness at its roots, at the 'head and limbs' of the Bundeswehr and society, can decisively raise the fighting power of the army."[70] In essence, these army generals ignored de Maiziere's request to mention something as fundamental as the Basic Law. Their request was simple. They wanted more power to run the armed forces without outside interference.

The so-called Schnez study assumed tremendous importance from late 1969 to mid-1971. It was seen as the military's manifesto—its challenge to internal reform. The officer corps reportedly supported the study, and it shaped the nature of the debate for the next eighteen months. There was never a danger that the military would act against political authorities. Such an action was unthinkable. However, there was little chance of the two sides working together to solve their problem: the military's symbols and tradition. From the military's standpoint, the Kiesinger government was not helpful. It was not a good period for civil-military relations. Instead of shared responsibility, the politicians on the left launched a variety of attacks on military culture.

Willy Brandt, SPD (Coalition) (1969–1974)

THE POLITICIANS COUNTERATTACK

When Brandt became Chancellor in 1969, he appointed Helmut Schmidt defense minister. Schmidt was a member of the SPD and a man who knew a lot about military affairs and the Bundeswehr. He was a former combat officer in the Wehrmacht in World War II, fighting both on the Russian and Western fronts. His military experience gave him credibility with the military and insights that many politicians lacked. German officers trusted him. He had been the SPD's primary spokesman on defense affairs and had defended their interests. He was seen by many military officers to be a moderate, someone they could relate to, even if he was a member of the SPD. The bottom line was simple: there were serious problems in the military, and growing unrest was unhealthy. Unrest was not limited to a general here or there.

According to one study, Schmidt believed the Schnez study was "politically very naive."[71] He was at best unenthusiastic about it. Despite their unhappiness, the loyalty of the generals was not the problem. Schmidt's task was to find a way to open a "permanent open discussion with leading soldiers."[72] He wanted to avoid a confrontation. With this in mind, on January 6, 1970, he told the army leadership that he did not believe that the Schnez study raised a serious question about the primacy of politics.[73]

Also in January, a group of lieutenants at the army's officer school in Hamburg wrote their own paper. It contained nine theses, and it attacked the Schnez study. It was especially harsh in criticizing those who opposed efforts to strengthen ties between soldiers and society, dismissing those who claimed that virtues such as bravery, chivalry, and self-sacrifice were uniquely military. These officers had a different goal in mind. "I want to be an officer of the Bundeswehr that does something not for itself," but for a greater goal. The officer should carry out his mission in order to "optimize society."[74] They dismissed the importance of the tradition debate. However, their nine theses found very little support among their military colleagues.

Shortly thereafter, General Eike Middeldorf took over command of a division in Unna. He asked his captains to come up with a paper criticizing military practice. The paper was finished in March 1971 and promptly leaked to the press. In it, the 30 captains cited a number of complaints and then turned to a key military concern: "They spoke of inadequate material, political and legal means to fulfill their mission."[75] They also complained that it was becoming impossible to maintain discipline. They complained about Innere Führung arguing, as had a number of other officers, that integrating the soldier into society should not be their primary concern. By not pushing for this integration, they were attacking the very raison d'être of a Bundeswehr soldier. The captains believed the soldier's profession is fundamentally different from civilian professions and demands that he live in a special world. They commented that the civilian leadership seemed to believe that "the integration of the soldier into society is judged to be a higher good than his value as a fighting man."[76]

These captains also made it clear that they mistrusted their political and military leadership. The most serious charge came at the end, where they accused their military, especially their civilian leadership, of political opportunism. Instead of standing up for the troops, they were primarily concerned with currying favor with different political parties, and, as a result, the parties were getting undue political influence over the military. This was leading, in Helmut Schmidt's case, to a "politicization" of the military.[77] The result: "under the present conditions our mission can no longer be carried out."[78]

General de Maiziere and Colonel Eberhard Wegemann (who played a major role behind the scenes in the development and evolution of Innere Führung) went to Dortmund to talk with them. The meeting did not go well. According to Abenheim,[79] the captains acted like a bunch of university students placing a demand on the president. They spoke about their frustration: training soldiers was hopeless. De Maiziere made reference to his experience as a general staff liaison officer to the Führerbunker[80] in April 1945. "He said that a hopeless situation existed when an army had to fight off the armed might of the whole world while its leading officers had been accused of trying to kill the head of state."[81] While he realized the situation facing these officers was difficult, it was far from hopeless.

Schmidt's primary response was to hold a number of seminars with company-grade officers to permit them to express their views. As far as the standing of the 30 captains in the army were concerned, more than 800 of the 9,000 captains in the Bundeswehr wrote in support of them; "114 captains and general staff officers candidates at the Armed Forces Command and Staff College in Hamburg, the best captains in the Bundeswehr, were among the first."[82]

The incident with the captains from Unna tended to end the crisis between the military and its civilian leadership and demonstrated how one individual, in this case Helmut Schmidt, even though he came from the leftist SPD, can make a difference in civil-military relations, especially if he understands the military, its traditions, culture, and thought process. Generals Grashey and Karst retired in 1970, and Schnez, who Schmidt defended, retired at the end of 1971. Middledorf, however, was relieved of command.

After 1970–1972, military resistance lessened. A generational change took place in the Bundeswehr, because most of the key military actors had retired. There were few generals in the Bundeswehr from year group 1928, and only every tenth colonel was from the years from 1928 to 1937. The majority of those who had served the Third Reich had done so primarily as members of an anti-aircraft auxiliary or in the *Volkssstrum*,[83] in other words, they had not served at the front during World War II.

REFORMS?

Despite the less contentious attitude on the part of the military, problems remained. While it had been a year since the captains from Unna had spoken out, in his report to the Bundestag the parliamentary commissioner Fritz-Rudolf Schultz spoke of "disappointment and bad temper on the part of the officers."[84]

One reason was the increasingly poor quality of recruits. According to one officer, when he was a lieutenant there were two or three disciplinary cases a month. Now illegal absence had become a major disciplinary violation: "70 percent of the stumbling comes from difficult surroundings and individuals who had been often convicted of a crime prior to military service. Many soldiers, who come from Billstedt or St. Pauli, will have a better reputation in their rock groups if they are sent to jail."[85] The officer went on to talk about an armor soldier who was present six times during the last eight months of his service. Without living parents, he had been raised by his grandparents. Another soldier, a special student, was absent for five months in a year. He usually did not come back from weekend leave. His mother was a prostitute. To quote one captain, "The soldiers ignore uniforms and ranks. Today, that no longer impresses."[86]

Another problem facing the Bundeswehr was the "Battle of the Hair" in

1972. Because of the long hair worn by many soldiers, on March 13, 1972, Defense Minister Schmidt issued an order that soldiers with long hair must wear hairnets. Manfred Woerner, a senior member of the CDU, criticized Schmidt, arguing that long hair is indicative of lax discipline and that Schmidt had not done enough to strengthen the authority of commanders. Once again, this was a battle of military versus civilian culture. Civilians wore long hair, but the military did not for a number of reasons beyond just discipline, for example hygiene. It was a constant struggle between the soldiers who would wear their hair as long as possible, and their NCOs and officers who had the task of making sure that it wasn't too long.

SHAKING UP THE EDUCATIONAL SYSTEM

One of Schmidt's more important targets in reforming the military was the educational system. While the Bundeswehr marked a radical change from the past, there was little change in the old-style educational process.[87] On May 5, 1972, Schmidt introduced a proposal to create Bundeswehr colleges. In contrast to the past, the Bundeswehr would not provide officers with a strictly military education, but rather an education on the level of civilian universities, one that would award graduates a *Diplom*.[88] Not only would it make it easier for military officers to understand the civilian world, it would give them a degree that would help them find employment after their military career.

A Commission for the Reordering of Training and Education in the Bundeswehr, chaired by Thomas Ellwein, a civilian political scientist, was formed to oversee the creation of such higher educational institutions. Ellwein's appointment created a storm of protest over a civilian overseeing the creation of a new educational system. Further aggravating the situation, the committee included "soldiers of all ranks, civil servants and experts from independent groups."[89] Many in uniform were outraged. One former officer "asked whether Ellwein was intent on 'ruining the officers of the Bundeswehr.'"[90] Many believed that this commission was "a bastion of leftist ideological politicos."[91] The commission tried to straddle the fence arguing that:

> The curriculum of the universities of the armed forces ought to teach skills, knowledge, and attitudes of behavior which are common to civilian professions too, but it ought not to neglect the fact that the challenge of education for the military profession demands specific answers. Therefore the curricula had to include a military professional core of general learning objectives such as participation, creativity, flexibility, critical rationalism, the capability of get-

> ting information and organizing it, the capability to communicate and exchange information, but also concepts such as social sensitivity, evaluation of one's own behavior and its effect on others, endurance of conflicts and tensions, the readiness to take on responsibility and criticism, the capability to inspire corporate unity, and the like.[92]

The states of Hamburg and Bavaria each agreed to host a university. The Ministry of Defense relinquished control; the universities were basically autonomous. In areas such as standards for examinations, faculty, and keeping student records, the universities turned to other universities and the various states' culture ministries. The education would have a military content, but it would also meet the standards of the civilian world, practically foreign to the German military. For centuries, military education had focused primarily on military topics; this was a complete break with the past, and many officers remained unconvinced. In a resolution dated March 7, 1973, the German Bundeswehr Association's governing board argued, "any reform should be oriented toward the concrete tasks of the armed forces and should not be transformed into scholarship for the sake of scholarship."[93] Despite such complaints, the reform of the German military educational system continued to advance. German society had changed. Simply issuing orders no longer sufficed. An officer had to convince the troops that what they were doing was important, and that necessitated a knowledge of pedagogy and the social sciences.

Schmidt also attempted a better definition of Innere Führung by issuing a new instruction called *Zentrale Dienstvorschrift 10/1: Hilfen für die Innere Führung* (Central Service Regulation 10/1: Help for Innere Führung), issued in September 1972. The regulation made it clear that Innere Führung was based on the country's Basic Law or constitution, and it emphasized that the Bundeswehr was an army within a democracy. While it listed soldiers' rights, the heart of the regulation focused on leadership. Bald argues that while it stated what Innere Führung meant for the first time, definition of the term remained ambiguous.[94] According to one account, the effort was largely unsuccessful and was too technocratic.[95]

Schmidt's issuance of 10/1 was useful in focusing attention on this critical concept, but ambiguity remained. Schmidt was helped by the passage of the old generation, and it appeared for a while that civil-military relations were on the upswing. His most important accomplishment, however, and the one that would have the most far-reaching impact on the officer corps, was his creation of two Bundeswehr universities. This fought against the closed nature of the military and guaranteed that officers would be better able to successfully interact with the civilian world.

During the two years he spent as defense minister, Schmidt was good for civil-military relations. He was faced with a major upheaval by the military, which believed that members of the SPD were out to destroy it. Despite his SPD membership, he was respected by men and women in uniform, listened to those in the military who had grievances (including the captains from Unna), then made decisions. He showed respect for military attitudes, even if he issued unpopular instructions. He also contributed a path-breaking modification of the educational system. He was a defense minister who made a difference, and the military respected him. He believed in shared responsibility, and as his time as defense minister came to a close, civil-military relations where in much better shape than they had been when he took over. It was not a situation of joint responsibility, but Schmidt had laid the groundwork for such a development.

CHAPTER 5

From Helmut Schmidt through Angela Merkel

> A new time in military strategy and tactics naturally demands a *sui generis* type of soldier. The citizen in uniform . . . has served its time.
>
> JÜRGEN ROSE

The period after 1974 witnessed a major shift in the focus of civil-military relations. While the issue of tradition gradually moved into the background, focus changed from that of staffing and outfitting a military prepared to face a mass onslaught by the Russians to an expeditionary military. That meant not only a change in psychology on the part of the military, but the construction of a very different kind of armed forces: an expeditionary military, where many of the weapons systems held by the Bundeswehr were no longer relevant. That meant not only changing the types of weapons held by the military, but convincing the country's civilian leaders to pay for it. It also marked the entrance of the Bundeswehr into a number of conflicts, most notably in Afghanistan.

Helmut Schmidt, SPD (1974–1982)

Helmut Schmidt became chancellor on May 16, 1974, and held that position for eight years. His first defense minister, Georg Leber, was not effective in dealing with the uniformed military, while his successor, Hans Apel, had an important influence on military tradition. However, the most important impact the Schmidt Government had on civil-military relations was Schmidt's continued willingness to stand up against the far left wing of the SPD (Social Democratic Party), an action that endeared him to senior military officers.

ATTACK ON MILITARY TRADITION

By the mid-1970s opponents, mostly on the left, took aim at tradition by focusing on the military's practice of allowing members of the Bundeswehr to have contact with veterans, especially those from World War II. The impetus was the 1976 visit of the air force hero Colonel Hans-Ulrich Rudel to a German squadron. Rudel was a dive-bomber pilot during World War II (he destroyed 519 tanks and a battleship) and was shot down thirty times. He was a member of the National Socialist Party and had been slow to repudiate it. He was also an active member of a number of right wing parties.[1]

In spite of opposition from the Ministry of Defense, Rudel was invited to an air force function after air force officers enlisted the assistance of a number of Christian Democratic Union (CDU) politicians to get permission for him to take part. When Rudel's attendance became public at the end of October, Major General Karl-Heinz Franke, one of the officers responsible for the visit, commented that he could not understand why Rudel's visit was controversial. When the head of the air force, Lieutenant General Walter Krupinski, was asked about it, he also said he could not understand why there was any opposition to the visit. Given the outcry by a number of politicians, Defense Minister Leber placed both men on the retired list. In the wake of the crisis, State Secretary Hermann Schmidt also resigned.[2]

Chancellor Helmut Schmidt responded to the Rudel affair by ordering the military to take another look at the issue of tradition and focus more attention on events and personalities during the Bundeswehr's more than twenty-year existence. As far as most of the public was concerned, the pre-1945 past was history. This meant that the average German found it hard to understand why the Bundeswehr kept looking to the pre-1945 period for its tradition. "In the wake of the Rudel affair, the broader public discussion about military tradition took on a new character, which increasingly disparaged any personal or symbolic connection with the Wehrmacht."[3] This attitude was even more pronounced in the SPD, especially among those on the far left. They demanded that the Bundeswehr do away with its oath of allegiance and all ceremonial activities. One SPD parliamentarian went so far as to suggest that the Bundeswehr do away with the salute, troop flags, and all military formations. This was an attack on the heart of military culture, aimed to integrate the Bundeswehr into civil society by abolishing any values that differed from those of society at large. If these proposals had been adopted, civilianization would have triumphed. Military culture at this level would cease to exist.

Of all the ceremonies carried out by the Bundeswehr, the one that was most spectacular was the Grand Tattoo (Zapfenstreich), a centuries old military formation similar to what is referred to in other militaries as taps or retreat. It had not been held since 1956–1957. To quote Abenheim:

> These customs had taken hold in the German armed forces of the nineteenth century. In the twentieth century, a growing emphasis on military pageantry had filled the swearing of the oath and the grand tattoo with ever greater formal and symbolic meaning. After much debate, these customs were carried over into the Bundeswehr, where they tended to be confined in one event.[4]

The tattoo was popular in many parts of Germany because it permitted the local townspeople to have direct contact with the Bundeswehr. Others were offended by any reference to the Reichswehr or Wehrmacht, claiming they were "offensively oriented militaries." Since the Bundeswehr was defensive in nature, their logic ran, it could not use symbols from the past.[5]

In 1978, the armed forces Chief of Staff Harald Wust gave a speech, "Tradition in the Bundeswehr," to a group of graduates from the command and staff academy. In it, he maintained that it was impossible to separate tradition from esprit. "And it is overlooked that the Federal Republic of Germany has a German and European history that goes far back, which at the same time is also the history of the Bundeswehr." Toward the end of his speech, he added, "The Bundeswehr also included in its tradition the many soldiers who were not guilty of the criminal deeds of National Socialism, but who courageously, valiantly, and in exemplary fashion carried out their soldierly duty, not knowing that they had been shamelessly misused." And he named names: "Molders, Freiherr von Fritsch, Feldwebel Lilienthal, just like Jewish officers from the First World War, Frank and Frankel, after which bases in Nauburg and Hannheim are named."[6] There was no doubt on which side of the debate he stood.

However, there were those, especially in SPD-leaning towns in the northern part of Germany, who wanted nothing to do with such ceremonies and tried to stop them. Eventually, matters came to a head. A swearing-in was scheduled for Bremen leading local SPD leaders to complain. The event took place on May 6, 1980, with the country's president, Carl Carstens, present. A pitched battle resulted between the police and demonstrators in a major football stadium. Then on the twenty-fifth anniversary of the founding of the Bundeswehr in November, the regime scheduled a public swearing of the oath of allegiance in Berlin. Police were brought in from all over the country to ensure that the ceremony went off well. "Over eight thousand police were needed to protect fewer than two hundred soldiers."[7]

Complaints from the left wing of the SPD kept flowing in:

> It is surprising that more than 20 years after the founding of the Bundeswehr and more than ten years after the appearance of the Tradition Instruction that a number of units have "Tradition Rooms" where the soldier's heritage from the Reichswehr and the Wehrmacht are brightly honored and comradely ties to traditional units of the Afrika Korps and to the Waffen-SS are maintained. . . . Then the right wing of the Wehrmacht invites Colonel Rudel to a traditional celebration of an Air Force squadron of the Bundeswehr and this is approved . . . and then in 1978 in Saarbrücken formally displayed the uniforms of v. Seeckt, v. Rundstedt, and Trettner. The one created in the Reichswehr, but kept his distance from the Weimar Republic, the next was CinC in the West, and was probably involved in shooting some of the 20th July plotters, and the third walked out when union membership was granted to soldiers.[8]

Apel faced a dilemma. Even though he was a member of the SPD, he did not want to be seen giving in to the left wing of the party.

Supporters of the Bundeswehr were hit with another problem, the slow ebbing of the Soviet military threat. "The classical picture of the threat began to break down. Many found themselves even more threatened by the mere existence of and concentration of nuclear weapons than they did from the highly armed ideological enemy in the east."[9] The result was a strengthened peace movement whose aim was to stop the Allies from stationing intermediate range missiles in Europe. All of these factors taken together led to a widening gap between the Bundeswehr and a significant part of the German population.

THE 1982 INSTRUCTION

In an effort to find a compromise, Apel invited 50 representatives to a meeting on military tradition in April 1981. The invitees included individuals from political parties, youth groups, labor, education, local governments as well as serving and retired military officers. As one might expect, primary focus was on the role of the Wehrmacht in creating military tradition. A retired general spoke in favor of the Wehrmacht, maintaining that it would be wrong to exclude it. He emphasized that soldiers rarely have the luxury of choosing the political masters they serve. He argued that focus should be on "the values in themselves," regardless of what regime they served.[10] It soon became obvious that there was little chance of reaching a compromise.

Apel decided to take matters into his own hands and issued guidelines on tradition on September 20, 1982, just before the Social Democratic–Liberal coalition broke up. "The overall tone of the guidelines emphasized that soldiers should derive their tradition from democratic examples."[11] The most important modification was to refocus attention on the principles of the Basic Law. It stated that the only soldiers who could be honored were those whose attitudes and basic orientation accorded with the principles in the Basic Law. "Meetings within the framework of facilitating tradition may only take place with such persons or units who in their political orientation are in accord with the values and goals of our political system."[12] The same was true of any association with former Wehrmacht units.[13] In the future, the minister of defense would have to agree before any object could be named for an individual.

Some Bundeswehr members were unhappy with Apel's instructions, even though they were not strictly enforced. To quote a lieutenant colonel who was serving on the General Staff, "The Bundeswehr is . . . according to its structure not an industrial entity, but to the contrary, a fighting force and of necessity must have unity. . . . The demand that the Bundeswehr must reflect all of the effective values and norms in society, cannot be seriously combined with the goal of the armed forces: destruction."[14] Despite unhappiness of many in the armed forces, the approach to tradition suggested by Apel has remained unchanged to the present. There was one aspect of the new instructions that pleased many in uniform and irritated those on the left: the maintenance of the public oath of allegiance and the Grand Tattoo.[15]

While many in the military were upset at the push by some in the SPD to destroy what they believed was best in German military culture, the important factor was the willingness of the Schmidt government to stand up to them. The swearing-in ceremonies in Bremen and Berlin were carried out despite cries on the left against militarism. The same is true of the Grand Tattoo. It would have been easy for the Schmidt government to give in, but Schmidt permitted Apel's instructions to stand. This decision had less to do with ideology than practicality. Soldiers and officers needed clearer guidelines with regard to tradition, however, the real issue was how extensively would the government enforce them?[16] The two sides were at least communicating. They were far from a shared responsibility in which both sides were working together to create an acceptable form of tradition, but the atmosphere between the military and civilians with regard to tradition had improved.

Helmut Kohl, CDU (1982–1998)

On October 1, 1982, Helmut Kohl and the Christian Democrats (CDU) came to power. Kohl served for 16 years, the longest serving chancellor since Otto von Bismarck. The new defense minister, Manfred Woerner, was a reserve Luftwaffe pilot, who ultimately reached the rank of colonel. He served for six years and then went on to serve as NATO's secretary general.

Woerner was most interested in bringing military values such as performance, duty, service, and order again to the fore.[17] He made it clear at the outset that he believed that the ten previous years of military reform had an antimilitary character, and that he intended to reverse the SPD's efforts at enforcing civilian values on the military. He wanted the Bundeswehr to be a "real" military. Recognizing Woerner's goal, one of his greatest critics claimed that the Bundeswehr was developing a "counter culture." As he put it, "It demanded as its highest goal 'sufficient combat carriage.' The general in charge of training took exception noting that military exercises must be utilized every day so the soldier doesn't bring anything else into the situation. The magic word was 'training under wartime conditions' [*kriegsnähe Ausbildung*]."[18] It is hard to imagine a clearer statement of the fundamental differences between the culture of the left-wing of SPD and the majority of those in uniform, who believed that to prevail in combat, training should be as realistic and as hard as possible.[19]

In December 1982, retired General Heinz Karst undertook a study of the Bundeswehr with the goal to determine how to rebuild it. His study placed emphasis on the military aspect of civil-military relations. As the study stated, "Only when society identifies with the constitutional duty of the military will the soldiers be integrated."[20] This negative feeling toward the SPD appeared widespread in the armed forces. Two other general staff officers commented that under the SPD the Bundeswehr had become a "peace army." Once again the difference between military and civilian values came to the fore. As they put it, there is no such thing as common values between the military and civilians. Both can believe in and defend the Basic Law, but if soldiers are going to be effective in combat, they need a different set of values, ones that ensure the soldier's success in battle.[21] The draft was submitted to Woerner in 1984, but his position had been weakened by scandal—General Günther Kießling, deputy supreme allied commander in NATO was accused of homosexuality (a charge later proven false). Woerner immediately retired Kießling but in the process was wounded politically. As a result, he was hesitant to take on a sensitive issue like rewriting tradition in the Bundeswehr. He resigned on May 18, 1988.[22]

The battle over civilian values and military tradition continued. In 1991, Major General Johann Adolf Graf von Kielmansegg, a former Wehrmacht officer involved in the July 1944 plot against Hitler, and an officer who would later become commander in chief of central forces in NATO commented in a widely read journal that, "There is no question: The possibility of civilianizing an army, which is supposed to be combat capable, faces very narrow boundaries." And he added, "Naturally the soldier should have most of the values and rights that he is defending in the armed forces. But not quite all of them."[23] Civilianization was not the only problem. There remained the issue of how to treat the Wehrmacht. A retired general, Dr. Jürgen Schreiber in an article entitled "The Naive and Malicious," blasted civilians, especially "the smoking and coffee-drinking journalists, historians and lawyers," who misrepresented the role played by the Wehrmacht. The response by Hans Schüler, published in *Die Zeit*, returned the favor by arguing that the Wehrmacht engaged in the killing of innocent men, women, and children.[24]

THE NATIONAL PEOPLE'S ARMY AND INNERE FÜHRUNG

One of the most unexpected events in recent German history was the collapse of the German Democratic Republic and with it the National People's Army (NVA). Out of the 90,000 still serving on October 3, 1990, when the NVA went out of existence, 18,000 of them were taken over into the Bundeswehr: 6,000 officers, 11,200 NCOs, and 800 enlisted men. Of that number, 15,000 requested that they be taken over as extended service length soldiers (*Soldaten auf Zeit*). However, only 10,200 were actually allowed to stay in the Bundeswehr, including 3,000 officers.[25] Few on either side grasped the differences between soldiers from the two armies. The former East Germans tended to be looked down upon by officers in the Bundeswehr. The more officers in the West knew these *Ossies* (a derisive term referring to those from East Germany), the more they questioned whether they would be able to serve in a democratic army that relied heavily on initiative. They set up special courses for those who joined the Bundeswehr in an effort to help them make the transformation.[26]

The West Germans made it very clear that the East German military experience was not a basis for tradition. Indeed, it is hard to see how they could have done anything else. They had outlawed the Wehrmacht's experience because it was not a democratic military, and honoring people or units from the undemocratic East German military would have legitimized them.

There was also concern over the fate of Innere Führung, especially given the turmoil the Bundeswehr was going through as the Cold War ended. Toward this end, on February 18, 1993, the Bundeswehr issued a new document, which reaffirmed its importance—*Innere Führung, ZDV10/1*. One of its primary purposes was to explain how that concept was to be implemented. It even included a section on the role to be played by chaplains as well as the importance of political education that stressed the role of a military in a democracy.[27]

CHANGING THE ROLE OF THE BUNDESWEHR

The most important implication of the collapse of the German Democratic Republic was that it signaled the end of the Cold War. This was to have a profound impact on the Bundeswehr. For more than 25 years, the Bundeswehr was legitimized as a mass army, set up to help stop masses of Russian and East European troops from invading the West. It was a tank-heavy army, one that had deterrence as it sole justification in the eyes of the German population. However, the threat from the East had evaporated. Not only was Eastern Europe no longer a threat, but the Soviet Union had collapsed. As with other NATO armies, the question was what role it would now play, a point Heiko Biehl made:

> During the Cold War one could refer to the threat to the homeland by foreign armies. The Defense of the FRG in case of attack was the reason for the existence of the Bundeswehr. Clearly, this is no longer sufficient. Defense of the homeland remains a mission. . . . But it is necessary to have another means for justifying military action.[28]

One of the key individuals involved in redefining the role to be played by the Bundeswehr was its inspector general, General Klaus Naumann. His goal was to move the Bundeswehr away from a territorial army (i.e., its commitment within NATO) toward a crisis intervention role (which in the end would involve sending German troops outside the NATO boundaries)—not an easy job given the structure of the Bundeswehr and the prevailing antimilitary feelings on the left.

Chancellor Helmut Kohl agreed with Naumann and, in 1992, decided to make Volker Rühe the country's defense minister, because he was impressed with his drive and bureaucratic skills. The 1992 Defense Policy Guidelines clearly stated what Rühe had in mind, stressing the importance of restructuring the Bundeswehr. The Federal Republic's first chance to play a new "crisis" role came in May 1992, when German troops set up a hospital in Cambodia for victims of the Khmer Rouge. A year later they were in Somalia.

Both Rühe and Naumann emphasized the importance of Germany's role within NATO and the Alliance's increasing concern for dealing with crisis situations around the world. It faced a situation similar to that in Canada. If it hoped to remain a key player in the alliance, it was vital that the Bundeswehr do its part. In a landmark ruling, the Supreme Court stated that "out-of-area operations," were legal. It decided that Germany "is at liberty to assign German armed forces in operations mounted by the North Atlantic Treaty Organization and the Western European Union and to implement resolutions of the Security Council of the United Nations."[29] Its only condition was that the Bundestag had to approve such actions. The Bundeswehr had a green light to continue to engage in such operations.

Rühe and Naumann still faced the question of structural changes in the Bundeswehr. The tank-heavy army was backed up by obsolescent F-4s, of limited use in complex contingency operations. In 1994, a new white book was issued. It focused on the Bundeswehr's new structure, which split it into three parts. First was the basic military organization, primarily intended for training and supply/logistics as well as personnel, military schools, and the Bundeswehr's research institutes. Second was the main defense force, the majority of the troops, a defensive force made up of 54.5 percent conscripts, and 45.5 percent longer-serving soldiers (*Soldaten auf Zeit*). Third were the crisis reaction forces. These would contain about 50,000 troops at a high degree of readiness. This force would participate in NATO, EU, and UN operations, and would be made up primarily of career and longer-serving soldiers.[30]

ANSWERING QUESTIONS ABOUT THE BUNDESWEHR'S HISTORY

In November 1995, Defense Minister Volker Rühe gave a speech entitled, "40 Years of the Bundeswehr—Self-Understanding and Tradition." In it Rühe pointed out, as had others in the past, that the Wehrmacht was an organization of the Third Reich. Solders were involved in many of the crimes of National Socialism. For this reason, the Wehrmacht could not be the basis for tradition. Turning to the critical issue of individual heroism, Rühe commented that he recognized that many behaved honorably and bravely during World War II, and we cannot condemn them. However, he noted, it is not possible to look only at military behavior; it is also necessary to look at the person's personality and overall behavior.[31] From this point on, there was no question of using individuals or units from the Wehrmacht as unit names. Rühe had drawn the line, and his action was welcomed by a brigadier general writing in *Die Zeit*.[32]

Innere Führung came into focus again because its role would have to change. Primarily focused at conscripts, it was clear that there would be fewer of them in the future. Second, at least one component of the military would be almost entirely professionals, and not the "Citizen in Uniform," which had been primarily aimed at conscripts and was a major reason for initially creating Innere Führung. The professionals would focus their attention primarily on military culture. The officers and NCOs would be fighting wars, not sitting back in a base in Germany reading a book on how they should treat their troops. Two authors argued that officers in elite units have problems with Innere Führung and attempts to integrate the troops into society.[33] In an effort to remain relevant, the Center for Innere Führung began to offer special classes to help soldiers deal with the many new and extreme situations they would be facing. In addition, it began to publish special publications to help them deal with the new reality. One writer raised the fundamental question in 2005: "The question is not one of modifying Innere Führung; it is a question of whether or not Innere Führung is compatible with an expeditionary army."[34]

The naming of bases reemerged. This time it was a facility named for Eduard Dietl in Füßen. There was no evidence that Dietl, the hero of Narvik who later commanded German troops in Finland, had committed any war crimes. However, he had been a willing member of the Nazi Party. Rühe entered the debate in 1996 when he announced that the bases named in honor of Dietl and General Ludwig Kübler, who had been hung as a war criminal, were being changed.[35]

MODIFYING THE ROLE OF THE BUNDESWEHR

From the German perspective, the situation facing the Bundeswehr was becoming increasingly difficult and complex. General Naumann maintained that the expanded task "is becoming more differentiated, but in no way has it become easier; from a military point of view it is even more demanding."[36] The Bundeswehr was structured for one kind of combat but was told to transform itself to carry out a much different mission. The transformation process was both complex and very expensive. The situation facing the Bundeswehr was so bad that one writer stated the force was in a state of collapse.[37]

Given the chaos that seemed to surround efforts to transform the Bundeswehr, Rühe issued what in German is called a *Denkverbot*, a ban on thinking. He was getting tired of all the different ideas that were floating around. Then an air force officer, Jürgen Rose, a researcher at the George C. Marshall Center, questioned Rühe critically about conscription. That was followed by an article by Rose in the *Frankfurter Allgemeine Zeitung* stating that "conscription must end."[38] This was more than a one-time action of defiance.

Rühe had taken control of the policy process in the Ministry of Defense and needed to show who was in charge. Rose was disciplined. As Dyson put it with regard to territorial defense and conscription, "Promotion and career advancement were consequent upon support for these concepts."[39]

REFORMING THE EDUCATIONAL PROCESS

While there had been significant changes in the *Führungsakademie* from the pre–World War II period, there remained similarities. Both institutions placed emphasis on creating an effective and efficient military, while glorifying events and personalities of the past. Political subjects were seldom taught: the curriculum was apolitical. According to Bald, both Generals Heusinger and Speidel agreed with Baudissin in 1969; their first effort at reform had failed.

Officers could not afford to be only mechanical experts on equipment and tactics. Knowledge of things political was key to German civil-military relations. According to Bald, this meant primary focus on the Basic Law: officers should understand the constitution thoroughly. What the German officer corps needed in essence was what in the U.S. is called a liberal education, or as one German writer put it, "The complexity of old and new tasks of the Bundeswehr requires a new balance of professional skill and political education."[40] This had become even more evident in the aftermath of the Cold War. During that period, there had been a structure of good and evil: the West was good, while the East was evil. Now, however, the Bundeswehr would be called to fight wars in which there was no clearly defined good or evil. Rather it would be a case of peacekeeping—trying to separate warring groups—while not taking sides. Officers would actually have to lead soldiers into battle, and it was critical that they understand something other than brute force. They would also be required to understand leadership, which requires a knowledge of the social sciences. Indeed, the Academy was preparing officers for jobs such as,

> political advisor in the ministry; leading command positions; security-political participation in official discussions and by their expertise in staffs; participation in international organizations, cooperation with parliamentary panels, parties and groups, evaluating the possibility of conflict; the uniqueness of international alliances and the process of legitimating systems.[41]

To prepare officers for these jobs as well as to lead soldiers in combat, a second revolution in military education was required. Seen from the perspective of American joint military education, the program has been successful. A U.S.

military officer investigated the program in 2001, using an evaluation system accredited by the chairman, Joint Chiefs of Staff. The results, according to the author, were:

> The findings conclude that the Führungsakademie meets the majority of requirements for joint professional military education accreditation. In many cases, the Führungsakademie exceeds the established American standards and more appropriately educates and prepares field grade officers for their command and staff duties than do American command and general staff courses.[42]

This was quite a departure from the old Prussian apolitical style of focus strictly on military topics.

This was a period of major change for the Bundeswehr. Not only was its role fundamentally changing, questions were raised about the utility of sacrosanct policies such as Innere Führung. If anything, the absorption of the NVA into the Bundeswehr made a firmer policy regarding tradition more urgent, and it came in the form of Instruction 10/1, which defined what was acceptable in the area of tradition and what was not with a new specificity. Education was also upgraded to be in accordance with U.S. military standards. The most important development, however, was the fundamental change in German strategy, from deterrence to a military capable of carrying out what is often referred to as expeditionary army actions. The key problem, however, was the constant underfunding of the Bundeswehr. Making such a fundamental change in strategy, operations, and tactics is very expensive. A lot of the old equipment (heavy tanks, for example) become less important, while the role of other weapons systems such as helicopters play an even more important role. However, when it came to military issues Kohl was not helpful. To quote Dyson, "Kohl . . . was not about to claim that there was a need to reorient the role of the Bundeswehr, fearing a political backlash."[43]

Gerhard Schroeder, SPD (1998–2005)

Gerhard Schroeder, who also had little interest in security matters, took office on October 27, 1998.[44] Rudolf Scharping, who had hoped to become foreign minister, lost out to Joschka Fischer, and instead became defense minister, a position he would occupy until July 2002. The military leadership was very concerned about the new government and about Scharping in particular. This was the first center/left (SPD / Green Party) coalition government in postwar history. The Bundeswehr had already had problems with the SPD. Now it faced a government with an even more leftist party, the Greens, in power. Schroeder's selection of Rudolf Scharping was unfortunate. He was a man of limited leadership skills who went out of his way to alienate the uniformed military. His successor, Peter Struck would have to work hard to overcome the cultural gap between the military and the political leadership.

KOSOVO

As Schroeder was elected president in October 1998, he immediately came under pressure to commit German troops to the Kosovo War. He and Joschka Fischer agreed to deploy German forces. As Dyson argued, this war gave Scharping an opportunity to push hard for change—from the territorial army to the now badly needed expeditionary force.[45] The Bundeswehr was fighting a different kind of war, and Scharping could have and should have made the case for a major infusion of money to move the Bundeswehr toward reform and restructuring. Unfortunately, he missed the opportunity with the anticipated consequences.

In early 1999, a few German planes (ECM Tornados, German crewmen on NATO AWAC aircraft) joined NATO forces in action against Serbia. On October 8, 1999, for the first time, a German general, Klaus Reinhardt, assumed command of the NATO-led peacekeeping force, and German forces began to arrive in theater on June 12, 1999. But performance by the German forces showed they were not up to the challenge with regard to weapons, cultural knowledge, and personnel performance. If anything, the Kosovo War made it clear that there was an urgent need for change. The result was increased pressure on the government to get rid of territorial defense and conscription. It also made it clear that the Bundeswehr was not prepared for such a conflict, and it increased domestic pressure for change.[46]

Conscripts were an obvious target from the generals' standpoint. What good were soldiers with only a few months of training in a professional army that had to perform complex tasks in places like Kosovo? Russia had ceased to be a threat. Why have territorial defense forces at all? To quote an article in *Die Zeit*, "It is clear that in the future 'Alliance help' would more closely resemble the kind of crisis intervention they engaged in the Balkans. What was needed were mobile, flexible and quickly transferable units. The heavy tank units—the pride of the Bundeswehr—were history."[47] As an incentive to get soldiers thinking, the *Denkverbot* was lifted. To make the transition, the MoD needed all the help it could get.

NEW IDEAS

In May and June of 2000, three reform proposals were published. The first was presented by former Federal President Richard von Weizsäcker, who had been wounded twice in World War II while serving largely on the Eastern Front. Also a seasoned politician, he had credibility with Germany's military. The second was by the Chief of the Defense Staff Hans-Peter von Kirchbach, and the third was by the Minister of Defense Rudolf Scharping.

The Weizsäcker Commission issued its report on May 23, 2000, recommending that the Bundeswehr's central role should be crisis management and prevention. It called for a reduction to a peacetime strength of only 30,000 conscripts together with 140,000 troops in the operational units ready for use by the Alliance. The report highlighted the problems facing the Bundeswehr when it stated, "The way the Bundeswehr looks today, it is not capable of coping with the tasks it has to fulfill."[48] Combined with events in Kosovo, the Weisäcker Commission's Report gave Scharping a golden opportunity to push for a significant budget increase. Instead, he refused to support it.

Von Kirchbach immediately ran into problems with Scharping, and relations between the two were icy at best.[49] The general argued for an army of 290,000 despite the Weisäcker Commission's much lower suggestion. As a consequence, Scharping fired von Kirchbach on May 24. While he had the right to fire him, the way he did it made it clear he was not interested in shared responsibility. He wasn't even interested in considering his senior general's position on transformation. "According to one source, von Kirchbach felt he was being used as a 'political football.' "[50] The impact on civil-military relations was negative. "It severely undermined his personal credibility within the ministry, dissipating the trust and loyalty he had sought to develop by retaining Rühe appointees."[51]

Scharping came out with his own paper in June, a proposal more cautious than that put forth by the Weisäcker Commission but a bit higher than that suggested by von Kirchbach. He proposed only cutting the Bundeswehr from 338,000 with 135,000 conscripts to 277,000 including 178,000 regular troops and 77,000 conscripts (with 22,000 others in educational institutions and training). Scharping's leadership style was called into question as he was openly criticized for his refusal to consider plans other than his own.[52] However, his goal was to control the reform process while avoiding the kind of radical change called for by the Weisäcker Commission, much less that proposed by von Kirchbach.

While the Cabinet approved Scharping's plan in June, his cautious but autocratic leadership style combined with his effort to maintain control over all aspects of defense policy had alienated many. He did not reach out to others in the MoD or to different organizations for the political assistance he needed. He seemed to think he could pay for modernization on the cheap, primarily through the sale of bases that had to be closed—bringing in, he hoped, up to DM 1 billion.[53] But Scharping's plan fell far short of what was needed by the Bundeswehr. Not wanting to upset matters, he vetoed just about every serious plan for reform.[54] By 2001, he was thoroughly disliked, not only by the military, but by almost everyone in the MoD. To quote Dyson, "Enmity towards Scharping and the process of Bundeswehr reform reached such critical levels that a substantial number of important figures within the ministry were active in leaking politically sensitive information to the CDU/CSU, in particular to Volker Rühe, in an attempt to undermine Scharping and the SPD."[55]

The most obvious question was just how much transformation was needed by the Bundeswehr? Clearly it would have to be much more mobile. As *Die Zeit* put it, "What Should German Soldiers Fight For?"[56] Then there was the question of conscription. Was it still necessary at a time when the Bundeswehr was moving to greater reliance on professional soldiers? The problem, however, as Dyson pointed out, was that the SPD's continued support for territorial defense was evident in its purchase, despite the lack of available funds, of heavy, immobile artillery, an action that infuriated other members of the Alliance.[57]

It was becoming clear that the Bundeswehr was in even worse shape than many observers believed. One source pointed out during 2001 that in the Bundeswehr as a whole, 1,412 officer and 4,138 NCO posts were not occupied. When it came to the lower ranks, 17,418 posts were vacant. Seventy-five percent of the vehicles were 20 years old, 15 percent more than 30. "Many experts even state that with more than 30,000 Bundeswehr troops stationed in the Balkans at various times, 'Die Truppe' " ("the troops," as they are called in the Bundeswehr) "are already operating beyond their capabilities—even on the verge of collapsing." Simply put, the Schroeder government was not paying much attention to the military.[58]

The 9/11 attack on New York City and Washington, DC, underlined just how poorly off the German military was. *Die Welt* carried an article on September 12, 2001, noting that Germany puts only 1.6 percent of its GDP on its armed forces, almost as little as Canada.[59] A couple of months later, a group of German security experts expressed concern about the ability of the Bundeswehr to carry out alliance obligations, not to mention foreign deployments.[60] For example, in Afghanistan by the end of 2002, the army had only four "Dingo" armored vehicles, and they had to be given to a driving school in Hammelburg. As for the Eurofighter, it was built to fight the Russians and now had to be modified, an expensive process, if it was going to be used in a place like Afghanistan.[61]

Scharping continued to push an idea, popular in the SPD, that the military should do its best to emulate civilian business culture. He said, "Cooperation with entrepreneurs, industry and trade centers as well as centers for handwork can build the basis for the necessary renewal of the armed forces."[62] One can only imagine how an officer in a front-line unit in Afghanistan would react to being told that he and his troops should act more like civilians. Such a policy would be a recipe for disaster.

Well aware of the problems in the military, the government carried out a survey. The results were troubling. Investigators found that no one in the military cared about Innere Führung or the "citizen in uniform." To quote one respondent, "Our last chief was here only a very short time. One has the feeling that he did not identify with the unit and had this posting only because it was needed for his career."[63] Once again, the problem was a lack of money. When the yearly report from the inspector for education and training went to the Chief of Staff General Harald Kujat, he was so upset that he requested another one. In the meantime, several copies of the report leaked out. Everyone who read it, including Defense Minister Scharping, was upset. According to General Dieter Löchel, the situation was "desolate. We have no spare parts, and, what we have only gets older and older. . . . We are not even in a situation to put together one single unit that can carry out its mission 100%." Morale was at an all-time low. "In the 64th Officer Candidate Class there wasn't a single one who wanted to become a professional soldier [*Berufssoldat*]."[64] Publicly, at least, Scharping continued to deny that problems inside the Bundeswehr were as bad as reports like the one sent to Kujat suggested. Taking aim at future CDU Chancellor Angela Merkel, he commented, "You know, this morning . . . I heard that conditions in the Bundeswehr are disastrous, or so Frau Merkel stated. I am sure she understands something from many political areas, but not much from this one."[65] One suspects that many, if not most, of those in the Bundeswehr would have agreed with Merkel on this point regardless of her lack of expertise.

In the first half of 2002, the Ministry of Defense began to face the problem head on. It carried out another in-house assessment, which maintained that the most likely future tasks for the German armed forces would be outside the

Euro-Atlantic area. In a significant shift, the assessment maintained that Germany should not construct its armed forces to deal with a particular threat: it was no longer a case of deterring a single enemy. Now it was important for the armed forces to become a mobile and flexible instrument of German foreign policy.[66]

However, to make the armed forces a viable tool of German foreign policy money would be needed, and there was no sign the SPD government was about to come up with it. Based on a report from June 2002, "around 4.5 billion Euros were lacking in order to carry out the Bundeswehr reform through 2006. In 2003 alone, 720 million Euros were lacking."[67] Regardless of how forthcoming the military might have been, given Scharping's stance, there was little chance of creating joint responsibility.[68]

PETER STRUCK TAKES CHARGE

Scharping resigned in July 2002, amid rumors that he had accepted more than $72,000 from a public relations firm together with pictures of him cavorting with his mistress in Mallorca as the Bundeswehr was about to go into Macedonia.[69] He left the Bundeswehr in disarray. He was succeeded by Peter Struck, who had a reputation as a consensus builder close to Chancellor Gerhard Schroeder. Struck immediately went to work to bring order, primarily by redefining the Bundeswehr's new crisis management role through the new defense policy guidelines. He gave only lip service to conscripts, Innere Führung, and territorial defense. His focus was on moving the Bundeswehr away from the past, both psychologically and in practice. He wanted German soldiers to see themselves playing a critical role in support of Berlin's foreign policy. As Struck put it, "Germany is no longer being defended on our Eastern borders, but is being defended around the world as the Bundeswehr, together with other states and organizations, helps prevent countries from turning into bases for terrorist attacks."[70] Struck's first priority was to modify the equipment procurement process, which he did when he offered his new budget in February 2003. Given the tremendous financial limitations facing the armed forces, he pushed to cut down the military's inventory of weapons.[71] The navy lost control of its aircraft and the air force had to disband two squadrons. The tank inventory was cut significantly, and almost all other programs lost personnel while the military focused on expanding programs such as army transportation and armored personnel vehicles. This was followed in March by Directive 21, which marked the death of the old Bundeswehr. It was now becoming an expeditionary army.[72] One complaint from the military was that when Struck came up with the motto "Germany will be defended in the Hindukusch, he neglected to explain publicly what was entailed." The concern was not the creation of a more expeditionary force, but that his new motto ended discussion of the matter.[73] The task of implementing this directive fell to chief of staff, General Wolfgang Schneiderhan, who was to become an important player in the development of the Bundeswehr during the next six years.

In May 2003, Struck presented new defense policy guidelines. The document made two critical statements. First, defense was no longer understood in a territorial context. Second, in the "foreseeable future there is no conventional threat to Germany."[74] The document made it clear that in the future, the Bundeswehr would focus on conflict management operations. Terrorism had become the main topic of concern, and territorial defense had taken a back seat at the highest levels. This was followed in January 2004 by a proposal by Struck for a new categorization of Germany's armed forces, in an effort to clear the air from Scharping's battle with von Kirchbach and his ignoring of the Weizsäcker Commission. He suggested that Germany's armed forces be reduced from 283,000 to 250,000 and be divided into three categories. Category I would have 35,000 quick reaction forces from all three services. Category II would include 70,000 soldiers for low- and medium-intensity conflict. Category III troops would include 145,000 support forces serving in the Federal Republic of Germany (FRG), as well as those involved in training.

Schneiderhan shared Struck's view of the Bundeswehr defending Germany abroad—"in the Hindukush."[75] He also supported the continuation of conscription. In contrast to his predecessor Harald Kujat, he was reflexive and politically adept.[76] He became one of the Federal Republic's most influential chiefs of staff. He was a strong Atlanticist, and commissioned a number of papers by like-minded officers. Schneiderhan and Struck would ask the Bundestag to repeal its requirement for prior approval so that the Bundeswehr could be "mobilized quickly and effectively, and be deployed domestically, to deal with a terrorist attack,"[77] a good plan, that never saw the light of day.

Struck endeared himself to those in uniform. For example, Scharping had been prepared to compromise on the Panther tanks the Bundeswehr wanted. Struck was not. Despite his concern for an expeditionary force, he pushed the Bundestag's budgetary committee to purchase all 410 of them. He emphasized the need for tanks and the need for modernization of German military capabilities by arguing that the Bundeswehr was in such bad shape that it would soon be unable to fulfill its international obligations.[78]

Some military officers were opposed to seeing their services cut back, and in some cases watching their jobs disappear. Struck and Schneiderhan tried to work diplomatically, but they ran into opposition from those in uniform. As a consequence, Struck felt he had no alternative but to relieve some of their positions. Gert Gudera, the inspector general of the army, and Vice Admiral Lutz Feldt, the chief of staff of the navy, were retired in favor of officers more amenable to Struck's plans for the Bundeswehr. The cutbacks were massive. According to one report, Struck announced in beginning of November 2004 that the military needed 48,700 fewer soldiers. As he reportedly stated, "When the threat demands fewer tanks, then we do not need as many tank battalions." Whereas the Bundeswehr had seven divisions, by the time the reform was complete, it would only have five. The civilian world was impacted as 105 installations around Germany were closed (for example, Schleswig-Holstein had nine installations, all of which all were closed). He also made it clear that if conscription were ended, a further 50 installations would be closed.[79]

Schneiderhan's push for radical, structural changes began toward the end of December 2005. He proposed merging the three services into one. The generals were furious. One called it "unacceptable," and it was opposed by members of both the CDU and the SPD. In the military itself, one heard comments such as, "In the end many don't know where their place is."[80] Schneiderhan quickly retreated recognizing, one assumes, that he had crossed the line when it comes to military culture. Members of all three services are proud of the uniform they wear, and the idea of everyone wearing the same one is unacceptable, as the Canadians learned when they attempted to go down that path in the mid-1960s.

Major changes were also underway in the educational field. For example, at the *Führungsakademie der Bundeswehr* changes in the curriculum were introduced, giving more attention to the social sciences. General Hans-Christian Beck, who was transferring command of the academy to his successor, noted that "already 80 percent" of the courses are taken together by the students from the army, navy, and air force.[81]

THE FIGHT OVER TRADITION REEMERGES

Brigadier General Reinhard Günzel, commander of Germany's crack special operations forces, was fired because he praised a speech by Martin Hohmann, a right-wing member of the Bundestag. In his speech Hohmann had compared the actions of Jews in the 1917 Russian Revolution with those of the Nazis. In his letter, Grünzel stated, "You can be sure that with your opinions, you are speaking from the soul for a majority of people. I hope you will not be put off by criticism from the left that you will hold your course with courage."[82] As Struck put it, "I have decided to relieve him of his command and to dismiss him. With that, the case is closed for me."[83] Grünzel complained openly about the way he was fired, arguing,

> If one shows a backbone, he loses access to the active troops. In the first instance that does not mean the loss of an Eintopf or a weapon on the base, but to the contrary above all else the chance to win new cadres. Which young officer, NCO or soldier joins a group of German paratroopers when a prohibition is hanging over the base?[84]

Despite Grünzel's fame throughout Germany, Struck's response was not surprising. I doubt if any other defense minister or chief of staff would have reacted differently under these circumstances.

The battle over Innere Führung continued. Professional officers, especially those serving with Germany's new crisis reaction forces, continued to question its relevance. It, together with the concept of the citizen in uniform, was introduced as a way of ensuring the German conscript military would avoid becoming isolated from society, as in the past. Almost 40 years had passed since creation of the Bundeswehr: there were very few conscripts and they would not be serving in crisis management units, which would be almost entirely professional. To quote one young officer, "to be sure, fine for peace, but too demanding and for that reason, not useful in combat."[85] According to Uzulis, Struck asked the Innere Führung School in Koblenz to look into the issue: is Innere Führung really necessary when an army is primarily professional?[86]

SCANDALS

Unfortunately for those who wanted to get rid of Innere Führung, several scandals tarnished their efforts. The first dealt with the training of recruits in Coesfeld. It involved trainers hitting recruits, stepping on them, and prodding them with electric prods. Some held it was one of the worst criminal actions by the Bundeswehr.[87] The argument of the trainers was that it offered the recruits realistic training. However, it was the opposite of the Innere Führung training concept, which outlawed such methods. Those who supported Innere Führung immediately criticized this scandal, arguing that it demonstrated the need for more emphasis on training. One proponent argued, "Instead of promoting and demanding constitutional patriotism, free, independent thought and open public discussion, a false understanding of the primacy of politics, there is a swearing of allegiance to a purely personal understanding of loyalty and to a rigid spirit. In place of retraining procedures, courage and civil courage, opportunism . . . and careerism have appeared."[88] Struck suspended 23 trainers, and the situation was carefully investigated.

One of the more radical proponents of Innere Führung argued that these incidents showed that the Bundeswehr was becoming a mercenary army and that only politicians could reverse the process.[89] The same author claimed that there were reports that a third of Bundeswehr soldiers had never heard of Innere Führung.[90]

Another scandal involved the base named after Colonel Werner Moelders, one of the most decorated German fliers of World War II. An elite fighter squadron and two military facilities were named after him, as well as a monument and a navy destroyer. However, it was discovered that prior to World War II, Moelders had flown with the Legion Condor in Spain. On April 24, 1998, on the 61st anniversary of the bombing of city of Guernica, Spain, by the Legion Condor, the SPD, the Greens, and the PDS (the former East German Communist Party, the Party of Democratic Socialism) passed a resolution stating that no one who participated in the Legion Condor should be so honored. Nothing happened despite comments from scholars such as Bald to the effect that "Moelders is an example of the criminal Wehrmacht."[91] Finally, on January 28, 2005, Struck removed Moelders's name from Fighter Squadron 74. There were protests, but to no avail.

Scharping's tenure as defense minister did little to improve civil-military relations. His refusal to treat von Kirchbach with respect alienated the inspector general and a good part of the military. As he was permitted, by virtue to his position as defense minister, he forced his plan for the future of the Bundeswehr on the organization, showing little respect for either the Weizsäcker Commission or the views of the military. He left the armed forces in a mess and with little cooperation between those in uniform and senior civilian officials.

Peter Struck was a refreshing change. He was prepared to make the difficult decisions that went along with the major transformation that the Bundeswehr was undergoing. Many whose positions were impacted or eliminated were opposed to his actions, as he was cutting positions and also changing chains of command. Egos were hurt as senior officers saw their power and authority evaporate overnight. The inspector general, Wolfgang Schneiderhan, understood the importance of the decisions and supported him. Although more than 50 years had passed, questions involving the past continued to haunt the civil-military interface, as the issue of Colonel Moelders demonstrated. Retired General Reinhard Günzel did something that no defense minister could permit to go unpunished, supporting the view that the action of Jews in the Russian Revolution was as bad as the actions of the Nazis. The scandal in Coesfeld provided strength to those on the far left who wanted to "civilianize" the military.

Angela Merkel, CDU (2005–)

Angela Merkel took office on November 22, 2005. Independent observers had expected Merkel and the CDU/CSU to win the election handedly; in fact, she won by a narrow margin and was forced to enter into a coalition with the SPD. She managed to get Franz Jozef Jung, a member of the CDU, appointed as defense minister, but given the distribution of power in the Bundestag, her ability to make major changes in the Bundeswehr was limited. Jung believed in the need for the country to restructure the military while at the same time restoring morale and pride. He soon became the administration's point man for German troops in Afghanistan.

Military tradition did win one battle as Merkel was about to come to power. In October 2005, in the face of opposition from the left, Berlin permitted a Grand Tattoo in spite of 1,200 demonstrators who opposed it. As outgoing defense minister Struck put it, "The *Zapenstreich* has nothing to do with the Nazis or the Wehrmacht, but to the contrary, it is an old Prussian tradition. I can understand that someone who is generally against the military will attack such a ceremony, but I know that the great majority of the population considers the *Zafpenstreich* to be a good event."[92]

In 2006, the MoD issued a white paper that dealt with tradition, stating, "The cultivation of traditions in the Bundeswehr focuses on the Prussian army reforms, military resistance to the National Socialist regime, and the history of the Bundeswehr itself."[93] The government's policy was now in concrete: Even the thought of honoring heroes from World Wars I and II was out.

Nevertheless, tradition continued to be a problem. In 2009, the left wing media reported that two Bundeswehr training manuals used GI jargon to describe the actions of antiarmor units during 1944. In another case, the left wing of the SPD zeroed in on the comments of a young officer, who highlighted the importance of fighting spirit among the troops surrounded in Stalingrad. An instructor stated that the manuals are "a goldmine for the extreme right wing."[94] The army general in charge of training, Walter Spindler, said, "Each trainer must be in a position to place examples in a rational montage." "Besides fundamental military truths also existed during the 12 years of a totalitarian regime."[95] Those on the left were not happy. Detlef Bald stated that the textbooks "were an absolute scandal and make the Bundeswehr look horrible."[96] From a practical standpoint, while Innere Führung lectures continued to emphasize traditional themes, more and more Innere Führung was being used to help prepare German soldiers going abroad to understand different cultures and how to deal with them. The days of blind obedience in the German military were long gone. These lectures and discussions played an important role in helping the soldier understand the nature of the operation and its importance.[97]

In 2009, Merkel and the Christian Democrats again won the national election to the Bundestag. In the face of a somewhat chaotic situation in the SPD, she joined forces with the Free Democratic Party (FDP). On September 4, 2009, German Colonel Georg Klein, who commanded a German base in the Kunduz region of Afghanistan, called in an air strike. The attack focused on two large tanker trucks that had been hijacked by Taliban insurgents. Up to 142 civilians were reportedly killed during the air attack.[98] The German military on the scene reportedly informed headquarters in Bonn that there were civilian casualties, but this fact was withheld from the public. However, word about the civilian casualties leaked out, and it soon became a hot political issue in Germany. Jung's top deputy in the Ministry of Defense, State Secretary Peter Wichert as well as General Schneiderhan resigned, accepting responsibility for the "cover-up." While both had violated military protocol by not reporting this incident, they complained about their treatment by the new 37-year-old Defense Minister Karl-Theodor zu Guttenberg.[99] The latter went on to maintain for several weeks that the attack was "justified."[100] However, on December 3, 2009, Guttenberg admitted that the attack on the tanker trucks, was "not justified."[101] Colonel Klein was relieved of his command and when sent back to Germany took personal responsibility for the action.[102] Schneiderhan was succeeded by General Volker Wicker as inspector general.[103] It was not a case of shared responsibility, in which both sides take responsibility.

SCANDALS

In October 2006, the German newspaper *Bild* published five photographs it said showed German soldiers in fatigues in Afghanistan playing soccer with human skulls. General Schneiderhan tried to explain by noting that the pressures in Afghanistan could not be compared with those prior to 2005, when the Bundeswehr's role was relatively passive. That was accompanied by a statement by the country's military leaders that such behavior was unacceptable.[104] General Schneiderhan commented that he had ordered increased training "for those in authority on their ethical and moral responsibility" in the performance of their duties.[105] In an interview he admitted the seriousness of the leadership problem, and again insisted that training, especially by the Center for Innere Führung, would be strengthened. For Schneiderhan, it was a matter of leadership and training.[106] From the standpoint of civil-military relations, that this minor incident became the subject of national importance, rather than a quick correction by a lower level officer, indicates just how sensitive the German public had become about the military and how ready the media was to publicize such events.[107]

Then the son of one of the country's leading generals (Jürgen Ruwe, the deputy inspector of the army), made some right-wing comments at the Bundeswehr University. The general who should have responded, Hans-Heinrich Dieter, the deputy general inspector, let the event pass. Several officers were astonished, as such comments by a regular officer would have seen him fired. Schneiderhan believed both generals were obstacles to reform, and he went to the political leadership. As a result, Ruwe and Dieter were forcibly retired. Dieter complained that he was "unjustly, unfairly, and improperly" treated.

On February 9, 2010, the German media reported that a soldier had complained that he was forced to drink alcohol until he vomited, and to eat raw pigs' liver as part of an initiation process in the Mountain Troops base in Mittenwald.[108] This latest incident demonstrated that this kind of action would probably continue in the Bundeswehr—as it does in most other militaries—and that media outlets like *Die Welt* are always looking for an incident in the military they can sensationalize.

MORALE PROBLEMS

In 2007, a survey of those in uniform indicated that 73.5% would not recommend the Bundeswehr to their friends. Every second soldier would choose another occupation. These problems could be reduced to the issue of financing. Only 3 percent believed policymakers supported them, and among career soldiers it was only 2.8 percent. The situation was especially bad among those serving abroad. Only 24 percent believed that they were adequately supported materially.[109] As another bad sign, Schneiderhan reported to Jung in a 65-page document that "The extremely badly needed material modernization cannot be carried out in accordance with the planning document." For 2008, the military would be given 630 million Euros less than the previous year.[110] At a meeting of the German Bundeswehr Verband (an organization of retired military and others who support the military), to which many individuals from a variety of military installations were invited, two conscripts criticized the *Bundesregierung* (the Federal Government) because, reading its official comments, they could not make sense out of the Afghanistan deployment. From their perspective, the only reason soldiers served there was for the extra money.[111]

Low morale was understandable, given the kind of equipment and weapons systems the German forces had in Afghanistan. For example, the primary transport plane for German forces was the 40-year-old C-160; the CH-53 helicopter was 30 years old. The Germans had to rely on the Americans for medivac services or for helping to relieve German troops under attack. In many cases they were prevented from taking offensive actions against the Taliban.[112]

The situation was so bad that a top German general branded the FRG's efforts in Afghanistan "a failure." He singled out the poor job the Bundeswehr had done training the Afghan police and in delivering and allocating development aid. He then pointed out that while the U.S. had given more than $1 billion to train the Afghan army and police, Germany had provided a mere 12 million Euros. "At that rate it would take 82 years to have a properly trained police force."[113] The general was not alone. Schneiderhan reported in March 2008 at the 41st Commanders' meeting in Berlin that the German military could not do everything it was being asked to do. The money given by parliament together with production problems meant that planning did not square with the reality of combat readiness. Attention was focused on the delay of the transport aircraft Airbus A400M and the helicopter NH 90.[114]

In addition to the changes under way, the military was exhausted.[115] As another source put it, "About 9,000 troops are active in Afghanistan, Lebanon, Kosovo and elsewhere, and there have been more than 200,000 deployments in the past 10 years."[116] In 2007, 73.2 percent of soldiers would not recommend service in the Bundeswehr.[117]

Much of the talk about Afghanistan centered around the word "war" (*Krieg*). Was Germany fighting a war in Afghanistan? In the past, it was labeled a civilian developmental assistance program. However, German soldiers were being attacked and killed in increasing numbers, and they were responding in kind. If Germany was fighting a war, then a stronger military presence, and a higher degree of sacrifice on the home front was in order. However, given the unpopularity of the conflict in Germany, if war were declared, it could lead to the withdrawal of German troops from Afghanistan.[118] The military commissioner from the Bundestag, who is the Bundestag's liaison member with the military, quoted a German soldier stating, "Currently, we are not building here any bridges or drilling any wells, We find ourselves in a war."[119] The commissioner Reinhold Robbe demanded from German society that it provide more support for the Bundeswehr.[120]

The Bundeswehr was coming under increasing pressure to do more to protect the Afghan population, a situation made worse by the Taliban's increasing its activity in the north where the Bundeswehr was deployed. On April 29, 2009, one soldier died, and four were wounded. According to General Schneiderhan, this attack had a new "quality." "This was a planned, one could almost say, a militarily planned action."[121] In a similar situation the following month, 30 German soldiers were attacked, four attackers were wounded, four others killed.[122] Since the deployment of German troops to Afghanistan in 2002, 32 German soldiers had died, 13 as a result of hostile action.[123]

In June, Berlin modified its strategy in Afghanistan. With the agreement of the SPD, the Bundeswehr began deploying heavy equipment. In addition, it gave the air force a free hand to provide ground support using its Tornado reconnaissance aircraft.[124] Schneiderhan also approved howitzers, in place of the "star shells" in use to that point. He also allocated additional armored transport vehicles, and he specifically mentioned the Marder armored personnel carrier.[125] In addition, at the request of its allies, Germany agreed to deploy two AWACS aircraft to Afghanistan to help allied forces locate Taliban units.[126]

An incredulous aspect of German service in Afghanistan was that German soldiers had to warn the opponent before they fired at an enemy. Soldiers had to say in Pashto, "United Nations—don't move or I will shoot"—absurd from a military standpoint.[127] After all, a Berlin police officer can utilize a weapon when he or she feels threatened. Fortunately, this policy changed. Shortly after the death of four soldiers who drowned after their vehicle was hit by a rocket, Defense Minister Jung announced he was asking that the old policy be reexamined with an eye to permitting German soldiers to operate under the same conditions that U.S. and U.K. troops did, so they could fire on Taliban forces without waiting for them to fire.[128]

During his time as chief of staff, Schniederhan came down very hard on soldiers he believed were not up to the job. In a speech on June 15, 2009, he criticized those who were unhappy with their equipment, for example a soldier in the Congo complaining about his sleeping bag or some professionals claiming they were denied numerous items, and he observed that too few soldiers and officers were prepared to take responsibility. He argued that while equipment was not always perfect, deployments abroad are part of the job, and NCOs and officers are supposed to be leaders and accept personal responsibility for carrying out the mission.[129]

In its search for tradition, one aspect of the Afghan War could have a positive impact on the Bundeswehr. On October 20, 2009, four German soldiers who had distinguished themselves in Afghanistan were awarded the "Cross of Honor for Bravery" (*Das Ehrenkreuz für Tapferkeit*), Germany's new highest medal for battlefield courage.[130] Ever since it was created in 1955, unlike other NATO members, the Bundeswehr did not have an equivalent of the Medal of Honor (U.S.) or Victoria Cross (U.K.). Thanks to Merkel and Jung's efforts, however, the medal was struck and awarded. While the criteria for the medal are not as strict as in the U.S. or U.K.—requiring extreme valor in the face of combat—it marks a step forward: Germany is beginning to recognize those who have performed outstanding actions in the Bundeswehr, beginning the process of building its own hall of heroes.

Merkel made the future of the Bundeswehr a part of her election strategy when she asked for a debate over the future of the armed forces during the 2009 election campaign.[131] Klaus Naumann probably stated Germany's problem best in a recent book, *Combat without a Goal: The Political Need for the Military* (2008). Until Germany answers that question there will be constant problems as the military continues to find it difficult to relate to the evolving civilian attitudes.[132] At the troop level, the German populace does not support the Bundeswehr, especially its efforts in Afghanistan, and this has had a serious negative impact on those in uniform. The *New York Times* article entitled "No Parade for Hans"[133] gives the impression that the reception for returning German soldiers mirrors that of American soldiers returning from Vietnam.

MODERNIZING THE BUNDESWEHR

The modernization process was not working. In late 2006, Defense Minister Jung was enraged by a report on the situation among German soldiers in Afghanistan. First, it had lain on General Schniederhan's desk for several weeks before Jung saw it. Schneiderhan's report stated that "the situation is disastrous, the Bundeswehr is hardly combat ready for new missions around the world." The problem was partly financial. In the 2007–2014 budget, there was a gap of 8.4 billion Euros,[134] the amount the Bundeswehr needed simply to carry out its mission.

In January 2008, the German high command received a 55-page report on external operations of the Bundeswehr that demonstrated how poorly organized the Bundeswehr was to deal with contemporary issues, because it lacked a political-military strategy. Seven of the highest former Bundeswehr generals wrote the analysis, including the former commander of forces in Afghanistan, General Norbert van Heyst. From February to July 2007, he and his colleagues visited about a dozen Bundeswehr bases and spoke with the commanders who had led the foreign missions. Their conclusion: "The Bundeswehr is good at ceremonies; militarily it is ineffective, and it is poorly controlled."[135] One suggestion was to create a General Staff to which critical questions could be staffed out and proposals made. There appeared to be a gap between the MoD and those in the field. Another criticism was that in the ministry, "there was too much talking and too little deciding." Another critic noted that "even when it involves questions of life and death, it can take years for the bureaucracy to make a decision." One example was the Störsender, an apparatus that helps neutralize roadside bombs. The request for such a device was made in 2003, but in 2008, the Bundeswehr was still waiting for it.[136] The report argued that the chief of staff should be given the authority to control the deployment and transfer of troops.

The situation did not improve in 2009. In his report in March, the parliamentary commissioner commented that the forces in Afghanistan did not have enough armored vehicles, and there were not enough armored all-terrain vehicles for training. As a result, Bundeswehr personnel had to learn how to operate and maintain them after they arrived in Afghanistan.[137] Money continued to be a major problem: according to one source, budget allocations for foreign and defense policy have "decreased by about 40% in real terms since their peak in the late 1980s."[138]

CONSCRIPTION

From a military standpoint, conscription made little sense. Conscripts served for far too short a period to learn to operate the weapons and equipment needed in modern war. But the military held on to it because it saw it as a means of attracting young men to serve extended tours in the Bundeswehr.

A conscript could extend for several years, or he could decide to become a longer-serving soldier (*Soldaten auf Zeit*). A strange paradox was also created. Over the years, Germany's social services became dependent on young conscientious objectors to staff their facilities. "If conscription ended tomorrow, parts of Germany's social system would simply collapse—that's why groups like the Red Cross vehemently oppose calls for an end to conscription."[139]

GUTTENBERG

On October 24, 2008, Struck became Minister of Labor and was replaced by the flamboyant CSU politician, Karl-Theordor zu Guttenberg. Seizing on the position as a possible stepping stone to the top, Guttenberg soon made the military and its problems a public issue. From his first day in office he used the term war (*Krieg*) to describe the situation in Afghanistan. One colonel commented that after seeing Guttenberg, he had the impression that he "will lead." He was further quoted as stating, "After the Jung era, a media savvy minister such as Guttenberg gives the Bundeswehr a chance."[140] Guttenberg defended the military by claiming that a mistaken attack on two tanker trucks stolen by the Taliban, but which were being looted by the Afghan populace, was "militarily justified."[141] He was determined to create a positive relationship with the military.[142] He fired Schneiderhan, who criticized him for the way he was treated.[143] As noted above, the latter was replaced by a new chief of staff, General Volker Wicker.[144]

THE DISPUTE OVER WEAPONS

During the middle of April, General Harald Kujat, a former chief of staff, criticized the government for failing to provide the troops in Afghanistan with the needed weapons and infrastructure, because of "a misunderstanding of the conditions in the field and ignorance of the necessities needed by the armed forces."[145] This was followed the next day by a similar piece by former Defense Minister Volker Rühe.[146] Then the new ombudsman from the Bundestag joined the chorus.[147] The problem was in Berlin. The problem for the government, in turn, was the lack of civilian support for the Bundeswehr.

Guttenberg set up a commission to deal with the weapons and equipment issue, and he flew to Afghanistan to assure the troops they would be receiving better weapons.[148] That was followed up by a visit by President Horst Köhler—the first such visit in 40 years.[149]

It was clear to Guttenberg that it was not just a question of public support, major structural changes were in order. On May 27, in a speech before the Bundeswehr Academy, he made his case. The Bundeswehr did not have the money to do everything; it would have to make choices, and toward this end he announced the creation of a commission to investigate the Bundeswehr, its structure, and its capabilities to determine the number of personnel, getting rid of old weapons in favor of newer ones, and closing of a number of bases.[150] Radical changes were coming, changes that many would not welcome.

Several models were discussed to restructure the Bundeswehr. Most agreed that 150,000 was the lowest the Bundeswehr could be reduced. This restructuring was entangled with the debate over conscription. On July 1, 2010, conscription was cut to six months. From a military standpoint, having a young man for only six months made little sense. At this point, the Bundeswehr consisted of about 247,000 active duty soldiers, 187,000 professionals or volunteers for a shorter period of service; the remaining 60,000 were conscripts.[151]

General Wicker entered the debate in September when he criticized the management of troops from the standpoint of weapons and equipment. He also criticized industry. There were cost overruns, the weapons were late, and they failed to meet the necessities of combat. He was especially critical in his attacks regarding the Tiger helicopter; the Germans were still relying heavily on the Americans for medivacting wounded personnel.[152] Furthermore, the most troops the Germans could deploy abroad was 7,000, whereas it should be in a position to send at least 14,000.

The commission set up by Guttenberg in October, the Weise Commission, was named after its chairman Franz-Jürgen Weise, a colonel in the reserve. Hanging over this commission was the determination of the Merkel government to save as much as $111 billion by 2013. For its part, the military was expected to contribute 9.3 billion Euros over the next three years.

Guttenberg found himself in the midst of a scandal. Inquiries by several German newspapers revealed that his doctoral dissertation at the University of Bayreuth had been plagiarized. He had openly copied newspaper articles to obtain the much desired PhD—in Germany often seen as a major asset for one entering politics.[153] The University of Bayreuth took away his PhD, and, despite strong support from Chancellor Merkel,[154] one of the most popular politicians in Germany was forced to resign on March 3, and to the surprise of many, moved to the U.S., only later returning to Germany. Despite the concern of many in the military about the forthcoming structural changes, Guttenberg had been the first defense minister who took the war in Afghanistan seriously and let the public know what was going on there.[155] He was replaced by Thomas de Maiziere, who had been serving as Minister of the Interior. De Maiziere was the son of the late general of the same name who had such a profound impact on the Bundeswehr, and a close ally of Merkel. His systematic style was the opposite of the flamboyant Guttenberg.

The military was in an uproar, and officers continued to worry about their careers. General Wicker commented, "There is definitely no need for so many different and competing command units in the Bundeswehr." "In my view only half the people we have in leading positions right now are required to do a proper job."[156]

The military stood at a crossroads. The report of the Weise Commission, released in October 2010, was to have a major impact on the armed forces. This report foresaw a new role for the general inspector, who was to become the commander of all of the military forces. The report complained that the military was marred by inefficiency and that reorganization was critical if it was to serve abroad in areas like Afghanistan. Toward this end, the report suggested structural changes: it suggested that the leadership of the Ministry of Defense should consist of a minister, a state secretary, and the general inspector. Each service would have its own commander, but in contrast with the past, the services would be overseen by the general inspector, who would be in charge of operational matters.[157] Also there would be a drop in the number of personnel in headquarters units from 3,000 to 1,500. The number of civilian state secretaries would be reduced from two to one. As far as the overall numbers of troops, Guttenberg had called for 180,000 to 185,000. The Commission suggested 163,500.

De Maiziere accepted Guttenberg's number of 185,000 troops, and set about making major cuts in the military. Navy submarines were cut from ten to six. He also planned to cut ten other ships, including supply ships, mine sweepers, and frigates. The army would go to two divisions, each with three brigades apiece, while the number of its Leopard I tanks would be reduced to 200. The air force would eliminate five of its thirteen squadrons. This meant the end of numerous careers.[158] Meanwhile, the five services (the army, navy, air force, medical service, and rear services, *Streitkraftbäsis*) would retain their independence as separate services. He further refined the number of troops as follows: 170,000 professional soldiers serving for shorter times (*Zeitsoldaten*) and 5,000 volunteers. Civilian personnel were to be cut from 76,000 to 55,000.[159] In October it was announced that 31 bases would be closed and others would be downsized.[160]

As this book goes to press, the Bundeswehr is in a state of semichaos. Old structures are being replaced by new ones, upsetting careers, families, and the whole concept of military service. But there appears to be a healthy relationship between the military and its civilian leadership, which has consistently stood up for the military, fought for resources, and done its best to improve its standing in German society.[161] However, from the military standpoint, the civilians could be doing far more to support it in carrying out its missions.

PART III / Canada

Canada's defence problem is that it has no defence problem.

JOEL SOKOLSKY

CHAPTER 6

From Paul Hellyer through Pierre Trudeau

> If a Canadian saw an admiral, let's say in the front lobby of the Hotel Fort Garry, he would hand him his bags because he would think the admiral was the bell-boy.
>
> COLONEL YORAM HAMIZRACHI

One of the main themes underlying civil-military relations in Germany was fear of a resurgent armed forces that could represent a danger to the civilian population: in Canada the populace ignored the military and saw little use for it in the furtherance of national interests. For many Canadians, the armed forces were a unnecessary and expensive organization, useful only during wartime. With the advent of nuclear weapons and the balance of terror, the Canadian military became less and less important. What difference would it make if the Canadian military showed up during an exchange of nuclear weapons? The answer for many Canadians was, "none."

The development of Canada's political-military culture has been influenced by issues that make the Canadian experience different from that in Germany, the U.S., and Russia.

First, foreign policy and defence policy have seldom held high priority in the minds of most Canadians. As one author put it, "For the last hundred years or so, Canadian leaders and the people they represent have not had to concern themselves about direct security threats to Canada."[1] The lack of interest in security policy and the military is evident in the memoirs of the various prime ministers.[2]

Second, Canada's defence policy has always been vulnerable to domestic concerns, and it has tended to be an irrational undertaking. As one of the country's former chief of the defence[3] staff commented:

> The formulation of explicit and detailed policy is never a simple or easy matter, and in some circumstances may not even be desirable; that, however, should be a matter of choice. Canadian defence policy, conversely, has probably never

> represented a deliberately chosen course of strategic direction, or a thoughtfully integrated element of national purpose and objective.[4]

According to General Theriault, Canadian defence policy is seldom the result of a carefully thought-out, planned strategy, rather it is often a budgetary afterthought or, as Jeff Tasseron put it, "defence policy is largely an adjunct to other elements of governmental concern."[5] Money is allocated, not to carry out a certain mission, but to replace worn out weapons or hire more soldiers. Then, the military budget is the first place Canadian politicians look when it comes to cuts, something that would not happen in the U.S. or Russia.[6] Senior Canadian military officers have never had the predictability that is so critical for planning military operations. As a result, key weapons programs have often been delayed or cancelled. Hence, the military often has been unable to carry out the tasks assigned to it by the political leadership, either because it does not have the requisite weapons systems or the personnel.

Third, Canadian politicians are generally ignorant when it comes to defence issues. They almost never have a military background. They accept a position of authority because the prime minister has asked them to, and in general have used it as a stepping stone to a higher political position. When they leave the defence portfolio they know as little about defence as they did when they arrived. They don't stay for four or five yeas as has been common in the U.S. or Russia. They are not competent to deal effectively with senior military officers, and often are not respected by the uniformed military. Their lack of expertise also undercuts their ability to represent military concerns abroad and to other members of the cabinet.

Fourth, in contrast to most American and Russian leaders, Canadian politicians "when in opposition seem unable to resist the temptation to use national defence policy as a whip against the government, and governments seem unable to see national defence as more than a liability against which they must protect themselves."[7]

Fifth, there is a belief among many Canadians that they do not have to do anything to ensure their own defence. The United States is a close neighbor, and any country that would try to invade Canada would quickly come up against the U.S. military. Even when the U.S. political leadership might not respect the Canadian political leadership, Washington would not permit another country to invade Canada.

Sixth, Canada does not have any traditional enemies. Ottawa may be upset from time to time with U.S. policies, but the U.S. is Canada's number one trading partner, and the two have worked together not only in matters of defence but often in foreign policy as well. When it comes to threats, the raison d'être for them "has almost always been defined by its allies, notably Great Britain and the United States."[8]

Seventh, for many Canadians, the military is an organization about which they know little. As Murray commented, "In many ways, the military operates outside the mainstream of society in Canada."[9] It is tolerated, respected, but not often considered an important part of Canadian society. In contrast to the other three countries discussed here, Canada does not have a long, deep rooted military tradition.[10]

The Institutional Structure

The National Defence Act (NDA)[11] is made up of two parts. Part one focuses on the Department of National Defence. It identifies the positions of the minister (MND), the deputy minister (DM), and the judge advocate general. The governor-in-council has the responsibility to "make regulations for the organization, training, discipline, efficiency, administration and good government of the Canadian Forces and generally for carrying the purposes of the Act into effect."[12]

The second part of the NDA runs 140 pages and focuses on the Canadian Forces, which are defined as "the armed forces of Her Majesty raised by Canada and consisting of *one service* called the Canadian Armed Forces (CF)." Here the important point is that the NDA makes a clear distinction between the Department of National Defence and the CF. The only military position identified is that of the chief of the defence staff (CDS) who has the "control and administration" of CF, under the direction of the minister. Finally, the legislation stipulates that "all orders that are required to carry out the directives of the government of Canada or the Minister shall be issued by or through the CDS."[13]

Unlike the United States and Russia, Canada does not have an institution like a security council. Instead, the defence minister is responsible to the Cabinet and the prime minister for defence. However, unlike the Russian, German, and American counterparts, the prime minister does not have his or her own expert staff to provide advice and assistance on defence issues that come from the National Defence Headquarters (NDHQ). Rather, he relies on the

CDS and the DM. Parliament's role is limited to the approval or rejection in toto of the government's policies.[14]

Canadian Military Culture

In many ways the culture of the Canadian Forces is similar to that in the U.S. military. As one noted Canadian analyst put it:

> Traditionally, military organizations are highly structured and ordered meritocracies. They are stable, conservative, and resistant to change. They operate under a special set of rules, have their own history and customs, and are governed by strict laws. Everyone knows his or her rank and place in the general scheme. On each soldier's uniform are the campaign and service ribbons that summarize his or her career. Status is transparent and palpable. At the same time, the military provides companionship and a built-in support system. A military organization is tough on individualists. It demands imaginative conformity.[15]

Soldiers are warriors, which in the words of two Canadian officers means, "Whatever the environment, the nature of military personnel policies must have its roots in the battlefield."[16] This could be a point of conflict between the military and some civilians who saw the CF more as a peacekeeping force. However, the military viewed the situation differently:

> From the very beginning, the Canada Army took the point of view that good peacekeepers can only be fashioned from soldiers who have been well trained to fight wars. Canada's soldiers rightly believe that troops who know how to defend themselves, who are trained in fieldcraft, weaponry, small-units tactics under fire, and who have had a good sense of field discipline instilled in them can be taught the art of peacekeeping.[17]

They went on to argue that military culture by definition is a subculture in any society. "What kind of a subculture are we talking about? Perhaps we can begin by saying what it is not. It is not a subculture which puts the individual before the group. It is not a materialistically or commercially oriented subculture. It is not a part of the 'mainstream' of Canadian society. It is therefore a distinctive social organization with its own characteristics that can be clearly identified."[18] This means that attempts to civilianize the Canadian military the way the left in Germany tried to do with the Bundeswehr will meet the same kind of resistance in Canada as it did in Germany.

Symbols and myths play a key role in the Canadian military, thus the requirement for ceremonies, medals, regimental colors, and such, as well as the perpetuation of the history of the group and the deeds of its heroes. Above all, one's acceptance within the "tribe" must be perceived as particularly significant. As for traditions, they give an emotional as well as a rational component to one's "self-image." They include distinctive dress, and the particular quirks that regulate military life on and off the job.[19]

In Canada as in the other three countries discussed here, the military is considered not merely a profession but a "calling." For most officers, ceremony and esprit de corps are considered vital to combat effectiveness. The bonds formed in peacetime between members of the military are critical when it comes to serving in combat. As English put it in reference to the CF's ethos, "It is in part a warrior's code, and it is based on four precepts: duty, integrity, discipline and honour."[20]

There is one area where Canadian military culture differs significantly from that of the U.S. and Russia. Canadian Forces are more amenable to adopting changing social norms. For example, the CF have been more accepting of both women and gays in their midst than is the case with Russians and Americans.[21] In this sense, the values of all three militaries closely resemble those in their societies.

Until recently, most of all Canadian Army ceremony and etiquette, "including its style 'on parade,' dress, awards, mess life, and even officer/senior NCO relations mimicked the style of the British Army. Cohesion and esprit de corps were, until very recently, entirely dependent on a strong regimental system that encourages a 'cradle to grave' system of rewards, sanctions and supports the bosom of the regimental 'family.' "[22] In time this would change, first because the government decided to abolish the regimental system, and second, because of the increasingly closer ties with the U.S. military.[23]

This British background has been the source of major problems in Canada, because for many years, French Canadians tended to consider the military a foreign army primarily interested in furthering the interests of the English-speaking regions of Canada:

> The Canadian Army of the 1960s was quite different from Canadian society in its ethnic and social composition. Men of British heritage or origin were over-represented compared to the rest of Canadian society, while Francophones and other ethnic groups were under-represented. This was especially true of officers, some 73 percent of whom could trace their roots to the British Isles, com-

pared to only 44 percent of Canadian society as a whole. Francophones were not only under-represented in the army but they were especially under-represented among the officer ranks.[24]

Brooke Claxton, Defence Minister (1946–1954)

Claxton was the first defence minister in the aftermath of World War II, at a time when the Canadian military needed to make major cuts in its armed forces—to the chagrin of many of the country's military leaders. He also was one of the few defence ministers who took his job seriously and remained in office long enough to have a significant impact. His primary accomplishment was his success in unifying many military functions. For example, he unified the separate service ministries into the Department of National Defence. Similarly he created the office of chairman, chiefs of staff committee, as well as the Defence Research Board. He also oversaw the evolution of Canadian forces through Canada's involvement in the Korean War, as well as in the creation of NATO. As Bland put it, "Claxton was unique in Canadian defence politics; he was active, inventive, competent and wise."[25] His primary goal was to "bring Canada's armed forces, the control of which had been more or less usurped by the Allies, once again under Ottawa's control."[26] In the process he was determined to unify them.

Toward this end he reopened the Royal Military College (RMC), which had existed since 1876, but was closed during World War II. He modernized its curriculum and he made it a tri-service academy. He also oversaw the opening of the College Militaire Royal de St-Jean in Quebec in an effort to attract Francophone officers into the army. Cadets attended either the College Militaire or Royal Roads in Victoria for the first two years and then went to RMC for the remainder of their education. He also established the National Defence College at Kingston.[27]

He streamlined the way the services did business, even if it meant working at a frustratingly slow pace. He unified several of the military's support services, including the dental and medical services, the chaplains, food procurement, and postal and legal services. In the process Claxton constantly fought with the postwar officers. The clashes were so serious that "Claxton was forced to warn the officers that henceforth there would be 'one department and one boss. . . . If an officer cannot be loyal [to the government] and silent he should get out [of the service.]' . . . 'I am,' he declared more than once, 'all for silent soldiers and sailors too.' "[28] In 1953, a new Defence Act was passed that established a common pay and welfare system for all three services. When Claxton retired in 1954, "his goals of a single defence budget, tri-service personnel policies, a single system of military law, and a single Defence Research Board had been achieved."[29] Two years later, Lieutenant General Charles Foulkes, chairman of the chiefs of staff committee proposed a three-phased process "to amalgamate the armed forces and the department into a new, leaner structure, so that the armed forces would operate 'with decisions taken on the basis of available facts and not on the basis of [service-inspired] compromise.' "[30] However, a year later Foulkes's proposal was lost in the change of governments; it would be almost 15 years before the Canadian high command would be forced to accept any further unification.

The Canadian Military (1956–1964)

Until the late 1950s, the Mobile Striking Force (MSF) served as Canada's key military force. It was originally conceived of as an air-droppable force that could be sent to anywhere in Canada's vast territory. But the MSF was more of an idea than a reality. It was, as Bercuson put it, a way for Canada to "make do."[31] In August 1950, Washington, London, and Canada's Commonwealth Allies put tremendous pressure on Ottawa to provide the brigade it had promised to fight in Korea. But all Canada had was the MSF forces, and if they were sent, however limited their abilities, Canada would be left defenceless. In response to this pressure, Ottawa decided to create a special force made up primarily of World War II veterans. It was sent to Fort Lewis, Washington, for training. It was not much of a fighting force.

> The Canadian Army was unready for the Korean War. . . . The brigade suffered constant, serious disciplinary problems in the first months in the field. A number of Korean civilians were murdered by Canadian soldiers. The Canadian troops had the highest crime rates of the Commonwealth force, the highest VD rates, and the highest desertion rates.[32]

While the Canadian military fought bravely and were awarded a U.S. presidential citation, the experience was not a positive one, and it did not enhance their reputation as an army, either at home or abroad. But then the military was not a priority for the Canadian government.

The real action for the Canadian military was in Europe. With the creation of NATO, pressure was again on Ottawa to provide troops. Toward that end, a brigade was raised, trained, and designated the 27th Canadian Infantry Brigade. To support these new obligations, between 1950 to 1953, the Canadian defence budget was increased from 3 percent of GNP to 8.8 percent.[33] As a result, the Canadian Army almost tripled in size.

From a practical military point of view, Canada's contribution was merely symbolic. Up to 1967, the plan was for Canada to augment its brigade with two others. Until 1967 it was part of a British division. Thereafter it became an independent brigade, first under British and later American command. Politically, however, the Europeans appreciated the presence of a second North American military force in NATO.

THE GLASCO COMMISSION

If anything has characterized civil-military relations in Canada, it has been the creation of one commission after another, all attempting to bring rationality into the defence process, especially when it came to command and control, the budget, and the inefficiency of the bureaucratic process. One of the first commissions was appointed by Prime Minister John Diefenbaker—"a Royal Commission on Government Organization"—in September, 1960.[34] J. Grant Glasco chaired the commission. At the time, the defence process required coordinating three chiefs of staff and the chairman of the Defence Research Board. Each had veto power over policy, and the result was often procrastination. As Bland said, it "undermined any chance of achieving significant military effectiveness."[35]

The Commission's conclusions were, as a noted Canadian historian put it, "unflattering."[36] The commission noted that there were more than two hundred committees in the Department of National Defence, and they were bottlenecks. Because all three services had their own intelligence organization, recruiting systems, pay systems, and public relations, there was a clear triplication of efforts leading to higher costs. Each of the service chiefs had direct access to the minister. However, neither he nor the chairman of the chiefs of staff committee could evaluate requests from the military. One result, the Glasco report observed, "was a shift in defence spending from new equipment to wages. In 1954, capital spending took 42.4 percent of the budget; by 1962 the share was 18.9 percent and falling."[37]

The message from the Glasco Commission, which published its findings in 1963, was clear: "save dollars wasted by bureaucratic inefficiency and put them to better use."[38] A consequence of this commission's work was the decision to replace the chairman of the chiefs of staff by a committee appointed by the Canadian defence staff to direct the armed forces "and control their common elements; the assertion of civilian control by giving the deputy minister greater responsibilities for reviewing the department's organization and administration on behalf of the minister; and the requirement to review civilian and military power needs in each of the three services."[39]

Because so little weight was placed on the Canadian military, the restructuring was based almost entirely on the premise that it would save money. Since cutting money from the military rang a positive note with the public, it was generally politically effective and would be used over and over in the coming years. The Canadian economy had been weak since 1957, and Canadians were demanding that more money be spent on social programs: "6 percent decline in industrial production in 1957 and growth of unemployment to 7.5 percent foreshadowed six years of weak economic performance."[40] "In 1963, the defence budget represented the most significant non-statutory federal expenditure."[41] If there were to be cuts in the budget, the defence budget was the obvious choice. Cutting defence might save money, but the military would fall farther behind. Something had to be done. The military could not simply be emasculated—the Americans would protest. Perhaps another reorganization was in order.

On April 22, 1963, Lester Pearson and the Liberals came to power. In the words of one Canadian scholar, Bercuson, when Pearson came to power, "the notion took hold that the government had a specific duty to re-engineer Canadian society."[42] This meant turning Canada upside down. Again to quote Bercuson, "The new Canada would be rights-driven. It would be bilingual. It would 'understand Quebec.' It would be multicultural. It would be a 'peaceable kingdom.' And the Canadian forces would lead the way."[43]

Paul Hellyer, Defence Minister (1963–1967)

When Paul Hellyer became defence minister in 1963, he had a mission to change the way the ministry did business. The government had to find a way to get the military under control, and most of all, rationalize the budgetary process. In his autobiography, he observed:

> A critical point that disturbed me greatly was the realization that witting or otherwise, each service was preparing for a different kind of war. The air force was thinking in terms of a three-to-five day all-out thermonuclear exchange. The army was thinking in terms of a long war. Only one of its four brigades was up to strength, and even it was ill-equipped. The other three would require months to buy equipment and call up the reserves in a general mobilization,

> not unlike what was done in the First and Second World Wars. The navy had one foot in each camp, with their emphasis on the type of anti-submarine warfare essential to convoy duty, as in World War II.[44]

It was clear to Hellyer that coordination and joint planning had to be to improved. The services could not go off in three different directions. From his perspective they were different fiefdoms, each jealous of its own territory. He was convinced that something had to be done to help rationalize the decision-making process. Canada was not a superpower, and its services were relatively small—between 60,000 and 80,000 troops.

For Hellyer, there were two options available to the Pearson Government. It either had to increase defence spending or reorganize Canada's armed forces. The government could increase the military budget to cover the cost of complex weapons systems, but for Hellyer, that was unacceptable. As he stated, "[the] impact of sharply rising costs for personnel, maintenance, and operations had been observed for some time, and its consequences for Canada's defence were strongly emphasized in the policy discussions of 1964."[45] If Canada was to be able to allocate more money to social programs, military outlays would have to be cut.

Thus, the decision to reorganize was made.[46] What did reorganization mean for the Canadian armed forces? Bland noted, "The essence of defence policy is to define defence objectives, identify resource requirements commensurate with those goals, establish rules governing the uses of force, and provide the process by which the civil authority will oversee the armed forces and defence officials."[47] The problem was that defence policy had not been approached in a holistic context; the fight was generally over this or that weapons system. Hellyer believed the answer was to centralize control and administration of the CF under one CDS, resulting in a single, integrated Canadian defence policy. There would be one CFHQ and one CDS.[48] Opposed by senior officers, this approach ignored several components of defence policy. For example, little attention would be paid to the issue of why? What was the purpose of Canadian Forces? Were there rules for the application of force? Indeed, future prime ministers would send Canadian troops abroad with little or no attention to their ability to carry out their assigned tasks. Hellyer was determined to restructure the armed forces, even if he faced stiff military opposition.

When it came to the senior uniformed officers, Hellyer intended to take charge, creating a special relationship. He refused to sign any documents during his first 30 days in office,[49] suspended equipment purchases while a defence review was underway, and cancelled the RCAF CF104 aircraft replacement program. He also demanded a "comprehensive review of defence policy and administration."[50]

THE *1964 DEFENCE WHITE PAPER*

Hellyer's review of defence policy and administration was the focus of the *1964 Defence White Paper.* It relied heavily on the material in the Glasco Commission's report. The paper focused on practical steps to alleviate the problems facing the Canadian military. According to Kronenberg, there were two underlying premises behind Hellyer's white paper. Canada is guarded by the United States, "It is for the foreseeable future, impossible to conceive of any significant external threat to Canada, which is not a threat to North America as a whole." Secondly, if there should be aggression against Canada, Ottawa could rely on the United States to support it.[51] Therefore, many argue that Canada's primary focus in the world was diplomatic. Canada would never have a big enough military to be taken seriously on the world stage; it was and would remain a middle-level power. It would only be involved in military activity in concert with other military organizations. Hellyer didn't realize that Canada needed a credible military if it expected to be taken seriously in the international community. There are many middle-sized countries in the world, and their militaries are not much bigger than those in Canada, but if the military were called upon and could not function effectively, Canada would run the risk of becoming an embarrassment.

To have an effective system of command and control, Hellyer believed there had to be a clear single line flowing from the MND and the CDS to the services and the commands in the field. The current system was too rigid. The services had to cooperate with each other, and although they claimed they were working together, Hellyer believed they were only giving such coordination lip-service. The services often circumvented the defence minister, treating him as only of symbolic importance. Hellyer felt the generals and admirals only pretended to listen to him. Now, however, he intended to get serious, outlining his intentions in the *1964 White Paper.* He argued that the "traditional pattern of organization by individual services" was out of date.[52] The alternative was a joint command structure combined with service unification. He would create a new kind of armed forces. This meant eliminating the chairman of the Chiefs of Staff Committee, as well as the three service chiefs, who would be replaced by a single CDS together with a joint headquarters, which would be called Canadian Forces Headquarters. To further systematize the process, Hellyer maintained that the headquarters should be based on functions. This meant all-service units in areas such as personnel and logistics, rather than the service-specific categories. This would help rationalize headquarters procedure and enable the military to replace many officers who were working in headquarters with civilians. Replaced officers could then be transferred to the field in combat functions, or go to sea. As a result, according to Hellyer, "sufficient saving should accrue from unification to permit a goal of 25 percent of the budget to be devoted to capital equipment being realized in the years ahead."[53]

MILITARY OPPOSITION TO HELLYER

Hellyer's refusal to pay any attention to senior military and naval officers in the 1964 document was especially irritating. Like Robert McNamara and Donald Rumsfeld in the U.S., and Yeltsin and Serdyukov in Russia, Hellyer was convinced that he understood the problems better than those in uniform. He would make the critical decisions on unification whether or not the military liked it. Kronenberg, an expert on the 1964 document, commented,

> Whatever the advice he got, there appears to have been a genuine feeling in his own mind, not always shared by others, that the "Hellyer solution" to the problem was the correct one. To this may be added two minor factors, which may explain some later events. The first was a growing awareness of the uniqueness of the Canadian venture, together with a feeling that other countries would shortly follow the same road. The second and related one was the political realization that the successful management of such a large undertaking could not but enhance the political career of the architect.[54]

This meant that Hellyer was constantly interfering in practical military matters, arguing that a change was necessary here, or not necessary there.

Hellyer ignored the generals and admirals on the issue of military tradition. The military believed it was a critical component of military culture, vital for morale and esprit de corps, which were, in turn, vital to combat efficiency and readiness.

Hellyer, dismissed such concerns out of hand.

> Unification of the Canadian Forces does not imply the abandonment of tradition, of pride in the unit and other ingredients of esprit de corps. The preservation of the intangible factors which support and sustain any fighting unit

> is an essential goal but along with this it is important to foster innovation. The stimulus of new ideas and methods injects enthusiasm and vigour into any organization. . . . The development of clearly defined roles, the provision of better equipment to carry out those clearly defined roles, and the anticipated public recognition of the efficient and useful defence concept being developed, should have a beneficial effect on the morale of service personnel in the unified force. They will have the added satisfaction of knowing that they are setting the pace for the world in modernizing the organization of military forces.[55]

In the white paper, tradition is mentioned, but quickly dismissed. Hellyer believed that instead of basing morale and esprit de corps on individual services, those in uniform would transfer their sense of tradition to a new unified Canadian Forces. According to Kronenberg, the document took the position that, " 'worthwhile' traditions on which *esprit de corps* was based would not be eliminated and . . . furthermore, morale should remain high or even rise as a direct result of the improved effectiveness of the integrated service."[56] It was, however, a recipe for political-military conflict.

Hellyer met with senior officers to learn of their objections to unification. He claimed that military opposition was "purely emotional" and "pretty silly."[57] However, he seemed to recognize just how sensitive the issue was, noting that during a meeting with two and three stars, his secretary, Ron Sutherland, "prepared two sets of minutes, one unexpurgated, of which there were only three or four copies, and another totally innocuous version that stands on the record." Hellyer then used unfortunate language in response to MG Bill Anderson's concern over tradition by suggesting he was worrying about "buttons and badges." For senior officers who had watched men fight and die for those button and badges, "the names of units and corps and the peculiar, particular traditions of services had real meaning."[58] He dismissed them, arguing, "Important as these are, one is scraping the bottom of the barrel to include them in a serious discussion."[59] Unification was far more important than the military's concern over "buttons and badges."[60] Hellyer refused to understand that many of those buttons and badges were earned as a result of the soldier, sailor, or airman putting his or her life on the line. To quote Granatstein, "It might be peripheral to the Minister, but it was heritage, tradition, and hard-earned distinctions to fighting men."[61] Brushing them aside as buttons and badges was a great insult.

Hellyer's most blatant attack on tradition came with his order that all members of Canadian Forces should wear the same uniform, with a common rank structure. His logic, as expressed in his autobiography, was that technology had unified the military, it had "erased the neat divisions between land, sea, air, and space warfare."[62] However, despite technological advances, the primary loyalty in the army, navy, and air force is to corps and regiments, to ships and squadrons, not to the DND. Most soldiers and airmen in Canada, as in the United States, did not even understand navy ranks, let alone feel much loyalty to ships none of them had ever seen. This was even more true in the army, where focus was on the soldier's particular regiment, in which some soldiers spent their entire military lives. As to uniforms, the mere idea that sailors all over the world would wear any color uniform but blue was heresy. Sailors had unique uniforms developed over the centuries to reflect the evolution of the naval service. As Granatstein put it, "Sailors in particular revolted at the idea that colonels would command ships and that a green uniform would replace the traditional bell-bottoms. How would that look when they went ashore in Plymouth or New Orleans?"[63] The whole process was made worse when Hellyer announced that the united rank structure would be that of the army. Sailors were not only losing their unique uniforms but their rank structure as well.[64]

Military officers were taken aback, in fact insulted, by Hellyer's attitude toward tradition and uniforms—not what they had anticipated from the Liberal government. The result was predictable: the adoption of a single green uniform resulted in "the corresponding severe damping effect on esprit de corps. Unit cohesion, that almost mystical mix of the warrior's psychology, family dynamics, and something more ethereal or intangible, that all good armies and their commanders coveted, was casually thrown to the wind by Monsieur Hellyer."[65]

Each service was focused on its own new weapons systems; the army needed new tanks and armored personnel carriers, while the navy was in desperate need of new destroyers to replace its outdated World War II ships, and the RCAF was in need of a long-range patrol plane. The generals and admirals were shocked by Hellyer's refusal to work with them in coming up with a new plan for restructuring the military. On occasion senior officers heard about "the latest [unification] development through press releases."[66] The bottom line was simple. As Morton argued, "Whatever their view of integration, few senior officers accepted Hellyer's major premises for unification. In peace and war, Canada's armed forces had been fated to work separately save when the RCN and RCAF cooperated in anti-submarine warfare."[67]

To a certain degree, Hellyer was trying to civilianize the Canadian Forces in much the same way as some members of the SPD had tried with the German Bundeswehr. A base administrative officer said, "Fundamentally, I don't think we operate a business. . . . Fundamentally, what we are doing, or should be doing, is training for war. . . . You won't be successful at war if you operate as a business, always concerned about the bottom line and the dollar sign." This was the same kind of response German politicians received from German soldiers. As German officers argued in dealing with their civilian masters, cost effectiveness and combat efficiency are not necessarily the same thing.[68] Cost effectiveness meant reforming the military for the sake of political and bureaucratic issues, instead of the promotion of military effectiveness, a point Bercuson made when he noted that unification had little to with creating an efficient military. The head of the Defence Research Board, O. M. Soldant, called unification "an act of mayhem committed in the name of administrative madness."[69] Or as another author put it, "We now have an army in which war fighting is of secondary or tertiary importance. Which is absurd."[70] From the military's standpoint, Hellyer was putting the cart before the horse. The simple fact, one officer claimed, was that the reform was not thought through, even though Hellyer may have believed that he knew exactly what would happen. To quote this officer, "Those who had initiated the reform, about which they talked non-stop for two years, had not given sufficient consideration to its overall implications,"[71] to which an outside observer can only respond by saying "Amen."

BILL C-90

Hellyer had no intention of limiting his efforts to the white paper. His goal was to give teeth to the changes outlined in the white paper, and he got Parliament involved in his plan to restructure the military. On June 7, 1963, Parliament created a Special Committee on Defence.[72] The Special Committee met 45 times between June 18 and December 11, 1963. Dozens of military and civilian officials, experts, and analysts were called to testify. The committee also visited a wide range of defence establishments in Canada, the U.S., and Europe, asking questions and taking notes. The primary focus of the Special Committee was on the importance of Canada continuing to participate in organizations such as NATO, NORAD, peacekeeping, and the defence of Canada. The committee only touched briefly on issues related to the centralization and unification of the armed forces.

In 1964 the committee's first action was to create Bill C-90.[73] The keys to the bill were economic—structural changes would save money, and continued focus was on a centralized command and control system. Too many individuals had direct access to the minister. Decision-making responsibility would be centered in a revised Defence Council (or as he reportedly called it, "The Cabinet of the DND").[74] It included the minister, the parliamentary secretary, the deputy minister, the associate deputy minister, and the Chiefs of Staff Committee. Depending on the issue, other officials could attend meetings of either the Defence Council or the Chiefs of Staff Committee. Hellyer intended to introduce better central control by making it the nerve center of the DND and thereby help stop the many end-runs that were made around the bureaucracy directly to the minister. Now the defence minister and the deputy defence minister would be directly involved in any decisions regarding defence policy, and they would have the advantage of getting advice from experts, who would presumably be less partisan than the service chiefs. The service chiefs would still have a chance to make their viewpoints known through the Defence Council, but their role would be advisory, and their primary function would be administrative. To quote Bland,

> Hellyer did not reject the need for "specialized"—that is service—input to decision making. In fact he recognized it in appointing deputies throughout the new structure. The point was, however, that these specialist viewpoints were not to get to the Minister before they had been coordinated by the CDS into a coherent military view. The assumption that a single military view could be logically and rationally arrived at was the essential act of implicit faith inherent in Hellyer's concept of defence administration.[75]

There were military voices who supported Hellyer's call for a more integrated military. For example, former Chairman of the Chiefs of Staff Committee General Guy Foulkes and former Chairman of the Chiefs of Staff General Guy Simmonds endorsed the legislation. Others, however, strongly opposed it. According to Granatstein, what made it difficult was the unwillingness of many in the service—and almost everyone who had once been in the military—to accept unification.[76]

Critics feared that the CDS would become too powerful or that the military's views would not reach the minister. Hellyer dismissed both concerns as unwarranted. The bill was passed on July 7 and came into effect on August 1, 1964. According to Hellyer, "The transition was so smooth that it didn't create a ripple."[77] However, while Hellyer had changed the command and control structure, he had done little to unify the services.

CANADIAN FORCES HEADQUARTERS (CFHQ)

The new structure was created in 1964, part of Hellyer's restructuring. It had a number of units such as intelligence, strategic plans, continental plans, force development, operational requirements, programs, operational training, and operations.[78] Then on July 7, 1965, the service chiefs disappeared and were replaced by the commanders of Air Defence Command, Air Transport Command, Mobile Command, Maritime Command, Training Command, and Material Command. Communications Command was subsequently added. A single base pay system was introduced, and all Canadian military bases became Canadian Forces Bases.

From a military position, the enactment of Bill C-90 meant that the CDS would henceforth be the senior military officer and the conduit through which orders would be issued. The Armed Forces Council, which met for the first time on August 10, 1966, provided him with an opportunity to hear from the main functional commands as well as the chiefs of the services. Two civilians, the deputy minister, and, in certain cases, the chief of the Defence Research and Development Council were imposed on the military.[79]

MORE MILITARY OPPOSITION TO HELLYER

It was the navy that led the charge against Hellyer. Admiral William Landymore, who commanded the Atlantic coast, led the opposition. In an address to his sailors and in testimony in mid-1966, Landymore "left no doubt that he thought that unification would destroy the RCN and its effectiveness."[80]

Landymore testified before the House of Commons on June 23, 1966. A transcript of the testimony taken from Hellyer's memoirs follows:

> Mr Matheson (MP for Leeds): "Admiral, in comparing the presentation we had today with a presentation we received in the previous Parliament from the Chief of Naval Services, I tend to see an enormous emphasis on a specialty, a fighting capability. Am I correct in thinking that with the navy, the senior service, there is, of course, some reluctance, to this tendency toward unification of service? Would you be frank with us on this matter?"
>
> Rear Admiral Landymore: "Well, the answer to that is yes. I think there is great reluctance on the part of the navy."
>
> Mr. Matheson: "Is it love of tradition and love of the sea? Or does it actually go beyond that to tactics and strategy?"
>
> Rear Admiral Landymore: "I do not think it enters into the operational field.

> I think that generally navies are very close to one another and find their way of doing things and their manner of presenting themselves and in their identity. If there is reluctance, and there is, it is due to that factor more than any other."[81]

From Hellyer's standpoint, this again was nothing but "silly" tradition on the navy's part. According to Granatstein, Landymore did testify that unification would destroy the RCN's effectiveness; it was not just a matter of tradition as Hellyer implied.[82]

As a result of his outspoken opposition, Hellyer sacked Landymore. Landymore went to the media, arguing that "unification had demoralized the officer corps." In return, an exasperated Hellyer said that the admiral had been fired for " '18 months consistent disloyalty to the policy of the people he was paid to serve,' a charge he subsequently withdrew."[83] Granatstein, however, maintained that Landymore and others who opposed Hellyer, "resisted unification . . . in ways that fit within the traditional rules of Canadian civil-military relations. They avoided the defiance exhibited in the 1962 Cuban missile crisis, when the Royal Canadian Navy put to sea without government orders to work with its United States Navy ally."[84] Hellyer may have thought that Landymore was out of line and that he was violating the rules of civilian control of the military. "Integration was the policy of the Government of Canada, and it was the responsibility of serving officers to implement rather than oppose it."[85] However, it was clear that by this point, a significant number of Canadian officers were not interested in a shared responsibility.

Landymore's open opposition led to the creation of antiunification organizations all over the country, formed by veterans, reservists, and most importantly by TRIO, the Tri-Service Identities Organization. These groups had media support as well as backers in the House of Commons. "At this time, twenty years after V-E Day, there were still many MPs who had served during the war."[86] Landymore also claimed publicly that he had carried out a survey of naval officers of the ranks of lieutenant commander and up. He claimed that only three of the 367 surveyed had supported unification.[87]

Canadian service tradition dictated that officers who felt they could not support the unification policy should resign. Thus, between January 1965 and August 1966, 28 general officers left, including all three of the "three stars," and 79 senior officers. These officers included Air Chief Marshal Frank Miller, Hellyer's first CDS. Opposition was not limited to senior officers. A total of 26,300 other officers and senior NCOs also left. By August 1966, only two of the thirteen most senior officers had been in their commands more than a month.[88] The man who became CDS at this time said,

> I feel obliged to say, however, that the departure of several senior officers who, in 1966 opted for the same course as Landymore, was unfortunate and much regretted. The greatest harm was caused by the gesture in itself and not by the skill or experience we were losing, for replacements were as well-qualified and as capable as those who, since 1964, had laid the foundations of the programme.[89]

There were also practical problems with unification. One could not simply substitute an army mechanic for a navy mechanic on board a ship. Problems arose, even with seemingly transferable jobs. Take the case of an army cook. It would be difficult to put him on a ship, because he would not be part of the "group," and because he would not know how to do the many other jobs a navy cook is required to do in the event of combat or an emergency. Then there was the simple issue of defining jobs, for example, a musician was defined as an individual who could play two instruments. What about those in the army who were pipers?

BILL-243

In 1966, the Canadian Forces Reorganization Act was introduced by the government. This bill foresaw the elimination of the three services: the Royal Canadian Navy, the Royal Canadian Air Forces, and the Canadian Army. Instead of the individual services, there would be "elements." In the future, the three of them would be combined under the term Canadian Forces. According to Bland, during the discussion of this bill, Hellyer stage managed matters so that civilian authority became the key issue. "He effectively deflected criticism and 'successfully presented himself as the champion of progress over the rebels of reaction.'"[90]

In presenting the virtues of Bill-243, four elements were singled out. First, it would create a common identity on the part of all Canadian servicemen and women. Second, it would open up larger avenues for highly motivated officers and other ranks (since they wouldn't be limited by the confines of their own smaller services). Third, the new force would be more adaptable when it came to meeting new requirements as a result of military technology and the international situation. Fourth, because of the demands for quick decision in contemporary warfare, a unified force would be preferable.[91]

From 1964 to 1967, Parliament debated both Bill C-90 and C-243. Numerous witnesses appeared before the various committees. One source argued that as military opposition to these bills increased, suspicion and resentment of Hellyer grew in the parliamentary committees.[92] Bill C-243 was approved by a vote of 127 to 73, with the Tories forming the heart of the opposition. It went into effect on February 1, 1968. General Allard commented that he told the members of the military present that "because the essentials had been preserved, the resignations of 1966 had been quite useless."[93] He then presented the new Canadian Forces emblem to the Commander in Chief Governor General Roland Michener. However, as far as most of the population was concerned, Desmond Morton noted, "Few Canadians cared."[94]

THE FRANCOPHONE ISSUE

The Liberals won the election of April 1963 and soon showed that they were serious about addressing the Francophone issue. A Royal Commission of Inquiry on Bilingualism and Biculturalism was created. Quebec nationalism came increasingly to the fore. The commission held numerous discussions and invited a variety of witnesses, both British-Canadian and French-Canadian.

From a military standpoint, the Francophones had a legitimate complaint. Prior to the mid-sixties, French was hardly ever used inside Canadian garrisons. The only option available to a French-speaking Canadian who wanted to retain his language and his culture was to join the Royal 22nd Regiment stationed in Quebec. If he or she hoped to move up in the service, the only option was to abandon the French language and culture and adopt the culture of the English-speaking regiments in other parts of Canada.

GENERAL JEAN ALLARD, CHIEF OF DEFENCE STAFF (1966–1969)

Of all the CDS to hold the position from the mid-1960s to the present General Jean Allard ranked near the top among those officers who had the most profound impact on Canadian Forces. Allard was a Francophone who had fought and commanded Canadian troops in World War II and in the Korean War and who had a good reputation in Canadian Forces. Allard was one of the very few Francophone officers who had risen to the top ranks of the Canadian military. Indeed, there were several English-speaking officers who reportedly resigned at the sight of a Francophone officer taking command of Canadian Forces. Hellyer claimed that he picked him because he "was a very handsome man with a first-class war record. Fluently bilingual, Jean was an ebullient leader of men, an optimist who radiated enthusiasm."[95] Hellyer also noted somewhat jokingly that Allard was obsessed with the Francophone issue. For example, he reported that at the end of March, 1965, he threatened to resign because the CF had not paid enough attention to the status of the Francophones. Hellyer said,

> It started off with Jean Allard telling me he is going to resign as a result of the failure in respect of bilingualism in the Armed Forces. I tried to convince him of the "truth" that the proposed command structure had no real connection to the problem of making French-speaking Canadians feel "at home" in the Armed Forces.[96]

The cabinet approved his choice, and Allard was appointed CDS on July 15, 1966.

While serving as CDS, Allard had one overriding mission: to improve the position of French-speaking officers and enlisted personnel in Canadian Forces, He knew better than almost anyone what it meant to climb the promotion ladder as a Francophone. He saw unification as an opportunity to promote the French side of the Canadian equation. He seized the opportunity to press bilingualism in Canadian Forces, recognizing that it was a lack of English that both discouraged Francophone officers and kept them back from promotions. In his memoirs, Allard stated that prior to accepting Hellyer's offer to him to become CDS:

> I wished to know what the Minister's opinion was on the subject and to obtain from him the guarantee that I would be able to set up, within as short a time as possible, the study group I had been dreaming of and which must have the means of examining the subject in depth. I would be able to make concrete gestures, based on the results of the report, to ensure and guarantee equality of opportunity for the advancement of Francophones at all levels, within the structures that the armed forces were about to adopt.[97]

Allard was not alone in his concern over the way French-speaking citizens were being treated in the military. In fact, a new, more nationalistic group was growing in Quebec—one demanding equal rights if not independence for French Canadians. The Liberal Party, meanwhile, had made it clear during the 1963 election campaign promised to examine the French issue. It was only a matter of time before the issue came to the fore and the military would have to deal with it. Given hostility on the part of the Anglophone officers, it would be a difficult task.

Statistics showed just how difficult life in the military was for a Francophone officer. As Allard noted, in the infantry, Francophone officers constituted 21 percent of officers, whereas in the more technical artillery, the percentage fell to 5.5 percent. "It took no wizardry to conclude that outside the R22ndR, a Francophone infantry unit, there was no salvation for my compatriots. At the various staff schools, we were underrepresented. Among the other ranks (NCOs and men) we noted the same phenomenon. Altogether, the Army had 14.5 percent Francophone officers, owing to the major role played by the infantry. . . . I was the only French Canadian officer at my senior level."[98]

With the cabinet's support, Allard's study was carried out. In spring 1967, it reported back with some 39 recommendations aimed at upgrading conditions for Francophones in the Canadian military. The study covered issues like the status of Francophone soldiers and officers, and also the recruiting process, their social lives once they joined the military, and the training process, for example, how did Francophone soldiers do in training courses that relied primarily on English-language textbooks or English-language instructors?

The Declaration of April 1968 contained a number of improvements for Francophones. Those who could not serve outside of Quebec for family or education reasons saw their career opportunities increased. Those Francophone soldiers stationed outside of Quebec would see an improvement in their social and cultural environments. Those in English-speaking sections of Canada would see their opportunities to learn French expanded.

On April 2, 1968, the first real results of the study came to light in the form of unit and base relocations. French-speaking units were created. "The most concrete result was the creation of 5 *Grupment de combat* at Valcartier, the manning of a vessel in Halifax with a French-speaking crew, the formation of a Francophone fighter squadron at Bagotville and the establishment of a French-language recruitment training centre. . . . Finally, between 1966 and 1972 great strides were made in another field—that of the French-language education of the children of Francophone servicemen serving outside Quebec."[99] In September 1969, before his retirement, General Allard was able to submit to the Defence Council a "Long-term Program for Bilingualism in the Canadian Forces." It focused on the presentation of a program for the integration of French Canadians into the mainstream of Canadian Forces over the next ten years.[100]

The issue then became one that is often attached to social quotas—what percentage of French Canadians should be part of the CF to ensure that it is representative of Canadian society? At that time, French Canadians accounted for 28 percent of the population. Thus, the idea was that French Canadians should compose 28 percent of the CF.[101] This was a major social action. For example, in 1967, there were not even 16 percent French Canadians in the CF.[102] An effort was made to ensure that the implementation of Francophone policies did not create injustices for English-speaking forces.

Pierre Trudeau (1968–1979)

On April 1968, Pierre Trudeau, a man who was one of the most anti-Canadian military political leaders since the end of World War II, became prime minister. He had avoided military service during World War II. As one of his foes, the later prime minister Brian Mulroney observed, "When Canadians were off fighting the Second World War . . . Trudeau was back home swatting black flies in Ourremont,"[103] Trudeau knew almost nothing about the armed forces.

> The new prime minister was even less informed about the Department of National Defence. He had never served in the armed forces, and during the war he had managed to make a lark out of his rudimentary cadet training. To him, the military was completely foreign, a world populated by men who trained to kill. One revealing sign came in the middle of the 1968 election when Trudeau asked Bill Lee, formerly a wing commander in the Royal Canadian Air Force but then the Liberal campaign tour organizer, "Why would a guy as smart as you waste his time in the military?" The incomprehension was total.[104]

On another occasion he reportedly confided to friends that he "viewed soldiers as unintelligent thugs." The military was an "alien nation of almost no importance. Money spent on the military was money wasted."[105] As far as his personality was concerned, it soon became clear to everyone that "he was not a diplomat."[106]

In accordance with what was becoming standard procedure in Canadian politics, when the new government wanted to make changes, the first thing they did was reject the last white paper, and create a new one. The cabinet decided on May 15, 1968, to carry out "a comprehensive review . . . [of] Canada's armed forces policy, including alternative forces' structures and costing." It was to be completed by July 15 and specifically structured to determine if it was possible for the new government to introduce an alternative policy to that suggested in the *1964 White Paper.*[107] To achieve the above, the review "sought to ascertain what Canada's national interests were, and then attempted to determine the role of Canada's military interests in helping to fulfill those interests."

From the perspective of Trudeau's primary assistant, Ivan Head, there were major problems with all three elements. All of them had become very specialized in their fulfillment of NATO and NORAD goals. In Trudeau's mind, the U.S. and Russia were moral equivalents.[108] Often, their missions had little to do with protecting Canada. As Trudeau put it, "Our paramount interest is to ensure the political survival of Canada as a federal and bilingual sovereign state. This means strengthening Canadian unity as a basically North American country. Canada's problems were genuine and serious enough, but the hint that Canada was going to turn inwards must have chilled many in External Affairs and National Defence."[109]

The navy, for example, was dedicated almost entirely to the North Atlantic. This meant that it did not possess "a single hull capable of navigation in ice-infested waters, and utterly opposed to performing—even contemptuous of—many of the paramilitary roles discharged by the Coast Guard, by fisheries protection vessels, by the RCMP."[110] The situation with the army was similar. They were primarily trained and equipped "to engage in tank combat on the German plain, an activity entirely alien to peace-keeping or to support the civil power."[111] The air force was flying obsolescent planes and primarily focused on NATO. "The Canadian Arctic, for all intents and purposes, was an area of indifference, except for the ever-changing commitments to the detection and interdiction of incoming bombers, and the conduct of sensitive electronic activities."[112] The problem of this special focus on NATO in Trudeau's mind was that almost all of Canada's forces were committed to a conventional response to a Soviet attack, but the West would be incapable of doing so without reliance on nuclear weapons. As a result, Trudeau sent a number of fundamental questions about NATO to the Departments of External Affairs and National Defence. From his standpoint, the problem was that NATO was determining Canada's defence policy. He believed that the situation should be reversed. They were Canada's troops, not NATO's.

In February 1969, External Affairs, which was very conscious of Canada's close ties with NATO, sent back a paper that in Head's words, "justified completely the current policies and argued strongly for their retention and continuation."[113] It was almost a year since Trudeau had requested the review, and here was External Affairs, the primary drafter, telling the prime minister that everything was fine. Rather than creating a confrontation, Trudeau simply stated that the review was unsatisfactory. He told Michael Sharp from External Affairs and Leo Cadieux from Defence that he would not even let the cabinet look at it. He told them to take it back and reconsider the recommendations in light of his wish to reexamine alternatives to current policy. That meant coming up with new proposals. Instead of modifying its report, External Affairs had only reaffirmed the earlier proposals. Canada's commitments to NATO were not changed.

Faced with bureaucratic opposition, Head proposed that the government set up a group to come up with a new set of proposals. The bureaucrats claimed that the proposals were so radical that they did not "deserve further attention."[114] The navy, already upset over unification policies, was especially adamant in rejecting the new proposal. It rejected any role for itself except antisubmarine warfare, in accordance with the tasks assigned to it by NATO. The army felt similarly, insisting that it must retain heavy armor.

When Cadieux and Sharp arrived for a meeting of the Combined Committee on Defence and Foreign Policy on March 26, 1969, they were surprised to see that instead of their departmental briefs they were presented with a "Canadian Defence Policy—A Study." "It proposed a drastic cut of 50 percent in the armed forces, greatly reduced commitments to NATO, an end to a nuclear role, and more emphasis on North America and peacekeeping."[115] The meeting quickly adjourned, and Cadieux phoned Trudeau and told him that both he and Sharp would resign if it went forward to the Cabinet. Trudeau withdrew the study, but it was clear to both of his ministers that he intended to make major changes in defence policy.

On April 3, 1969, Trudeau announced his decision. The process clearly established two principles. First, he was the one in charge, and second, Canada was adopting new policies in the defence field. The most important decision was that Canada would reduce its forces in Europe. "In the view of Trudeau and Head, that element was insignificant compared with the major decision to retire from the nuclear-strike role."[116] It was clear that Trudeau was prepared to accept neutrality, although he paid tribute to NATO. It was clear that cuts would be forthcoming in the future. Instead of Canada maintaining expensive forces in Europe, "Canada could, in essence 'free ride' on its allies, especially on the United States."[117] Trudeau believed the United States would never permit any foreign power to attack or occupy Canada, and that if the American nuclear deterrent should fail, the presence or absence of Canadian forces would matter very little.

On April 30, 1969, Cadieux recommended that Canadian NATO forces be reduced to about 3,500. However, in the end, the final figure was 5,000 to 10,000.[118] In essence, it was a 50 percent cut in Canadian troops in NATO.

The military budget was also frozen at $1.8 billion. This led to a drop in the percentage of the national budget devoted to defence from 18 percent in 1967–1968 to 13 percent four years later. "The percentage of gross domestic product spent on the military similarly declined from 2.5 to 2 percent. The strength of the Canadian Forces fell between 1968 and 1974 by 17,000 all ranks to around 80,000."[119] As inflation rose, "the financial policy of the Trudeau government directly contributed to inflation—and to the miseries of the military."[120] Trudeau was deadly serious about cutting back on—in his mind unnecessary—defence spending and reallocating the money to social programs.

LEO CADIEUX, DEFENCE MINISTER (1967–1970), AND THE OFFICIAL LANGUAGES ACT (1969)

Leo Cadieux, the minister of national defence was the first French-speaking defence minister during the twentieth century. He assumed the post on September 19, 1967, after having served as associate minister since 1965. Within a very short time, he proposed to Prime Minister Lester Pearson that Canada create French-speaking units and station them at Valcartier, Quebec. While Pearson and Allard generally supported the idea, given the danger to Canadian sovereignty represented by the separatist movement in Quebec, there was concern that in a crisis this could give Quebec its own army.[121]

Bill C-120, the "Official Languages Act," passed in June 1969, had a major impact on the military. It was presented as a directive ("Long-term Bilingualism Program in the Canadian Armed Forces") by Allard during his final appearance before the Defence Council on September 9, 1969. For him, as a Francophone, it was the crowning jewel in his service in the Canadian military. Among its provisions were the following:

- Both French and English were equal in CF.[122]
- No injustice should be caused to servicemen (Anglophone or Francophone) currently in the CF.
- All ranks, enlisted and officer, were included, and the percentage of Francophones in the CF should equal their demographic weight in Canada.
- The plan was to be implemented in 18 months.

- Tampering with the merit promotion system was permitted to quickly increase the number of Francophones at higher rank levels.
- By 1980 all officers and senior NCOs were to be "functionally" bilingual.

There was opposition to the act on the part of English-speaking officers, many of whom deeply resented Francophone officers taking positions for which the former did not consider them qualified. Indeed, resistance to the new military culture was deep-seated:

> One Royal 22nd Regiment battalion commander had the task of moving his unit from northern Germany to Lahr after the reduction in the Canadian NATO force in 1969. The Van Doos were French speaking, of course, but the air force operating the new base was unilingually English and resistant to change—so resistant that when General Laubman inspected the Van Doos in 1969 he was astounded to discover that the men spoke no English. "The joke's gone on long enough," he told the battalion commander. "Tell your men to speak English to me." Protests that the men were unable to do so were to no avail. Similarly, the regiment's officers were told not to use French in their mess. Only the sheer weight of numbers forced a change in policy, the Van Doos' Commanding Officer remembered.[123]

It is not surprising that those raised in an English-speaking armed forces with strong British traditions would resent the new bilingual military culture.

The goal was to have 28 percent of the armed forces be Francophone, mirroring the Francophone population in Canada. This meant that in an army of 83,000, there should be 59,760 Anglophones and 23,240 Francophones. In fact, the situation was even more complex: 33,347 service personnel were to serve in English language units (72 percent Anglophones / 28 percent Francophones) and 11,620 Francophones were to serve in French units, with an Anglophone component of 14,525.[124] The problem was the CF's inability to recruit Francophones. Few appeared interested in serving in the military. The plan went beyond just recruiting Francophone officers, however. It dealt with a variety of issues such as "language training, translation and terminology services; the military colleges and staff colleges; annotation of servicemen's files to the language of education desired for their children; bicultural services; dependent's education; an information program; and costs among other things."[125] It was to be an all-inclusive policy.

THE OCTOBER CRISIS (1970)

Of all the events that have shaken Canada since the end of World War II, none was more dangerous than the crisis in Quebec in October 1970. The new defence minister Donald MacDonald had only been in office for two weeks when the crisis erupted as a result of the kidnaping by Le Front de Liberation du Quebec (FLQ) of British Trade Commissioner James Cross and then of Quebec's Labour Minister Pierre Laprote. Quebec's premier, Robert Bourassa, called Trudeau and said, "Pierre, you are going to have to send in the army, and you should think about invoking the War Measures Act."[126] Trudeau called out the army.

On October 13, Trudeau ordered the Canadian military to defend public officials, foreign embassies, and some private homes in Ottawa. At his request up to 7,500 troops were moved in quickly to assist the Quebec Provincial Police and the RCMP. On October 15, two Hercules transports left Edmonton loaded with men from the First Commando bound for Quebec. Eventually, the entire airborne regiment was flown in and based at St-Hubert. They returned to Edmonton in mid-November, as the crisis lessened. Trudeau lauded the army's performance, noting, "the Cabinet, Parliament and the army carried out their roles extremely well."[127] The army must have been in shock because, "For the first time since Trudeau came to power in April the Canadian Armed Forces felt themselves needed and wanted by the Canadian Public."[128] Regardless of how much Trudeau may have appreciated the work the CF did in Quebec, it did not lead to an increase in the military budget.

Trudeau was also asked to invoke the War Measures Act. At first he hesitated, but when he asked both Bourassa and the mayor of Quebec if they were sure they wanted to invoke the Act because "only a state of war, real or apprehended, or insurrection, real or apprehended, can justify recourse to the War Measures Act. Are you, Bourassa, and you Drapeau, ready to declare in writing, that you are under such an apprehension? . . . The affirmative response was immediate."[129] The War Measures Act gave the police more power to arrest and place individuals in detention. This enabled them to stop and question members of the FLQ.

Trudeau also became a larger-than-life figure because of the way he handled this event. Several human rights activists were upset at the swift way Trudeau acted to put down this uprising. On October 13, as Trudeau left his limousine to enter the House of Commons, Tim Ralfe of the CBC asked about the presence of soldiers in the city. Ralfe expressed concern about "living in a town that's full of people with guns running around." The two bantered back and forth with Trudeau responding,

> "Yes . . . Well, there are a lot of bleeding hearts around who just don't like to see people with helmets and guns. All I can say is, go on and bleed, but it is more important to keep law and order in the society than to be worried about weak-kneed people who don't like the looks."
>
> "At any cost?" Ralfe interrupted. "How far would you go with that?"
>
> "Well, just watch me." His smile replaced by an icy stare. Trudeau continued: "I think society must take every means at its disposal to defend itself against the emergence of a parallel power which defies the elected power of this country, and I think that goes any distance. So long as there is a power in here which is challenging the elected representatives of the people, I think that power must be stopped, and I think it's only, I repeat, weak-kneed bleeding hearts who are afraid to take these measures."[130]

"Just Watch Me," in particular would become a slogan indicative of Trudeau's willingness to make difficult decisions and his determination to see his policies enacted.

DEFENCE POLICY IN THE 1970S

Donald MacDonald, the new minister of defence, decided that it was time to bring Canadian defence forces up to date by providing a policy framework. According to Granatstein and Bothwell, he turned to a recent graduate of MIT, Gordon Smith, asking him to come up with a new white paper.[131] Smith constructed a list of Canadian national interests. First, there was no direct military threat to Canada in an age of detente. The only possible danger was a Soviet–American war and that appeared unlikely. However, it did require Canada to maintain an antisubmarine capability, and its role in NORAD remained important. There was also an implication that Canada's role in Europe remained important. As far as the uniformed military was concerned, MacDonald let it be known that he was not interested in their views. The new policy was approved by the cabinet.

The 50-page white paper was released on August 24, 1971. The paper acknowledged the critical role that the CF might play in the event of an internal crisis, and it listed the defence of the Arctic as well as the role the military could play in dealing with "national development. That included assistance in natural disasters, scientific research, communications, and protecting the environment."[132] Imagine a CF officer or NCO who had devoted his or her entire life to the profession of arms being told that in the future your primary function was or could be dealing with national development. From a military standpoint, the implication of this paper was to turn Canada into "a pseudo neutral in the ongoing Cold War."[133]

From a budgetary standpoint, Canada had put itself in an increasingly difficult position. It was doing little to maintain the CF, while at the same time continuing to accept commitments, including peacekeeping. In this regard, the white paper signaled a new effort to streamline administration. MacDonald was convinced that if he restructured administration in CF and DND, it would be possible both to save money as well as to more efficiently allocate scarce resources.

Unfortunately, MacDonald's approach toward his subordinates only made matters worse. He saw any questions from the defence staff as open rebellion. MacDonald provided little guidance to the military on how it was to balance its ongoing commitments with the new ones. Given the way the DND was structured, the civilian and military sides were isolated from each other, hindering communications. The civilian side, including the deputy minister, controlled spending while the military side was only responsible for operations. As Bland commented, "This difficulty and the failure of the minister to build a consensus within the defence establishment for the new policies soon fractured relations between the government, senior officers of the armed forces, and defence officials."[134] Infighting was rampant. "The civilians fought with the military, and the Treasury Board, Privy Council Office, and other deputy ministers, naturally enough, preferred to accept the advice of Elgin Armstrong, DND's deputy until 1971, over that of the generals."[135] Showing the military so little respect ensured they would never achieve a shared responsibility.

THE MANAGEMENT REVIEW GROUP (1971)

Faced with what appeared to MacDonald to be bureaucratic chaos in DND, he announced in June 1971 that he had appointed a Management Review Group to evaluate the bureaucratic process in DND. The group made several recommendations. First, while CF in the field had impressed it, management in DND did not. It then went on to criticize one problem in particular:

> lack of unity of purpose due to a high degree of parallelism and duplication of management responsibility among its three major divisions—the Deputy Minister's staff, the Canadian Armed Forces, and the Defence Research

Board—and instead *the development of adversary relationships and undue compartmentalization.*[136]

The group recommended that DND be completely reorganized by integrating the military and civilian sides. The hope was that this would make it possible for the department to work as a unit. The deputy minister and the CDS were supposed to share authority. Problems arose when the two were at each others' throats. Most members of the group were businessmen, and they devoted most of their attention to overcoming bureaucratic inefficiency.

The group submitted its report in 1972. The primary focus was on integrating civilian and military members in the DND. CF became part of a unified ministry that was jointly directed by the CDS and the civilian deputy defence minister. In the process, it clouded lines of responsibility and accountability for defence-related issues. Since both men shared responsibility, who was in charge? There were also problems farther down the chain of command. Who sat at the top of the chain of command just below the minister? In contrast to the military world, if something adverse happened, who could they hold accountable? If a ship hits a reef, it is clear who is responsible—the ship's captain. If a unit is not locked down when it is supposed to be, then the senior officer in charge is guilty. The situation was made even more difficult by the tendency of CDS and other officers to remain in their post for only three years, while the civil servants could remain in DND for a lengthy career.

Officers complained about the civilianization of military policy as well as civilian interference in policy and operational decisions. A new post, Assistant Deputy Minister (Policy), was created. To fill it, DND brought a senior civilian official from External Affairs, leaving military officers furious that someone from the outside was brought in to fill a position that a number of military officers could have easily filled. In time, staffing it with military officers would have helped produce a new and different type of military cadre, exactly the political-military officers that a CDS needs to help him prepare for testimony before Parliament or the media and to ensure that the CF's concerns were addressed in government policy papers. The mass civilianization in DND was creating what the military feared would become "civilian generals," many of whom had never served in the military; and yet they would make military policy. Two CF officers articulated the feeling of many officers when they observed:

> Civilians, and specifically civil servants, should have only advisory roles in determining the policies for military training and education, for the selection, distribution and use of military equipment, for the administration of the armed

> forces, and for strategy and tactics. To give civilians positions of authority in the military hierarchy is to create civilian generals, a contradiction in terms and a combination of incompatible concepts—it would as well have laymen in the College of Physicians and Surgeons.[137]

Many officers feared that the 1972 decision was undermining the uniqueness of the CF and making it into another form of public service. This year-long study of the military was further evidence to senior officers that Trudeau and his government did not trust them. Rather, they believed his goal was to incapacitate them. Civilians also complained equally about military officers, who they saw as incompetent managers, individuals who knew very little about administering bureaucracies.

Often senior officers and military professionals were not certain about their role in this newly restructured bureaucracy. Was it to protect the Minister from criticism, even if he was going against military advice? In the past, they had worked in a structured military bureaucracy. Now, however, lines of authority as well as an officer's job description were blurred. Was the officer to "get along" with civilian colleagues by compromising the advice they had planned to give the minister? To quote Bland, "civil control of the armed forces was compromised, military advice was buried in efforts to forge bureaucratic collegiality, and some officers in the headquarters lost touch with the operational and human needs of the Canadian Forces."[138] There is nothing wrong with good management and compromise. However, when it becomes the end all and be all of an organization like the military, it undercuts the raison d'être for the armed forces—conflict and war. In times of conflict, military officers argued, the soldier cannot simply turn off the light and go home for the evening. He has unlimited liability—the lives of many men and women are entrusted to him. He does not want that situation affected by the involvement of a civil servant who does not understand the problems on the ground. "In the meantime, accountability suffered because it became increasingly difficult to identify who was responsible for what decisions. As a result, operational planning fell by the wayside."[139]

Another result of the 1972 management decision was that the size of the National Defence Headquarters (NDHQ) grew. However, the increased numbers did little to solve the key problems of operating the military. If anything, the increased size made it even more difficult to coordinate actions and policy. From the military's standpoint, one of the best comments on the confused situation represented by the new structure came from the head of the Defence Research Board, who called it "an act of mayhem committed in the name of administrative madness."[140]

BACK TO BILINGUALISM

In 1972, the language program faced a problem. Despite the favoritism to Francophones in promotion, they were leaving the service as previously. Five years after the plan was instituted, only 40 percent of generals were bilingual, 30 percent of other officers, 20 percent of senior NCOs, and only 15 percent of privates. By 1987, the plan called for the percentages in these four categories to be 60, 50, 40, and 25. The only way to achieve this end was to raise the ratio of Francophone and Anglophone officers to 50, 50. In addition the proportion of Francophones of other ranks was raised to 40 rather than 30 percent.[141]

Ottawa's affirmative action policy also produced resentment on the part of English-speaking officers. "While planners at NDHQ were busily adjusting targets, unpleasant reports were filtering back from the hinterlands that Anglophone troops were getting restless." Many Anglophone officers who were fully qualified for promotion were becoming bitter when they were passed over. The problem was acerbated by the reorganization of the NDHQ. Even the planners in Ottawa, often far removed from the regular field units, knew that the problems were worsening. Ottawa did not need disruption among its officer corps. In December 1973, Colonel James Hanna, a deputy in NDHQ, prepared a study that showed

> that Anglophone officers were becoming increasingly bitter over accelerated promotions for Francophones, and morale was becoming a serious problem. The promotion issue had sparked fist-fights between English- and French-speaking servicemen, and the commanders of several units in English-speaking areas had not made attendance at the briefings compulsory as ordered because the "morale" of personnel is already too low to risk generating further discontent.[142]

English-speaking officers and NCOs resented the entire program that held first-rate officers back while promoting second-rate officers, just because they were French speaking. The report was "hushed up."

Trudeau's administration was determined to make the program work, regardless of the consequences. By October 1, 1977, the CF were on their way to having 28 percent Francophones in the military. "Since 1970 the proportion of officers had increased from 10.6 percent to 19.2 percent, and men from 19.1 to 24.9 percent."[143] However worthwhile the program was from a social standpoint, it had cost money at a time when the CF commanders could not afford fuel for their planes or ships. One source claims that the program cost $500 million. In addition, soldiers were placed in language programs. In 1975, more than 5,000 regular soldiers were involved in language training.[144] The English-speaking officers continued to hate the quota system.

THE DEFENCE STRUCTURE REVIEW (1974–1975)

In 1974, the services were no longer bound by the three-year budgetary freeze that Trudeau had imposed. CF was in desperate need of money. Double-digit inflation had wiped out the small increase Trudeau had given them by the middle of 1974. The military was in bad shape, its weapons worn out and obsolete. One of the first decisions was to cut the military to 78,000. Rank structure was also a problem. In June 1976, there were 106 generals, one for every 170 privates. Privates were outnumbered by corporals by two to one, and there were 120 full colonels.[145] The situation was so serious that General Jacques Dextraze, the CDS, publicly stated that he had "advised the Minister that we could not reduce below that assigned level without running a grave risk of being unable to carry out all of our assigned tasks as well as of denuding the Canadian military profession to an unacceptable point."[146]

Trudeau ordered a review of the CF. The committee, composed of senior officials and chaired by the secretary to the cabinet, laid down the peacetime structure of the forces. On November 27, 1975, the military requested a 102 percent budget increase, which the cabinet denied. The review reaffirmed the four basic tasks of 1969, categorized in accordance with their "hard operational needs," to quote Dextraze.[147] They also called for a 12 percent increase in the military budget per year over a five-year period. The military could begin to plan rationally for its needs; a significant budgetary expansion was essential for the maintenance of the CF.

In January, 1977, the government launched an ambitious fifteen-year plan, the Defence Services Program. The goal was to reequip the CF with some 400 badly needed items, everything from ships and planes to bullets. As Porter noted,

> The budget would remain indexed to inflation, and the capital portion would be increased by 12 percent a year *after* inflation until it constituted 20 percent of total defence, optimistically by 1981. "It is widely accepted," the government

agreed, "that a modern military force must spend a minimum of 20 percent of its budget on new capital equipment if it is going to keep pace with technological change."[148]

However, defence was Trudeau's lowest priority; government spending increased from $10 billion to $45 billion between 1969 and 1978, but defence's share only increased from $1.8 billion to $3.8 billion, "the smallest increase of any department."[149]

Given the financial strain, budgetary problems, and Francophone issues, the situation inside the CF continued to deteriorate. As Brigadier General D. G. Loomis, the CF's senior policy analyst, told a closed door meeting with White House Fellows in Washington, DC:

> While I have suggested that unification *per se* has not adversely affected our military operational capability, other factors such as force reductions and consequent reorganizations, increased emphasis on civilian management systems as opposed to military command and control and changes in our military roles, activities and tasks have an impact on our forces.[150]

The CF even had to go to elaborate ends to replace its main battle tank through a deal worked out by Dextraze, Sylvain Cloutier (the Deputy Defence Minister), and German Chancellor Helmut Schmidt to obtain new tanks. Trudeau was against the new tanks, but Schmidt convinced him that the West had to have a military deterrent. Ottawa worked out a deal with the Germans for the sale of 128 Leopard tanks that Germany no longer needed.

During the mid-1970s, the budgetary situation improved, closing "the credibility gap."[151] But when it came to NATO, Canada's policy was to keep forces in Germany, but to give them minimal support, satisfying both NATO allies and the Canadian population, who were concerned with cutting the defence budget. Tasseron said,

> If defence policy has no particular purpose or inherently desirable outcome beyond that of simply demonstrating a rudimentary ability, and willingness to participate as Bland contends is reflective of general political and public service belief, actual capability is largely immaterial. As long as the troops can deploy to the desired location and function there in reasonable safety without embarrassing the Minister, the strategic objective may be considered met.[152]

This policy may have satisfied the Allies and cabinet members, but it was not a boost for the CF's morale.

Joe Clark's Short Interregnum (1979–1980)

Joe Clark was prime minister for a little less than a year. His defence minister, Allan McKinnon, a retired CF major, initiated the Fyffe Review to "unscramble the unification of Canadian Forces."[153] The Clark administration produced a document entitled *Canada in a Changing World* intended to replace the more pacifistic document produced by the Trudeau government. Unlike the Trudeau government document, it identified the Soviet Union as a problem because of its nuclear weapons and power projection capability. This document, unlike that of the Trudeau government, avoided left-wing verbiage like "harmonious natural environment."[154] The world was a tough place, and Canadians needed to recognize that.

The Fyffe Review focused on problems with NDHQ that continued to plague the military. Did headquarters represent the interests of those in the field? There had been some beneficial results from the 1972 amalgamation of CFHQ with DND, but the most important fear by the military was that the NDHQ had been "civilianized." "The commanders and many officers with experience in Ottawa believed their *professional* advice was being second-guessed by public servants and they resented this intrusion."[155] Civilians were making decisions on issues they did not understand, and they were inclined to tell the minister and deputy minister what they wanted to hear. "At the heart of the controversy, however, was a profound worry that the CF had lost control of its professional direction."[156]

The task force report was turned in on March 15, 1980, almost a month after Trudeau and the Liberals were returned to office. It made some thirty recommendations, including a call for a return to distinctive uniforms for the three services. They also called for greater army, navy, and air force input in the decision-making process. The officers seemed especially concerned about the assistant deputy minister level. "Civilians were making or were contributing to the making of decisions of a military nature and that control by the civil power should not mean control by the Public Service."[157] The military worried that many civilians at senior posts could lead to a "blurring" of the chain of command and control.[158] Might the civilians exceed their authority, and pass down orders, even though their understanding of the military was rudimentary? Senior officers pointed out that they were in charge of three different services. Those in charge of the services should be treated separately as independent advisors, a point accepted by the review. The Fyffe Review supported maintaining unification with a goal, "to retain the integrated systems currently in use in National Defence Headquarters, but at the same time . . . to ensure that the systems respond to the needs of the three environments."[159] But NDHQ ignored one of the key concerns—that is, given the problems they found, how could Canadians be confident that the CF would perform well in the future? "Unfortunately, the warning was dismissed in NDHQ as an indication of misperceptions in the ranks and not as a signal of any fundamental flaws in the defence structure of politics."[160]

The major morale problem was not unification, but the low budgets during a period of high inflation. The armed forces were staggering in the aftermath of having been neglected and their organization transformed, with no indication that the result was a better armed forces. The opposite was true. The bottom line for the Fyffe Review was that none of the goals Hellyer had spelled out were realized. "A blunter estimation, and in accordance with all the soldiers this writer has talked to, would have to state that the Hellyer plan was an unmitigated disaster for Canada's Armed Forces."[161]

Trudeau Returns (1980–1984)

Trudeau's new defence minister, Giles Lamontague, who assumed office on March 3, 1980, was dubious about unification, but he was determined to keep military matters out of the media. When he received the report he set out to dispose of it quickly and quietly. However, as Bland pointed out, "the report had too high a profile and the task force had raised expectations for change to such a level that the minister could not simply throw the report in the waste basket."[162] The deputy defence minister then suggested that he and the chief of the defence staff put together a National Defence Headquarters task force to look at the Fyffe Review. This gave Lamontague more time to plan. The deputy minister was determined to neutralize the recommendations concerning the decision-making process in the NDHQ.

The new task force's first observation was that contrary to Hellyer's prediction, no country in the world had followed Canada's decision to unify its military services. As a result of what was called the Task Force on Review of Unification of the Canadian Forces, delivered on August 31, 1980, the three senior environmental commanders (the commanders of the Mobile Command, the Maritime Command, and the Air Command) became members of the Defence Council and the Defence Management Group, increasing the number of military officers on these senior committees. This gave military officers a majority on each committee, but they were not present in the many impromptu meetings at which business might be conducted. Traveling back and forth to Ottawa was a problem, along with keeping up with the sheer multitude of studies, documents, information, and briefings that were part and parcel of life in Ottawa.

Despite the modifications Lamontague was instrumental in seeing adopted, such as the greater power for military representatives, the officers remained unhappy. Many of them wanted the traditional military staff and headquarters systems to be recreated in Ottawa. Senior military officers continued to worry that they were losing control of their services.

During the early 1980s several nongovernmental and parliamentary reports revealed the problems facing the CF.

> These studies argued that Canadian commitments to NATO and Western security exceeded the ability of Canadian Forces to enhance a deterrence capability. More importantly, the Canadian Forces lacked sufficient military means to fulfill assigned roles and missions under wartime conditions. Despite this untenable situation, Liberal governments either ignored the problem or argued that Canada continued to meet its requirements in a viable manner.[163]

Then a report by Peter Kasurak argued that the weakness of the military's base was a result of the pushing of public service into areas that had previously been occupied by the military. Accountability, a key component of military culture, is elusive when no one knows who is making the decisions. "[Kasurak] found that 'a significant number of the armed forces [had] come to believe that Canadian Forces [had] adopted civilian norms and standards to an unacceptable degree and that civilian [*sic*] public servants exercise undue influence over matters that are (or should be) exclusively military in nature.'"[164]

By 1983, the situation with the CF had deteriorated so much that it became a major issue with the Canadian population.

> Canada's military capabilities, once very significant, declined slowly throughout the Cold War era, but very serious retrenchments began around 1964 under the Liberal Government of Mike Pearson. Indeed, the decline continued in the 1960s and then in the 1970s under Pierre Trudeau, when some major capabilities were eliminated entirely. By the early 1980s, the rustout of the Canadian Forces was so pronounced and allied criticism so loud that the matter became a major issue in the 1983 election campaign.[165]

By 1983, the size of the CF was up to 82,000, and all three services continued to face major equipment and personnel problems. "The navy was in the worst shape. Only four of its twenty-three warships were less than twenty years old, a few verged on being unsafe to put to sea, and some navy electronics systems required vacuum tubes available only in Eastern Europe."[166]

The other services were also in bad shape. The German tanks, for example, simply masked a Canadian shortcoming, and there was no way to replace the navy's obsolete antisubmarine vessels. Maloney observed,

> In terms of defence and national security, Canada under the Trudeau government was a liability to any effort to counter Soviet or Soviet-inspired communist influence or expansion. Its younger members . . . schooled in 1960s leftist rhetoric, and its selectively plaint older hands, steeped in obsolete strategies and frightened of nuclear extinction, were philosophically disabled when it came to understanding the nature of the threat, let alone developing a means to deal with it. Canada was, by the early 1980s, a powerless victim waiting to be victimized, not the global player it had once been, defending its values and security from a forward posture.[167]

The prime minister was not interested in the military, the budget was a shambles, and few Canadians, including the opposition, acted as if they cared about the fate of the CF.

CHAPTER 7

From Brian Mulroney through Stephen Harper

In Canada over the years it appears that the politics of defence matters more than national defence itself.

DOUGLAS BLAND

After fifteen years of the antimilitary Pierre Trudeau and the machinations of Defence Minister Paul Hellyer, the Canadian military was hopeful that the newly elected Conservative Brian Mulroney would be more supportive. At least, the armed forces believed he could not be worse than Trudeau or Hellyer had been. He was making some positive comments about the importance of the Canadian Forces. Perhaps he would see the value of a modern, well-equipped, combat-ready Canadian Forces.

Brian Mulroney and the Progressive Conservatives (1984–1993)

Brian Mulroney and the Conservatives took power on September 17, 1984, after the three-month reign of John Turner, the shortest in Canadian history since 1896. The military's first disappointment came with Mulroney's choice of a defence minister, Robert Coates, "a lackluster Nova Scotia MP whose only claim to preferment was his opposition to the previous conservative leader, Joe Clark."[1] Coates was deeply suspicious of the department, and within a few weeks he and his personal staff were fighting with other officials in the department—both military and civilian.

Canada was at least five years behind the rest of the West. Although the Mulroney government wanted Canada to play a more active role, the neglect of the military during the 1970s made this almost impossible. When the Trudeau government took over in 1980, it destroyed the entire print run of *Canada in a Changing World;* the only way Canadians could access it was through the one copy that was read into *Hansard*. Ironically, it was to form the basis of Mulroney's foreign policy—rejecting the liberal stance and taking a more realistic two-fisted approach. In contrast to the Trudeau approach, the key area of concern was Europe, where:

> "a formidable, conventional and nuclear adversary" and indeed "the most direct threat to Canadian security [was] derived both from the Soviet Union's military capabilities and antipathy to Canadian values." Outside Europe, "the main problem areas were Afghanistan, Poland, the SS-20 deployment, and human-rights violations in Warsaw Pact countries. . . . Notably, international terrorism was examined as a threat to Canadian interests."[2]

THE *1987 WHITE PAPER*

The Mulroney government wanted to come up with a long-term plan that would reinvigorate the CF in terms of money, equipment, personnel, and morale. Reform began in 1985, and within three months a white paper was issued, the first since 1971, entitled, *Challenge and Commitment: A Defence Policy for Canada*. In this document, care was taken to separate foreign and defence policy. The goal of the latter was to compliment diplomatic, economic, and cultural policies. If Canada hoped to exert influence in Europe as well as the U.S., then it had to be a reliable military partner. During the Trudeau years, Canadian credibility abroad had eroded. To turn things around, "The Canadian government had to re-establish the neglected armed forces; it was immoral to commit units like the Canadian Air-Sea Transportable (CAST) Brigade in support of NATO without adequate resources."[3]

The white paper outlined a 15-year plan. "All elements of the Canadian Forces are to augment existing capabilities. Priority will be given to three clusters of military activity such as the maritime forces, surveillance and control capabilities, and the reserve forces."[4] Structurally, the document argued that NATO and NORAD were key organizations in which Canada needed to have credible military forces. It was critical that Canada be in a position to help defend against Soviet strategic attacks, which could best be done through Canada's association with NORAD and its forces in Europe.

To implement this white paper, Canada's continental forces had to be upgraded—that is, maritime patrol aircraft, fighters, and surveillance capabilities. The Arctic was also important because of Moscow's undersea capabilities. Toward that end, "Canadian naval forces would be modernized with SSNs and some twenty-four Canadian patrol frigates equipped for 'Three Ocean operations.' In addition, Ottawa's CF-18s would have to have forward operating bases in the Arctic."[5] The most controversial issue was the construction of nuclear submarines. One fear in dealing with the civilian leadership was that External Affairs Minister Joe Clark did not understand the differences between SSNs and SSBNs. While defence was concerned about the SSNs (which did not carry ballistic missiles), Clark thought they were the latter and that purchase of them would make Canada a nuclear power.

The paper called for nuclear submarines, an acquisition program for a new battle tank, additional long-range patrol and fighter aircraft, and enough weapons and material to be able to send a mechanized division to central Europe in a crisis.[6]

MULRONEY AND THE DEFICIT

Immediately upon becoming prime minister, Mulroney calmly noted that the 1985 deficit would be $37.1 billion, $9 billion higher than the Trudeau government had predicted. As Mulroney put it, "In our centennial year the net federal debt was $18 billion. . . . By the end of this fiscal year it will be $190 billion."[7] A couple of months later, Finance Minister Michael Wilson announced that defence spending was being reduced to $9.37 billion which was $154 million less than the budget Trudeau's minister of finance had presented only a few months earlier.[8]

Once again the CF was let down. Mulroney had promised to rebuild Canadian Forces, but he went back on his word given the size of the deficit. As Granatstein said, "Just as Mulroney pledged to fix the country's budget but signally failed to do so, he raised the military's hopes repeatedly, but failed to deliver."[9] The 1986 budget was limited to an increase of only 2.75 percent more than in 1986–1987, and a 2.5 percent increase the following year.[10]

In June 1986, a new defence minister, Perrin Beatty, was appointed. An ambitious politician, he hoped to use the DND as a stepping-stone a higher position. With that in mind, he instituted the return of traditional uniforms in 1986.[11] A year later, the service chiefs were reinstated and returned to NDHQ.

Beatty argued that Canada could not afford to constantly replace large numbers of ships, aircraft, tanks, and other weapons systems. However, he agreed that CF planners could continue to count on a two percent increase per annum (compensated for inflation). When new major items were purchased, the government would attempt to provide additional funding. Beatty himself maintains that he had returned rationality to the defence process. "Our defence planners can proceed in a systematic way to match our capabilities to our commitments."[12] Throughout his time in office, Mulroney continued to accept peacekeeping operations, ignoring that the forces and their equipment were being exhausted by their constant deployments.

THE LITTLE-HUNTER STUDY

A problem that arose from the restoration of the service chiefs was their desire to plan and implement missions. They often considered themselves to be operational commanders, which made either the CDS or the service commander redundant: this raised the question of who was in charge, as Bland noted,

> The centre as provider and the periphery as commander fit the heroic model. It also appealed to those who would separate policy from administration, or, in this case, military operations from politics. Some officers argued that the far-flung and diverse missions of the Canadian Forces precluded command from the centre, but they dared not carry the argument too far because they and their staff were as far removed from their subordinate commanders. One argued strongly for a unification model. The deputy minister had little opinion on the matter so long as it did not affect his domain. The potential loser in the discussion was the NDHQ operational staff which would soon find itself without any reason for being and no place in the decision-making process of the Canadian Forces.[13]

Little and Hunter proposed separating political leaders and senior officers from direct control over the CF. The problem, however, was bureaucratic. To be effective, the commanders needed direct contact with the ministers and the key politicians. Instead, the NDHQ bureaucracy retained control over the most sensitive aspects of decision making, retaining for itself the right to decide which operational orders to pass on to commanders. "The DNHQ created the worst of all worlds where the commanders had limited but undefined authority and little control of resources and NDHQ carried the responsibility to assure ministers without much influence over the detailed direction of events."[14] This study did little to solve the command problem. Relations between NDHQ and the service commanders remained ambiguous. No one knew for certain who was in charge.

BUDGETARY WOES

It would only take two years to invalidate most of the findings of the *1987 White Paper*. The collapse of the USSR and end of the Cold War hit every military in the world. It was difficult to support a defence budget in Canada when

Moscow was threatening to send tanks into Western Europe. It was worse when Russia no longer posed a threat, as the rest of Russian society began clamoring to have defence funds reallocated for domestic, civilian purposes. There was no way the Canadian SSNs could be defended in the aftermath of Moscow's collapse. Budgetary problems continued. Ottawa was cutting $2.74 billion from the defence budget over five years, a budget in which there was very little "wiggle room." "Some 8 percent of expenditures are statutory, 38 percent is for personnel, 24 percent is for operations and maintenance, 26–28 for capital expenses."[15]

Canadian officers were caught off guard when the 1989 defence budget was announced. Instead of a carefully thought out plan, it seemed to Canadian officers that decisions had been made by the prime minister and defence minister without their input. The officers accepted civilian decisions, but to them the cuts in military systems appeared arbitrary. Why are we getting rid of this system, and not that one? "Officers and soldiers were first surprised, then resentful, and finally sullenly resigned to the idea that no one valued their contribution, understood their needs, nor represented their points of view."[16]

TAKING STOCK—1990

In the aftermath of the 1989 budget together with other cuts in defence spending it was clear that the *1987 White Paper* existed only on paper. Budgetary cuts made the acquisition of weapons systems the white paper called for irrelevant. It was an abrupt policy change. Ironically, these budget cuts came at a time when CF were being used more and more around the world. For example, according to a *Globe and Mail* article, "By 1991 Canada was providing 10% of the UN peacekeeping force." How could Canadian Forces carry out these assignments with worn out weapons?

The service chiefs were gaining greater authority at the expense of NDHQ, almost to the point their predecessors had held prior to Hellyer's unification plan. "The navy effectively ran its own promotion system, as did army regiments, all but bypassing the unified promotion system. The army created its own staff college system to hand down service-specific knowledge not taught by the Canadian Forces Command and Staff College in north Toronto."[17] The situation inside the CF was chaotic. It was impossible to determine where decisions were made, and given the irrelevance of the *1987 White Paper*, Canada lacked a coherent, logical security policy.

Ottawa kept getting the CF involved in more overseas operations. When the First Gulf War was on the horizon, General John de Chastlain "advised

Cabinet not to commit land forces for reasons of Canada's inability to deploy and sustain these forces as well as the unlikelihood these forces will fight under Canadian command."[18] Canada's participation was negligible, primarily involving several ships sent to the Persian Gulf to provide air cover against a nonexistent air threat.

Unlike its allies the CF faced a desperate situation, especially having endured under-capitalization for the last twenty-odd years. The military's capability to carry out missions in the future was questionable. As before, defence policy seemed independent of national security policy. To quote a former CDS,

> The greater problem, however, is that too little, if any, of the excellent extra-governmental analysis of Canadian and international security finds its way into policy development. This is a serious shortcoming in the Canadian process that is increasingly out of keeping with the times, that is its internalized and closed character. In this respect, it is unfortunately only a reflection of a larger structural problem which affects the Canadian political system and machinery.[19]

The problems were deep-seated and would be brought home later that year by an incident involving the CF in Somalia.

SOMALIA DEPLOYMENT (1992)

On June 24, 1992, a change of command of the airborne regiment took place. The new commander Lt. Col. Paul Moreault had previously been deputy commander of the unit and was a neophyte when it came to leading men in battle, never having commanded a battalion-sized formation. His predecessor had called him "an excellent administrative officer but a 'procrastinator' in matters of leadership, training, and discipline."[20] He was eligible for command only because the commander of Land Force had reduced the regiment to the size of a regular infantry battalion, requiring a Lieutenant Colonel, the rank he held.

UN operations overseas had grown tremendously, and Ottawa had agreed to send troops. Although it was good politics, the size of the Canadian military had not increased in the face of its new responsibilities. Public pressure was for cuts in the CF so that the money could be used for social programs.

In spite of all the peacekeeping missions it had at the time (including Cyprus, Golan Heights, Cambodia, El Salvador, Kuwait, Western Sahara, Nicaragua, and two battalions in former Yugoslavia), Ottawa agreed to send troops to Somalia, to assist the UN in feeding the starving population of a failed state. The CDS spent two months trying to decide how to staff such an operation, settling on what was called Operation Cordor. Canada's assignment was to patrol Bossasso, a small port in northeast Somalia. On August 28, 1992, Ottawa informed the UN that it would send a unit of 750 soldiers to Somalia.

NDHQ and Mobile Command (under which the Airborne Regiment fell in the chain of command) thought the elite paratroopers were ready. It needed a mission to sustain unit morale, even though others, including its previous commander Colonel W. M Holmes, thought otherwise.[21] On October 2, a part of the unit celebrated the end of a training cycle by getting drunk and rowdy at the Kyrenia Club. It also had a reputation of being an assignment for troublemakers. An exercise from October 14 to 18 tested the units' readiness for the UN mission. The results were unfavorable: "it was weak on intelligence gathering; its chain of command did not function properly, especially in passing information about procedures for dealing with armed verses unarmed Somalis; they were still too aggressive"[22] to carry out such a mission. Peacekeeping not only requires soldiers who are trained to use force, but troops who are also trained not to use force unless absolutely necessary. This is especially true when dealing with an army that is already "reeling under the strain, its commitments vastly exceeding its capabilities."[23] It was clear that this unit should not have been sent to Somalia, but the prime minister wanted to send a unit, and the CDS agreed to send the paratroopers.

In December 1993, an 850-man battle group came to the city of Belet Nuen as part of a much larger American-led force called UNITAF (United Task Force), consisting of the Canadian Airborne Unit, a squadron of the Royal Canadian Dragoons, and an engineer squadron. The Canadian paratroopers soon began to hate the Somalis, who they believed were good only for stealing from them.

On March 16, 1993, several soldiers from the airborne regiment captured, tortured, and killed a Somali teenager they suspected was about to steal. From a military standpoint, an inexplicable aspect of the case was that other officers and noncommissioned personnel heard the teenager's screams but did nothing to stop the torture. "Once the crime was known, officers covered up the crime in a chain extending from Somalia to various levels in National Defence Headquarters in Ottawa. Such an action is despicable and unacceptable in any army, but even more so in one that is supposedly part of a democratic polity." As the historian of the Canadian Airborne put it, "a conscious decision was made to control any political damage rather than see public justice done."[24]

The airborne regiment should never have been sent to Somalia, but the CDS, General John de Chastelian, wanted to please his political masters. The generals knew that Mulroney was an activist when it came to peacekeeping. He was also using this latest action as a way to get the U.S. involved in peacekeeping, thereby lightening the load on Canada. However, the problem went far deeper than Somalia. A campaign carried out by noncommissioned officers "uncovered wide-spread fraud, deception and dereliction of duty in the officer corps."[25] Yet none of the officers stepped forward. It was the NCOs who were worried about the state of ethics inside the CF. Increasingly, promotion depended on relations with senior officers, and no one wanted to upset the status quo. The officer corps became increasingly incapacitated, exposing major problems that could destroy the CF—or so many believed.

In March 1995, the Chrétien government set up a commission of inquiry to investigate the Somalia incident. The commission was headed by a judge who was unable to focus on the issues. Ottawa had to become involved. As Bercuson put it, "The most important story of the Somalia affair has been the most ignored: How and why did the Airborne get 'totally out of control' in the words of Colonel Peter Kenward, the regiment's last commander?"[26]

The problem was related to the exhaustion of the CF, with their constant overseas deployments, the chaos caused by unification, and the role played by NDHQ. Bercuson was especially hard in suggesting the reasons for the CF's situation.

> The crisis was caused initially by the deliberate bleeding of the defence establishment to near death by successive, mostly Liberal, governments. *It was made a great deal worse by unification and imposition on the Canadian Forces of a structure designed to ease political and bureaucratic burdens rather than a promise of military effectiveness. These sins of unification were compounded by the creation of National Defence Headquarters, designed to murder military initiative.* With NDHQ safely ensconced at the top of the defence structure, it was not long before soldier-managers took control of the army and soldier-warriors were shunted aside. We now have an army in which war fighting is of secondary or even tertiary importance. Which is absurd.[27]

Most observers agreed that the Canadian military was in dire straits and that something had to be done if Ottawa wanted a competent force that could be used to improve Canada's image both at home and abroad.

Jean Chrétien (1993–2003)

Prime Minister Chrétien was similar to Trudeau in that he did not see the need for a big military. His senior advisor, Eddie Goldenberg, for example, wrote a memo in 1976 indicating "strong anti-military bias," and he told Chrétien that being a soldier is not "that demanding a task." Furthermore, he maintained that Canada did not need an efficient army.[28] At his first meeting, Chrétien cancelled the Conservative government's order for 43 new EH-101 military helicopters, even though that incurred a penalty of $500 million dollars. As Chrétien commented,

> Given the size of the deficit the Tories left us, we would have to borrow $6 billion to pay this additional bill and, as a result, been that much farther from balancing the books. Indeed, when all items were accounted for, we would have had to borrow even more than that: it's a reasonable calculation that those helicopters would have cost the people of Canada at least another $6 billion in interest over ten years. Compared to that bill, the penalty didn't look quite so bad.[29]

The Sea King helicopters the CF wanted to replace were 40 years old. Ironically, the Chrétien government's *1994 White Paper* noted, "There is an urgent need for robust and capable new shipborne helicopters. The Sea Kings are rapidly approach the end of their operational life."[30] One observer blamed Chrétien's tendency to make thoughtless decisions. "Chrétien hears the issues at hand and decides, bang, bang, bang, without much debate and sometimes without much thought."[31] Chrétien's lack of foresight would count heavily because soon, the CF would have around 2,500 troops fighting in Afghanistan.

By the end of 1993, morale in the CF had reached its nadir. No one was prepared to disclose the events in Somalia, nor were senior officers ready to accept responsibility for recommending that the airborne unit be sent to Somalia in the first place. The military had fallen to less than 80,000, and by the end of Chrétien's administration the CF would be down to 50,000. Unfortunately, Mulroney continued to accept UN requests for peacekeepers.[32]

Military writers argued that the CF had to be upgraded. It could not, for example, fly 40-year-old helicopters to carry out its missions. When David Collenette became defence minister in 1993, one of his first actions was to deal with was the Somalia affair. It wasn't long before pictures of the CF soldiers' cruelty and torture were appearing in the media.

In September 1994, U.S. President Bill Clinton asked Chrétien for Canadian Forces to be sent to Haiti. Chrétien agreed: "Okay, I send my soldiers. And then afterwards, I ask for something in return."[33] The revelation that soldiers were bargaining chips to be sent whenever it suited the prime minister revealed a serious lack of concern for the lives of the CF. Chrétien continued to refuse to provide the CF with the weapons and troops it needed to carry out his orders.

1994 DEFENCE PAPER

According to Martin, other white papers had also been prepared without outside involvement. He claimed that the *1987 White Paper* was written inside NDHQ, primarily by the deputy minister for policy Bob Fowler and a small group of civilians and military officers. It was not long before the *1987 White Paper* became the topic of controversy, in Martin's opinion because there was no public input during its preparation.[34] Few cabinet members, including the new defence minister, had ever met a serving CF officer; they had shown little interest in defence matters. The same could be said for Parliament and also for the Canadian public.

Collenette introduced his white paper in 1994. It outlined further cuts in defence spending, but as usual said nothing about increasing military capabilities so the military could carry out its assignments. When asked about the new white paper and the cuts involved, the CDS, General John de Chastelain, commented, "I learned a long time ago not to draw a line in the sand over which I could not step."[35] This approach was not well received by the CF, since Chastelain's job was to support the military. Here was a case when the defence minister was cutting resources just as CF was being asked to do more. Why didn't he draw a line in the sand?

The Cold War was over. For practical purposes, that ended Canada's overseas commitments. Canada did not need to field forces to stop Russians, as the Soviet military had collapsed. Now, where was the *peace dividend?*

There were those who opposed cutting the Canadian Forces again because of the uncertainty of the future. To quote one observer,

> The Government must resist the pressure and the inclination towards a radical restructuring of the Canadian Forces to suit the "flavour of the month." In the new, uncertain world of the 21st century the roles and missions of the forces are unlikely to be significantly different. Indeed, it is ironic that the Forces have been more involved in *active* military operations *since the end of the Cold War* than they had been in previous decades. National security writ large and

> sovereignty have always been in the forefront of Canadian defence policy, and the certainty over the next few decades is that this effort will draw forces into yet more active operational roles.[36]

Canada needed general purpose forces. Whether for peacekeeping or for protecting Canada, men in uniforms were critical. Police units had their role, but when it came to the application of military force, only trained and educated military officers, NCOs, and enlisted personnel could do the job.

A white paper of this kind hit at the heart of military culture. To Collenette, the military was not a special occupation. He did not consider the hours of training and the hardships suffered by families and troops during long deployments, whether on the ground, in the air, or at sea exceptionally demanding.

The document committed the government to "doing its part to ensure global security." Then the ministers discarded the idea of peacekeeping. The document had different language, arguing that Canada should have "the means to apply military force when Canadians consider it appropriate." Canada would not have an all-purpose military. Rather, it would be smaller. The budget would be reduced to less than 60 percent of what it had been prior to Chrétien coming to power. Personnel would be cut by 32 percent. "Major capabilities such as the CF18 fighter fleet and maritime helicopters would be eliminated or greatly scaled back." For practical purposes this meant that the minister would have a smaller, aging, and not very flexible armed forces.[37] But as early as 1993 it was becoming clear that, contrary to Collenette's vision, the world was getting more dangerous, and Canada would be called on for many foreign missions, for example, in Somalia, Bosnia, and Rwanda.

THE WAR IN THE BALKANS

Canadian troops were already in the former Yugoslavia when the Liberals came to power. The phrase that characterized Canadian Forces ability to act was "risk-adverse," avoiding conflict whenever possible and thereby avoiding casualties. General Rick Hillier's opinion was that a risk-adverse policy had been in force in the CF for over 30 years, so that almost all the country's senior officers had been avoiding conflict. "We put battalions in place on the ground, but because of the nervousness of Ottawa, those units were, more often than not, reluctant to take on missions, slow to carry them out or unable to get approval for them, despite the fact that the soldiers would see how necessary they were."[38]

The Allies mocked Canadians and their inability to carry out their assignments. As is normal in the military, each battalion was given a call name. The Russians became Rusbat. The Canadian battalions were "Canbat 1" and "Canbat 2." After several months of the Canadians refusing this task or avoiding that job, "because they were more concerned with what was happening in Ottawa than something going on in Gornji Vkutim, the Canadian battalions were quickly and cynically renamed by other nations 'Can't bat 1 and Can't bat 2.' "[39] This demeaning name told the world, and the CF, that the rest of the countries involved in the former Yugoslavia considered them cowards. "An increasing number of 'significant incident reports' arrived in NDHQ detailing reports of soldiers and officers who were often drunk on duty, fighting with local citizens, abusive towards women and others, and generally behaving outrageously."[40] Other reports noted that plans were inadequate, that equipment was obsolete, that command and control was inadequate, that soldiers were exhausted, and that a number had contacted some strange sicknesses.

In Bosnia, as an example, Hillier cited the "Battle of Medak Pocket" as a case of governmental coverup—war at its worst. Scores of Canadian soldiers were involved in heavy combat, an event that was hushed up. "Individual casualties were covered up and some, allegedly, were reported as accidents."[41]

> The government's policy is to participate in peacekeeping missions and they assume them to be free from human costs. We [officials] moreover assumed that Canadians are allergic to "body-bags"; that is to say, they would not tolerate continued participation in missions that result in casualties. If, therefore, we were to report publicly, say in Parliament, the real cost in people of these operations, then Canadians might have asked the government to withdraw from them. Then the government's defence and foreign policies would be threatened. So we did the best we could to make sure the news never got out. After all, our job is to protect the interests of the government of the day.[42]

SEARCH FOR A NEW CF OFFICER CORPS

Chaos reigned inside the armed forces. As part of Collenette's reform plan, more than 30 bases were being shut down, operational forces were being withdrawn from Europe, military personnel were being cut by 31 percent, civilian by 46 percent; wages and salaries were frozen for six years, combined national and command headquarters were being cut by 50 percent, support slots were cut by at least 15 percent, and R&D and construction was cut by more than 25 percent.[43]

Civil-military relations were at a low, "floundering and uncertain," as described by Bland. The reason, according to Bland, was that the defence team concept, which recognizes the DND and CF, has no basis in law. He believed that the NDHQ also had to be reformed because it is an "assertive organization that has thwarted the effort of many senior officers and officials to change the nature of defence policy, of command of the CF, and of the administration of defence." That was problematic in Bland's view because "the political leaders have regularly 'failed in their basic responsibility to supervise the armed forces of Canada.'" Finally, Bland noted that the "relationship between the command of the CF and political control of the armed forces is so critical that it must be a first-order concern of the minister of defence and Parliament; however, few ministers have grasped the importance of this point."[44] Most of them seem to feel that as long as the United States is prepared to defend them, why should they care about conditions in the CF?

The situation in Quebec again became unstable in October 1995. Francophone groups raised concerns over conditions in Quebec. However, at least one writer claimed that Collenette was aware of how serious the situation was and in 1970 was ready to call out the army to protect federal property and assets. As he put it years later, "I was in a tough position." . . . "I was minister of defence. There were things that went on that we have to be prepared for that I don't even want to talk about."[45] Others deny that such a situation ever took place. Members of the cabinet denied that there were any plans to send in soldiers. Chrétien, who was in Thailand at the time, speaking in French, called the whole idea "bullshit."[46] Regardless of the truth of the matter, it shows that the country's defence minister at least thought about using the CF once again against domestic foes.

In 1996, General Jean Boyle, scandalized that the CF personnel were lining up at food banks to feed their families, let it be known that the CF lacked the equipment, training, and reserves to carry out the tasks assigned to it by the white paper. He pledged that he would seek a pay raise for the troops. On April 1, 1996, Collenette announced a 22.2 percent increase for noncommissioned personnel, in spite of a freeze on government salaries. He also allowed commanders to manage their own budgets. "Solutions ranged from privatizing messes to buying tools and parts at a nearby hardware store."[47]

THE SOMALIA INQUIRY

On January 25, 1995, Collenette ordered the airborne unit disbanded. In August, the chief of the defence staff, General Boyle, appeared before the Commission. When asked if he was responsible for his subordinates' actions, he said, "yes." When asked if he was responsible for tampering with documents? he said, "no." If there were problems with the report, then it was his subordinates who were guilty. Accountability and responsibility are sacred canons of military culture. Boyle refused to accept responsibility for the actions of his subordinates. "Military veterans expressed shock. Major-Generals Vernon and MacKenzie denounced Boyle personally." For his part Collenette stood by Boyle, but on October 4, the minister resigned over a minor conflict of interest matter, and two days later Boyle resigned—six years short of a full pension.[48] Because no one would assume responsibility for either sending the airborne regiment to Somalia, or for their actions there, the Board was unable to assign responsibility for what happened in Somalia.

DOUG YOUNG REPLACES DEFENCE MINISTER COLLENETTE

The first thing Young did after he was selected to replace Collenette was to terminate the Commission's work. From his perspective, there was nothing to be gained by letting the Commission continue hashing out more criticisms of the CF. However, something had to start the CF on the path to recovery. As General Jeffery noted, "The army was *forced* to change . . . I mean 'forced' due to the institutional failures revealed by the Somalia affair."[49] Toward this end, Young appointed a Special Advisory Group on Military Justice and Military Investigation Services. The group was headed by a former chief justice of the Canadian Supreme Court, Brian Dickson. The group was given until January 1997 to provide Young with suggestions on revising the military justice system. He also appointed a four-person group (three Canadian military historians and a political scientist) to report on what they believed was wrong with the Canadian Forces. On March 25, 1997, Young issued a report to the prime minister that included 35 recommendations from the Dickson Commission and with 65 of his own. The prime minister approved all 100 recommendations. The task then was to implement them.

Young's recommendations focused almost entirely on the educational system. In his view, it had to be revamped from top to bottom, a radical change in officer education. Officers should have degrees. He also recommended that DND create an independent professional military journal (i.e., *The Canadian Military Journal*), an Ombudsman (who reports regularly to the CDS), and the Canadian Forces Staff College liberalize its course offerings and begin defining the ethos of the CF.

When Art Eggleton took over as defence minister in June 1997, he created a Monitoring Committee to oversee the implementation of these changes in the CF. In late 1997, a major revamping of the curriculum at the Royal Military College (RMC) began. This meant adding courses in the arts, humanities, and social sciences—a change that has occurred in all four of the militaries discussed here. The RMC distance learning program, which made it possible to earn an MA, was expanded. In addition, the RMC introduced new compulsory courses in national security studies and strategic planning, much like the program at the National War College in Washington, DC. The program was so successful that by 2009, of those at the rank of captain in the army or lieutenant in the navy over 90 percent held university degrees and over 50 percent had graduate degrees. As in the U.S., formal education is usually a requirement for promotion.[50]

In June 1999, the defence department adopted a new policy called "Shaping the Future of the Canadian Forces: A Strategy for 2020." It outlined goals and purposes for the CF, making it clear that the purpose of the CF is to defend Canada and Canadian interests and values. At the same time, it was to contribute to international "peace and security," contribute to the government's priorities, and continue to play a role in NORAD and NATO. "This means that Defence must keep pace with new military concepts, doctrine and technological change" In contrast to past practice, the suggestion was that DND would play an important role in Canadian foreign policy.[51]

MAKING USE OF THE CF

The CF were still in bad shape. By 1999, the budget had been reduced by 23 percent in real dollars. Regular forces had shrunk from 88,000 to fewer than 60,000. Civilian jobs had been cut from 37,000 to just more than 20,000. By the time the CF was deployed to Somalia in late 1992, the CF were in deep trouble: short of funds, short of equipment, poorly trained, and undermanned.[52] The CDS, General Maurice Baril, combined a modest thank you for a modest increase in the budget with a request to reduce CF commitments overseas and not to accept new ones.[53] But the prime minister was determined to spread Canadian influence by sending CF regardless. When the former Yugoslavia collapsed, it was prime minister Chrétien, like his predecessors, who immediately volunteered the CF to help keep the peace. By the end of May 1999, the first Canadian forces left Canada to go to Macedonia. In June, 400 soldiers left from CFB Edmonton to help keep the peace in Kosovo, so that CF had between 750 and 800 soldiers in the region.[54] In addition, Chrétien sent Canadian Forces to help after a devastating earthquake hit Turkey. In September, he sent a ship, aircraft, and 600 CF personnel to join an Australian-led peacemaking force in East Timor. In addition CF personnel were sent to East Africa and Haiti. But the CF were still flying the 40-year-old Sea King helicopters, with no replacement in sight. One source described them as "ten thousand nuts and bolts flying in loose formation." Moreover, these old planes were costing the tax payer $60 million a year in service costs.[55]

By 2000, almost every piece of equipment in the CF inventory was worn out, but the cabinet would not agree to replacements. The main reason, according to Hillier, was that Chrétien knew that the CF did not have a constituency. He could make cuts and the average Canadian did not care. To quote Hillier,

> My beef was that while all that was occurring, they were continuing to ask more of us; in fact, they were asking a *lot* more of us. We were being asked to do everything we had done before the cuts of the 1990s and to do it all over the world with less money, fewer students and outdated equipment. The Government of Canada and Canadians wanted their cake and wanted to eat it too, and we paid the price for it. If the government decides to have a Canadian Forces of only ten people, it's their right to make that decision. You can agree or disagree with it, but when a government decides to have an army of ten and wants that armed forces to continue to do the work of ten thousand, that's a different kettle of fish. That's what really caused the decade of darkness.[56]

Canadian Forces had been told years earlier by Hellyer that unification would save money and make it easier to argue for increases. But the savings that were supposed to accompany unification never occurred, according to Middlemiss and Sokolovsky.[57]

However, Art Eggleton gradually began to address some of the military's problems. On November 10, 2000, he announced that 28 new helicopters would be delivered in 2005. In the meantime, he ordered a $50 million refurbishment for the Sea Kings to keep them flying until their replacements arrived. The next day he announced a series of reforms aimed at improving Canadian military medical care. General Baril brought the point to his attention after a year-long study indicated there were not enough military doctors and that the delivery of services was hurt by red tape and years of budget cuts.[58] But major problems continued to haunt the military. Shane Henry, a retired colonel, claimed that the decision to pull out of Kosovo and East Timor was motivated primarily by the inability of the CF to deploy 3,000 troops overseas.[59]

9/11

From a Canadian standpoint, the major message from the 9/11 attack on New York City and Washington, DC, was that Canada had to get serious about security. It would be dangerous to allow defence to float, subject to the whims of the cabinet. While the United States would help, it could not protect Canada from this new kind of war. On March 1, 2001, Ottawa announced an infusion of $624 million into the Canadian military. Part of this money would go toward a pay increase. This followed a report from Canada's auditor general, who concluded that the CF budget was overextended. He stated that the CF, in fact, needed an additional $750 million per year just to maintain the status quo.[60]

OPERATION APOLLO

On October 7, 2001, Prime Minister Chrétien visited President Bush in Washington. That evening Canada's CDS issued a ten-day warning for Operation Apollo, the code name for Canada's participation with the United States in responding to the 9/11 attacks by hitting al Qaeda and the Taliban in Afghanistan. Ten days later, Commodore Drew Robertson and three of his four ships cleared Halifax for the Arabian Sea. The HMCS Halifax later joined these three. When they arrived in the Persian Gulf after an eight-thousand-mile passage, the Canadians were assigned the task of escorting ships of a U.S. Marine expeditionary unit off of Pakistan.

With memories of Canada's nonperformance in Kosovo, none of the Allies was keen on having Canadian forces beside them in battle. " 'We were shunned. Part of the reason was that the Europeans, and the British in particular, remembered our risk-adverse approach . . . had no faith that Canada would pull its weight. . . . They did not want us as part of the alliance.' As a result, Canadian forces were subordinated to an American battalion in a US division."[61] In December, Canada secretly deployed elements of its special operations force Joint Task Force 2 (JTF2), its elite fighting force to southern Afghanistan.

General Raymond Henault seized on the events in Afghanistan to plead for more resources. On October 16, he gave a speech before the Committee on National Defence and Veterans Affairs, emphasizing the importance of recruitment and retention; he also noted that CF had finally received new equipment. He pointed out the Army's new Coyote reconnaissance vehicles, the LAV III armored personnel carriers, and the Victoria class submarines the Canadians had purchased from the British.[62] But polls taken in spring 2001 indicated that while Canadians understood the desperate condition that the CF was in, "money to improve the situation was not on their priority list."[63]

By 2002, it was clear that the CF was in deep trouble. It was involved in missions all over the world, and it was still short of money. In September 2002, the Council for Canadian Security stated that while the government was providing a military budget of about $12 billion, Ottawa should spend an additional $1.5 billion immediately. To quote Granatstein, "We've all been moved to act by the sense that the Canadian Forces are in crisis and literally on the very edge of collapse."[64] What was especially important was that the new defence minister John McCallum endorsed the demand for more money.[65] The number of missions assigned to the CF skyrocketed in the past decade, from 24 between 1948 and 1989 to 79 between 1990 and 2002,[66] but the army was given only 40 percent of the money it needed to maintain its bases and equipment.

On April 16, 2003, at the urging of the Germans, the Netherlands, and Canada, NATO agreed to take responsibility for the ISAF (International Security Assistance Force) mission in Afghanistan. Canada had previously agreed to become the lead nation in Kabul, beginning that summer. The Commander of NATO troops was Canadian General Rick Hillier. He was a "general's general" having commanded troops from the platoon level to multinational formations, including a stint as the Deputy Commander of US III Corps at Fort Hood, Texas.

THE BUDGET

By February 2003, the Canadian military's share of defence spending was a meager 1.1 percent, the second lowest in NATO.[67] Yet Canadian troops were carrying a heavy load in Afghanistan. The problem was not only equipment. Canadian Forces had fallen from 80,000 to 60,000. All of Canada's three regiments were understrength. In addition, the operation tempo was exhausting the troops and convinced some well-trained troops to leave the service.

The situation was so serious that Douglas Bland, one of Canada's leading military experts, edited a book entitled, *Canada without Armed Forces* (2004). The message was clear:

> Numerous studies, both public and private, point to the stresses and strains on members of the armed forces and military capabilities resulting from an unprecedented operational tempo and from policies that have demanded for a decade that members of the Canadian Forces "do more with less." It is the crisis of "the present force"; a commitment capabilities dilemma brought on by

> the gap between the quantity and quality of people, equipment, logistical support, and funding available today and the demands of current defence politics and operations.[68]

Politicians in Ottawa needed to understand that given the situation inside CF they would soon be deprived of the military aspect in foreign policy. "Canada in a few years will be effectively unarmed."[69] Canadian defence planning was chaotic. As a danger would appear, the Cabinet would rush to call for new weapons systems, but once the danger passed, just a few of the planes, ships, or armored vehicles would be produced. The weapons procured were not coordinated with a strategy for their employment. What money there was went to support the existing forces, thereby taking money away from new weapons and personnel. As Marsh commented, "The Canadian Forces has lost so much momentum in core areas that bringing major capabilities to a full operational scale is likely to take one or two decades."[70]

Prime Minister Chrétien's comments on defence spending show just how low military spending stood among his priorities:

> But when asked about defence spending . . . Chrétien said the government was doing the best it could. "Last year, we gave them virtually a billion dollars," he said, prior to touring the main Canadian Camp southwest of Kabul. . . . "But it is never enough. I have never seen an army anywhere in the world who returned government money anywhere. They all need more and they all have plans for more. It is a question of priority."[71]

Chrétien's memoirs give the impression that he did not believe the defence minister or the CDS when they begged him for more money. He felt that he was giving enough, perhaps even too much. The military, however, saw it in a far different light. Martin Chadwick observed,

> Most importantly, he failed to fundamentally reassess defence requirements in response to changing international circumstances. He also offered pat utterances on defence that were unfortunate or unworthy (e.g., references to peacekeepers as "Boy Scouts") and the infamous year-end interviews which implied that supporters of increased defence spending were mere shills for the arms industry.[72]

Chrétien's last defence minister, John McCallum, recognized the extent of the problem and was successful in getting more money for the military. For example, he spent nearly $600 million on new armored vehicles while at the same time cutting almost $100 million from military headquarters in Ottawa.[73]

Paul Martin (2003–2006)

In December 2003, Chrétien was succeeded by his Liberal Party colleague, Paul Martin. It was clear to those in uniform that he had a whole new approach to defence. Where the Chrétien administration had looked upon the CF as a peacekeeping institution, and structured it accordingly, the Martin government saw it as a war-fighting institution and changed its structure and size accordingly.

The new approach was welcomed by the military. The CDS General Ray Henault was well aware that fundamental changes had to be made before the CF would be in a position to deal with the different kind of combat coming over the horizon. Transformation and change were the main themes in his annual reports to Parliament. The term transformation would become a constant theme in military commentaries on CF in coming months and years.

In January 2004, the new defence minister, David Pratt, publicly stated that it was time to rest Canada's soldiers. In the past two years, for example, soldiers of the Princess Patricia's Light Infantry were sent once to Afghanistan and three times to Bosnia. The request for rest came from the unit commander himself. As Colonel Tim Grant put it, "We would be challenged to go off to do an international operation of any magnitude. . . . This brigade needs time to get its house in order, to take that breath to refresh ourselves."[74]

In March 2004, the new budget committed $4 billion for new spending on military equipment, including modern fixed wing aircraft and rescue aircraft, maritime helicopters, three naval supply ships, and mobile gun systems to replace the aging Leopard tanks. At long last, the ancient Sea King helicopters were to be replaced. Fifteen new CH-149 Cormorant helicopters were now in Canada and would be operational by December. Almost all of CF's shortcomings were finally being addressed.[75]

The opposition was pushing even harder for more money for the military. Future prime minister Steven Harper argued in May that "For too long, Canadian defence policy has wallowed in the throes of strategic drift," Harper suggested that a Conservative government would inject an additional $1.2 billion a year for the next three years followed by an increase of $1.6 billion in the fourth year. This would increase the CF to about 80,000 personnel (versus the 52,400 it had).[76] While Harper blasted Martin, and Martin complained

Harper was going overboard even to the point of bringing back helicopters, defence did not catch the public interest. Paul Martin won the election, but he presided over a minority government. Some of his ministers, including his defence minister David Pratt, lost their seats.

RICK HILLIER, CHIEF OF THE DEFENCE STAFF (2005–2008)

General Rick Hillier did more to change the way Canadian Forces were treated in Ottawa than any senior military officer in the postwar period. Transformation was his key concern. Like the German forces in the aftermath of the Cold War, Hillier believed that CF must be reorganized. They had to be reequipped, and they had to be reconnected with the Canadian people.

As he took over as CDS, Hillier had four goals. First was to restructure the organization; second, to bring back the warrior class of the army, navy, and air force while working toward a more vibrant CF culture; third, to improve operational effectiveness; and finally, to overcome the "bureaucratic fog" that is inherent in NDHQ. As Stein and Lang observed, "In a few weeks' time, a soldier from Newfoundland had outclassed and outrun the best minds in Canada's august Department of Foreign Affairs."[77]

Hillier also stressed the CF was not some sort of public service organization. Its job was simple—to kill people, what CF was doing in Afghanistan. He was determined to show Canada and the world that the Can't bats in Bosnia, had become the Can'bats in Afghanistan. The first thing he did was to split Canada into three commands: Canada Command (CANCOM), for all actions inside Canada including humanitarian actions; Canada Expeditionary Command (CDECOM), which replaced the Deputy Chief of the Defence Staff at NDHQ, and assumed responsibility for all troops abroad; and third, Canada Special Operations Command (CANSOFCOM).

Personnel remained a serious problem, both retention and training. The CF needed competent pilots, ground crews, and sailors. "The proportion of the population with 1–4 years of service is too large; that with 6–11 is too small; and the portion with 12–18 is also too large."[78] Hillier believed that the first step should be increasing the CF to 85,000. Another problem was the need to reinstitute the kind of service pride that existed prior to Hillyer's time as defence minister. This remained a critical component of military culture, something that was critical to service pride.

In addition to numbers and competency, Hillier was concerned about the mental state of these forces; CF had been deployed almost steadily for the last several years. Still living in a Cold War world, it was time to bring them into the twenty-first century. It was also time for both the country's military personnel and its civilian leadership to understand that CF could not do everything. Why, for example, was Canada still spending millions of dollars on antisubmarine warfare? Hillier also raised questions about the utility of Canada's aging Leopard tanks and its fighter aircraft.

To his defence minister, General Hillier was a visionary. He was not trying to build a military that would make all of the service chiefs happy. To the contrary, he was taking Canadian foreign policy as his starting point and using that as the basis for his transformation of Canadian Forces. Hillier made an equally strong impression on the prime minister. After meeting with him, Martin wrote, "General Hillier had a vision for the Armed Forces and a plan—including a capability to deploy forces quickly when needed. I had given a lot of thought to the role and capabilities of our armed forces when I was out of office, and I found that General Hillier's views—admittedly based on a deeper understanding—were very similar to my own."[79] In addition, he paid Hillier one of the highest compliments a soldier can receive.

> Hillier's appointment would fundamentally change the philosophy, the strategy, the organization and the culture of the Canadian Forces. He would become the most important and influential CDS in living memory. . . . Hillier would make defence policy his first priority. Defence policy was historically and quite appropriately, the domain of civilian officials, and it was unprecedented for a chief of defence staff to be given this responsibility.[80]

The appointment of a dynamic personality like Hillier made it clear to everyone that the situation inside defence had changed. Hillier had the strong support of his prime minister.

Hillier had only been CDS a month when he devised a new plan for using Canadian troops in Afghanistan. He pushed for a widening of Canada's role—not just sitting in Kabul, but carrying the action to the enemy. As Janice Stein and Eugene Lang noted, "It was heavy lifting. And it was an initiative that would impress the Pentagon and even George Bush."[81] U.S. policy also figured prominently. Canada made it clear that it would not join the Ballistic Missile Defence Program. As a result, Hillier and those in External Affairs were looking for something to do for the U.S. Sending more Canadian troops and putting them in harm's way was a step in the right direction; it would be the main focus for the Canadian Forces for the next six years.

Military culture and tradition began to reemerge. For example, the helicopter crews deployed to Afghanistan in 2008 began to paint pictures on the nose of their helicopters: skeletons, hockey sticks and even a few naked women—an old tradition among pilots in all countries. As Hillier noted, "It wasn't so long ago that it would have been unthinkable for pilots or aircrews in combat to show a little esprit de corps, pride in what they do and the aircraft they fly. Regulations and procedures would have ensured that it never happened. This rebirth of tradition signaled the rebirth of pride."[82]

2005 DEFENCE POLICY PAPER

Under Hillier's guidance, DND issued a key policy paper outlining Canada's new defence policy. In this document, Hillier played up the importance of failed states, as well as the dangers presented by global terrorism. As happened in Germany, Hillier stressed that the Canadian Forces would have to undergo a fundamental transformation. He also called for new unified commands with a unified approach to dealing with problems. The document was published in the spring of 2005, and as soon as it was, Hillier began working on the changes he felt necessary. In contrast to the *1964 White Paper*, Hillier's paper contained a detailed and comprehensive list of tasks for the CF. The 2005 document is an "integral part of the government's International Policy Statement, rather than a separate government white paper."[83] The 2005 document also argued that CF should play a prominent role in Canadian foreign policy. While the public was becoming increasingly impressed with Hillier, Martin was playing an equally important role behind the scenes. He recognized the problem of underfunding the military and its low status with the public. One of the first things he did was to visit defence headquarters and to meet with the soldiers and staff. As Martin put it, "It was a signal of the importance I placed on our Armed Forces. My view was that we needed to have a larger military with an ability to deploy rapidly, and with the latest equipment for the men and women we were putting in harm's way."[84]

BUDGET 2005

The defence budget was substantially increased. "In Budget 2005, the Government made the largest investment in Canada's military in over 20 years, totaling approximately $13 billion."[85] The money gave Hillier the wherewithal to begin replacing critical equipment and weapons systems, for example, the C-130 Hercules, which were older than the pilots who flew them. But when Hillier and his boss took these issues to the cabinet, the trouble began. As Hillier described it:

> Despite all the meetings and briefings we'd given Cabinet, suddenly they became a bunch of worrywarts. Clearly ministers had heard concerns from their staff, because all I heard in that meeting was objections. "Oh my goodness—you know, this is big money"; "We can't do this, can't do that"; "We've got to do it another way"; "We've got to avoid sounding like we're sole-sourcing."[86]

Hillier was angry. As he told Minister of Defence Graham, "Well you know, Minister, actually I'm not just a little bit upset." I said. "I'm pissed off."[87] The preparatory work had been done, and people who knew absolutely nothing squashed everything he did. Hillier made it clear that if he felt he could not support policy, he would resign:

> First, let there be no doubt, I work for the Government of Canada and as CDS, I take direction from them—from the Minister of National Defence and from the Prime Minister who appoints the CDS. I am in fact the sole advisor for the PM. The Government of Canada sets the agenda and it is our job to provide military advice and counsel on that agenda and how it can affect Canada's military capability. I either support or, if at significant odds with that agenda, I resign.[88]

Hiller's conversation with Graham had an impact, because the next day the C-130s were back on the table, and within a couple of weeks that project was formally announced. Unfortunately, the project died because of the election. Despite his strong feelings, Hillier never tired of pointing out that he was working at the behest of civilian authorities. "First, let there be no doubt, I work for the Government of Canada and, as CDS, I take direction from them—from the Minister of National Defence and the Prime Minister who appoints the CDS."[89]

Stephen Harper (2006–)

Stephen Harper won the election, despite a blistering ad against him, claiming, "Stephen Harper actually announced he wants to increase the military presence in our cities. Canadian cities. Soldiers with guns. In our cities. In Canada."[90] The ad backfired. It outraged most Canadians that the Liberals were presenting such a picture of the CF, and second, many found it hilarious. At first, Martin admitted that he approved the ads but later claimed that he had not seen it before it was released. Martin was right about one item. Harper made national defence and security the center of his campaign in the 2005–

2006 election. Harper pledged to commit five billion dollars to the CF's budget over five years.[91] After all, Canadians understood that CF were fighting and dying in Afghanistan.

While most Canadians opposed sending the CF to Afghanistan, Harper identified with the deployment. He flew to Afghanistan, slept with the soldiers on the desert base, and visited Kandahar where Canadians were in the process of rebuilding. Back in Ottawa, he permitted a debate on the topic, and on May 17 the House of Commons held a vote on whether to permit Canadian troops to stay in Afghanistan for two years after the current commitment ended in 2007. He won, but only by two votes.

Unlike most of his predecessors, Harper's view of foreign policy was that a strong military strengthened the government's hand. In practice, this meant having the military play a far more important role in the area of peacekeeping than was envisaged by Martin and his Liberals. That meant expanding the size of the military as well as modernizing its antiquated equipment and weapons. In addition, he also believed strongly in patriotism.

HILLIER VERSUS HELLYER

At this time, Hillier and others began a revaluation of Defence Secretary Hellyer's actions in the late 1960s. Most observers, including Hillier, agreed that unification made some sense by getting rid of some redundancies. The idea of centralized leadership also made sense, even though NDHQ was often a problem. However, there were major negatives in Hellyer's actions. Hellyer over-centralized authority. There is something to be said for keeping the three services independent—while clearly subordinate to the CDS. As one author put it, "The reality is that the unique operating environments of the three services make them look at their capabilities and contributions through a different lens, and differing strategic perspectives and doctrines between the services almost guarantee that there will be service competition and disputes with respect to operational roles and mission."[92] Hellyer simply did not think matters through. He never asked himself, what would be the long-term implications of his policies. He was not concerned about creating a top-flight combat organization. His primary goal was to find an organizational change that would save money.

In contrast, for Hillier transformation of the CF began in the middle of the command structure, at the operational level. It was only peripherally focused on NDHQ. "Operational effectiveness and in particular operational command, was at the heart of the transformation agenda."[93] Where Hellyer's policy had been put together in a haphazard fashion, Hillier was carefully implementing a predetermined policy.

However, the new government refused to accept the 2005 Defence Policy statement, and Hillier was forced to implement parts of the country's defence policy without being able to see how it fit into the larger picture. He was able to work his way through this confusing situation, thanks, he said, to the new defence minister, Peter McKay.

> I had, at this point, worked for two different defence ministers and two prime ministers, and we still had to come up with a coherent strategic plan, all while we were at war (even though we weren't calling it that). Continuity of approach is important, particularly when your people are fighting and dying in a foreign land. It was only in the last six months of my appointment that the vision, with the strategy and details in it started to emerge. Much of the credit for that is due to Peter McKay, Defence Minister as of August 2007.[94]

In the eyes of the military, it was frustrating the Canadian public still did not understand the critical role played by the military in international affairs. As Jones and Kilgour observed, "What Canadians have not yet come to terms with really is that conflict is and will be a part of global reality now and for many years to come."[95]

AFGHANISTAN AND THE BUDGET

In June 2006, the government announced it would be spending $17 billion on the military. As a senior Canadian officer put it, that amount "represents a huge investment in equipment and support activity over a long period."[96] Peter McKay brought the message to military units all over Canada, "expectations are growing that the Government is truly committed to investing in core military capabilities."[97]

At about the same time, the security situation in southern Afghanistan had deteriorated significantly. In the area around Kandahar, the CF was faced with a new, more intense insurgency. This was combat that neither Canada, the U.S., or NATO had expected. On the one hand, Harper claimed that this experience "had turned Canada's military into a better fighting force and improved Canada's standing on the world stage."[98] Canada was paying a high price for the high quality of its troops, however. "Canadian deaths in Afghanistan were proportionately higher than those from other NATO countries. On the positive side, the mission in Afghanistan changed the public image of the Canadian Forces from a military largely engaged in peacekeeping and humanitarian work—a public perception that ignored Canada's long military history—to one of an army engaged in full-scale combat and counterinsurgency work. Canada's military was at war, and it was at war in ways the whole country could see and feel."[99]

It was a far cry from the dismal days of Bosnia. However, conflict in Afghanistan consumed soldiers and equipment. Hillier had promised Paul Martin that starting February 2007, the CF would be in a position to fight two different wars at the same time. Hillier was well aware that the Afghanistan mission would be challenging, but he did not anticipate the extent of the problems. "By the spring of 2006, as the conflict in Kandahar escalated, the new government began to signal that this optimism was no longer warranted."[100] Hillier himself publicly stated that the CF would be unable to undertake a second mission in the foreseeable future.[101] The mission in Afghanistan was consuming resources far faster than Hillier had anticipated. "I underestimated the demands of the Afghan deployment, what it would consume. . . . It includes a conventional force component—which I did not foresee—which demands so many enablers [support elements]. Our C-130s are dying by the month, and we have no replacement in sight. The intensity of the fighting required all our enablers."[102]

For Canada, the Afghan war ended in June 2011, except for a group of Canadians who stayed on to help train Afghan troops. It was a momentous occasion:

> Canada leaves the Kandahar mission with a reputation for having the best small army in the world. Canadian soldiers are respected around the globe for their battle-hardened professionalism, innovative application of counterinsurgency doctrine and holding their nerve in Kandahar, while other NATO allies cowered on heavily fortified bases munching lobster instead of fighting insurgents. The Americans, who led the mission, have noted: Jon Vance, a Canadian general, was entrusted to command thousands of American troops when the US surged into Kandahar last summer.[103]

RESTORING MILITARY CULTURE

To Hillier, all of the aspects of military culture were critical. With years of operational experience, one of his goals was to strengthen command and control. In accordance with military culture, that meant to have "a distinct and unambiguous chain of command, with the key being the allocation of mission-specific capabilities to operational and tactical commands/formations to increase the ability to deploy rapidly."[104] That meant changing the way NDHQ operated. The CDS took charge of development by strengthening control of force development, increasing the control exerted by the VCDS branch, and strengthening the authority of the central structure that dealt with such issues. In addition, Hillier created a Military Personnel Command, directly subordinate to the CDS. The most significant change in NDHQ was the dismantling of the DCDS group and the transfer of a lot of power to the military via a Strategic Joint Staff (SJS) that reported directly to the CDS. This meant that, for the first time, there was one unified chain of command for both routine and domestic operations. "The key difference between this model and the pre-transformation command structure is that the JTF commanders are empowered, during an emergency or contingency operation, with the command over all CF assets within a given region, thereby increasing responsiveness."[105] As a result, there was a major change in the decision-making process in the direction of restoring one of the key principles of military culture:

> Hillier's highly visible role in shaping defence policy, in articulating persuasively defence issues to the Canadian public, and in exercising the command of the CF has considerably strengthened the role of the office of the CDS. Today, the CDS's power and authority inside the CF is unparalleled, and it is essentially unchallenged by the services and their constituencies. The establishment of a strong unified staff, a shift in the institutional power of the DM on operational matters, and the decreased influence of environmental commanders have prominently placed the CDS as the sole military advisor to the government, strengthening at the same time civil control of the military.[106]

He also worked to restore service loyalty and pride. "The younger—and older—members of the CF are proud and dedicated to their military duties and responsibilities, and they clearly identify with their unit, regiment, or service."[107] In contrast to Hellyer, Hillier understood the importance of the psychological aspects of service life and loyalties. As Gosseln observed, "It took 40 years for the CF institution to articulate properly *Duty with Honour*, something the three service chiefs of staff could not get Hellyer to understand during the 1960s."[108]

In 2007, the CF began the process of modernization, purchasing 100 more modern second-hand tanks from the Germans. During the years 2006–2007, CF's regular forces increased by 1,000 while the reserves increased by 1,300.[109] Hillier criticized the previous Liberal government that failed to live up to its promises. During a speech at the Conference of Defence Association Institute in Ottawa, he pointed out the "negative legacy" of the defence spending cuts that began in 1994 and left "deep wounds." He went so far as to call the last ten years "a decade of darkness."[110] While Hillier did not mention the previous Liberal government, he was letting it be known that he would not remain silent when the military was given impossible tasks while being denied the wherewithal to carry out missions. Then, with the horrendous experience in Bosnia in mind, Hillier made it clear he would not put up with civilian interference in the conduct of operations in Afghanistan:

> As the mission in Afghanistan began heating up in 2007, various folks around Ottawa became very focused on our actions there and wanted command of Canadian Forces units on the ground to fall under civilian jurisdiction. These field marshal wannabes wanted to have a say in every single tactical mission in Kandahar province by having the ambassador in Kabul or another representative actually take command of our troops. These civilians' time on the diplomatic cocktail circuit undoubtedly had prepared them well for those challenges, but the mere fact that they proposed it indicated a superficial understanding of what was at stake. I essentially told them to get lost. I was responsible for the lives and limbs of young Canadian men and women and was accountable to their families, the Minister of Defence and the Prime Minister. The Civil Service had no say in the matter.[111]

One reason for the improved performance of the CF was Hillier's change of the power relationship inside the defence bureaucracy. He made the CF forces proud to be soldiers. "As far as the troops are concerned, Hillier doesn't have to walk on water—water simply makes sure it gets out of his way. After more than a decade of our military being mislabeled as mere peacekeepers, Hillier has made the rank and file proud to proclaim themselves soldiers again."[112]

Although slow, there was progress in purchasing new weapons systems. In 2007, a contract was signed for C130J transports to replace the C-17s. Progress was made on the Joint Support Ship, and work was moving ahead for the purchase of medium-sized trucks for the army and a Chinook medium/heavy lift helicopter fleet. Work was also proceeding on sustaining the Navy's twelve frigates as well as the purchase of new ice-capable ships to work in Canada's north.[113] However, while new weapons systems were promised, the CF were still flying 40-year-old airplanes and driving 25-year-old trucks.

There was pressure to increase the size of the CF, particularly the ground forces. They totaled 20,000, but there were calls for them to be doubled. At the same time,

> Canada's nine infantry battalions should be organized for deployment in permanently affiliated battle groups; and the JTF-2 unit should be increased to full strength. Indeed, Canadian Forces need more JTF-2 soldiers and a full strength Special Operations Forces Regiment to back them up. At the same time, the army requires more combat engineers and the Land Force reserves need to be increased.[114]

Given the past problems faced by CF, and the interest shown by Harper in the military, supporters seized on the opportunity to emphasize the need for the long awaited weapons systems, and to stress the importance of expansion in those areas the military considered critical.

GENERAL WALTER NATYNCZYK AND THE CANADA FIRST STRATEGY

On May 12, 2008, Harper announced the Canada First Strategy, which led the future chief of the defence staff, General Walter Natynczyk to comment, "In my 35 years of service, we had never had a blueprint for Canadian forces." It had four pillars, which Natynczyk argued had to be kept in balance: "people, capital, readiness, and infrastructure." What was unusual about this strategy was that it was closely tied to weapons, personnel, and the budget.[115] It called for 70,000 regular forces, up from 64,800 in 2007–2008. It also called for an increase of 4,000 in reserve forces to a total of 26,000.[116] There was opposition to structural modifications: the then retired General Hillier blasted the plan, arguing that it created the conditions for "a system of micro-management." As he continued, "The National Defence Act is clear—our sons and daughters need to have direction from the leaders that Canadians have elected, and they need to have that direction passed through the chief of defence staff without interference from bureaucrats who have no preparation or training for this task, and no responsibility for those lives." And he concluded, "Any governments who permit anything different should have their rear ends booted out of office by moms and dads of those serving sons and daughters."[117] His conditions for a shared responsibility were clear.

Meanwhile, the situation inside the military was again desperate:

> Canada's air force needs new fighter jets, and more than just the 65 F-35s the government has said it intends to purchase. . . . The air force also urgently requires more helicopters, both to carry supplies at home and abroad, and to (if necessary) transport troops into battle. The navy is rapidly rusting out, with virtually every type of ship in the fleet needing either upgrades or outright

> replacement. The army has benefitted the most from the Afghan-era urgent purchases, but still should be expanded, to reflect its duties at home and abroad. And this is far from a complete list.[118]

On June 19, 2008, the Harper Government released financial details on its new 20-year defence plan. It included $490 billion in spending over the next two decades. While the number appeared large, it was to be spent over 20 years, and 51 percent would go to salaries. Then there was money for training, as well as modernizing old equipment and purchasing new weapons.[119] While the increased funding came as a welcome development to Hillier and the CF, it did not meet the immediate needs of the CF. One specialist said,

> While the overall dollar figure of about $45 billion for recapitalization over the next 20 years is probably about right, more—much more—of the money needs to be allocated at the beginning of the twenty-year period. Reduced investments in defence in the 1990s have led to a situation in which a whole range of major military platforms—supply ships, destroyers, marine patrol aircraft, fighters, battlefield helicopters, light armored vehicles—must be replaced within the same five-year window of about 2012 to 2017. The CF needs approximately $30 billion for capital acquisitions over the next 5 years to the procurement process. After that, the CF will need about $15 billion over the period to 2028 to maintain the equipment.[120]

Despite the problems with money, there was limited progress. On August 11, 2009, Ottawa finalized a deal to acquire 15 new heavy-duty US-built helicopters with a $5 billion price tag. Delivery is set for July 2013.[121]

On July 2, 2008, General Natynczyk assumed the position as chief of the defence staff, replacing Hillier, who retired. Natynczyk is an army officer who served extensively in a variety of posts. He attended the U.S. Army War College, and was deputy commanding general of III Corps at Fort Hood, Texas. Unknown to many Canadians, he deployed with III Corps to Baghdad in January 2004, and commanded American forces in the First Gulf War.

Despite the problems, after more than fifty years struggle, the CF had attained some sense of predictability and logic. Canadian Forces now had a road map. Natynczyk said, "it's the first time certainly in my 33 years—and so we can actually do the planning. In the past, if you wanted to buy a ship, our best track record is 10 years. So unless you know how much money you're going to have in 10 years' time, how can you show government you can afford to purchase this ship and then run the ship."[122] The question was could the CF keep the money, or would Ottawa take it and use it for other purposes? And there were grounds for concern. By December the CF was cutting back on training, travel, maintenance, and the purchase of new computers—because it had to save $80 million between December and March 2010.[123]

TROOP EXHAUSTION

While a rational, sufficient budget was a major concern for Natynczyk, there was another even more important concern. Canadian troops in Afghanistan had been carrying a heavy load for years. They were exhausted. According to a report prepared for the CDS, "the army can't continue at the current pace, which demands it deploy 4,000 troops a year to Afghanistan while preparing and training 12,000 others for combat rotation. 'The Afghanistan mission is particularly taxing on army capabilities, and the current operations tempo is not sustainable.' "[124] The situation was made worse by many servicemen, specialists, and officers who were leaving the service. There were too many deployments, one after another, and the equipment was breaking down. "The army recently estimated that it is going to need $5 billion to spend on new armored and transport vehicles, and a good part of that will simply replace or repair equipment broken or worn out in Afghanistan."[125] This led Lieutenant General Andrew Leslie, the army chief, to tell the Canadian Senate that the army was so strained that it may need a one-year "pause" to regroup and rebuild after Canada withdraws from Afghanistan. The situation in the navy was so bad that there were concerns that the two Canadian 40-year-old oil tankers "risk being barred from docking at European or American ports over environmental concerns."[126] Natynczyk agreed, observing, "It's an army that's undergoing an incredible operational tempo right now."[127] Faced with such severe problems, Ottawa announced in November 2009, that Canadian Forces would be withdrawn from Afghanistan during 2011, and that preparations for their withdrawal had already begun.[128]

CONTINUING EFFORTS TO FINANCE CF

The Harper Government's 2010 budget cut $2.5 billion from the $5 billion previously promised to the military.[129] As a consequence, several high-cost systems will probably be cut. One of the first items that drew attention was the F-35 stealth bombers. The argument in favor of the GOC spending $16 billion to replace the aging F-18s with the purchase of 65 of the stealth jets is that they enable the military to "sneak up on an adversary at the edges of domestic airspace and use that potential for surprise as a deterrent."[130] But others argue that they are not needed because planes from Russia would be aimed at the U.S., not Canada.[131] On January 21, 2011, General Natynczyk added his name to supporters for the plan, commenting, "From my perspective, the F-35 is the best aircraft with the best value for Canada."[132]

Then on November 22, 2010, it was announced the decades-old Sea King helicopters would not be replaced by 28 Cyclone helicopters as soon as anticipated. Instead, the Cyclones would first begin arriving in 2012.[133] Most important, on October 20, the government announced that it had awarded a $25 billion contract to a firm in Halifax to build 22 combat vessels. A firm in Vancouver was awarded $8 billion to build two noncombat vessels. It appears that help is finally coming.

However, some way had to be found to pay for these new weapons systems. In the face of continued financial problems, a Canadian officer, Lieutenant General Andrew Leslie, who was in charge of military transformation, put forth a plan that called for major changes. As he put it, "If we are serious about the future—and we must be—the impact of reallocating thousands of people and billions of dollars from what they are doing now to what we want them to do . . . will require dramatic change." His proposal suggested 44 changes on how "to reduce the tail of today while investing in the teeth of tomorrow."[134]

The bureaucracy was strongly opposed—since they were targeted for a major downsizing.[135] General Natynczyk backed up Leslie, calling the cuts needed to save $1 billion (including the elimination of 11,000 civilian positions) painful, but necessary.[136]

REESTABLISHING TRADITION

In August 2011, the Harper Administration announced that it was reversing one of the remaining parts of Hellyer's 1968 change. Instead of using the name Canadian Forces, the military would go by its old names: the Canadian Army, the Royal Canadian Navy, and the Royal Canadian Air Force. As the *Globe and Mail* commented, "The decades-long attempt to erase the historic designations, and unique identities, of the RCN, Canadian Army, and RCAF was a failure."[137] The change of names was welcomed by veterans, although there was concern that the use of the term "Royal" would alienate some, especially those in Quebec. One Liberal senator, who served in the navy, stated that he would have preferred leaving the term Royal off, but commented, "If we're going to get a title that has Navy in it, well then God bless them."[138]

PART IV / Russia

Fighting bureaucracy in Russia is a very difficult undertaking.

VLADIMIR PUTIN

CHAPTER 8

From Boris Yeltsin through Vladimir Putin

> If a lion stands at the head of an army of lions, victory is assured. If a lion stands at the head of an army of asses, the chances are fifty-fifty. But if an ass stands at the head of an army of lions you can call it quits.
>
> GENERAL ALEXANDER LEBED

The collapse of the USSR in 1991 ushered in a revolution in Russian civil-military relations. When Gorbachev came to power, he was willing to take on one of the country's most sacred institutions—the Soviet Army, the organization that had saved the country from the German onslaught in World War II, and one of the most trusted and respected institutions in the country.[1]

Gorbachev's time in office was marked by constant attacks on military culture. First, perestroika undermined the military-industrial complex on which the military depended. Second, glasnost had a disastrous impact on military cohesion and combat readiness. Third, the military was unaccustomed to the public criticism emanating from the civilian media. Many officers believed that the armed forces were on the verge of collapse, and the generals saw Gorbachev and his policies as part of the problem. He did not seem to care what was happening in the military, and a joint relationship was the last thing on his agenda. This opened the door for Boris Yeltsin, the president of the Russian Republic, to appeal to the military for support. Although the military had limited contact with him, given Gorbachev's lack of concern, the generals believed Yeltsin would do a better job protecting their interests.

Reality would turn out to be much different from what the generals and admirals expected. If the senior officers thought Gorbachev had attacked military culture, it was nothing compared to what Yeltsin had in store for them.

Boris Yeltsin (1991–1999)

Yeltsin was a difficult person, stubborn, arbitrary, and unpredictable. He was also impulsive and would make decisions on the spur of the moment. He was irascible, and his primary focus was on his political power—maintaining his position as president. He cared little about creating new political institutions or strengthening the old ones, including the military structures that would help consolidate the new, postcommunist political system. That was his successor's problem.

His operating style immediately caused problems for the creation of shared responsibility. His impulsiveness and unpredictability flew in the face of the military's need for clear and concise orders. The generals wanted clear instructions on what the political leadership expected of them, assurances that the necessary supplies would be available when the time came, and assurances that political authorities would not dictate operations or tactics.

The generals expected Yeltsin to approve of military reform and provide guidance and financial and political support, while leaving the details to them. They also expected the president's word to count for something. If he asked them to make plans to deal with event *x*, they would do so. But Yeltsin's erratic and undisciplined behavior made that impossible.

During the coup attempt in August 1991, the military played a critical role, one that was far more important than Trudeau's use of CF in Quebec in 1970. Given their grievances against Gorbachev, one might have expected the military to line up against him. Initially, they refused to become involved as Russia and the Soviet Union had a long apolitical tradition in which the military stayed out of politics.[2] Also they were astounded at how inept and incompetent the coup plotters were.

Recognizing the military's desire for leadership, Yeltsin used his position as president of the new Russian state to issue an order placing the Soviet Army under his control. He immediately launched a purge. "Thirty generals from the high command, nine deputy ministers of defense, ten military district and fleet commanders, eight heads of major [Defense Ministry] departments, and three other lower-rank and 316 additional generals who actively supported and promoted the coup were retired."[3] A new generation of generals came to the fore; Yeltsin rebuilt the Army by putting officers loyal to him in positions of authority. He wanted a cadre of generals he could count on in a crisis, aware that if they owed their positions to him, they would likely support him in the event of domestic political problems.

General Yevgenni Shaposhnikov, an air force general who was defense minister, faced a daunting task: how to hold the army together while the country was falling apart? He understood only too well the dangers that accompany splits in the military. He was counting on the political leadership to help him maintain unity. Shaposhnikov soon gave up on Gorbachev. The latter seemed only concerned about Yeltsin, his bid for power, and the danger the military presented to his power. Besides, Gorbachev was president of a country that no longer existed. Yeltsin was constantly praising the army, and he gave the impression of being decisive and seemed to represent the future, not the past. The military soon went over to Yeltsin's side.

The generals were in for a shock, however. The country's senior military leadership soon decided that Yeltsin's only interest was to ensure the military's political support against potential domestic enemies. As far as a joint relationship culture was concerned, he was no more interested in their welfare than was Gorbachev.

Like his Canadian counterparts, Yeltsin was convinced that the Cold War was over and that the threat facing Russia had diminished. Who was going to attack Russia? Why worry about Russia as a superpower and the Russian military? Moscow's biggest problem was that it might collapse internally. The available scarce funds had to be spent on social and economic programs, not on the military. Yeltsin's goal was to keep the military off balance as he played one political card and then another. Russia had nuclear weapons, and as long as that was the case, no one would attack it.

Yeltsin decided that the best way to deal with the military was to leave it alone, a strange form of civil-military relations. If the generals wanted to continue to fight the Cold War, that was fine. But there were problems in letting the generals live in the past. The budget had been severely cut, but the generals resisted the chance to revise current military strategy in order to deal with this new fiscal reality. The generals understood the need for reform in theory, but not in practice.

The generals faced a new problem. On September 1, 1991, Shaposhnikov abolished the Main Political Administration. With that, the key officer in charge of dealing with disciplinary infractions, morale, and other personnel-related issues at the unit level was eliminated, and no other structure was created to deal with these issues. Junior officers were expected to handle such problems in their already overworked schedule.

Shaposhnikov and Yeltsin were running into difficulties. Shaposhnikov made it clear that he would not issue an order to use force against civilians. "I will never permit our Armed Forces to be used against its people either to settle inter-ethnic or political disputes."[4] Second, Shaposhnikov was conscious of the past. Gorbachev had issued the military orders to restore order in Tbilisi, Baku, and Vilnius, only to later deny he gave such orders. He then blamed the military for what had happened to the civilian population, As a consequence, much to Yeltsin's chagrin, Shaposhnikov informed him that in the future any orders involving the use of the military against civilians would have to be in writing. Like Donald Rumsfeld in the U.S., Yeltsin quickly and quietly removed the strong-willed Shaposhnikov in favor of a more pliant airborne officer, General Pavel Grachev. Yeltsin wanted a loyal officer, one who would carry out whatever orders Russia's president might give. On May 7, 1992, Yeltsin signed the orders that officially created the Russian Army.

Grachev inherited a mess. As one source put it, "The Air Defense had lost the majority of its bases and the army had lost most of its first line troops and weapons—up to 70 percent of its latest weapons, according to General Grachev."[5] Many of the units resembled "Swiss cheese because all of the holes there are after soldiers simply went back to their home countries in the Caucasus or Central Asia."[6] The army was unhappy and frustrated. Alexander Lebed, commander of the 14th Army in the so-called Trans-Dniester Republic, a secessionist enclave of Moldova, criticized the Yeltsin regime when he noted, "It's time to stop fooling around in the swamp of little-understood politics. . . . It is time to get to work; the interests of the people must be defended."[7]

THE MILITARY CONFRONTS PARLIAMENT

By early 1992, it was becoming obvious that a major power struggle was underway in Moscow. On the one side was the Duma or legislature, while Yeltsin, the president, was on the other. Which side was going to run the new Russian state? In October 1991, parliament had given Yeltsin the power to issue decrees that held the force of law, regardless of the legislature. However, on March 12, 1992, the legislature took back Yeltsin's power to issue such decrees. The situation between Yeltsin and the Duma continued to deteriorate, leading Ruslan Kasbulatov, the senior official in the legislature, to declare that Yeltsin should be impeached. Ultimately, a referendum was held to determine who Russians preferred, Yeltsin or parliament.

When the referendum was held, "58.7 percent expressed confidence in the president, and 53 percent supported his social and economic policies. Only 31.7 percent of the voters favored early presidential elections, while 43.1 percent of voters favored early parliamentary elections."[8] It was a victory for Yeltsin. He followed up on May 7 by stating that henceforth the vice president would not have any duties, effectively neutering him. Then on September 1, Yeltsin had him locked out of his office. Finally, on September 25, police and Interior Ministry troops moved into position to blockade the parliamentary building.

General Grachev was well aware that the military might be asked to intervene as the army was the only service that had heavy weapons such as tanks. He held a meeting with his deputies on September 20, and warned the generals of the impending political crisis. Grachev met with them again on September 22 and warned them to stay out of the conflict unless they received his written orders. He said, "The Army must be left in peace, outside politics. It guarantees Russia's security and will not meddle in questions of internal security up to the point where political passions cross into general confrontation. If the blood of innocent people is spilled, the Army will not remain neutral."[9]

Recognizing the importance of a military in crisis, Yeltsin followed up his promises of financial assistance to the armed forces with a statement that was published in *Krasnaya zvezda*: "Dear Soldiers of the Russian Armed Forces, My Sons!," it began. "I appeal to you at a critical moment for Russian statehood and our Fatherland." His message was simple: refuse to get involved in his battle with parliament. In the conclusion he observed, "Remember that the prevention of national collapse and civil war and the prospects for the revival of a great Russia depend on your firm, responsible position."[10] Only about "some forty or fifty active-duty personnel rallied to Parliament. Some two million did not."[11]

On October 3, the Duma arranged a large demonstration, and there were calls for a march on the Kremlin. Yeltsin thought the army had already begun to move into Moscow, but was told they had not. Furious, he went to the Ministry of Defense to discover that an emergency meeting of the Collegium of the Defense Ministry was already underway. Looking at the generals, it was clear that, "They obviously understood the awkwardness of the situation: the lawful government hung by a thread but the army couldn't defend it—some soldiers were picking potatoes and others didn't feel like fighting."[12] Grachev turned to Yeltsin and asked:

> "Boris Nikolayevich, are you giving me sanction to use tanks in Moscow? I looked at him in silence. At first he stared me right in the eye, then dropped his gaze." Chernomyrdin, unable to contain himself, turned to Grachev, "Pavel Sergeyevich, what are you saying now? You've been assigned to command an operation. Why should the president decide what precise means you require for it?"[13]

Grachev was determined to get Yeltsin to sign an order regarding the use of tanks. Yeltsin responded, "I'll send you a written order."[14]

Tanks began to move on the parliament building early the next morning. Shortly thereafter they began firing on the building. In short order, those occupying parliament surrendered to the police and security services. While they did not get directly involved in dealing with the prisoners, from a civil-military standpoint, the military had crossed the line. "No longer could it remain neutral in a time of intense political struggle. . . . A tradition had been broken and a precedent set."[15] Despite the action by the military, Grachev, who understood how to play politics at the highest level, warned his colleagues to stay out of politics. Barylski said, "Officers could not afford to ignore his warning that those who want to build successful military careers should not attempt to combine them with politics."[16] As the officers were being warned to stay out of politics, Yeltsin's new constitution, approved in December 1993, removed all parliamentary controls over the military. Yeltsin was now in charge.

THE ARMY FACES PROBLEMS

The military that the new Russian state inherited was chaotic. Yeltsin either did not recognize the depth of the problem or did not care. As far as leadership was concerned, from the military's standpoint, Yeltsin was what the military calls a "no-show." The situation inside the military was deteriorating. The group of Soviet forces in Germany was withdrawn from East Germany, and more often than not troops were dumped in Siberia, where the temperature was often was -30 degrees Fahrenheit. There were no accommodations for the soldiers, officers, or their families. Yeltsin permitted the military budget to collapse. In 1991 the official figures for the military budget stood at $324.5 billion. In 1992 it was down to $86.93 billion; in 1993 it was $74.1 billion; in 1994 it went down to $71.7 billion.[17] The military did not get what it was promised by Yeltsin: in 1993 the budgetary shortfall was one billion rubles, in 1994 it was 12.2 billion rubles.[18] What money the military did receive was primarily spent on personnel. To quote Grachev, "Our budget for 1994 was corrected in an attempt to tackle, first, the social problems of 120,000 homeless officers, thousands of people without jobs. This will consume 50 percent of our resources."[19]

The quality of the army's officer recruits was dropping to the danger point. For example, in 1989 there were 1.9 applicants per space in the officer schools. By 1993, the number had dropped to 1.35.[20] The quality of students was also declining. In 1987, 4.1 percent of students at military officer schools were expelled for failing to study; in 1993, that number rose to 13.4 percent.[21] More army personnel problems became evident: an August 1990 poll in the army revealed that "only 40 percent of officers regarded their jobs as satisfactory, and 24 percent wished to change their career."[22] The situation was so bad that a junior officer's family was living below the poverty line unless his wife was able to work.[23] Three years later, the situation among officers had worsened: "92 percent of officers polled 'had no faith in tomorrow,' 50 percent noted worsening living conditions, 35 percent mentioned an increased lack of social protections and saw no point in continuing to serve."[24]

Yeltsin made a half-hearted effort to address the problem on November 25, 1994, when he issued Decree No. 2113, permitting the Defense Ministry to annually recruit officers who graduated from civilian universities to serve for two years as reserve officers. Furthermore, in a throwback to World War II, a network of short courses to train junior officers was created. But the situation among officers continued to worsen. The MoD planned to downsize the officer corps by 36,000 during 1993, however, 59,163 quit voluntarily.[25] 1994 was even worse. The MoD's plan called for the discharge of 19,674 officers; 60,033 left on their own accord.[26] Thus, between 1992 and 1994, "over twice as many officers left the army than was forecast (155,000 compared to 71,000)." To make matters worse, more than half were under the age of 30, the young officers who would be critical in reforming the military. In an effort to improve the situation, on September 16, 1999, Yeltsin issued Decree 1237, reducing the number of years required for promotion to the next rank. Lieutenants and senior lieutenants were promoted in two years instead of three, and captains and majors could be promoted in three years instead of four.[27] However, the army continued to lose an average of 45,000 officers annually.[28]

There were also problems among enlisted personnel. Almost everyone wanted to avoid the draft, given the brutality of the process called *dedovshchina*, whereby those who had served longer brutally beat up, raped, and stole from junior conscripts. To quote one report from the Academy of Sciences, "For any man entering the Army, there was an 80 percent probability of his being beaten up (30 percent in a particularly savage or humiliating form), and a 5 percent chance of being the victim of a homosexual rape."[29] In 1992, draft avoidance had doubled over the previous year. In Moscow only 7 percent of those eligible were drafted. The manning level had dropped to 50 percent in some units. By October, some units had only 8 to 10 percent of their slots filled.[30] In addition to concerns about numbers, quality was also dropping. In 1994, Grachev said, "Last year 34,000 conscripts had a criminal record," Only 76 percent of those called up had completed secondary education. Faced with such opposition from the civilian world, the Yeltsin government agreed to cut conscript service from two years to eighteen months, even though most of the country's senior military leadership was opposed. They believed that eighteen months was not long enough to train and prepare soldiers to deal with modern weapons.

While the government cut the service time for draftees, it faced another problem—the shrinking draft pool, especially those healthy enough to serve in elite units. The high command decided to try to convince young men to stay in the military voluntarily after signing a contract. Called *kontraktniki* (contact soldiers), this program began on December 1, 1992. If the army could attract 100,000 individuals, the high command believed they would be able to offset the six-month reduction in time for draftees. In the beginning, the high command was optimistic. By April 1993, there were 45,000 troops serving on contract, and by June it was up to 110,000. Getting quality young men to enlist in a country with no tradition of a volunteer army was not easy. Besides, there were serious problems with the young men who were joining the service. In 1993 alone, 15.8 percent of the contracts were cancelled, first because of the poor quality of the recruits. Second, the *kontraktniki* were soon disillusioned. The pay was low, and their living conditions were not much different than those of a conscript. The military was unable to help given its low budget.[31]

If the armed forces faced only these problems, it could be called a crisis. However, the issues went deeper. Corruption and crime were rampant. In 1992 there were 3,923 reported thefts from weapons depots.[32] Yeltsin's public mention of the problem was a further indication of just how bad it had become. "The embezzlement of weapons and military hardware with a view to their resale has acquired menacing proportions."[33] Grachev stated that 459 men were dismissed for selling military weapons and equipment, while 3,711 had been disciplined, and criminal charges were leveled against 31.[34]

Other types of crime were also getting out of hand. According to one source, "the number of premeditated homicides increased (by 71.4 percent; 26 servicemen have already died), as well as rapes (up by 60 percent), and crimes associated with the acquisition, possession, and sale of narcotic substances (up by 80 percent)."[35] Discipline was also collapsing. In the Far East, several sailors starved to death because their superior officers forgot about them. There was also a report that a soldier on guard at a strategic missile site went berserk and killed several of his comrades.[36]

The most telling indicator regarding the collapse of the Russian military was the end of training exercises. They were almost nonexistent, and according to a senior officer, "For me to predict some kind of breakthrough in this area in the near future would be, at very least, unprofessional."[37] The lack of training was especially difficult for pilots. They were getting only 25 to 30 flight hours a year. In one case, a commander went out on a limb and ordered 26,000 tons of fuel oil on credit at a personal cost of 11 billion rubles.[38]

> The reality was that by 1994 the situation had seriously deteriorated to the point that troops' material provision has been cut by nearly 60 percent as a result of which approximately 70 percent of games and maneuvers had to be scrapped; combat flying practice had been reduced sharply from 100 to 120 hours to 30 to 35 hours a year; and only one to two divisions are deemed fully combat-ready in each military district, and one to two ships in each fleet.[39]

By this point, it was clear, both to Russian generals and Western observers, that the combat readiness of the Russian military had dropped precipitously. In 1992, the high command believed that over 70 percent of the army could not perform the "basic task of stopping a combat vehicle in its designated place."[40]

Yeltsin seemed unconcerned and any talk of a shared responsibility was nonsense. Yeltsin saw no need to work with the military in resolving national security issues.

The First War in Chechnya

Yelstin's refusal to take the military seriously was especially evident in the First War in Chechnya. Yeltsin seemed to think that all he had to do was to order this increasingly nondescript army into battle and all would be fine. However, Moscow's inept ground forces, supported by a weakened air force, would soon prove that the Kremlin's generals were right—the mighty Russian Army was in no position to fight a rag-tag military unit such as the Chechens fielded. Even his defense minister, General Grachev, was concerned and warned Yeltsin:

> Unless there is respect for the Army, unless the very approaches to its financing are changed, unless the armed forces are provided for without interruption, unless staffing by conscription is changed, unless social programs provide for them, and unless legislation is improved, there will be in the near future an irreversible loss of combat ability, a real disintegration of the army.[41]

Yeltsin was not listening. He did not care about military culture and the problems facing the army; his main concern was to remain in power.

The relationship between Chechnya and Moscow had never been good.

Stalin did not trust the Chechens and removed most of the Chechen population to Central Asia during World War II. Khrushchev eventually permitted them to return to their homeland, but the bitterness lingered. Thus it was no surprise that as the Soviet Union was collapsing, the Chechens proclaimed independence on September 1, 1991. Dzhokhar Dudayev became the country's first president.

Yeltsin quickly declared a state of emergency in Chechnya, warning Dudayev that he had three days to disarm. Dudayev ignored Yeltsin, so Yeltsin sent 600 Interior Ministry troops to Chechnya. These troops were seized by the Chechens when they landed in Grozny, Chechnya's capital. The idea that a part of Russia could unilaterally declare its independence—and in the process undermine Russian sovereignty—was unacceptable to Yeltsin. If Chechnya were permitted to succeed, it would only be a matter of time before other groups in this multiethnic country attempted the same thing.

A legitimate criticism of Yeltsin's and the high commands' thinking, is that they did not understand substate conflict. Most Russian officers saw World War II as the model, but they should have learned from their unhappy experience in Afghanistan that it presents a different kind of conflict. As one scholar noted, "Russian military thinking found it difficult to internalize forms of conflict involving irregular operations, especially those undertaken by sub-state military formations. It was easier to view irregular operations as an extension of state policy."[42]

Determined to bring Dudayev and his colleagues to "justice" the Security Council named Grachev to be the commander in chief of Russian forces in Chechnya. Grachev worked to defuse the conflict by negotiating with Dudayev. However, Yeltsin, was displeased at Grachev's efforts at private diplomacy. He stripped him of his Chechen portfolio, although he remained in command of Russian troops there. Despite Yeltsin's action, Grachev continued his policy in Chechnya.

Although he knew better, Grachev told Yeltsin that a military operation would be "a piece of cake; that he could take Grozny with a single airborne regiment in two hours." In fact, the majority of Russian battalions were only manned at 50 percent, and there was a serious problem with the quality of troops. Most officers would have agreed with the legendary military scholar General Makhmut Gareyev when he said, "It can be confidently said that if [World War II] hero Marshal Georgiy Zhukov had been the defense minister in 1994, the war in Chechnya would not have occurred. In any case, he would not have offered his assurances that execution of the mission in Chechnya would be a simple matter. The same applies to the day-to-day affairs of the Army and Navy."[43] Given the enormity of the problems, many officers thought that Grachev should have gone into Yeltsin's office and handed in his resignation.

INVADE CHECHNYA!

If ever there were a case of total incompetency in leading a military operation, it was the first invasion of Chechnya. Officers were standing guard duty because units were so understaffed. The only way Moscow could put units in the field was to pull them from all across Russia. Naval Infantry units from the Northern and Pacific Fleets, airborne units, troops from the Border Guards, some regular infantry, as well as reservists were called up from all over the country. This violated one of the cannons of military culture: soldiers who have not trained together should not be expected to fight together. General Eduard Vorobyev, deputy commander of ground forces, refused Grachev's order to take command of the troops about to invade Chechnya:

> When I heard about all these people, and met them personally, I decided the operation was not prepared. There were no reserves organized, which is the most important part of an operation. They had not considered weather conditions, the snow, rain, mud, and slush. The strength of these forces was based on aviation, which could not operate in such conditions; they could not work in the fog and they could not use their laser weapons. They could not drop bombs. Helicopters could not fly and could not provide the corresponding support.[44]

True to the dictates of military culture, Vorobyev resigned his commission rather than lead troops into battle in Chechnya. The commander of airborne forces was excluded from discussions, and a number of deputy defense ministers were forced to resign, because Grachev feared they would also oppose the action. In the end, a total "of 540 generals, officers and NCOs resigned rather than serve in the 1994–1996 Chechen War."[45] Yeltsin was unimpressed.

On the morning of December 11, 1994, 4,000 Russian troops advanced in three columns. The goal was to meet and seal off Grozny. The Chechens did not accommodate them. Snipers fired at the Russians, and roadblocks were set up to stop them. On December 21, Russian forces began storming Grozny, the heart of the rebellious republic. The Russians did not expect a fight. The first 4,000, plus another 2,000 Russian troops that entered Grozny were in for a surprise. The Chechens knew Grozny far better than the Russians. The Chechens would fire at the Russians and then quickly move to another location. The battle turned into a "turkey shoot" for the Chechens. They trapped Russian units in the street while destroying the armored vehicles that were not made for street fighting. According to a Chechen, "the Russians soldiers stayed in their armor, so we just stood on the balconies and dropped grenades on their vehicles as they drove by underneath. The Russians are cowards. They just can't come out of their shelter and fight us man-for-man. They know they are no match for us. That is why we beat them and why we will always beat them."[46] The battle was a disaster for Moscow and the Russian armed forces.

> According to an interview with a participant in the operation, the 131st Motorized Rife Brigade (MRBde) and the 81st Motorized Rifle Regiment (MRR) took the brunt of the losses. In one column alone 102 out of 120 armored personnel carriers and 20 out of 26 tanks were destroyed by Chechen anti-tank fire, and all six "Tunguska" surface-to-air missile systems were also destroyed. Seventy-four servicemen, including a corps' operations officer, were captured. The commander of a division surface-to-air missile platoon, LTC Aleksandr Lezenkom added that "they were not trained to fight in cities and an enormous amount of armored equipment, thoughtlessly left in narrow streets without any cover, was not protected by infantry. . . . There is a lack of even basic co-operation between different subunits and their commanders and subordinates."

Of all the generals who publicly attacked Grachev and Yeltsin over their actions in pushing the war in Chechnya the outspoken General Alexander Lebed was the most vociferous:

> The whole world has come to know the main Russian military secret. The reforms of the armed forces under the leadership of *the best defense minister of all times and peoples* has ended up with their complete collapse. It is terrible and bitter to understand Russia no longer has an army—what it has is only military formations and boy-soldiers which are hardly capable of handling anything.[47]

The military had strongly opposed the operation in Chechnya, to the extent that one report at the beginning of January 1995 said, "the Russian Army was on the verge of refusing to obey the ridiculous orders of its commanders and government."[48]

Despite having ignored the generals' warnings that the invasion of Chechnya would be a disaster, Yeltsin blamed the army for its problems in Chechnya. On February 16, 1995, he criticized the military in his annual address to the Duma, calling its performance "unsatisfactory." Then on February 23, he criticized it again claiming, "The army is slowly beginning to get out of hand—

the conflict in Chechnya convinced us once more that we are late with reform of the army."[49] This was an open violation of military culture—"commend in public, criticize in private."

There was support in the upper echelons of the military for reform. The problem, however, was that given the conservative nature of the Russian military, the reformers needed Yeltsin's support. The need for reform predated the events in Chechnya, something Yeltsin should have understood or as Colonel General Igor Rodionov, at that time head of the General Staff Academy, put it, "It ought to be well understood by all those on whom the future defense of the country and its armed forces of the twenty-first century depend."[50]

Yeltsin continued to speak in contradictions. On June 28, 1995, speaking at a graduation ceremony, he stated, "A lack of resources was partly to blame for the slow pace of military reform, but it should get moving." He also claimed that he would put a stop to the fall in the military budget. "In the 1996 budget we have laid down the principle that the allocation of resources for national defense must be preserved at the level of 1995."[51] The reality, however, was that the size of the budget fell. Where it was $46.6 billion in 1995, in 1996 it was $42.1.[52] This came at a time when the military needed 715 billion rubles for food alone, a situation that was forcing it to go into its wartime food reserves. By the beginning of 1996, 90 percent of those reserves had been eaten.[53] Yeltsin's reputation among the troops dropped to rock bottom as Timothy Thomas noted,

> Some 3,000 servicemen stationed in Novosibirsk were surveyed and asked what quality a Russian president must possess. Some 81 percent said he must have the ability to impose order on the country. For servicemen, this also includes an army properly financed, one with a proper manpower level, one outfitted with new types of weapons and military hardware, and one that did not get into situations such as Chechnya.[54]

Yeltsin and the 1996 Election

Yeltsin had a dismal approval rating of 5 percent as he approached the 1996 election.[55] Once again he turned against the military in an effort to explain away some of his problems. In a speech on February 1996, he accused the military of failing to reward professional competence and told the generals and admirals that he was planning to increase political control. The purpose was to demonstrate that Yeltsin was the one who was moving the country forward in the face of a conservative military that would not change with the times and was refusing to reward meritocracy. Grachev was told to turn members of the military into strong supporters—and voters—for Yeltsin, even if such an act went against the constitution. Since the constitution called for a secret vote, how was Grachev or any other senior officer to know how a soldier voted? This was a clear violation of military culture. Even Grachev understood that Yeltsin's policy toward the military was not working. He was also well aware that the patience of many in uniform was wearing thin. As he warned, "It is not wise to keep testing the military's patience and push it to the breaking point."[56]

But Yeltsin wanted to retain control over the military. The soldiers seemed to be docile, but one could never tell. On April 24, 1996, he convinced the Duma to pass a bill that would modify the relationship between the Ministry of Defense and the General Staff. Fearing a possible move by the military against him, Yeltsin changed the relationship. To further raise Yeltsin's suspicions, Interior Minister General Anatolii Kulikov had "expressed doubt about the ability to guarantee the loyalty of troops in case street clashes broke out."[57] Under this bill, "The Duma had no role whatsoever in the review of military appointments, the definition of national defense policy, or the use of military force at home or abroad."[58] There was no doubt in anyone's mind for whom the military worked—Boris Yeltsin.

Yeltsin was always prepared to use the military for his own purposes. For example, almost no one in Russia liked the draft. Yeltsin issued Decree No. 722, ordering the Ministry of Defense to end conscription by 2000. No one in the military seriously believed that he would do it. As General Lebed noted, "It is a purely populist decree and nothing will be achieved."[59] General Rodionov, who became Grachev's successor, called it "dangerous and irresponsible electioneering rhetoric that at best would never really be implemented and at worst could cause the final downfall of the Russian army."[60] Yeltsin's order appealed to many civilians, especially those who wanted to avoid military service. It also made it more difficult to recruit young men. Why not avoid the draft until 2000, when it would go away?

To the surprise of many, Yeltsin won the first round of the election, although he did not win the election outright. In accordance with the Russian constitution, a run-off election had to be held, and Yeltsin was worried. What if the other three candidates united against him (the Communist Gennadi Zyuganov, the nationalist Vladimir Zhirinovski, and the former General Alexader Lebed)? Given his lack of popularity, he would never win such an election, especially if the final candidate were the charismatic Lebed. Yeltsin made overtures to Lebed, whom everyone knew was very ambitious. Lebed's response was positive, especially when he was offered the position of presidential national security advisor and secretary of the Security Council. Yeltsin's health was a problem, and Lebed could position himself to become Yeltsin's successor.

Lebed and Grachev did not get along, even though both had come from the airborne troops. Lebed, in particular, disliked Grachev, with whom he had served previously. He believed Grachev was unqualified to be defense minister and convinced Yeltsin to fire him. For many in the military, it was a relief. Grachev was so disliked that his continued presence as defense minister would have become an election issue. Yeltsin appointed General Igor Rodionov to replace Grachev. He also fired a number of Grachev's deputies. Yeltsin's strategy of appealing to the military helped him, as he won the run-off election with 53.82 percent of the vote.

Despite Lebed's entrance into the political arena, his actions did not represent the armed forces. There were numerous areas where he and the General Staff and the Ministry of Defense did not see eye to eye. Thus, the armed forces remained outside of politics.

YELTSIN AND THE GENERAL STAFF

Despite the military's record of staying out of politics, Yeltsin worried that some general would try to grab power. With this in mind, Yeltsin held a meeting on January 11, 1995, that was attended by Prime Minister Chernomyrdin and the heads of both chambers of the Federal Assembly. To deal with the possibility that the military might get out of line, he introduced a new structural modification. Instead of the General Staff working for the Minister of Defense as is normal in most militaries, Yeltsin decided to create two parallel institutions, both reporting to him. The military was well aware what Yeltsin had in mind General Rodionov said:

> The assertion is made that in attaching the General Staff directly to himself, the President will be able to neutralize it, and, if necessary, forcibly suppress any external or internal threats to the security of the current political regime.

Rodionov recognized that this action would weaken command and control throughout the army, a critical component of military culture. Rodionov asked the rhetorical question, "How long will this change last?" What about the future of the military? What if it so weakened command and control that the military's combat effectiveness collapsed? In essence, Rodionov complained, this meant that in many cases, the generals will only learn about key decisions from the newspapers.

> Pulling the General Staff out of the Defense Ministry will immediately cause the creation of a different administrative structure, since not a single ministry, as practice has shown, can get by without them. Will the Defense Ministry in its new form really correspond to its name better than now?[61]

It was not only Rodionov who was concerned about the possible change in structure. General Makhmut Gareyev made the same points:

> In countries where there is no developed civil society, the direct subordination of military departments to the president, as the supreme commander-in-chief, results in a situation where the army turns out to be in a special position, outside of civil and parliamentary control, and often all relations between the minister of defense and the head of state, or party, are built on principles of personal loyalty, which is not only dangerous in the political sense, but harms the army, for, as much as any organization that is hidden from the light of day and the public eye, it begins to decay without noticing or covering up its flaws.[62]

Yeltsin ignored the military warning about the impact of his latest idea on military readiness and went ahead with his plan. His reasoning was simple. The danger of an external conflict was close to zero in the aftermath of the end of Cold War, but who knew what the military might do in a domestic crisis, especially considering his numerous violations of military culture?

Article 13, paragraph 2, of the 1996 Law on Defense stated, "Oversight of the Armed Forces of the Russian Federation is carried out by the Defense Minister via the Defense Ministry and the General Staff of the Armed Forces, which is the main body of operational supervision for the Armed Forces."[63] This change in supervision created confusion and had the effect of setting one official against the other. The Defense Minster would issue an order, and the chief of the general staff would ignore it. After all, he really worked for the president and besides, the minister's orders were general statements. It was up to the general staff to implement it, and the generals could interpret (and modify) the minister's orders however they wished. Instead of the clear chain of command that goes to the heart of military culture, Moscow would have a split command with all of the problems that entailed.

MORALE IN THE ARMY

Morale continued to plummet among the military rank and file, given the conditions and the way they were being treated. In December 1994, Deputy Minister Valeri Mironov commented, "Nihilism, lack of spirituality, and moral degradation have reached an extreme point that poses a danger to both the army and navy combat readiness and security of society and the state."[64]

With the drop in budget, the military was soon short of just about everything, including items from food to fuel to fly planes or drive tanks. Ships were tied up for lack of fuel and the supplies necessary to sustain a crew. Civilian society was aware of the problems in the military, resulting in a drop in their ability to attract and retain junior officers. In 1995, over 50 percent of students at officer schools left prior to commissioning.[65] "By 1995, the Russian army was reportedly facing a shortfall of officers as high as 25 percent with the greatest problems at junior officer levels where the shortfall was as high as 45 percent."[66] The next year, 50 percent of all junior officers left as soon as their obligated service time was up.[67]

Senior officers also left the service. In a 1995 survey of officers at the Gagarin and Zhukovski Academies (usually at the major or lieutenant colonel level), "Eighty percent . . . were pessimistic about the future, and 87 percent were disturbed about the decline in the prestige in military service. 40 percent wanted to resign and only 3 percent expressed a desire to continue service."[68] There were even questions concerning the political reliability of field grade officers in case of internal instability.[69]

Housing seemed to be an unsolvable problem in the post-Soviet military. Hundreds of thousands of officers had been moved almost overnight from Eastern Europe, and there wasn't housing available for them in Russia. In 1994, 180,000 officers were without apartments.[70] Inflation ate at the pay raises officers received every six months. Pay was almost always late, and it was not unusual for pay to be months behind. In 1996, there was a report that "80 percent of all officers had gone without pay for five months or more."[71] This led a number of officers to take on additional jobs, often as cab drivers, even though military regulations forbade such actions. Consider the following comment that moonlighting

> is winked at by senior officers; indeed, according to *Red Star* (*Krasnaya zvezda*), commanders now often organize job opportunities "on the side" for their officers. A good posting is one that offers the best outside job opportunities, for example, the military academies in Moscow. The majority of officers are forced to take demeaning manual jobs, and because their work is illegal they cannot complain about pay.[72]

The Ministry of Defense argued for a 208 percent increase in military pay, while the Ministry of Finance only offered a 25 percent increase. Morale dropped. From the perspective of officers in the military, the outside world did not care about them. "Society has withdrawn the respect and prestige they normally accord to officers, and junior officers are resigning in droves. Older officers are being forced into premature retirements."[73] There was very little attraction for a military career—a war in Chechnya, no pay, no housing, no respect. In the eyes of many officers—and a good part of the public as well—officers would have to be either too dumb or too lazy to work in the civilian economy.

Faced with the downturn in military morale, the Duma did the only thing it could to retain numbers. It lengthened conscription time to twenty-four months retroactive for those drafted, starting in 1993–1994. Students were also subject to conscription, making it necessary for college students to spend one year on active duty, regardless of whether or not they had taken reserve officer training courses.[74] Unlike Germany, in Russia draft evasion was a major problem. There were two draft pools a year, spring and fall. In spring 1996, there were 26,000 draft evasions, in spring 1997 there were 32,000, and in autumn of 1997 there were 40,000. What infuriated the army was that of the 66,000 draft evaders, only 110 were prosecuted. Yeltsin had closed his eyes to the problem, much to the bitterness of the generals.[75]

The food situation also worsened. By 1995, the army was out of food. "By winter many garrisons in the North could simply starve—but [the generals] were told to borrow some money from local banks."[76] But the generals' credit standing was poor and the situation grew so serious that in the latter part of 1995 twenty soldiers died of malnutrition.[77]

Food was rationed and war reserves were utilized. One of the strongest statements came the following year, "The soldier does not have enough to eat. He is hungry. And it is painful to see young guys in uniform begging in the streets."[78] Soldiers in the three other armies covered in this book never reached this point of abject starvation: deprived perhaps, but not denied the basics of life. These conditions in the Russian army resulted in 3,000 soldiers deserting from January to June 1995.[79]

The Russian military remained beset by a problem only occasionally found in other militaries. That was the so-called *dedovshchina* ("brutalization of recruits"). By the mid-1990s the situation had deteriorated to the point that one observer noted, "The atmosphere reigning in army barracks can easily be compared to the microclimate in correctional labor camps."[80] The situation was no better among the *kontraktniki* ("contract soldiers"). Between 1993 and 1995 "about 50,000 contract servicemen resigned."[81] They quit for many reasons. Some could not meet the Army's physical and mental standards. Living accommodations remained below what the army had promised. Most important was salary: in September 1995, the average Russian salary was 550,000 rubles, almost twice the average salary for a contract servicemen of 278,000 rubles (including supplements), and below the subsistence wage in Russia of 300,000 rubles (excluding the big cities).[82] Some men not only faced the reality of living like a recruit, they faced the reality of being sent to Chechnya.

Crime and corruption were also major problems. By the end of 1994, one source noted, "in recent years the number of thefts [of arms] has increased by a factor of 25. While in 1987–1988, a little more than 100 items were stolen, now this is thousands of gun barrels, including not just pistols and rifles but machine guns, grenade launchers, portable surface-to-air-missiles, air-to-air missiles, and armored fighting vehicles."[83] By 1995 it was reported that, while the overall crime rate in Russia had risen by 5.6 percent, in the military it was up by 30 percent.[84] The situation had deteriorated to the point that the military prosecutor called on Yeltsin to establish military police, as exist in Germany, Canada, and the U.S. To quote one noted specialist, "given the growing levels of random and organized criminality in the Russian military—and the corruption at all branches, and services—the creation of an effective military police force or other political entity is clearly critical for creating a cohesive military institution."[85]

Corruption also permeated the military commissariats where young men registered for and reported for the draft. Alexandr Golts noted that the payment of bribes to members of the commissariats and to physicians was so out of control that it involved 87 percent of the youth and that "It is an industry with the turnover of tens of billions of dollars."[86]

Combat readiness in the Russian military continued downhill, even in the Strategic Rocket Forces, one of the elite branches. As one commentator reported, "The command posts and control centers were in worse shape than the missiles."[87] In 1993, only 20 percent of all tanks were usable, and "the supply of combat aircraft had fallen twenty times." By 1995, they were down 90 percent in comparison with 1991.[88] Pilots spent most of their time sweeping runways and some them were reassigned to other branches—it made no sense for them to remain around planes if there were none to fly.

Even if there had been money for training and exercises, Russian equipment and weapons or the lack of them presented a major problem. For example, in 1991 the air force purchased 585 aircraft, but in 1993 it bought only two.[89] During the same year, the army received only twelve new battle tanks, whereas it should have received 300, just to keep its armor at its current level.[90] How was the Russian army to proceed without new weapons? The best-trained soldiers in the world cannot stand up to their enemies if their weapons systems are inferior. From the military's standpoint the current situation was disastrous, and it was getting worse.

Igor Rodionov, Defense Minister (1996–1997)

Yeltsin appointed General Igor Rodionov to be defense minister on July 17, 1996. Lebed and other military officers thought highly of him. To quote one General Staff officer, "It was the best possible decision. . . . He enjoys deep respect both among the troops and in the central apparatus of the Ministry of Defense."[91] Rodionov's name was well known as the commander of Soviet troops during the massacre in Tbilisi under Gorbachev. The Sobchak Commission was established to investigate these events and found him responsible for the brutal loss of life that took place. It would have been hard to find many in the military who accepted this verdict. To them he was a scapegoat for Gorbachev's sins. Rodionov was also remembered for standing up to Yeltsin, criticizing him for not making military reform a priority. To quote Rodionov, "If military reform is now at an impasse and the Armed Forces per se [i.e., the army and navy] have been reduced to a desperate state, this is primarily the fault of the country's political leadership, which has completely removed itself from the management of military reform."[92] From Rodionov's point of view, Yeltsin's improvisation strategy when dealing with the army was a disaster.

As head of the General Staff Academy, Rodionov tended to look at problems from an intellectual standpoint. He was enough of a politician to stand up to Yeltsin. He also had an analytical mind, and he tended to look for logical answers. He believed that nothing would improve in the military until and unless the country came up with a realistic plan to deal with its many problems.

Rodionov was different from many Russian officers who regarded the military as a closed world. They thought civilians knew nothing about the techniques of fighting and winning wars, and that they should be kept out of military matters. Rodionov, however, believed that civilians should be welcomed. The famous German theoretician Karl von Clausewitz was right when he observed that war is "a continuation of politics by other means." What better way to ensure the military was moving in the right direction than by listening to senior civilian officials. The military might not like what it heard, but political factors were becoming an increasingly important part of warfare. A failure on the part of civilians to understand operational and tactical issues would guarantee that they would try to interfere in such matters. Mutual understanding was critical. Rodionov had even suggested that the General Staff Academy should be transformed into an Academy of National Security and Defense. The goal would be similar to the war colleges in the U.S., which were created to train military officers and civilian officials together, to give them an opportunity to interact and learn the other person's point of view, while studying national security affairs. He believed in shared responsibility and was prepared to meet Yeltsin half way.

Another area that set Rodionov apart from most of his colleagues was his support for a professional cadre of noncommissioned officers (NCOs). He noted the Western experience, where NCOs played a major role in training and attending to the enlisted personnel. This left the officer corps free to focus on other problems. He was convinced that the key to a professional military would be the development of NCOs. Unless and until the Russian Army had such a military, it would never be up to Western standards. The introduction of NCOs would help eliminate the brutal tradition of *dedovshchina*. Without senior professional enlisted personnel around conscripts, the hazing would continue.

Budgetary issues were also a problem. The Russian army was massive and difficult to control. Given the way it was structured, the only way it could win a war would be by the use of mass. A military that was smaller, but armed with high tech weapons would be both more mobile and more lethal. As Rodionov noted, "It is essential to increase the number of fully manned, combat-ready large units by sharply reducing the number of military formations of reduced strength."[93] His first accomplishment was to convince Yeltsin to postpone the end of the draft planned for 2000 to 2005. This provided the military with breathing space so it could plan for such a contingency.

Rodionov was a person of high moral standards. He even believed in God, which set him apart from most of his colleagues.[94] He also supported the appointment of a civilian defense minister, a change advocated for years. The military, however, was opposed. The Soviet Union had always had a military defense minister. Andrei Kokoshin of the Institute for the Study of the USA and Canada had long been a proponent of such a plan. If nothing else, Yeltsin was a politician, and he did not want to alienate the armed forces. So to satisfy both sides of the debate, Rodionov retired from the army on December 11 and became Russia's first "civilian" defense minister.

As the head of the General Staff Academy, Rodionov had been thinking about military reform for some time. In contrast to Grachev's simplistic ideas, Rodionov's proposals were thought through and straightforward. For example, Rodionov argued that there was a difference between military reform and reforming the armed services. As he put it, "Military reform is the process of bringing the entire defense activity of the state into conformity with the new political, economic and social changes in society."[95] Rodionov's idea was to make fundamental changes, but carrying out such reforms required political support, because it would impact Russian society.

Militarily, it meant changes in military doctrine, the document that controls everything: training, weapons, personnel, strategy, operations, and tactics. Toward this end, Rodionov suggested the creation of a new structure—a Defense Council. "This new body was given a mandate to gather information from all the actors involved, and to draw proposals concerning the future tasks of the Armed Forces, as well as the other troops."[96]

Rodionov was also out in front of most of his colleagues by calling on the Russian army to prepare for "low-density" conflicts, such as the First Chechen War. Primary attention in most military institutions continued to be on the deployment of mass armies, reminiscent of World War II. He was also against the idea of using nuclear weapons. "The first blow could be devastating. The task was to absorb the first attack, to make it possible for the country to move from peacetime conditions to wartime conditions. For this reason the main task for [the] military organization of society was the presence of ready reserves."[97] Rodionov saw military reform as a part of a larger process involving society as a whole. Rodionov's approach was expensive, and the military continued to face a major financial crisis. When he became defense minister, the military's debts accounted to almost 30 percent of its operating budget.[98] The situation was so bad that civilian power companies had turned off power to many military installations because they failed to pay their bills.

Yeltsin jumped on Rodionov's idea of a Defense Council, believing he could control it and that it would become a political counterweight to the Security Council, headed by Lebed. The new Defense Council was created on July 25, 1996. Yeltsin wasn't taking any chances and put a civilian, Yuri Baturin, his national security affairs assistant in charge. In the typical Yeltsin fashion of turning one policy maker against another, Rodionov would spend the ten months of his time as defense minister arguing with Baturin.

Rodionov's problem with Baturin was simple. He considered the latter to be ignorant when it came to military affairs. But Baturin's ignorance did not stop him from violating military culture by interfering in the military reform process, making one ill-informed proposal after another. In February 1997, Rodionov accused Baturin of "conducting a misinformation campaign about the state of affairs in the armed forces." He even called on Yeltsin to dismiss Baturin.[99] Rodionov also believed that Moscow had to cut back on the size of Russian forces, and he was aware that would be expensive. If an officer was let go, he had to be paid a separation allowance and provided housing. In addition, new weapons systems had to be purchased and new organizations had to be created while the costs of operations and maintenance of weapons and equipment still had to be met. Rodionov refused to accept Baturin's argument that money was not critical for military reform. As he noted, "When I am told that reform can be implemented without financing, without money, this is pure demagogy."[100] Neither side was interested in shared responsibility.

Yeltsin told Baturin to convince the military to cut back on spending—the country was going broke. At one point, he argued that the budget should be cut by up to 30 percent.[101] As a consequence, until Rodionov was fired in May 1997, a virtual Cold War existed between him and Baturin. It continued to be the opposite of a shared relationship. Yeltsin sided with Baturin if the issue was the budget. Baturin was replaced in August 1997 by a civilian, First Deputy Minister Andrei Kokoshin.

LEBED IS FIRED

The ambitious Lebed was not happy about Yeltsin's decision to create the Defense Council, believing accurately that it was intended to undercut his position as head of the Security Council. He tried to use the situation in Chechnya to strengthen his position. In an effort to embarrass Yeltsin, Chechen forces had attacked Russian forces in Grozny just prior to his second inauguration. On August 10, 1997, Yeltsin went along with Lebed and appointed him to be Moscow's representative to Chechnya.

In short order, Lebed did what no other member of Yeltsin's administration could. On August 31, he signed a power-sharing agreement with Chechen leader Aslan Maskhadov. The agreement "covered withdrawal of federal troops, deferred the definition of Chechnya's status for five years, and called for a unified commission to supervise implementation of the agreement."[102] Lebed noted, "There are no victors in this war."[103] The agreement made Lebed an instant hero, and that upset Yeltsin. Lebed could become a political danger, something Yeltsin was determined to avoid.

Lebed was ordered to avoid the public spotlight. Given his lust for public attention, the chances of him doing so were slim, and he told that to Yeltsin.

He continued to fight with General Anatolii Kulikov from the Interior Ministry. Lebed wanted to take control of that institution. The conflict between the two generals became increasingly public, creating an impossible situation. As Yeltsin observed, "when generals fight each other, civilians as well as law and order can suffer."[104] The bottom line was simple. Yeltsin was determined to pick his own successor; he was not about to allow this upstart general take the prize for himself. So on October 17, Yeltsin fired Lebed. That was the end of the colorful general's political career in Moscow. He had overestimated his power. With Lebed out of the way, Yeltsin disbanded the Defense Council the following March.

RODIONOV PUTS THE RUSSIAN MILITARY BACK TOGETHER

When Rodionov became defense minister, he was convinced he had to change emphasis, from Grachev's glorification of the airborne units (VSV) to greater emphasis on combined arms operations. Russia could not meet every potential threat by just relying on its admittedly elite airborne forces. Rodionov's primary problem was political leadership. Like other senior military officers, Rodionov accepted civilian leadership. And that was exactly what he was trying to obtain—leadership from the Yeltsin administration.

Yeltsin remained unpredictable. His health was poor, and no one ever knew if he would survive the next week, month, or year. Yeltsin's drinking problems were common knowledge in Moscow, and he was often incapacitated because of too much reliance on vodka. The failing economy created another problem. The generals needed money to modernize and reform the Russian army. Finally, there was the problem of the generals' own making—their extreme conservatism, which translated into a desire to keep the World War II mass army—the multimillion-man-strong Soviet-type army, ready to repulse a supposed invasion by NATO.

In May 1996, Yeltsin ordered the Security Council to come up with a new national security concept, which was required before the military could draw up a military doctrine statement. The draft was complete in May 1997. At first glance, the document appeared to provide the necessary guidance. However, it was too vague. The Russian General Staff was looking for specific guidance, not hortatory political statements.

Lacking specific guidance, Rodionov decided to cut the size of the armed forces from 1.5 million to 1.2 million. Conventional forces including the airborne would have to be downsized. Most of the country's generals were opposed. Ground Forces Commander Vladimir Semenov commented, "As a person versed in these affairs I know that an early reduction of the armed forces to this figure will lead to the collapse of the reforms."[105] Rodionov's goal was to set up at least one combat-ready division in each of the military districts. "In the Moscow District, for example, a new division, the 3rd Motor Rifle Division, was created in 1997 from elements of two under-strength divisions which were originally part of the Western Group of Forces."[106]

Despite their many problems, the generals were encouraged when Yeltsin appeared to give in on the funding issue. In October, he ordered Prime Minister Viktor Chernomyrdin to create a special commission to analyze armed forces funding. Yeltsin's main concern was the constant need to come up with back pay for the officers, many of whom still had to wait four or five months for their back pay. For many, that was their only source of income. Rodionov asked for more. But with Lebed gone, Yeltsin struck back, violating military culture: on national TV, he blamed Rodionov and his deputy General Viktor Samsonov for the army's failure to reform. "I am not simply dissatisfied. I am indignant over the state of reforms in the army and the general state of the armed forces. . . . The soldier is losing weight while the general is getting fatter."[107] Yeltsin had openly violated one of tenets of military culture, "praise in public, criticize in private," and in so doing, humiliated his defense minister, who had not disobeyed Yeltsin, but had the audacity to defend the military in the face of the president's refusal to provide even minimal support. Civil-military relations were about as far away from shared responsibility as one could imagine.

GENERAL LEV ROKHLIN'S OUTBURST (1996–1997)

If there was any senior officer who was bold enough to openly call for Yeltsin's ouster it was retired Lieutenant General Lev Rokhlin, a hero from the war in Afghanistan as well as the attack on Grozny during the First Chechen War. He soon found himself a member of the Duma. His primary goal was to improve the situation inside the armed forces. Given his military background, Yeltsin's public attack on Rodionov and Samsonov infuriated him. He was even more incensed by Yeltsin's decision to cut the 1997 military budget by 20 percent. "This amount would not even cover the cost of six months of the salaries and benefits mandated by Russian law."[108] As far as Rokhlin was concerned, the Russian military had reached the point that it was no longer able to function as a viable military force. In December 1996, he made a speech openly criticizing the civilian leadership for failing to understand the need for military reform and failing to provide the necessary financial guarantees.[109]

He wrote a letter to Yeltsin accusing him of attempting to destroy the military, stating, "If this happened to the army of a well-to-do country, there would have been a military coup long ago."[110] He attacked Yeltsin in front of serving military personnel, sending out 900 copies of a letter to top military officers protesting the government's failure to properly fund the military.

In his effort to weaken Yeltsin, on July 9, 1997, Rokhlin founded a new organization, the All-Russia Movement for Support of the Army. Its purpose was to defend the military from Yeltsin's arbitrary actions. Shortly thereafter, he called upon Yeltsin to resign. The military had always tended to be apolitical, but in this case, there was concern among civilians that the military was coming perilously close to direct involvement in the political process. However, most of the organization's members were retired officers, and in any case, the defense minister quickly denounced its actions. This was the closest the Russian military came to taking action against Yeltsin. There was little doubt that most officers were fed up with him.[111] Civil-military relations worsened and the idea of a shared responsibility became even more unlikely.

Igor Sergeyev, Defense Minister (1997–2001)

Army General Igor Sergeyev became defense minister on May 22, 1997. Unlike Moscow's other senior defense official, Sergeyev came from the Strategic Rocket Forces (SRF). After his fight with Lebed, Yeltsin wanted a defense minister who would avoid the limelight and do what he was told. Sergeyev was perfect: he could be counted upon to argue and indeed fight with the outspoken chief of general staff, Army General Anatoli Kvashnin, just what Yeltsin wanted.

Yeltsin decided to cut the military budget from 5 percent of Gross Domestic Product (GDP) to 3.5 percent.[112] Given the extent to which Yeltsin had ignored military pleas for money during the past six years, Sergeyev felt he had no alternative but to introduce major cuts. He focused on conventional forces, an action that quickly drew Kvashnin's ire. With this in mind, he eliminated the Ground Forces High Command, the structure that many had long considered the heart of Russia's military. Kvashnin and his colleagues were angry. "Its functions were distributed among a dozen or more General Staff directorates, and the senior ground forces officer was now just head of the General Staff's main directorate of the ground forces. In theory this implied that the ground forces were no longer an independent branch of the armed forces ranking with the air force or navy."[113] Sergeyev went even further, ordering the ground forces to repair vehicles and equipment damaged in Chechnya out of their own budget. What money was available went to strengthening the SRF, which, as far as Sergeyev was concerned, was the heart of Moscow's deterrent.

Sergeyev cut numerous slots in the Ministry of Defense, and even cut the number of active duty generals from 1,700 to 1,298.[114] He reduced the number of military districts from eight to six (as of January 1, 1999, the Siberian and Trans-Baikal districts would be merged, and in 2001 the Volga and Urals districts would be combined). Military districts were given the status of Operational Strategic Commands, and the military district commander took over command of all the forces in his area of responsibility. This meant a shift in authority from Moscow to the field. He cut the size of the military by 500,000 to 1.2 million,[115] and shifted funds to support the less expensive nuclear forces, an action that Yeltsin surely welcomed. But Sergeyev's favoritism of nuclear forces put him and Yeltsin in direct conflict with Kvashnin and his conventional forces. Because of Yeltsin's change in the relationship between the MoD and the General Staff, Kvashnin reported directly to the president.

Few officers favored Sergeyev's approach. Why should they place all their bets on the nuclear forces? Terrorism appeared to be the major threat to Russia, and nuclear weapons would not help fight that threat.

THE OIL CRISIS

In 1998, the world's oil prices collapsed, and by May, Russia was facing a financial crisis. Stock prices dropped 10 percent on May 20, 1998. "Between October 1997 and July 1998, the Russian market lost more than 60 percent of its value."[116] The country's economy was in serious trouble. The International Monetary Fund (IMF) provided the Kremlin with a loan, but only after the United States exerted considerable pressure. The loan did not solve the problem, and by July there were rumors of social unrest. On August 10, Russian stocks dropped precipitously. On August 17, the "government announced a dramatically new approach to currency policy. The key components were a ruble exchange rate fluctuating with the new limits of the 'currency corridor.' "[117] The result was a 50 percent devaluation of the ruble. Despite rumors in Moscow that the military was planning a coup, the soldiers remained in their barracks.

From the military's standpoint, the most damaging effect of the economic collapse was that it undercut Sergeyev's efforts to reform the military. In 1998, 2.97 percent of GDP was allocated to the military, in 1999 it was down to 2.34 percent, and in 2000 it was only 2.63 percent.[118] Sergeyev commented, "To draw up a budget like Mozambique but demand forces like the United States is not entirely logical." To make matters worse, the military received only 55 percent of what it was promised in 1998.[119]

Sergeyev continued to publicly lament the lack of money for the military. On September 28, he stated that the situation in Russia was so bad that the army could not expect to "increase spending to the point needed to reequip the military until 2006."[120] Taylor noted the problems facing Sergeyev and the military when he observed that, "Russian defense spending declined from 142 billion dollars in 1992 to four billion in 1999, a ninety-eight percent decrease!"[121]

Sergeyev was not better at creating a joint relationship than his predecessors. Such a situation under Yeltsin was simply not possible.

CHECHNYA, AGAIN

By mid-1999, Chechnya had deteriorated to the point of anarchy. "It was estimated that as many as 1,300 people lost their lives in Chechnya between 1997 and 1999, and many thousands more fled the republic."[122] Kidnaping became a way of life. After the Russians killed Chechen President Dzhokhar Dudayev with a missile in 1998, chaos reigned throughout the republic. In time, the radical Islamic sect called Wahhabism began to creep into the region, a situation that raised alarm bells in Moscow. In August 1999, Chechen extremists led by Shamil Basayev and Emir al Khattab, invaded Dagestan, which borders Chechnya. Their troops occupied a number of Wahhabist villages. They were hoping to enlist locals for their army, but that did not happen. Murphy, describing the Russian response, said, "Thus Basayev and Khattab not only precipitated an act of war on Russia by invading Dagestan, but their new Islamic organization officially and publicly declared war on both Dagestan and Russia."[123] The Kremlin had no alternative but to respond.

Vladimir Putin as Prime Minister (1999–2000)

On August 10, Yeltsin ordered his newly appointed Prime Minister Vladimir Putin to "impose order and discipline," in the region.[124] In time, Russian troops were able to restore Moscow's authority in Dagestan as the rebels retreated into Chechnya. The Russian forces did a better job in the Second Chechen War than in the first. However, there was still a problem with cohesion in many units, and all too often the soldiers did not know the name of the person next to them until they were on their way into battle. In addition, many of the conscripts did not know how to utilize equipment or weapons.

Putin made good use of Yeltsin's decision to put him in charge of operations, and declared that he accepted personal responsibility for events in Chechnya. Putin's acceptance of accountability was important to senior military officers who worried that they would again be made scapegoats for the politicians. Then Putin flew to Grozny in a jet fighter, to emphasize his connection to the war.[125] He also promised to crush the Chechen "scum" and to restore law and order in Chechnya. He said that, "Russian forces will *be following terrorists everywhere. If we catch them in a toilet, then we will bury them in their own crap*."[126] Putin's handing of the Second Chechen War improved his standing in the public opinion polls.[127] As another observer noted:

> Another factor, perhaps the most important one for the success of the invasion was the resolve and direction demonstrated by the political leadership in Moscow, namely Vladimir Putin as acting Prime Minister. Putin's authorization of the fuel-air explosives in Tando in Bagestan was one example of his determined positive and *no-nonsense* response to the crisis.[128]

Putin's standing among the military escalated. For example, while politicians were always intervening in the First Chechen War, Putin made it very clear to the generals that they were running the second war. He was overseeing their handling of matters, but they were the professionals. Throughout the second war, Putin stayed in the background, providing encouragement or even help to the military or the interior forces. When there was confusion over who was in charge, Putin sat the leaders of both bureaucracies down and ordered them to come up with a clear chain of command.

As far as the generals and admirals were concerned, Yeltsin had been a disaster. He lied to them, he ignored them, he put them on starvation rations, and he sent them off to fight a war they were convinced could not be won. Hundreds of officers turned in their letters of resignation rather than take unprepared green troops into battle. By the end of Yeltsin's term in office, military morale had reached rock bottom. As the military's rations ran out, soldiers were going out in the fields to pick mushrooms to supplement their meager diet.

For the generals and admirals, Putin was a breath of fresh air. No one knew to what levels he would rise, but just having him keep Yeltsin off their backs was a major move in the right direction. He seemed to respect them, he provided the leadership they were seeking, and he ensured that there was a clear chain of command. The idea of shared responsibility began to seem possible.

The critical question, however, was how long would he be around? After all, Yeltsin had a reputation of tossing prime ministers to the wind the first time something untoward happened. Yeltsin resigned on December 31, 1999, leaving Putin as his successor.

What Yeltsin Left Behind

The military Yeltsin passed on to Vladimir Putin was in terrible shape. Given the displacements caused by the disbanding of twenty divisions in Germany, not to mention the loss of bases and factories located in the newly independent fourteen countries, separated from the Soviet Union, created both personnel and equipment chaos. *Dedovshchina* (hazing) remained rampant and led to massive efforts at draft evasion. Within the military, crime and corruption were out of control. Even the *kontraktniki* policy, aimed at attracting professional soldiers, had failed. The whole idea of developing noncommissioned officers (NCOs), so critical in Western armies, seemed to go nowhere, as officers had problems delegating authority.

Given these problems, the Russian Army had to be reconfigured and reformed. Instead of working with the military to help it adjust, Yeltsin ignored it. The budget was cut, and cut again. Even though an officer like Rodionov saw his budget for the coming year, it did not mean that he would actually receive that money. Too often, the civilian financial wizards would take back part of what had been promised. While demographic changes made it clear that the armed forces could not hope to rely on mass numbers of soldiers, both Yeltsin and the generals ignored the need for change.

Homeless officers and difficulty in recruiting either those on contract or new officers further undermined morale. The situation was made worse by the continued presence of crime. The lack of basic items such as food for the troops, or petrol for the tanks, ships, and planes sabotaged plans to conduct the exercises necessary if Moscow wanted a competent military. The same was true of personnel. The Russian Army was full of colonels who had never exercised anything larger than a platoon, and officers who had no combat experience. Morale hit rock bottom. Young officers were leaving in droves, while the more senior seemed to be waiting until they could get their retirement and then leaving for a civilian job.

Finally, every military needs modern equipment to survive. For ten years, the Russian military received almost nothing. For example, the navy received less than half of the money it required; the shipyards were in need of repair, and ships sat tied up to a pier because of equipment problems.[129]

Yeltsin did not care. His major concern was to stay in power. If that meant emasculating the military, so be it. He had little concern for military culture, violating it time and again. His orders were often unclear, he showed little or no respect for the military, and he did not care about the chain of command. If he wanted to talk to a lieutenant, it was none of military's business. If the generals did not like it, they could leave the military. Clearly, shared responsibility was not on his agenda.

CHAPTER 9

From Vladimir Putin through Dmitry Medvedev

> It is entirely up to the president whether true military reforms take place, or whether the military bureaucracy continues pretending that reforms are under way.
>
> ALEXEI ARBATOV

Putin understood military culture. He also made it clear that he was in charge, but he believed in attempting to create shared responsibility if possible. He had served as a KGB officer, which is structurally modeled on the armed forces. He knew the military mind differed from the civilian mind, and he understood that Yeltsin had violated just about every precept of military culture. He set out to deal with the military by respecting military culture, but the high level of corruption and the refusal of the high command to introduce serious reforms often led him to force major changes on the military, even if it meant ignoring shared responsibility. It would lead to one of the greatest and most massive civilian-induced changes undertaken in any of the four countries discussed here. It would also lead to considerable unhappiness and even hostility on the part of the officer corps toward Russia's civilian leadership.

Vladimir Putin, President (2000–2008)

Vladimir Putin assumed office with a heavy weight on his shoulders. Rising out of nowhere, he assumed the responsibilities of Russia's president when Boris Yeltsin decided to retire. He took the job of acting president three months prior to the upcoming presidential election. Given the internal chaos that had existed under Yeltsin, Putin was determined to right the listing ship of state, and in March 2000, he won the national election. Now he stood before the Russian people, who not only expected him to solve internal problems but to return Russia to its superpower status.

Almost nothing in the Russian state worked. The regions had become almost autonomous, ignoring Moscow whenever it suited them. The economy was in a shambles, not having recovered from the collapse in 1998. Education was not up to Soviet, let alone Western, standards. The military was in a dismal state and was especially defiant. Planes did not fly, ships did not sail, and tanks did not roll.

Putin was a very different leader from Yeltsin. He was not threatened by those around him; and he was not paranoid like Yeltsin, who saw everyone around him as a potential threat. He was an effective leader, and would not put up with anyone undermining his policies. One of the main reasons Yeltsin chose Putin to become prime minister and then president was because Putin did not appear threatening. He didn't seem to want Yeltsin's job.

Where Yeltsin tended to be impulsive and did little to create the stability and predictability so desired by the generals and admirals, Putin was cool headed and carefully calculated his every move. He was what in the West would be called a "problem solver."

Putin also understood the uniqueness of Russian political and military culture. As he saw things, the Russians wanted a strong leader, but a leader who would not repress the population. For Putin, this meant centralized control, which was why he was concerned with strengthening the Russian state. That was the kind of state he believed Russians expected. However, Putin was not ideological: he was pragmatic. His primary question in deciding which policy to utilize was "will it work?"

Putin was determined not to interfere in military matters, an approach that was welcome to the military. Rather than issuing orders, he stayed in the background, leaving the limelight to the generals. He expected all of the bureaucracies to implement his orders. From his perspective, the generals and admirals were the one's running the military. His job was to oversee the country's political-military future and avoid interfering in internal military matters unless it was absolutely necessary. This was a recipe for shared responsibility, a far cry from Yeltsin. The generals welcomed Putin, however, Putin was prepared to overrule the generals if he felt they were dragging their feet on an important issue.

Putin's approach became evident shortly after he was elected president. He immediately set up commissions to look at problems inside the army, problems accumulated over many years of neglect in a world where technology was changing so fast that it was hard for anyone, including the military, to keep up. Commissions were looking at improving management in the military, increasing combat readiness, restructuring the defense-industrial complex, upgrading the status of servicemen, increasing financial assistance to the military, as well as upgrading command and control.[1] The resulting proposals, which dealt with the period up to 2010, were approved by the Security Council. Unlike Donald Rumsfeld in the U.S. or Paul Hellyer in Canada, Putin welcomed the involvement of the military in these matters. He focused on one problem at a time, avoiding grandiose but meaningless statements, as often happened with Yeltsin.

CONFLICT BETWEEN DEFENSE MINISTER SERGEYEV AND CHIEF OF THE GENERAL STAFF KVASHNIN

Sergeyev and Kvashnin were different from one another. Sergeyev was a soft-spoken missile officer who spent the majority of his career working on Russia's nuclear deterrent. Kvashnin was an infantry officer who had briefly commanded Russian troops in Chechnya. While many considered Sergeyev to be diplomatic, Kvashnin could be abrasive, outspoken, and disrespectful. Despite their different personalities, one might assume that their relationship was formal and correct. Sergeyev was the defense minister and Kvashnin was the chief of the General Staff. Yeltsin's decision to put both structures directly under the president's office played a critical role—one of those strange relationships where the minister of defense could issue orders, but he was dependent on the chief of the General Staff, who had direct access to the president to implement them. As a result, the two men were constantly fighting. Sergeyev wanted primary reliance on strategic missile forces, which were a lot cheaper than conventional forces. Given the restrictions on Moscow's military budget, how could anyone expect the Kremlin to come up with the money necessary to modernize conventional forces? It was strategic weapons that deterred an outside power from attacking Russia.[2]

Kvashnin took strong exception to Sergeyev's emphasis on missiles. As Kvashnin saw it, the likelihood of a nuclear attack on Russia was minimal. Why waste limited resources on nuclear weapons, unlikely to be needed in a crisis? What if Moscow faced a problem on its periphery? What good would nuclear weapons be in such a case? The only weapons that would protect Russia in such a situation were strong, mobile, modern, and flexible conventional forces. At its heart, this debate was a reflection of a much more entrenched dispute between the traditionalists and the realists.

> A "traditionalists" school of thought was one that saw Russian's military potential as the guarantor of its international great power status and directed its pol-

> icies against any foreign policy losses or deterioration of Russian military power in general and of its Strategic Nuclear Forces in particular; and a more "realist" school of thought who favored aligning Russia's future with contemporary economic and political realities inside and outside Russia. Its continuation at the highest level inside the Russian high command led to a split of the military elite.[3]

The last version of Moscow's military doctrine had been adopted in 1993. The new 2000 doctrinal statement included important items. It strengthened the role of the president, who was given a key role in the training and the organization of the military—a sign that Putin would be heavily involved in dealing with military reform. The new document described the Defense Ministry as responsible for "working out concepts for the construction and development of other troops." This meant that Sergeyev was ordered to create blueprints to develop the other services, suggesting that Kvashnin, who had long wanted the General Staff to be in charge of such duties, had lost this bureaucratic battle.[4]

As an effective leader, Putin had no choice but to get in the middle of this intermilitary dispute. The issue came to the fore on July 12, 2000, at a meeting of the Collegium of the Defense Ministry. Kvashnin argued in favor of getting rid of the Strategic Rocket Forces, proposing that the number of ICBM divisions be cut from nineteen to two. The SRF's percentage of the budget would be reduced from 18 percent to 15 percent, with the resulting savings going to the Ground Forces.

Sergeyev responded in an interview on July 14. He bluntly called Kvashnin's plan "criminal stupidity and an attack on Russia's national interests." At this point, Putin had enough from these two generals. He ordered them to "silence their debate and come up with realistic policy proposals."[5] By the beginning of August 2000, many of Sergeyev's supporters had been removed from the high command.

In spite of Putin's warning, Krashnin attacked Sergeyev again at a Security Council meeting on August 11. He claimed that the SRF was getting preferential treatment. If nothing else, it became clear to Putin that he would have to take direct control. How could one have unity of command when the country's top two generals were constantly fighting? He began by criticizing all of the services. As Putin put it, "When pilots do not fly and sailors do not go to sea, can it be said that everything is right and proper in the structure of the Armed Forces today?" He then turned to the ongoing argument between Sergeyev and Kvashnin, noting, "I have been rather tolerant of the debates in the defense ministry and society as a whole. . . . Now is the time to bring them to a conclusion."[6] A new plan was adopted at the meeting for armed forces development to 2005. Playing the role of the good soldier, Sergeyev remarked, "The discussions are over and the Supreme Commander in Chief has made a decision. . . . Not a single booster rocket will be dismantled before it serves its full operational life."[7] However, Kvashnin had won. As he noted, "Our Main Objective is the harmonious development of all services of the Armed Forces."[8] That reference to harmonious development was code for treating the Ground Forces more equally.

At this meeting it was decided to release 365,000 soldiers and more than 100,000 civilians working for the military. The meeting also reversed Sergeyev's decision to abolish the Ground Forces as a separate unit. In addition, the SRF was downgraded to a command. Sergeyev was upset. As Golts tells it, it was not really a plan. On the contrary, it "simply strengthened the victory in bureaucratic channels of the 'combat and arms generals' over the missile generals."[9] This meant that attention and rubles would favor conventional forces. Despite the peaceful nations on Russia's borders, the Kremlin was convinced that the only way it could deal with potential threats was to have a modern army with modern conventional weapons.

THE KURSK

Then an event occurred that really upset Putin and the nation. On August 12, the submarine Kursk, the pride of the northern fleet, sank and with it came the loss of 118 sailors. This tragedy was an embarrassment to the Kremlin, especially because the Russian admirals refused offers of help from the U.S. and U.K. They claimed that it had been sunk by a foreign submarine. In reality, the submarine sank due to a defective practice torpedo. The military prosecutor blasted the navy for general incompetence in the way it handled the situation. It was the military, and not the civilians, who were responsible for this crisis.

Putin decided that in the future, the military would not lie about such events, and he let it be known that he intended to get more involved in military affairs. He decided he could not trust them to tell the truth. It was also clear to Putin that Moscow had to do more about modernizing and reforming the Russian military. This appears to be the first time he publicly raised the idea of permanent readiness units. As he put it in November 2000:

> The Army and Navy must be ready in all strategic directions to neutralize and repulse any armed conflict and aggression. And one important task—the cre-

> ation and stationing of groups of permanent readiness units in the South-Western and Central Asian strategic directions. Here the state of the general purpose forces is of primary importance. Such forces must have the latest technology.[10]

Permanent readiness units referred to military forces, mostly army infantry units, that could be deployed in a matter of hours, preferably manned exclusively by professional military personnel.

Putin was beginning to question the value of a shared relationship with the military. He was in charge. The Security Council met again on November 9, 2000. It was a critical meeting and it dealt with just about every military issue imaginable: management, combat readiness, the military-industrial complex, the status of servicemen, increasing financial assistance to the military, as well as command and control.[11] For Putin, the primary challenge was to improve the military's conventional forces. The plan adopted by the meeting focused primarily on personnel. By 2005, the total size of all of the Kremlin's security service (including the military) would be reduced by 19.7 percent. This meant a cut of 363,000 from the Ground Forces as well as 60,000 from the SRF.[12] Details concerning Phase II remained to be worked out, but Putin, in contrast to Yeltsin, attempted to rationalize the process. He refused to come up with a grand plan: given the mess he inherited, his primary concern was to solve outstanding problems.

Sergei Ivanov, Defense Minister (2001–2005)

Of all the problems Putin faced, none was more difficult or urgent than finding a way to end the endless fighting by Sergeyev and Kvashnin. Sergeyev would try to get Kvashnin to do something, but he could not order him to do so because he did not work for Sergeyev.

On March 28, 2001, the Kremlin announced that Sergeyev had stepped down as defense minister to become a presidential advisor—the Russian version of the golden parachute.[13] His replacement, Sergei Ivanov, was a long-time member of the KGB/FSB (Committee for State Security / Federal Security Service of the Russian Federation), but his strongest bureaucratic card was his close friendship with Putin. The two had served together in the KGB, and Putin apparently decided that it was time to bring in someone who understood the importance of military discipline, but who was not a member of the military. The disastrous actions of Russian troops in Chechnya had revealed the many problems, and many in the military believed that this tough KGB officer would quickly take charge and force Kvashnin to align himself with the MoD. Given his close ties to Putin, "Ivanov can make decisions and can make things happen." He hoped to emulate Putin—take charge, but remain open to creating a shared relationship. The problems facing him were formidable.

Ivanov wanted to implement the reforms the military badly needed and actually create a smaller, more capable professional army. One advantage was that he did not "have to deal with Moscow's corrupt defense bureaucracy."[14] All he had to do was to pick up the phone and call his close friend, the president. As another analyst observed,

> He is someone who is outside the armed forces, who had a lot of authority . . . notably from his [earlier] posts inside the security services . . . and so maybe he can impose decisions on the army that it might see as going against its interests. In other words, he may be capable of fighting the corporation of the military institutions that until now was largely responsible for breaking successive attempts at military reforms since 1991.[15]

Ivanov did not come into office with a magic wand. The military was a conservative and insular organization, and Ivanov was an outsider. To many in the defense ministry, he was a policeman whose only qualification was his friendship with the president. Kvashnin still had the right to go directly to the president. He worked for the president, not for Ivanov, and there was little likelihood that Kvashnin would start obeying just because Ivanov was the president's close friend.

It is ironic that one of Ivanov's first problems was a result of his close ties to Putin. Putin was an evolutionary president; he had no intention of coming in and making radical changes. Putin would have never selected Ivanov if he thought Ivanov intended radical change. Putin emphasized this by noting that he had no intention of becoming "a revolutionary" when it came to stabilizing and modernizing the military.[16]

Ivanov's job was to implement the changes Putin had made, and to do so in an evolutionary manner. Putin observed, "he was the head of the group which worked out the main parameters of reform."[17] It was becoming clear that as gradualist as Ivanov was, he expected progress. As he stated in May, "Today, the discussions are over. . . . The armed forces reform plans have been approved by the president; it's time to implement the approved decisions."[18] The Kremlin was clearly getting tired of the conservative and inactive high command.

Putin moved ahead on reform. On March 24, 2001, he signed Decree No. 337, "On Supporting the Plan for Conversion and Development of RF Armed

Forces and Improving Their Structure." As a consequence, the SRF was split into two commands (*rodi*): The Strategic Missile Troops and the Space Troops. The Ground Forces were also given back their independent command status that Sergeyev had taken away. In addition, the decree established the size of the Russian military at one million as of January 1, 2006.[19]

Social problems continued to beset the military. On May 11, 2001, a commission Putin had created to look into these issues provided him with a report on housing, military pay and allowances, medical services, and pensions. Putin tried to do something about pay, announcing that he would see to it that the military received more money. "Deputy Minister Alexei Kudrin, who was present at the meeting, said that an additional 4 billion rubles would be found for the army this year, and that funding for military procurement would be upped by some 27 billion rubles in the year 2002."[20] At another Security Council meeting focused on mobilization, Putin allocated another 34.6 billion rubles for pay and allowances, and said he would try to help the MoD repay some of its outstanding debts.[21] From the standpoint of the professional military, Putin promised to help the military, and he was doing just that. He was the kind of leader that military culture called for.

Putin did not want to interfere, but he wanted to be sure that the money was spent properly. He ordered the military to come up with a plan for spending the money, and the high command delivered its proposal on November 1. Putin approved the plan two weeks later. He also ordered the military to present him with a plan outlining what steps it planned to develop a "transition to a fully professional military by 2010."[22] This was another idea that would generate problems between Putin and the generals.

The generals had mixed feelings about moving toward a fully professional military. They were well aware that a professional military would produce a better army than the conscript-heavy force they had. Few of the generals wanted to fight a war weighed down by a conscript force of recruits with minimal training. Well-trained professionals translate into a more competent fighting force. There were generals who were less focused on the military's combat readiness, who liked the conscript-heavy military because it meant free labor for their commanding officers—when it came to building dachas or summer houses. A general could always loan out the conscripts to a labor-starved civilian enterprise—for a price. Finally, as in most countries, there were those officers who believed that by making service universal, the majority of young men would learn to love their country.

The situation with the professionals (*kontraktniki*) remained poor. In January 2002, there were 157,000 *kontraktniki* in the armed forces. Forty percent of them were women, forced to work because their husband's salaries were so low, in spite of Putin's efforts. In many cases women made better soldiers, if for no other reason than that they reported for duty sober. Normally, women were not sent to danger areas. "As a rule, men serve in Chechnya, Tajikistan, and other hot spots, where contract servicemen are paid more than the average 1,500 rubles a month."[23] That meant that only 94,200 of the total cadre of *kontraktnikis* were actually available to be sent to hot spots such as Chechnya. The situation was only getting worse; three months later there were only 132,000 *kontraktnikis* in the military.

The *kontraktnikis* tended to leave soon after they took their oath and discovered that, as in the past, living conditions were not as advertised. They were paid $100 per month, and their quarters and living conditions were primitive. This was a critical problem and one with which the General Staff wrestled. Money was scarce: who could afford to pay enlisted personnel when there often wasn't enough money to feed the troops?

PROFESSIONALIZING THE ARMY

A professional military continued to be the goal for Putin and Ivanov. However, Putin recognized that in the face of the objections he was getting from the generals and admirals, he would try an "experiment" to get matters moving, Putin intended to professionalize the 76th Airborne Division (7,000 soldiers stationed at Pskov, using this unit to show the generals that a professional military was both possible and militarily effective). The experiment began on September 1, 2002, and was to last a year and then be evaluated. The contracts signed by these soldiers bound them to fight—if ordered—in dangerous hot spots such as Chechnya. But the amenities were far below those the *kontraktniki* expected. Money was key: one could not expect to attract the "best and brightest" if such individuals were not paid more than most civilian occupations. To achieve that goal, one author maintained that the basic salary for a soldier would have to be increased to 4,000 rubles a month.[24]

Infrastructure problems continued. To the chairman of the Defense Committee of the Duma, "You cannot drive contract servicemen into dilapidated barracks."[25] As a consequence, the *kontraktnikis* were promised private apartments.

Many generals were distressed. First, they emphasized the extraordinary cost of a *kontraktniki*, pointing out that a conscript cost 17,900 rubles per annum whereas a professional, they claimed, cost 32,000. A professional military would cost twice as much as a conscript force.[26] To emphasize how "bad" this experiment was, while he was still chief of the General Staff, Kvashnin visited Pskov. In his evaluation of the unit, he made it clear that "No one intended to give apartments to soldiers."[27] To make matters worse, he stated, "The complex would be built without a kindergarten and school and that not all of those expecting flats would get them (of the originally slated eight apartment blocks, only five will be built)." After listening to Kvashnin, some forty *kontraktniki* NCOs immediately resigned from the program. Kvashnin then criticized the 76th Division Airborne Command, giving it very low inspection marks. He also made sure that these grades were leaked to the media. He was clearly working to undermine Putin's plan to professionalize the armed forces.

A battle was also going on behind the scenes between Kvashnin and Airborne Commander Georgi Shpak. Shpak's concern was to keep the airborne troops independent of the ground forces. Kvashnin's criticism was as much aimed at Shpak as it was at the experiment with professionalism. As one source commented,

> Kvashnin, who holds a special commission evaluating the combat readiness of the country's airborne forces, told airborne forces commander Colonel General Georgeii Shpak that he rates the readiness of Shpak's forces as "mediocre," *Izvestiya* reported. Kvashnin has long had antagonistic relations with Shpak and has proposed abolishing the airborne forces and creating instead a highly mobile rapid-reaction force capable of combating terrorism.[28]

Shpak lost this battle and was forced to retire in September 2003.

The main problem remained—how to make contract service more attractive to quality recruits? Shpak had attempted to approach the problem in a graduated manner. First, he wanted to make the 104th regiment combat ready. This meant that within three months the percentage of *kontraktnikis* would have to be up to 77 percent (1,500 officers and men). The following June the unit was declared ready and sent to Chechnya. The next unit was the 234th Regiment. There were not enough volunteers to staff this unit, and there were problems with the regiment as a whole as well as the division's operations and supply sections. It took until December 2003 before enough personnel were found to send the unit to Chechnya.[29]

Even though the military found sufficient recruits, the quality was abysmal. One writer referred to the city of Pskov, where the 76th Division was stationed, as "a criminal zone with marauding drunken *kontraktniki*."[30] Ivanov agreed. As he put it, "Last year there were forty-one deaths in this part of the

Armed Forces, and in the first half of this year, there have already been thirty-two deaths among the paratroops due to various accidents."[31]

While he was well aware of the problems involved in creating professionals, Putin took advantage of a meeting on November 26 to state that he had a "generally positive" outlook on efforts toward professionalizing the military. Still the generals resisted. They attempted to drag the process through three distinct stages. The first would end in 2004. The second would last seven years. The goal at this point was to have 50–60 percent of soldiers and sergeants serving on contract. The third was left undefined, no doubt, because the generals themselves had no idea how long it would last. "It is planned that all armed forces will be manned with 'contractee' during the third stage."[32] Putin was not happy. Since the time would run out after he left office, Putin believed that the generals were following one of the key rules of career bureaucrats—outlast those in power.

The generals had a point in that it took a year and four months just to man the 76th Division in Pskov fully with *kontraktniki*. Like a good bureaucrat, however, when Ivanov visited the unit in December 2003, he proclaimed the experiment a success. He said he recognized that the key would be housing, pay, and after hours recreation, issues that would continue to be a problem for many years to come.[33] As time would demonstrate, he spoke a bit too soon. The problems first encountered at Pskov would beset this program for years.

DEFINING THE ROLES OF THE GENERAL STAFF AND MOD

By the end of 2003, it was clear to everyone in the defense establishment that conflict between Ivanov and Kvashnin was as bad as it had been between Sergeyev and Kvashnin. Putin realized that structural changes had to be made if Russia's future presidents wanted to avoid this same type of conflict.

In January 2004, with Putin's support, Ivanov suggested an overhaul of the General Staff–MoD relationship. At the heart of his suggestion was a proposal that the General Staff not be directly involved in operational matters and that the generals be subordinated to the defense minister. On June 14, the Duma changed the key article, Number 13 of the Law on Defense. The new version mentioned only the Defense Ministry. "Oversight for the Army Forces of the Russian Federation is carried out by the defense minister via the Defense Ministry."[34] In addition, Article 15, which had listed the main functions of the General Staff, was declared null and void. Now there was less ambiguity. The chief of the general staff was no longer in charge of operational matters. He was in charge of whatever the defense minister put him in charge of. This meant that the General Staff could plan for every eventuality, one of its two primary functions (the other, planning for operations and mobilization), but it could do no more than that without authorization from the defense minister. As Ivanov put it, "In the view of the supreme commander, it is important that the General Staff focus more on future wars and the prospective development of the armed forces, and not be involved in routine affairs."[35]

Putin took advantage of the change in the law to get rid of Kvashnin. Seven years of him as chief of the General Staff was enough. The pretext for Kvashnin's firing was an attack in Inguishetia that killed 100 people to which the army took 12 hours to respond. As far as the military was concerned, no one was sorry over Kvashnin's departure. He was despised by most of his fellow officers because of his arrogance and refusal to consider alternative approaches. As one analyst put it, "When officers, both retired and still serving, speak of Kvashnin, they recall his total incompetence, bad manners, berating of commanders in front of subordinates, and so on. There is also much talk in the ranks about rampant corruption at the top of the defense establishment."[36] Kvashnin's replacement, General Yuri Baluyevskii, was a more modest and reflective officer. He would eventually run into problems with a future defense minister, but for Ivanov it was a great relief.

Putin was determined to work with both Ivanov and the new chief of the General Staff. He put bureaucratic efficiency ahead of concerns over bureaucratic intrigue. A key component of military culture in Russia, as well as throughout most of the Soviet Army's existence and the Russian military, has been the principle of "one man leadership" (*edinochalnie*). Since the 1920s, the military have operated under that principle: the commanding officer is in charge. Ivanov now had the power of *edinochalnie*. As he noted, "There is one immutable constant in military organization: the principle of one-man command and one-man control. Armed forces remain what they are only for as long as this principle prevails, and a rigid vertical command structure is ensured."[37]

CREATING PERMANENT READINESS UNITS

The Russian army continued to be undermanned; in fact, many units were only second- or third-level units. What this meant in practice was that they had a skeleton staff and would be fully manned only in the event of a crisis. This was an approach devised to deal with a situation such as occurred in World War II. The first-line units would absorb an attack while the second- and third-category divisions were brought up to fighting strength. The problem, however, was that the Kremlin was slowly recognizing that the military had to be ready to move in an instant. What, for example, if the threat were not a new world war, but a substate conflict as in Chechnya or elsewhere on the periphery? What would be important would not be the totality of the Russian military, but small, flexible, lethal conventional units that could respond in hours rather than weeks or months.

Toward this end, Moscow set up a two-tiered system. After 2008, the General Staff proposed that there be 144,000 volunteers serving in permanent readiness units (elite units like the airborne, naval infantry, and some infantry regiments). The conscripts would only serve for one year. Only professionals, the *kontraktniki,* would serve in combat, except in the most serious or threatening situations. The conscripts would go through one year of training and then move to the reserves, to be called upon only if the country faced a major external threat.

The problem of providing these professionals with the kind of creature comforts they demanded continued to be more difficult than many in the high command anticipated:

> In 2005 the task is to convert forty Defense Ministry units and subunits at once. In fact, this is where the difficulties have developed. We were allocated money to build hostels and mess halls and modernize firing ranges (79.5 billion rubles), but the social and cultural sphere was forgotten. After all, a contract serviceman is not a soldier on compulsory service. At 1800 hours, if he has no official duties, he is free, like an officer. And what is he to do? A fit 25 year-old cannot simply lie around the barracks looking at the ceiling.[38]

In other words, if you want individuals to serve voluntarily, make it worth their while.

Then there was pay. A 2004 survey indicated that most of those the military was trying to recruit would expect a salary of 10,000–12,000 rubles. A *kontraktniki* was paid only 4,600.[39] Recognizing the extent of the problem, the Putin administration raised the salary for *kontraktniki* serving in Chechnya to 15,000 rubles. But problems continued to haunt the program. As General Baluyevskii noted, "Despite the additional payment . . . it is mostly citizens, who as a rule have not established themselves in civilian careers, who apply for contract service, as well as residents from areas with poor economies and from the countryside, while many still consider the current reward for military work to be inadequate."[40] To make matters worse, 70 percent of those who signed up to become *kontraktniki* were conscripts extending their service. "Incidentally, the fact that the main bulk [of contract soldiers] are yesterday's drafted personnel is a problem. At the moment, our contract soldier is the same old compulsory-service soldier, remaining at the same level in terms of his education and training, but very expensive."[41] To make matters worse, inflation almost immediately wiped out wage increases.

In 2005, the Army launched an advertising campaign. At first, it appeared to be succeeding. For example, Ivanov noted that close to 16,000 young men and women had become privates and sergeants. This enabled the government to announce that the 42nd Motorized Division fighting in Chechnya had been completely manned with professionals and that housing had even been built for the unit.[42] However, problems continued to plague the system. In January 2006, the military announced that the 98th Airborne Division had failed to fill 500 positions "for privates and NCOs." Rather than going fully professional it was permitted "to retain one conscript battalion."[43] The 2006 draft budget specifically addressed the issue of *kontraktnikis*. "Funds allocated to the special federal program 'Transition to what the Russians call an All-Volunteer Force' (when they are discussing professional forces) in 2004 will amount to 22.3 billion rubles ($789 million) next year, which is bigger than the 2005 budget (19.7 billion rubles [$697 million]) and two-fold as much as the 2004 budget (9.6 billion rubles [$340 million])."[44]

ATTACKING THE IMPOSSIBLE: THE MILITARY BUDGET

A modern military force is expensive. Putin, made it clear from his first day in office that he intended to increase the military budget. The generals believed they needed at least a 3.5 percent of GNP for their budget. While Putin was not prepared to go that far, the military budget did increase substantially. In 2005, Ivanov maintained that defense spending would increase from 20 to 25 percent a year, "remaining at 2.5 percent to 2.7 percent of GDP,"[45] but the additional money did not solve the military's problem. To quote a retired general and member of the Duma, "The matter is that the government and the Finance Ministry particularly have forgotten about inflation and the steady growth of prices on fuel, energy, services, goods, and defense products."[46]

The problems were enormous, especially in the area of weapons. In contrast to NATO, whose new weapons made up between 60 and 70 percent of the total, in Russia they were only 15 to 20 percent. "There has been no mass production of new technology such as the KA-32 helicopter, T-90 tank, close-battle-radar location stations, and closed communications radio stations for the Russian Army,"[47] Russia was ten to twelve years behind the United States in the technology of weapons.[48]

This led the Putin administration to adopt a "State Program for Armaments for the Period up to 2010" aimed at increasing support for arms and research. "Klebanov said the procurement plan tops last year's expenditure by nearly 40 percent. . . . The 40 figure corresponds to remarks made last year [2001] by Finance Minister Alexei Kudrin, who said the 2002 procurement budget would likely increase by 27–79 billion rubles [from $850 million to $2.5 billion]."[49]

Despite the additional money, problems remained. Klebanov, minister of science, industry, and technology, commented, "In-depth modernization of combat aircraft, ships, nonstrategic missiles, precision weapons systems, and other military hardware on the existing basis will make it possible to carry out work in the sphere of (long-range) research and development."[50] It would be a long time—2010 according to the commander of ground troops—before new weapons would be available.[51] The situation in the air force was similar. In 2002, Lieutenant General Sergei Solnitsev, who was in charge of flight safety, stated that half of Russia's airbases were in need of complete refurbishment, while another report on the air force commented, "The share of up-to-date aircraft of the fourth generation amounts to less than 45 percent of the aircraft fleet. The share of operational aircraft has fallen to 60 percent. Only a little over 30 percent of airfields are ready for operation. The personnel's annual flying hours do not exceed 20 to 25 percent of the required number."[52] Still, by 2002, the military's budget tripled, from 109 billion rubles to 284 billion rubles.[53] This budget meant that the financial situation had begun to stabilize, providing the General Staff with a modicum of predictability.

While progress was minimal, the long-term job of replacing Russia's outdated weapons and equipment began under Putin. For example, the air force received 12 modernized Su-27 general purpose planes in 2002, and a further 20 in 2003.[54] The amount of money allocated to upgrading weapons increased. In 2002, the state weapons order rose to 80 billion rubles, and this target was also met. The next year, the state weapons order grew to 112 billion rubles.[55]

The military appreciated that money was being allocated for new, modernized weapons. However, this was only a start. The armed forces were in dire straits, and the generals openly complained. For example, the deputy commander of the air force, General Yuri Grishin, argued that the air force will "have to fly planes that are twenty to forty years old."[56] One source complained, "Some 80 percent of Russia's military-industrial complex is obsolete. . . . The average years of service for the machinery of the complex is thirty, as compared with seven to eight years in the developed nations of Europe."[57]

By 2004, some new weapons were entering the inventory, but at such a slow pace that it would take a long time before Russia's military was competitive. In July, the army announced that it had obtained 14 T-90S tanks, and it hoped to get another 20 to 30 tanks in 2005.[58] It received between 30 and 40 BTR-80 armored personnel carriers. The air force then announced it would receive one Tu-160 bomber, and a second would be repaired. In addition, it planned "to modernize seven Su-27 fighters, purchase four Topol-M strategic missiles, two Iskander tactical missile systems . . . one warship and one diesel submarine."[59]

By 2006, the weapons budget had grown to 225 billion rubles, an increase of one billion rubles over the preceding year. Among the weapons planned were seven Topol-M missiles and 17 tanks, while 17 Su-27 fighters were to be modernized.[60] There were also plans for the army's main strike helicopter, the Mi-28N to enter service.[61] These few weapons meant little to the country's generals and admirals, who were concerned about having an inventory to match that of the U.S. and NATO. As one observer noted, "We need to buy 140–150 planes, 60 helicopters, 200 tanks, 250 artillery weapons annually, but next year we will buy mere single pieces of equipment."[62]

Putin initiated structural modifications to improve efficiency and to fight corruption, a constant problem. A single-purchasing system was established. When Ivanov took over as defense minister, there were fifty-two entities inside the Defense Ministry that had the authority to purchase military equipment and weapons as well as to order research and development. The number was initially cut to twenty and then to only one.[63] However, corruption remained a matter of major concern. From 2001 to 2004, there was a 160–170 billion ruble shortfall. The reason was unclear. Some argued that it resulted from an annual budget that was trying to purchase weapons that required five or more years lead time. It would later turn out that corruption played a major part in this shortfall.

PAY AND CREATURE COMFORTS

Putin called for significant pay raises effective January 1, 2002. The raise was put off until mid-2003 for economic reasons. Then an increase in wages for rank and file was moved from 2003 to 2004,[64] at the same time the government decided to take away special privileges from the military such as free transportation on buses and trains. The rate of inflation in Russia was 18 percent, but despite Putin's efforts, the average officer's pay remained $100 per month.[65] A year later, one source claimed that the situation was so bad that "43 percent of officers lived under the poverty line, defined by a monthly wage of at least $59."[66] Given this low level of compensation, officers continued to leave in droves. In 2003, a report noted that "up to 50 percent of the graduates of military schools leave military service a year after graduating."[67]

Pay, however, was only part of the problem. In 2001, 92,000 officers in Moscow still did not have apartments, and another 45,000 did not have any official housing at all, which meant they were left on their own to find whatever was available.[68] The situation only worsened. According to one source, in 2003, 168,000 servicemen needed housing, while another 60,000 officers and warrant officers required housing, because the bases where they were stationed were about to be closed.[69] In an effort to understand the depth of the problem, the General Staff undertook a major study. It concluded that, "Every tenth medium-rank officer position is vacant and among petty officers, every third. In the last few months over 100 officers lecturing at the Ground Forces Academy have asked to be dismissed from military service, and if this trend continues, the Academy will have to close in six months. About 70 percent of the officers who resigned last year were 30 or younger."[70]

Given the problems with pay and housing, those who remained in the military openly complained about their treatment. One source noted that poor pay was a threat to the military's very "existence." In addition, predictions at the time called for the price index to increase by 25 percent.[71] In one case, a serving officer did what few ever do: he openly complained of the situation to Putin.

> The deprivation of servicemen and their families of the lost social benefits was not bolstered by a significant rise (by a factor of 3–4, at a minimum) of their pay and allowances. This has created critical social tension and is contributing to the outflow from the army of skilled regulars. Thirty-five officers, including 13 pilots, 3 maintenance technicians, and 19 ground-service engineers, left the service early in 2004 alone. The officer shortfall runs to 192, of warrant officers to 62, and of contract servicemen 20.[72]

The reception of such complaints in Russia was different from Germany or Canada. Putin took them seriously, as he wanted a shared relationship. He fully understood and empathized with the soldiers and sailors, but there were structural problems such as the inability of wives to get jobs at isolated military installations.

Putin also tried to deal with the housing problem. At the end of 2002, Ivanov stated that the government was "radically transforming the system of providing housing to servicemen."[73] The defense ministry planned to divide servicemen into categories. The first were those who had been discharged and who had to be provided with housing (i.e., those who had served 20 years, or had been discharged at the convenience of the service). The second focused on military personnel who had joined the service after 1998. They had to be provided with housing. This group would come under the new plan, in which the servicemen made deposits into a savings account and the government would put in 37,000 rubles ($1,300) per year. The plan provided that "Later on the sum will be revised on an annual basis taking into account the rate of inflation."[74] Nevertheless, the housing situation did not improve. For example, in 2005 Ivanov complained that there were "85,000 soldiers living in communal housing facilities; 49,000 are renting housing; and 1,300 families are taking shelter in offices and barracks of military units."[75] Putin complained about the housing situation again on November 28, 2005, arguing that "The average price of housing is 29,000 rubles per one square meter of floor space, while we assume it's 11,000 rubles. And we wish you good luck. Why are we pulling the people's leg?"[76]

CORRUPTION AND HAZING

Just as in civilian society, corruption raged rampant in the military. It was so widespread that one observer claimed that it was impossible to calculate just how serious the problem was.

> No one has ever been able to put a finger on the scale of theft in the Russian armed forces overall. Rations are sold while soldiers go hungry. Arms and ammunition disappear, perhaps to hunters, gangsters or terrorists, but no one knows. Fuel, spare parts, and vehicles can be bought. Recently, in Mulino, home of a permanent-readiness motor rifle regiment, tanks ran out of fuel on the ranges because it was being sold by the tanker-loader to local business. A motor rifle regimental commander sold all his unit's lorries [trucks], becoming, briefly, a millionaire.[77]

Senior officers were constantly being convicted of corruption and that included General Georgii Olenik, the Ministry of Defense's chief financial officer.[78] Russian air force planes even got into the corruption game. Air force aircraft were used to smuggle caviar. "We confiscated 5.5 tons of red caviar, 160 kg of black caviar, and 0.5 tons of sturgeon fish on board a Russian Tu-154 aircraft that was on the point of taking off for Moscow. Representatives of the military were unable to explain where this consignment came from."[79] In 2005, 5,000 officers, among them five generals, were convicted by Russian military courts.[80]

> Twenty percent of the draftees have primary education, and only 1.8 percent higher education. Every fourth conscript has grown up in a family without a father and 1 percent are orphans. Forty-three percent had studied and 37 percent had worked before army service. Eleven percent frankly confessed to alcohol addiction being their worst habit. Up to 4 percent of respondents used drugs and 11 percent already had police records for various reasons.[81]

The consequence was predictable. "Barrack room fagging and bullying is endemic."[82] The high command responded by posting morale officers to units, but to little avail. According to the young lieutenant who identified himself only as Dmitri, "The older soldiers educate young troops. . . . This is the way the army is built. We mustn't break established rules." In contrast to Western militaries, the young lieutenant made it clear that he enforced discipline by producing a "72-centimeter, hard-nosed baton he uses to punish unruly soldiers. He refers to it as an educator."[83] This process was so widespread that it impacted combat readiness. Senior soldiers took food from junior ones. But that was not the worst problem. According to the main military prosecutor, in 2002 some 800 servicemen from security agencies were killed by other soldiers. This led to desertions, and in 2002, 4,200 soldiers fled.[84]

Prior to 2002, commanders could send unruly soldiers to the guard house for up to ten days. However, the Duma decided to close military jails so that Russia would look better in the eyes of the European Union. While this political decision may have made sense from a foreign policy standpoint, it undermined the already serious discipline problem. It led to a situation in which officers, like the young lieutenant cited above, were forced to use their fists to enforce discipline. That, in turn, led to officers being arrested for beating up their troops. "Almost a battalion of officers [was] sentenced for violence with a general at the head and half of them are behind bars."[85]

THE WAR IN CHECHNYA

One of the biggest command and control problems facing the military in Chechnya had been the confusion over who was in charge of operations there—the Ministry of Defense or the Interior Ministry. Under Putin's direction, responsibility was gradually shifted to the Interior Ministry. By September 2003, Lieutenant General Valeri Baranov, from the Interior Ministry, had taken charge of all operations in Chechnya. In May 2005, the Interior Ministry began to take over command of all nineteen military personnel in the commandant's office in Chechnya. MoD forces were gradually withdrawn until there were only 30,000 army troops permanently stationed there, primarily with the 42nd Motorized Infantry Division.

PUTIN CALLS IT QUITS WITH THE GENERALS

Despite their efforts to create a working environment of shared responsibility with the generals, it was becoming clear to both Ivanov and Putin that corruption was out of control. However, neither of them was aware of just how serious the problem had become. Money was disappearing. As Russian journalist Pavel Felgenhauer noted, "To this day, it is unclear how the money was actually spent." It certainly was not going into the creation of modern weapons systems. To quote Felgenhauer, "We are talking about very large amounts of money that are disappearing—no one knows where."[86] One problem was that the Duma did not have oversight over the military budget. In 2006, 44 percent of the defense budget was classified, and only deputies with special security clearances could see the budget, and even they could not determine how all the money was spent.[87] The next year an article claimed that corruption was rife in the defense ministry.

> These efforts are never crowned with success because they are essentially going after themselves. The main military secret today is that almost all generals and officers constituting the ranking nucleus of the arms of military leadership from procurement subdivisions of the MoD and the General Staff through the corresponding agencies and combat arms of the Armed Forces are members of corporate boards of directors and sit on auditing commissions and are even appointed the general managers of corporations.[88]

Faced with what appeared to be a misappropriation of funds, Ivanov privately ordered an audit of the military budget to document how funds were spent. The result of the audit shocked him. On April 3, the Audit Chamber announced that over R164.1 billion had been stolen from the MoD by fraud and outright theft.[89] One source argued that 30 percent of the budget was being lost due to corruption.[90] Another report stated that the MoD "accounts for 70 percent of the budgetary resources used for purposes other than those officially confirmed," and an unnamed Duma member told Interfax, that "The Defense Ministry is the unchallenged leader in missing funds among federal budget agencies."[91] A separate Federal Security Service (FSB) report claimed that many defense enterprises refused to accept MoD orders because they had to pay back up to 50 percent of the value of the order as a kickback.[92] Faced with such overwhelming evidence of corruption in the MoD, Ivanov went to Putin.

Putin decided to make major changes. He had tried to work through the generals for seven years, only to find out that a major segment of the military budget that he worked so hard to raise, was being siphoned off. It was time for the civilians to take charge.

Anatolii Serdyukov, Defense Minister (2007–2012)

On February 15, 2007, Putin elevated Ivanov to the post of first deputy premier and brought in a previously unknown civilian tax official, Anatolii Serdyukov, to be defense minister. The country's senior generals were shocked: he was a civilian whose military experience amounted to service as a reserve lieutenant in the ground forces, who only spent a year on active duty. What an insult to military culture. While active duty officers avoided public comment, retired officers vented their outrage. Colonel General Leonid Ivashov, a well-known hardliner, said that the military had been "spat upon . . . and is now in mourning." Another critic argued that Putin "had turned the screws" on the military.[93]

While most observers were shocked by Serdyukov's appointment, few expected it to lead to major changes. Alexandr Golts, commented that it gave a "sham impression of civilian control over the armed forces." Vladimir Dvorkin, a retired general stated, "I think that in the situation we have today it is irrelevant who was appointed."[94]

> While active duty officers were careful to avoid public comment, it was clear that they did not take Serdyukov's appointment seriously. As one columnist put it, "The Russian Armed Forces are in confusion. Headquarters, barracks, and military on-line forums are caught up in heated debates about the newly appointed defense minister, Anatolii Serdyukov. The battles are intense." Some insist that this former "furniture dealer" is incapable of managing Armed Forces development—backing up their arguments with jokes about Serdyukov providing new tables and chairs in all barracks.[95]

It would soon become clear that they grossly underestimated this civilian tax collector. In time, he would turn the Russian armed forces upside down—

a revolution in military affairs comparable to what happened in the aftermath of the Russian Civil War.

One of Serdyukov's first decisions was to make it clear that he was serious and was prepared to fire those he considered incompetent, regardless of rank. For example, at the end of March 2007, he traveled to St. Petersburg where he paid an unscheduled visit to the Nakhimov Naval College. He entered the college unannounced through the back door, where food was stored and the trash containers were located. "During his snap visit, Serdyukov discovered horribly inadequate sanitary arrangements, damp college cadets' rooms, water in the basement, fungi on the walls, and crumbling plaster." Serdyukov's response was immediate. The chief of the college Rear Admiral Alexandr Bukin was dismissed from the service.[96] Still, senior officers did not take him seriously; they were convinced they could run circles around him.

Serdyukov's primary goal was to gain control of the budgetary process. He brought 20 tax officials with him to help him create "a more transparent system for the rational and targeted expenditure of budget funds allocated to the Armed Forces."[97] He was not about to rely on military officials, which irritated the generals. Serdyukov did not limit his tenure as defense minister to just rationalizing the budgetary process. He did not care about shared responsibility. He intended to make major changes such as downsizing the military, a commitment that most senior officers ignored. Toward that end, he began to reform the procurement and financial oversight departments by putting them "on a entirely different basis." He eliminated one of the worst forms of corruption: the assignment of military procurement officers to factories. As he put it, "military representatives have essentially turned into employees of these enterprises."[98] He also created auditing and inspection entities to operate independently while monitoring the flow of financial assets.

In comparison to the German, Canadian, and American militaries, Russian officers had carefully guarded their autonomy from civilian interference in purely military matters. Even during the communist period, when the party was active in the military, Soviet generals resisted civilian or party interference in what the senior officers considered military decisions. A civilian official getting involved in operational matters, tactics, weapons, structure, or many other "purely" military matters was unheard of. However, that changed under Serdyukov.

Serdyukov did not limit himself to firing one rear admiral. By the end of 2007, he had gotten rid of the commander in chief of the air force, Vladimir

Mikhailov, as well as his deputy, General Boris Cheltsov. In November, three more generals were sent into retirement, General Igor Bykov, chief of the Main Medical Directorate, General Anatoli Greceniuk, in charge of the construction of medical facilities, and Colonel General Vladislav Polonsky.

Then the National Strategy Institute issued a blistering report on the situation inside the Russian military entitled "The Crisis of the Russian Army." It argued that contrary to what the military claimed, "the Russian Armed Forces are in a very deep crisis, and the unfavorable trends in the development of the military sphere have assumed an irreversible nature." As the report emphasized, Moscow's weapons were too old. The navy had launched only three ships since the collapse of the USSR and all of them were based on 1980s technology. The command and control systems dated back to World War II. With the exception of a few aircraft, the SS-300/400, a new sub, the Topol ICBM, and the Bulava SLBN missiles, almost everything had to be developed anew. And even these weapons had problems. Despite repeated tests the Bulava missiles had continually failed, thus leaving a new submarine, the *Yuri Dolgoruky*, without its missiles.[99] Some major changes were needed if Moscow expected the Russian military to be taken seriously around the world.

THE BATTLE WITH GENERAL BALUYEVSKII

By the end of 2008, there were increasing rumors in Moscow of problems between Serdyukov and the Chief of the General Staff Yuri Baluyevskii. Baluyevskii did not appreciate Serdyukov's interference in what he considered military matters. He reportedly offered his resignation in November 2007, when Serdyukov appointed Oleg Eskin, a communications specialist to a newly created deputy minister post to oversee automated control systems and communications that had previously been the job of the General Staff. On January 9, 2008, Baluyevskii submitted his resignation a second time. When at the end of February he submitted his resignation for a third time Serdyukov was overjoyed, writing on the letter, "I do not object."[100] On June 3, 2008, it was announced that Baluyevskii was retiring and would become deputy chair of the Security Council.

Baluyevskii's response to Serdyukov's actions was much like the American military's response to Secretary of Defense Robert McNamara and his "Whiz Kids" in the late 1960s, or Donald Rumsfeld's involvement in operational and tactical issues during the administration of George Bush. It was a clear case of a clash of two cultures and made shared responsibility impossible.

Baluyevskii was replaced by General Nikolai Makarov, who came from the position of chief of armaments, an area of concern to Serdyukov. His appointment marked a clear break with the past because "formerly, chiefs of the General Staff were nominated from among combined-arms commanders."[101] Makarov was not the only new face among the country's top military leaders.

Despite some important changes that were underway, it was only after the war in Georgia that the reform program took on a sense of urgency. The war brought home to the military and political leadership that there was no alternative to radical reform.

THE WAR IN GEORGIA

The lessons learned from the war in Georgia in 2008 were so shocking and had such tremendous implications that it became the *causes belli* to announce the most radical and sweeping changes in Russian conventional forces since the end of World War II. The conflict served primarily to highlight the shortcomings, failings, and the decrepit condition of its armed forces. Reviewing events in Georgia showed that the forces then available to Moscow were in no condition to fight a modern war. The Five Day War represented the last Russian war of the twentieth-century fought exclusively with dated tactics, equipment, weapons, and structures better suited to waging large scale conventional warfare, typical of the massed armies of World War II.[102]

SERDYUKOV'S REFORM PLAN

Serdyukov and Makarov sent a clear message to the rest of the military: either go along with the changes in the Russian military or leave. Almost all of the senior officers in charge of major branches prior to Serdyukov's tenure were retired to be replaced by younger men. Serdyukov had no illusions of a shared relationship. His job was to transform the Russian military. He would work with Makarov, as long as the latter followed orders, but he was unconcerned when it came to creating a shared relationship with the rest of the military.

Serdyukov introduced draconian cuts in force structure. During 2009, he cut the number of officers on active duty from 355,000 to 290,000. About 140,000 more were discharged in the next few years. Having just cut 150,000 officers, he suddenly announced that he was expanding the number to 220,000 a few months later.[103] This changed the ratio of officers to enlisted from 2:2.5 to approximately 1:15, much like the average in NATO.[104] These cuts also aimed at reshaping the officer rank structure. The number of generals on active duty was cut from 1,107 to 886, and colonels went from 25,665 to 9,114. Majors were cut from 99,550 to 25,000, while captains decreased from 90,000 to 40,000. The only rank that increased was lieutenants—by 10,000.[105] There were 140,000 warrant officers still on active duty. That number was pared down to 20,000 all of which were in the Navy. Warrants were given the opportunity to become noncommissioned officers (NCOs) unless they were currently filling an officer's billet, in which case they had a chance of becoming an officer.

These cuts hit all parts of the military. In the medical staff, for example, the deputy head of the main military medical department confirmed that as many as 22 military hospitals were being closed, and over 10,000 officer positions were slashed in the Russian armed forces' medical service. "In the course of the medical military service reform, which is being pursued to reshape the makeup of the armed forces, 22 military hospitals will be liquidated and the officer staff will be cut to 5,800 from the current 15,953." He stated at hearings on May 27, 2009, that it was planned to cut civilian personnel as well. "We had 145,000 . . . civilian personnel in 2008, and this figure should be cut to 97,000 in 2010." By December 1, 2009, the Russian medical service will include 13 central and district military hospitals and 101 branches.[106] Eighty percent of all lawyers were let go, and all but 20 officers' positions in the military media were closed.[107]

The General Staff traditionally had been completely out of bounds to civilian involvement. It was the General Staff, that the legendary Marshal Boris Shaposnikov labeled the "brain of the army." Even when Khrushchev made all his cuts in the 1950s, he left the General Staff alone. This was not the case with Serdyukov. He decided that there were too many uniforms in Moscow, and, as a result, the number of officers in the Ministry of Defense and the General Staff would be cut by a factor of 2.5 over a four-year period. This meant dropping it from a total of 27,873 officers to only 8,500.[108]

The military's intelligence organization, the GRU (Main Intelligence Directorate), was cut by more than 40 percent, and equally shocking, one of the country's most elite units, the *Spetsnaz* was also cut.[109] The head of the GRU, General Valentin Korabelnikov, resigned in March 2009, to rumors that he could not accept Serdyukov's radical changes in the armed forces.

A final personnel-related change was the introduction of physical fitness tests. For years, it seemed that there was a correlation between an individual's girth and the number of general's stars he wore on his shoulder. Now, however, much to the unhappiness of Moscow's many overweight officers, all personnel were required to pass an annual physical fitness exam as is the case in the American, Canadian, and German militaries; in the first half of 2008, 26 percent of all young officers tested failed the exam.[110]

CREATING NCOS

The problems with *kontraktnikis* continued into the Serdyukov period. The generals continued to think they could fill sergeant billets in "permanent-readiness units with contract service members." Later on the plan was to "continue bringing the compliment of sergeants up to strength in permanent readiness units at training centers, and in the remaining command."[111] Yet, Moscow was convinced that the modern army would only work if it had a corps of NCOs as existed in the West. Moscow had such a corps in World War II, but these ranks were permitted to lapse. They were replaced by conscripts, who were made NCOs after a short period of training. They were useless when it came to the kind of military expertise, leadership, and initiative expected of an NCO in the West.

In addition to those warrants, which decided to revert back to enlisted status as NCOs, the Russians came up with another idea—they planned to set up a ten-month program to train NCOs in six military higher educational institutions. The program never got off the ground, however, because most of the applicants could not meet the academic qualifications. To quote one Russian source, "At the military VUZs in Ryazan and Omsk, as many as 60 percent of those tested were incapable of solving quadratic equations, while half of them were unable to do calculations involving simple fractions and decimals. Yet this is eighth- or ninth-grade standard in high school."[112] The program was postponed for a six-month period. Even then there were doubts about its potential success, as one Russian author noted, "Having spent nearly 85 billion rubles, they will form a professional NCO corps in 2009–2011. The fact that this is a complete utopia is obvious. Fifteen years at the very least will be required to train the needed number of professional NCOs."[113]

Faced with this problem, Moscow adopted another approach. Instead of the ten-month program, the defense ministry decided to put students through a two-year and ten-month training program at the Ryazan Higher Airborne School and provide them with diplomas on graduation. The graduates received R35,000 a month, the same pay as a general. The center opened on December 1, 2009, and the initial class totaled 248 students,[114] With only a class of 248 students it will take many years to train sufficient NCOs for an army with approximately 800,000 enlisted personnel. While these NCOs presumably will have good technical training, the kind of experiences that American, Canadian, and German NCOs gain going up through the ranks, the experience that gains them the respect of their subordinates, will be missing.

It was evident that the fifteen-year effort to produce *kontraktnikis* as the basis for NCOs was failing. Recruits came from the least educated parts of society, and they tended to be those who could not find a job.[115] Given the low pay and the difficult living conditions, Moscow could not attract high-quality individuals common to Western NCO corps. As the new Ground Forces commander Colonel General Aleksandr Postnikov put it, "It has not been possible to make contract service prestigious; those that could become true professionals have not been recruited, and units that have been brought up to strength with contract servicemen have done so to the detriment of quality."[116] Any question about the quality of the *kontraktnikis* was removed in the war in Georgia when "Contract personnel did not demonstrate the required effectiveness."[117] Then on March 6, Makarov announced that Moscow was cutting funding for the *kontraktniki* program by 86 percent.[118] According to Makarov, "very many mistakes were made and the task that had been set of building professional Armed Forces was not being accomplished."[119] According to another report, the General Staff has decided to reduce the number of *kontraktnikis* "by a minimum of one-and-one-half times, from 200,000 to 130,000–150,000 while increasing their pay." Provided such individuals have a technical specialty, they will see their pay go from an average of around R7,000 to an average of R35,000.[120]

EDUCATION

One problem inherited by the Makarov-Serdyukov team was the poor state of military education. To deal with this issue, Moscow cut the number of military educational institutions from 65 to three military-educational centers, six academies, and one military university. The Kremlin decided that it had too many schools, the majority of which would not be needed with a smaller military. Downsizing provided the Kremlin with an opportunity to raise the quality of the faculty and students. Many specialized schools dealing with issues such as electronics, communications, and logistics offered a common program until the student got to the level when his or her specific type of equipment was involved.

The pillar of the Russian military educational system has been the General Staff Academy, the key supplier of senior officers to the General Staff and other high level positions in the Russian military. In this case, however, Moscow had declared war on the General Staff, and on its hitherto sacred academy as well. Of the seventeen chairs at the academy, only two remained. Instead of graduating 100–120 officers a year, in the future they were to have only 16 students. They were to study both military and civilian topics, be at the rank of major general, and assume senior command positions upon graduation.[121] Then, in 2011, the Academy announced that the training term was being cut to ten months.[122]

CHANGING THE COMMAND STRUCTURE

Moscow also introduced major modifications in the command structure. In the past, the military had four levels of command: military district, army, division, and regiment. In an action reminiscent of what happened in the U.S., the Russians have moved to three levels: military district, operational command, and brigade.[123]

There was one exception—the airborne troops. They were commanded by 52-year-old Lieutenant General Vladimir Shamanov, who had spent most of his career in the airborne troops. He graduated from the Ryazan Airborne Troops School and served in Chechnya where he was chief of staff of the Novorossiysk 7th Division. He later left the military to become the governor of Ulyanovsk Oblast, but returned several years later. He is one of Russia's top military commanders, for example, in August 2008, he commanded Russian forces in Abkhazia—and they did not sustain any casualties.[124] Thus, Shamanov was successful in convincing the military to retain the divisional structure in the airborne forces.

CHAPLAINS AND POLITICAL OFFICERS

Ever since the collapse of the Soviet Union and with it the Communist Party, there had been a morale/moral gap in the Russian Army. The political officers raison d'être disappeared. If there was no party, then the military did not need political officers to preach its doctrines. However, the political officers did more than just spread ideological slogans. They played a critical role at the unit level where they functioned as morale officers. When they disappeared, problems such as *dedovshchina* worsened: there was no one for the soldier to go to with his problems.

The Russians reestablished the political officer in 1992, but there were only a few of them, and their positions were not well designed. This situation changed in the aftermath of the war in Georgia. Several political officers were singled out for their heroic actions "The title of Hero of Russia was conferred on two political workers, and 13 political workers were awarded the Valor Medal."[125] According to a senior defense official in Moscow, the new political officers are called, "Specialists for the Psychological Training of Soldiers." This function, however, is still on trial. Political officers are back at the platoon level in several combat-ready units.[126] Their task is to motivate soldiers and help in the maintenance of discipline. There was one area, however, where there was still a vacuum—the spiritual venue.

In July 2009, Serdyukov initiated a meeting with Russian Orthodox Patriach Kirill, in order to "consult" with him on defense issues.[127] On July 21, Medvedev shocked many in the West when he announced that the Russian military would be getting chaplains. The chaplains do not have a military rank, but are paid at the level of a deputy brigade commander in charge of educational work.[128] Serdyukov stated that he expected between 200 and 250 clergy from four religious groups to be appointed chaplains (Orthodox, Jewish, Muslim, and Buddhist).

TRAINING

The lack of training during the 1990s so crippled the army that when the War with Georgia began, Moscow had to search the country to find qualified ground commanders. According to Makarov, "Because the regular commanding officers, who, having sat there and commanded 'paper regiments and divisions,' were simply not in a position to tackle the issues that arise in a five-day war. When they were given men and equipment, they simply became flustered, and some even floundered, and some even refused to carry out their assignments. Do we need such officers?, I wonder?"[129]

One of the first steps Serdyukov took was to appoint General Shamanov to head the Directorate for Training. Shamanov believed that Russian military training was still behind the times. As he put it, even prior to the war in Georgia, "The experience of the Chechen campaigns and of combat operations in Afghanistan and Iraq showed that forms of warfare have changed substantially in the last 20 years, but our troop training has remained practically unchanged."[130] He made it clear that he was prepared to take foreign experience into account. If Russia could not produce modern training devices and simulators, then Shamanov was prepared to purchase them abroad. The entire training program was transformed. Money was poured into the program, and military exercises began to be held in 2008. By 2009, the Russian Army was carrying out a major exercise, Zapad 2009 to be followed by Vostok 2010. While Shamanov moved on to be in charge of the airborne troops, he managed to turn the training program around, although it will take some time before the military is back where it was prior to the collapse of the USSR.

The Future

The Russian military has a long way to go before a shared relationship will become a reality. Unlike the other three armies, the political leadership does not feel the need to consult with the uniformed military. Given the magnitude of the changes underway, a shared relationship may not be an option.

The military continues to be beset with internal problems, some so deep that it will take years to resolve these issues. However, any realistic attack on the problems that beset the military would require a plan. At this point, military reform appears to be a "floating" concept. If chaplains are needed, they are added. However, no one bothers to ask how they are going to fit into the overall picture of maintaining morale. The same is true of NCOs. Moscow is a long way from figuring out what they are, what they should do, and how they fit into the ranks of the military.

Putin's decision to bite the bullet and raise salaries significantly caused internal political problems—as Finance Minister Alexy Kurdin quit—because the only way salaries could be raised was by robbing money for social services.[131] Higher pay will not necessarily guarantee more soldiers, and the idea of volunteer military service has historically existed only among officer ranks. However, the much higher pay will certainly attract a lot of young men and women to serve. In areas such as crime and corruption the situation appears hopeless.

Seen from the outside, the decision by Putin and Dmitri Medvedev to change positions (Putin to be president, while Medvedev became prime minister) has not fundamentally changed the relationship between the civilian leadership and the armed forces. The two men appear to work together.

In November 2012, Serdyukov was fired. While the reason for his ouster was unclear, there is little doubt that his mishandling of military reform played a major role. He was replaced by Sergei Shoigu, who promised to work with the military. He also agreed to continue the military reform while getting rid of some of those in the MoD most strongly opposed by the military.[132]

Putin still exerts tremendous influence on the military, indeed it was Putin who obtained the 20 trillion rubles to modernize and update military weapons and equipment by 2020. It put the military in the driver's seat. The Russian generals and civilians understand the problems facing them. The problem is technological backwardness combined with semichaos in the ranks. Overcoming the first requires a major overhaul of the country's defense industrial sector. The Russians are at least a generation behind the West. The other issue is how to create a structure that will facilitate the creation of a better relationship between the country's senior civilian officials and those in uniform. Certainly, with the appointment of Shoigu, there is opportunity for a fresh start.

CHAPTER 10

The Search for Shared Responsibility

War is the continuation of politics by other means.

KARL VON CLAUSEWITZ

It is now time to return to the questions posed in the introduction. The thesis of this work is that shared responsibility is the most desirable form of civil-military relations. In such a relationship, the civilians are in charge, and there is no question that their policies will be implemented. But the environment in which the decision-making process takes place has a profound impact on these relations, in particular on the quality of decision-making. National security decision-making will be enhanced by the willingness of civilian leaders to create an atmosphere in which uniformed officers feel free to present their points of view, and the greater the degree to which different points of view are respected, even if not adopted, the greater will be the chances for a shared relationship. If the civilian society and the military share the same values, it is likely that a joint responsibility between civilian and military leaders will develop. Civil-military relations in the four polities discussed here are not so much about a struggle for power; rather they are about the nuanced manner in which civilians implement power in dealing with the uniformed military.

Eight key causal factors determine the nature of the civil-military relationship.

1. *Executive Leadership and Respect for Military Culture.* The greater the degree orders are unclear or senior officers are disrespected, the less is the chance for shared responsibility.

2. *The Military and Shared Responsibility.* Under a policy of shared responsibility generals and admirals must be willing to be involved in national decision-making policy, and accept the principle of civilian leadership and superiority.

3. *Military Symbols.* Failure by the civilian leadership to respect military symbols and tradition will lessen the chances for shared responsibility.

4. *The Need for a Military.* Failure on the part of the civilian elite to believe in the necessity for a viable, strong military force, will lessen the chances for a shared responsibility.

5. *Promotion Process.* Interference by civilian authorities in the promotion process except at the highest level will lessen the chances for shared responsibility.

6. *Civilianization.* Efforts to impose civilianization will be opposed by the military and lessen the chances for shared responsibility.

7. *Change.* Efforts to bring about radical change in the military may undermine any opportunity for shared responsibility.

8. *Dissent.* It is possible to have a shared responsibility with the military openly dissenting, provided this is part of the country's civil-military culture.

In each of the four countries discussed here, an examination of these causal factors sheds light on civil-military relations and the possibility of a fruitful relationship of shared responsibility.

United States

1. *Executive Leadership and Respect for Military Culture.*[1] Because of its stability over the past 70 odd years,[2] there is hardly a case when personal relationships in general and presidential leadership style in particular did not play a major role in the nature of civil-military relations. On only one occasion was there was a danger that the structure of civil-military relations was threatened—when the Joint Chiefs of Staff threatened to resign under Johnson. While there was a nuanced difference between the parties (with the exception of Nixon, the Republicans tended to come closer to having a shared responsibility relationship), the critical factor was the president's personality and leadership style.

John F. Kennedy exercised executive leadership. He was the one who made the major decisions, for example, to invade Cuba, to handle the Cuban missile crisis, and to become involved in Vietnam. In many ways, the problem during the Kennedy period was the military. Their advice was seldom useful, as in the Cuban Missile Crisis, or they were excluded, as in the Bay of Pigs. They had little or no experience in dealing with political-military issues, and were often naive in their approach to political issues.

Lyndon Johnson saw the generals and admirals as a distraction to his Great Society social agenda. He disrespected them, and he made it clear that he did not value their military culture or their years of military experience. The generals primary concern was to find a way to end the Vietnam War on American terms, and to them the answer was simple: bomb the North into submission, an option Johnson feared would bring the Russians and Chinese into the war. The generals returned the disdain he felt for them to the point of almost resigning en masse. Johnson provided leadership, but it was erratic, and on many cases he tried to micromanage operations and tactics. He did everything he could to avoid introducing a policy of shared responsibility.

Richard Nixon, appeared to respect the military and praised them and their service. The problem for the generals was not his leadership: he made it clear that he was in charge. He appeared to the public to work well with the military and to value their advice, but his extreme penchant for secrecy and his Machiavellian, conspiratorial approach to decision making made it impossible to create a shared responsibility relationship.

Gerald Ford worked well with the military on the two issues he dealt with: the withdrawal of troops from Vietnam and the Mayaguez incident. He understood military culture and made the key decisions, but requested and received input from the generals, especially when it came to the Mayaguez. He respected them and their point of view. It could be called a shared responsibility.

Jimmy Carter's election initially elated the military. However, in spite of having graduated from the U.S. Navy Academy, Carter made no effort to show even minimal respect for any of the three services, and he made key military decisions without consulting them. The one exception to his leadership style was the U.S. effort to free the U.S. hostages in Teheran.

Ronald Reagan made it clear from the day he entered office until he left the presidency eight years later that he respected the generals and admirals. He carefully listened to their advice on the invasions of Lebanon and Grenada. Once they had explained the operations to him, they were particularly appreciative of his willingness to leave the operational details to them. They often disagreed with him, for example, over Lebanon, but the relationship was one of shared responsibility.

George H. W. Bush knew the military, and one could argue that of all of the presidents since the World War II, he best understood how to work with both the military and the civilian bureaucracy. In turn the military respected him. He was clearly in charge, but his willingness to hear his generals out prior to making a decision was much appreciated by his colleagues in uniform. The two sides worked together smoothly in a joint relationship during the Panama and Kuwait operations. It was a period of shared responsibility.

Bill Clinton made little distinction between his civilian and military staff. He tended to blame others for foreign policy failures, with one exception—the threat to use military force in Haiti. When it came to Somalia, Bosnia, and Kosovo, he hesitated, but eventually worked well with the military. Even when he took actions the generals disapproved of, for example, "Don't Ask, Don't Tell," they respected him and the way he dealt with them. While it might be a stretch to call it a shared responsibility, by and large, it was a positive relationship.

George W. Bush's relationship with the military was determined by Donald Rumsfeld, who was a disaster as secretary of defense. Rumsfeld had little respect for the military and made no effort to hide it. He provided the worst kind of leadership. The generals and admirals were not only ignored (with the exception of the few who were prepared to do his bidding), they were regularly disrespected.

In 2006, Rumsfeld resigned to be replaced by Bob Gates, who continued into the Obama administration until July 1, 2011, when he was replaced by Leon Panetta.[3] Gates's relationship with the military was always correct. He made it clear that he was in charge, even firing officers when their performance was not up to his high standards. At the same time, he showed respect for the Joint Chiefs and their views. They had a shared responsibility. This was also true during the Obama administration. The decision over whether to surge American troops in Iraq was only made by Obama after he had heard views of both the civilians and the military.

2. *The Military and Shared Responsibility.* The attitude toward working with the civilian leadership was different from one president to the next. In some cases, as under Kennedy, the military was totally unfamiliar with what that meant. In other cases, such as Johnson, Nixon, Carter, or Rumsfeld, the military was prepared to work under them, but were rejected by the civilian leadership. In other instances, the military's willingness to work with civilians was reciprocated and the result was a shared responsibility.

3. *Military Symbols.* With the caveat that the civilian leadership would not accept any symbols critical of the civilian world, or one glorifying a person or event that reflected negatively on the country, the U.S. civilian world paid little attention to military symbols. In fact, like the military, civilians would draw on them when seeking to praise the armed forces.

4. *The Need for a Military.* While the need to use the military abroad ebbed and flowed, with one exception there was no effort to downplay its importance. The exception was Jimmy Carter, who slashed the budget to the point

where major weapons acquisitions atrophied and enlisted personnel were living on food stamps.

5. *Promotion Process.* Except at the highest levels, civilians stayed out of the promotion process with two exceptions. There were rumors that the military was "pushed" on occasion to promote women and minorities.[4] Other than those cases, the promotion process was not politicized.

6. *Civilianization.* The civilian leadership understood that a military professional was different from a civilian. There was no effort to make military service comply with a nine-to-five workday, as was attempted in Germany. However, on occasion, the civilian leadership forced its value system on the military. In the process, the military was forced to accept significant changes. The two major instances were the integration of women at all levels of the military and the struggle over gays, an action that eventually led to the end of the "Don't Ask, Don't Tell" policy. In both cases, the military resisted civilian efforts to force it to accept these changes, but neither had an unusually negative impact on the national security decision-making process.

7. *Change.* While weapons systems and force structure changed over time, in most cases it was gradual. The only attempt to introduce a whole new system of weapons was made by Donald Rumsfeld, and that process did not work. Indeed, it was a contributing factor to the disconnect between Rumsfeld and the army, in particular.

8. *Dissent.* There were two periods when this issue was prominent. The Joint Chiefs threatened to resign under Johnson, and retired officers (including at least one who appears to have resigned for that purpose) spoke out against Donald Rumsfeld. In both instances, there was no chance of shared responsibility.

Germany

1. *Executive Leadership and Respect for Military Culture.* The first years of the post–World War II German military were devoted to figuring out what could be salvaged from the past, while taking over a military made up in large part of former Wehrmacht soldiers. The country's top military officer's authority was limited to being an advisor to the defense minister. Even when the situation began to be stabilized and the chief of staff was given a more prominent role, he was still subordinate to a civilian under secretary who reported to the defense minister.

Adenauer's primary concern was creating a modern military as a contribution to NATO while ensuring that the new military rejected the culture of the past. Personal relationships were good, partly because the Bundeswehr was not a political actor in the traditional sense. The problems came from the opposition SPD (Social Democratic Party) and society at large, which objected to some of the ways the military portrayed tradition or carried out training. It was a relationship of shared responsibility, but only in the sense that Adenauer controlled politics and listened to the generals who worked for him.

Ludwig Erhard focused almost entirely on economic matters. He could have played a major role given the problems that beset civil-military relations, but he was nowhere to be found. This was especially true during the "Crisis of the Generals," which revealed considerable differences of opinion between civilian and military leaders over the question of civilian involvement in the internal affairs of the Bundeswehr.

Kurt Georg Kiesinger was also not interested in the military. At a time when the debate over military tradition came to the fore in the Grashey affair, it was General de Maiziere who saved the day by convincing the generals and captains to tone down the rhetoric and begin to work toward major reforms. It was not a shared relationship.

Willy Brandt's most important contribution to civil-military relations was his decision to delegate authority to Helmut Schmidt, his defense minister. Schmidt had credibility with the military. He opened a discussion with Bundeswehr officers while fighting politicization of the officer corps. Schmidt revamped the educational system, and took a personal interest in Innere Führung. When Brandt left office, civil-military relations were in much better shape. For the first time, German civil-military relations began to reach the level of a shared responsibility.

Helmut Schmidt followed up the work he had done as defense minister as chancellor. He remained opposed to contacts with those from the Wehrmacht as shown by the Rudel affair. He strongly opposed the left wing of the SPD's efforts to get rid of military traditions such as the Grand Tattoo. He and his defense minister, Hans Apel, were also the first to deal with the end of the Soviet threat and the changing military environment. Schmidt worked with the military and, in the process, created a shared responsibility even though he was from the party that usually opposed the military on issues like tradition and civilianization.

During his time in office, Chancellor Helmut Kohl remained in the background, leaving it to his defense minister, Manfred Woerner, to deal with the military. Convinced that too much of the military side of life in the Bundeswehr had been lost, Woerner worked to make the Bundeswehr a "real" military, not a "peace army" as it appeared to be becoming. He demanded appropriate changes in tradition, but Woerner's position had been weakened by other factors, and nothing happened.

One of the challenges confronting authorities during Kohl's time in office was transforming the military from a territorial to an expeditionary force. The new defense minister Volker Rühe, and the chief of staff, General Klaus Naumann, worked together to come up with a solution, including the possible end to conscription. If there were ever an action that demanded a shared relationship, this was it. And the problem was not only structural—it was also financial. Thanks to Naumann and Rühe, an effort to work together trying to deal with a myriad of problems was a step in the right direction.

Gerhard Schroeder sent German troops to Kosovo in 1998. Given their miserable performance, it was obvious that the country needed a professional army sooner rather than later. But the chief of staff and the defense minister did not speak to each other, and their antagonism soon became public. The defense minister refused to ask for a budgetary increase. It was not a positive period in civil-military relations.

Peter Struck became defense minister in 2002 and worked closely with the new chief of staff, General Wolfgang Schneiderhan. It was a difficult period: some officers found their careers jeopardized as their military branch or specialty was cut, leading to the forced retirement of senior officers. While Schneiderhan's support of Struck's actions drew the ire of some of his colleagues, he and the defense minister worked together in a shared responsibility.

Angela Merkel appointed Franz Jozef Jung defense minister. He began by refusing to cancel the Grand Tattoo ceremony in spite of strong agitation by the left. He was forced to deal with a number of scandals, and he worked closely with Schneiderhan at a time when the Germans in Afghanistan increasingly found themselves in a "hot" war. He changed the "rules of engagement" to enable German soldiers to operate under the same conditions as U.S. and British troops. Meanwhile, it was becoming increasingly clear that the Bundeswehr was in horrible shape, incapable of carrying out the missions assigned to it.

Karl-Theodor zu Guttenberg, a flamboyant politician from the Christian Democratic Party (CDU), became defense minister in 2009. He made working closely with the military a priority, protecting them while fighting for more resources. The killing of numerous Afghan civilians at the behest of a

German colonel put him in a difficult position politically that he handled by firing the chief of staff, General Wolfgang Schneiderhan. The latter was replaced by General Volker Wicker.

From the standpoint of the average member of the Bundeswehr, the most important problem facing the military was radical reform. Guttenberg even announced the nature of the forthcoming changes in a speech before the Bundeswehr Academy, the extent of which shocked serving officers: their careers were at stake. General Wicker provided him with bureaucratic cover when he criticized the management of troops and called for a restructuring of the armed forces. Guttenberg set up a commission in an effort to come up with an acceptable structural modification.

In the meantime, Guttenberg was caught up in a scandal over his doctoral dissertation, which, it turned out, had been plagiarized. He was replaced by Thomas de Maiziere, who continued Guttenberg's policy of shared responsibility, despite the major changes that were about to befall the Bundeswehr. Some, like the elevated role of the chief of staff, who would now be in charge of all the services, were greeted warmly by senior officers.

The radical changes in the services may have been a fiscal and military necessity, but they meant the end of many careers. The military was deeply involved in devising these changes (after all, the chairman of the Weise Commission was a reserve colonel), and the military's views were taken into consideration before changes were introduced. Beginning with Struck's tenure, relations between the military and the civilians have been characterized as a shared responsibility.

2. *The Military and Shared Responsibility.* The German military was of two minds in its first years. It wanted to work with political authorities, but often pushed back as one attempt after another was made to change its traditions. Later on, the issue became military reform. The generals understood the need to move from a territorial to an expeditionary military—with all the changes that meant. The problem was that it meant the end of many careers. Nevertheless, there was shared responsibility in that the military and civilians worked together in trying to find a way to implement change.

3. *Military Symbols.* The primary concern throughout the first half of the Bundeswehr's existence was to develop an acceptable military culture. How blind was obedience? A whole new policy, titled Innere Führung, was developed, which sought to reconceptualize the soldier's relationship to his superiors and the state. The issue was heavily fought back and forth, with the content gradually changing in the eyes of many from the Wehrmacht toward

the direction of a more permissive environment. If the fight over tradition did anything, it undermined efforts to create a shared relationship.

4. *The Need for a Military.* The Germans did not have much of a chance in deciding whether they needed a military or not. Despite some domestic opposition, it was a decision made by the Allies and Chancellor Adenauer; the German military was too valuable not to be used to counter the Russian threat during the Cold War.

The need for a military would be questioned several times during its first sixty years. The left-wing of the SPD was especially determined to rid the country of what it considered an unnecessary and dangerous vestige of Germany's darkest past. Yet, there were SPD leaders who understood the need for a military. The most notable example was Helmut Schmidt, who showed the tremendous importance a leader can play. He did not win over his left wing, but he maintained control of the ship of state. As far as he was concerned, the military was necessary, and that was that.

It is easy for political leadership to ignore the military if it is not a vital component in the implementation of foreign policy. Since the post-Schmidt period, none of the administrations have questioned the importance of having a military, although they have had different plans for dealing with it in terms of structure, funding, and deployment. In a recent interview with the current defense minister, Thomas de Maiziere, he commented that the point that impressed him about the decision to send German soldiers to Afghanistan was that it was supported by a left-leaning Green Party Bundestag representative and also by the Social Democratic minister.[5] Times have changed, and there are calls for Germany to pull back its troops, but the idea of German troops playing a role overseas is an established fact. The debate is over finding the funds to support the military so it can carry out these missions. The important factor is that the military and civilian elites are working together.

5. *Promotion Process.* There was minimal interference in the promotion process except during the 1960s and 1970s, when there were officers who openly defied political authority over issues such as symbols. It appears to have been a case of firing an officer rather than interfering in the promotion process, although there were instances when officers in favor of policies such as Innere Führung were singled out for special attention. One of the basic criteria of a shared responsibility is being observed.

6. *Civilianization.* More than any of the other countries analyzed in this paper, the Bundeswehr had to fight a constant battle against efforts by the left wing of the SPD, which was constantly trying to get rid of what German offi-

cers considered the heart of their culture. The left wing of the SPD maintained that being a truck driver in Afghanistan was the same as driving around Europe. It was only when German troops went to Afghanistan that the military began to convince their civilian colleagues that fighting the Taliban was different from a nine-to-five civilian job. Civilianization undermined efforts at creating a shared relationship. However, as with the Canadians, Afghanistan provided a proving ground for those who favored military culture.

7. *Change.* This writer was surprised to see how well German forces have adapted to the massive changes that they are experiencing as they move from territorial to expeditionary warfare. Many officers are bitter—after putting in 18 years of dedicated service, only to be told they are no longer necessary. However, the institution appears to be adapting. Most of the credit goes to senior political-military German leadership. Despite disagreements, since Peter Struck became defense minister, there appears to have been a genuine effort to create a shared relationship, which has made the transition somewhat smoother.

8. *Dissent.* Given its past, the German military has gone out of its way to permit dissent. The history of the Bundeswehr is filled with senior officers who resigned, especially in the 1960s and 1970s over the question of tradition. In some cases, the resignation was a result of civilian action, in other cases it was the individual's own decision.

Canada

1. *Executive Leadership and the Respect for Military Culture.* Of the four countries discussed in this book, Canada has experienced the stormiest civil-military relations. It went through periods of extreme distrust on both sides, to one of a shared relationship under Prime Ministers Martin and Harper.

Paul Hellyer is probably the most hated post–World War II civilian defense official in recent Canadian history. In an effort to save money, he set out in the mid-1960s to transform a conservative and insular Canadian military. He was not concerned about building bridges to the military, and as a result, his relations with the senior military officers were marked by conflict as they saw this civilian attempt to make drastic changes. He was determined to unify the services. This meant destroying the rich tradition of the Canadian Army, Royal Navy, and Royal Air Force in the face of strong, vocal opposition from uniformed officers. The services were united into Canadian Forces, and all servicemen wore the same uniform, an action the Navy found especially upsetting. The one area where there was civilian-military cooperation was in dealing with the Francophone issue: General Jean Allard insisted on giving more weight to the French language and was supported by Hellyer. However, that was an isolated issue, and one that the majority of those in uniform, who were Anglophones, opposed.

Prime Minister Pierre Trudeau did not improve matters. As far as he was concerned, the unification of the services was a closed issue. He had little interest in the services, turned away from NATO, sought major reductions in force strength, and froze the military budget. In this process, the views of the military were considered unimportant.

The only positive interaction between Trudeau and the CF was in 1970, when they were deployed to Quebec to deal with a domestic crisis. The military reacted to what they considered bureaucratic chaos in the military command structure, which they saw as an attempt by civilians to interfere in the conduct of normal operational matters, not to mention policy issues. No shared responsibility existed at this time. Besides, the largely Anglophone officer corps resented the push of the French language and what they saw as preferential treatment for Francophone officers.

The military, at the bottom of Trudeau's concerns, received little money, and was in a mess with its weapons worn out and obsolete. It was only Helmut Schmidt's intervention that helped the army purchase used German tanks. By the mid-1980s, the situation had so deteriorated that it became a major issue in the 1983 election campaign.

Brian Mulroney promised to do something about the military budget when he took power in 1984. The problem, however, was that the 1985 deficit was $9 billion higher than the Trudeau government predicted. From the military's point of view, one step forward was the decision in 1986 to permit them to return to their traditional uniforms.

The 1989 budget was formed without the military's input and, in 1992, Canada deployed airborne forces to Somalia with disastrous results. The unprepared troops should have never been sent, something the CDS should have told the prime minister.

Jean Chrétien made it clear at his first cabinet meeting that the military did not figure high in his priorities by cancelling a replacement for the 40-year-old Sea King helicopters. Morale plummeted, in large part due to the military's inability to deal with scandal over Somalia. What followed from the civilian standpoint was a several-year debate focusing on reasons why Canada did not need a modern, highly capable military, a debate in which the CF appears to have played a minimal role.

Conditions in the CF continued to deteriorate as civilian leadership failed to provide modern weapons while Ottawa interfered in military operations in the Balkans. Weapons were increasingly obsolete, soldiers were using food banks, while the CF faced demands from the prime minister's office to step up operations in peacekeeping missions—all in the face of a decreasing budget. The situation had become desperate, especially with the deployment of Canadian troops to Afghanistan on the horizon. Chrétien's time in office was anything but one of shared responsibility.

Paul Martin was different from Chrétien. Both of them were from the Liberal Party, but Martin saw the CF as a war fighting organization in need of change. The budget was increased in 2004, and the CF's shortcomings were addressed. Most important was the appointment of General Rick Hillier as chief of the defence staff (CDS) and Martin's willingness to work with him in correcting some of the CF's shortcomings. Martin worked well with his defense minister. As in Germany, realization of Hillier's plans for reorganizing the military meant upsetting those officers whose bureaucratic fiefdoms were cut back or eliminated. Hillier worked closely with his civilian superiors in revamping the CF.

Hillier put his ideas for reorganization behind a new defence policy paper in 2005, while his civilian superiors attempted to provide the funds needed, only to be turned down by the cabinet. Hillier was furious, not at Martin, but at his colleagues, who didn't seem to understand the importance of a highly technological and capable CF. As far as his most important civilian colleagues were concerned, however, they had established a shared relationship.

Even though Stephen Harper was from a different party than Martin, Harper believed a strong CF was vital for Canadian foreign policy. He supported Hillier's efforts to restructure CF, although Hillier did have problems with his new defence minister. That situation changed in August 2007, with the appointment of Peter McKay as defence minister. The two were to work together throughout Hillier's reign as CDS. As a result, in Afghanistan, the formally noncombative CF sprang into action, suffered the highest proportional rate of casualties among the Allies, and changed the Allied view of the Canadian soldiers, as Ottawa stayed out of the picture and permitted those on the scene to take command.

Another change Harper permitted was the reemergence of Canadian military culture by transforming the command structure. In addition, service loyalty and pride was increased, especially in 2011 when Harper reestablished the services' traditional names: the Canadian Army, the Royal Canadian Navy, and the Royal Canadian Air Force. Hillier was not afraid to stand up to civilian authorities when he thought their ideas were wrong, even making it clear that if he disagreed with policy, he would resign.

General Walter Natynczyk, the next CDS, followed up on Hillier's actions by continuing to maintain a shared responsibility at the behest of Harper, who won greater control of Parliament in the 2011 parliamentary elections. The Harper government announced a 20-year defence plan that called for spending CN$490 billion over the next 20 years. Shared responsibility became a trademark of the Martin and Harper administrations.

2. *The Military and Shared Responsibility.* In the early years, with the battles of World War II still fresh in mind, the military tended to see itself as an independent entity. That idea was crushed under Hellyer's leadership. His changes, hated by the military, together with the lack of respect on the part of the civilian leadership, did little to build a shared responsibility. It was only later, when Canadian political leadership began to take an interest in the status of the CF, that the political leadership began to elicit the military's opinion.

3. *Military Symbols.* One reason for the poor relations between the military and Hellyer was his open contempt for military symbols as "buttons and badges." As long as the defense minister expressed such views on a topic as sensitive to the military as the ribbons they wore, there was no chance that there would be a shared responsibility. While he did not articulate his views as bluntly as Hellyer, Trudeau also had little respect for military symbols. The Somalia disaster also uprooted respect for symbols—in this case, the fault was the military's. This approach changed under Martin and Harper who valued shared relationship with the military.

4. *The Need for the Military.* In this sense, Canada differed from the evolution of civil-military relations in the U.S. and Germany in which the military was always a critical part of foreign policy. As in Russia under Yeltsin, the military was not considered a critical component of Canada's foreign policy, except as a source of peacekeepers to provide the prime minister with a tool he could use to influence other political leaders, especially the American president. There was little respect for the CF among the Canadian population because few considered it critical to the nation's survival. This only changed with Hillier's emergence under the Martin and Harper administrations. The country needed the military if it wanted to be taken seriously on international issues. Respect for the military increased as exemplified by the public honor paid to CF soldiers who were killed in the conflict in Afghanistan. A shared relationship was the norm of the Harper administration.

5. *Promotion Process.* Hellyer made it clear that only those officers who supported the unified and restructured CF would be promoted to top positions. In addition, Canada introduced an affirmative action policy to help Francophone officers advance to more senior positions, a policy deeply resented by the Anglophone officers who opposed giving Francophone officers advantages because of their ethnic background. The criteria for promotion above lieutenant colonel (knowledge of both languages) still exists, but how strictly that policy is enforced is unknown. Shared responsibility does not appear to have been affected by the Canadian approach to promotions.

6. *Civilianization.* The CF fought a long battle against those on the left who made the argument that it was just a group of peacekeepers, and that much of its job was like that of civilians. One of the constant and most bitter battles in the upper ranks of the CF was over the role of civilians in the Department of National Defence (DND) and other structures. It was only with Hillier's rise, and the move to make the CF into combat soldiers under military command in Afghanistan, that the idea of civilianization slid into the background. These were soldiers who were highly respected for their fighting ability by their NATO colleagues. They fought and fought well. By the Harper period, this factor has pushed the civilians and military toward a shared responsibility.

7. *Change.* The first effort to bring about change by Hellyer was deeply resented by the CF officers not only because of its radical nature (e.g., forcing sailors to wear army-like uniforms), but because they did not consider themselves part of the process. Hellyer decided what changes to introduce and forced them on the military. Under Martin and Harper, some officers disagreed with their reforms, but in time the chief of the defence staff (CDS) was closely involved. This is similar to the approached taken in Germany. De Maiziere has called for radical changes (from territorial to expeditionary forces), but he has kept the military closely involved in the process, a key part of a joint relationship.

8. *Dissent.* Resigning or threatening to resign over policy is a well-established policy among senior Canadian officers. Admiral Landymore publicly opposed Hellyer's policies, and for a while he was tolerated. He was finally forced to retire, but few among the officer corps seem to feel that he had violated any rules. Then between January 1965 and August 1966, 28 general officers resigned, including three "three stars." General Jean Allard threatened to resign if Hellyer did not pay attention to the Francophone issue. Hillier stated that he would resign if he had fundamental differences with the civilian leadership. While there are still officers who disagree with policy and say so from

time to time, the open dissent and challenge to authority common in earlier periods is not present, creating one of the key aspects of a joint relationship.

Russia

1. *Executive Leadership and Respect for Military Culture.* Gorbachev did not understand the military, and his policies such as glasnost undermined military order. He permitted the media to openly attack the military. Many officers feared that the military was on the verge of collapse and that Gorbachev did not care. Then, he issued orders for the military to use force three times, but did not take responsibility for his actions. There was no chance for a relationship of shared responsibility.

Yeltsin appeared interested in the military during the chaos of the collapse of the USSR and made numerous promises. He even relied upon them in 1993 to save his administration by using force against those who had barricaded themselves in the Duma building. The problem was that in reality, Yeltsin was only interested in a military that would not pose a political threat. He paid little attention to their fundamental needs, as the military was starved in every way possible. He changed the structural nature of the relationship between the defense minister and the chief of the general staff in an effort to further undermine any attempt by the military to become a political actor.

Yeltsin interfered in the first Chechen operation, a disaster for the military, and he openly insulted the generals by violating a fundamental premise of military culture—"praise in public, criticize in private." The military came close to collapse, planes did not fly, ships did not sail, and tanks remained silent. It was so bad that servicemen were sent to look for mushrooms to supplement their diets. Yeltsin offered to support military reform, but he was not about to provide the money needed to support the reform process or develop a relationship of shared responsibility.

From the military standpoint, the only positive action he took was his appointment of Vladimir Putin as prime minister. Putin made it clear to the military that he respected them, giving them the green light to carry out the war in Chechnya as they wished. When Putin became president, he inherited serious problems in the military. He began by reestablishing order in dealings with the military and began to raise its budget. In the process, he gave the generals what they desperately sought—predictability and stability. While he would have to fire both his defense minister and his chief of general staff, he worked with the military in a smoother fashion than Yeltsin. He brought in a new former KGB general to serve as defense minister, and matters appeared to be moving in the right direction, toward shared responsibility, until it became obvious to Defense Minister Sergei Ivanov that corruption was rampant. Putin then moved Ivanov to another position and brought in Anatolii Serdyukov. While Putin and his successor Dmitri Medvedev worked well with the military, everything seemed to go through Serdyukov, thereby inhibiting any chance for a joint relationship.

Serdyukov was a different kind of leader, an accountant who set about trying to get a handle on corruption in the armed forces. One problem led to another, and Serdyukov gradually became convinced that radical changes were necessary if the military were to be brought into the twenty-first century. He replaced all of the senior leadership, convincing the chief of the General Staff to resign. That was followed by massive, radical changes. From the standpoint of civil-military relations he was not interested in shared responsibility. His changes were chaotic, lacking a plan or coherence. At one point he reduced the officer corps to 150,000, only to decide later to add 70,000 officers.

In theory, Serdyukov worked through his chief of the General Staff, General Nikolai Makarov. However, Makarov was often caught by surprise when Serdyukov made important decisions, leaving the impression that he too was not consulted. In 2011, Putin made it clear that Russia would devote a considerable part of its budget to rebuilding the military. While such an action was appreciated, as far as civil-military relations are concerned, Serdyukov was determined to carry out his plan to remake the military and had no intention of working with them. For practical purposes, as long as Serdyukov was defense minister, the creation of a joint relationship would remain nothing but a pipe-dream. The new defense minister appears determined to work with the generals.

2. *The Military and a Shared Responsibility.* The military was only given a chance to be heard when Putin and Ivanov were in charge. The military was prepared to work with Yeltsin and played a major role in his standoff against the Duma, but he quickly forgot them and insulted them. Once Serdyukov took over, he made it clear that he was not interested in working with the military. He did not care what senior officers thought; in fact, he began a process of getting rid of them.

3. *Military Symbols.* There is no indication that the Kremlin did anything against the symbolic life of the Russian military.

4. *The Need for a Military.* Yeltsin made it clear throughout his tenure that he did not need the military. From his perspective, Russia did not face a military threat, so he saw no reason to invest in or show respect for the armed forces. Putin felt differently. He was not consumed with building a modern

military, but he believed that a strong military was an important part of an effective foreign policy. That continued under Medvedev until 2011, when Putin decided to modernize the armed forces. This was clearly a sign that he felt a greater need for a modern military. Unfortunately, the personal open relationship that is critical for a joint relationship remains elusive.

5. *Promotion Process.* There is no sign that the Kremlin involved itself in the promotion process except by Serdyukov.

6. *Civilianization.* In spite of the way both Gorbachev and Yeltsin treated the military, there was no effort to civilianize the military the way the left had attempted to treat the Canadians and Germans.

7. *Change.* The changes introduced by Serdyukov have turned the Russian military upside down. The General Staff lost the stability and predictability that Putin had created during his first term as president. Serdyukov's lack of a coherent plan and his failure to consult the military led to a serious morale problem in the military. This is one of the major reasons why a shared responsibility was an impossibility.

8. *Dissent.* From Vorobyev and his more than 500 colleagues who resigned rather than lead troops in the First War in Chechnya to Baluyevskii's submission of three letters of resignation, Russian officers have repeatedly used resignation or the threat of resignation as a vehicle to influence or denounce policy. Russian military officers (usually, but not always retired) have repeatedly published articles criticizing Russian military policy. Given the acceptance of dissent in Russia today, it does not appear to be a problem for the development of a joint relationship.

Conclusion

What does the foregoing mean for the study of civil-military relations?

First, the basic assumption in this work is that a shared responsibility is desired from the perspective of both senior civilian and military officials. This means the generals feel comfortable expressing their views on national security issues. When civilian officials use persuasion, it helps create a situation in which senior civilian officials will enjoy a maximum interchange of information, views, and opinions with their military colleagues. It is irrelevant whether the military side agrees with civilian official plans. Without being concerned about retribution, it maximizes the opportunity for civilians to gain the full and enthusiastic cooperation of military officers.

Second, this book assumes that the senior officers accept civilian supremacy, although there have been exceptions like MacArthur. This approach is not relevant for the study of civil-military relations in a polity where the military seizes or threatens to seize power from time to time. Pakistan is a good example.

All decisions taken in the national security arena have political overtones, and it is critical that both sides understand these decisions are highly sensitive. When military officers are called upon to make statements that carry a serious political overtone (e.g., the American military commenting on the surge in Iraq), it is critical that they remember they are only advisors; the senior civilian must make the decision, and suffer the political consequences.

Third, the goal here has been to determine the key factors associated with the creation of a shared responsibility by focusing on trends and not statistics. To what degree are the factors discussed above present in a period of shared responsibility? Which factors are most important? The answer may depend on the country concerned. This model cannot be used to predict the exact and systematic nature of civil-military relations. Instead, it shows if there are trends toward or away from a shared relationship.

Fourth, none of the four polities discussed here are mirror images of the others. Each has it is own history, civilian culture, and military culture. It illustrates the continuing importance of history and culture. Some practices are permitted in one but not in another. One of the clearest examples is the case of resignation from active duty over a policy difference. Only in the U.S. has it been suggested that resignation over policy or speaking out against policy when retired is "against the rules." However, the main characteristics of military culture are similar enough in their role in all four militaries to permit comparison.

What is the relative importance of these causal factors?

1. *Executive Leadership and Respect for Military Culture.* Personal relationships are the most important factor in determining a shared responsibility. It was clearly the overwhelming factor in the U.S., and played an important role in Germany as exemplified by Helmut Schmidt and the Merkel administrations. The same is true of Canada between Hillier and Natynczyk, on the one hand, and Martin and Harper, on the other. In the Russian case, neither Gorbachev nor Yeltsin made any effort to establish a personal relationship with the military leadership. Putin created a better relationship, but found it necessary to bring in one of his former KGB colleagues to manage matters, and then brought in Serdyukov because of corruption. The latter made no effort to create shared responsibility.

2. *The Military and Shared Responsibility.* Officers in all four countries

accepted the principle of civilian superiority when they took their oaths of office. With a few exceptions, the military has been prepared to work with its civilian leadership. When that has failed, it is generally because the civilians did not want it to work.

3. *Military Symbols.* The German and Canadian cases suggest that a failure to respect symbols by a civilian executive makes a viable relationship almost impossible. In Canada, Hellyer was able to create a working relationship with General Jean Allard, but the latter was driven not by the normal aspects of civil-military relations, but by his almost fanatical determination to improve the status of Francophone members of the CF.

4. *The Need for the Military.* This factor focuses primarily on Canada and Russia. During the periods when there was no officially recognized need for the military in Canada (useful only as peacekeepers), there was no pressure to create a shared relationship. It was only when Afghanistan became a major issue, Hillier appeared on the scene, and he and Martin agreed on the need for a strong military to back up foreign policy that they began moving toward a shared relationship. In Russia, neither Gorbachev nor Yeltsin saw the military as an important structure, and so the military was ignored. Putin began working more closely with the military in an effort to restore it as a viable organization. This worked until Serdyukov became defense minister. He considered the military important, but his policies so destroyed the existing structure and evoked so much military opposition that it became impossible to create a meaningful civil-military relationship. Putin's decision to make a major investment in the armed forces in 2011 signaled that he considered the armed forces important, but it has yet to translate into an effort to create a shared relationship.

5. *Promotion Process.* With the exception of Canada, where the Francophone issue played a major role in the promotion process, and Russia under Serdyukov, the other three governments have not meddled with the promotion process except at the highest level. The integration of blacks, women, and gays into the U.S. military created some opposition, but few officers openly opposed it or, when they did with the gay issue under Obama, they made their objections clear, and once the president decided the policy, moved quickly to implement it.

6. *Civilianization.* Civilianization is the opposite of military culture. Military culture is aimed at killing people (and maybe getting killed), so the push for civilianization by the left wing of the SPD in Germany undermined efforts to create an even-handed relationship. It was only when Helmut Schmidt appeared on the scene that the Bundeswehr found a champion to give greater

attention to fighting wars, and this was especially true when German troops were sent to Afghanistan.

Civilian involvement in Canadian military affairs was a constant source of tension. Hillier appears to have had a major impact in this area, and the result has been the creation of a smoother relationship between the military and the civilian factions.

7. *Change.* Three of the militaries discussed here have undergone major changes. In Germany and Canada, the military has been closely involved in decision making at critical points. It has been disruptive and it has hurt a lot of officers' careers, but in both cases, the military has been permitted to voice its concerns, and they appear to have been considered. Russia is an example of the exact opposite. Serdyukov fired all of the country's most senior officers and replaced them with officers who supported his changes, undermining a shared relationship.

Rumsfeld's attempts to restrict the active duty military's involvement in devising new approaches or plans for the military resulted in numerous problems. When he left and Gates brought the military back into the process, the relationship improved.

8. *Dissent.* In three of the four countries discussed, resignation over policy is considered a normal part of civil-military relations. Hillier took the view that if he could not support the government's policy, then he would resign. That was also Landymore's view and the view of numerous other Canadian officers. German officers have resigned on numerous occasions when they believed they could not support the government's policy. The situation in Russia is the same, and officers have resigned. Contrary to the American case, German, Canadian, and Russian civil-military relations see no conflict between resignation over policy and the creation of shared responsibility. The same is true for retired officers who decide to speak out critically about the government's official policy.

Final Thoughts. As stressed repeatedly, the civilians are in charge and it is up to the civilians to determine the nature of the professional relationship. However, this study of four different polities suggests that civilians who are concerned about civil-military relations and who desire to create a shared relationship in dealing with their military subordinates would be advised to keep the factors discussed here in mind. Although in some cases I have simplified situations I would argue that this study helps lay the groundwork for a long-term positive relationship.

Future Research

This book was limited to four countries. There are other nations whose militaries are subordinate to civilian authorities, for example Australia, the U.K., France, Spain, Italy, Japan, Poland, and perhaps even China, Ireland, and Sweden. Do the same trends noted here also appear in these countries? To what degree do the civilian and military leaders deal with civil-military relations in a shared relationship? Do causal factors noted here play a greater or lesser degree of importance? How is resignation handled in other stable, developed polities? To what degree do different political and military cultures play an important role?

Civilianization is also a potential problem in a wide variety of countries. How real is the issue? In a polity like Russia, the civilians have taken over major military power, but paid minimal attention to the country's generals. Are there other examples?

One factor that appears predominantly in this study is stability. In three of the four cases, change was evolutionary rather than revolutionary. The one exception is Russia. It is hard to imagine a country in which civil-military relations have been more upset than in the Russian Federation. How will Putin create a situation of shared responsibility?

This study represents a stop along the way to a better understanding of civil-military relations and a beacon toward a better understanding of the process in a number of polities.

Notes

CHAPTER 1. A Conceptual Framework for Shared Responsibility

1. See, for example, the discussion of the surge in Iraq as presented in Bob Woodward, *Obama's Wars* (New York: Simon and Schuster, 2010), which displays an open give-and-take between senior military officers and civilians. In fact, not all civilians are on one side, nor are all military officers.

2. Sam Huntington, *The Soldier and the State* (Cambridge, MA: Harvard University Press, 1957).

3. For an excellent discussion of the problems involved in separating policy from operations, see Frank G. Hoffman, "Dereliction of Duty *Redux?* Post-Iraq American Civil-Military Relations," *Orbis* 52, no. 2 (Spring 2008): 219.

4. Huntington, *The Soldier and the State,* 11.

5. For an updated view of Huntington's relevance today, see Suzanne C. Nielsen and Don M. Snider, *American Civil-Military Relations: The Soldier and the State in a New Era* (Baltimore: Johns Hopkins University Press, 2009). One of the best critiques of Huntington's model is Peter D. Feaver, "The Civil-Military Problematique: Huntington, Janowitz, and the Problem of Civil-Control," *Armed Forces and Society* 23, no. 2 (Winter 1996): 149–78.

6. Michael Desch, "Soldiers, States and Structures: The End of the Cold War and Weakening U.S. Civilian Control," *Armed Forces and Society* 24, no. 3 (Spring 1998): 391. He repeats this approach in his book-length study of civil-military relations, *Civilian Control of the Military: The Changing Security Environment* (Baltimore: Johns Hopkins University Press, 1999), 3–6.

7. Kenneth Kemp and Charles Hudlin, "Civil Supremacy over the Military: Its Nature and Its Limits," *Armed Forces and Society* 19, no.1 (Fall 1992): 9.

8. Richard K. Betts, *Soldiers, Statesmen and Cold War* (New York: Columbia University Press, 1991), 5; Richard Kohn, "The Erosion of Civilian Control of the Military in the United States Today," *Naval War College Review* (Summer, 2002), http://findarticles.com/p/articles/mi_mojiW/is92745784/print.

9. For an essay arguing the critical importance of "influence" see Kobi Michael, "The Dilemma behind the Classical Dilemma of Civil-Military Relations," *Armed Forces and Society* 33, no. 4 (2007): 518–46. See also Peter Feaver, "The Right to Be Right," *International Security* 35, no. 4 (Spring 2011): 87–125.

10. Peter D. Feaver and Christopher Gelpi, *Choosing Your Battles: American Civil-Military Relations and the Use of Force* (Princeton: Princeton University Press, 2004), 1–5. As they state, "Military officer respondents report what they called a 'realpolitik' approach

to the issue, one that reserves the use of force for interstate issues that represent a substantial threat to national security such as control of territory, the maintenance of geostrategic access and positions, and the defense of allies" (5–6). See also Deborah Avant, "Conflicting Indicators of 'Crisis' in American Civil-Military Relations," *Armed Forces and Society* 24, no. 3 (1998): 384. She notes that "what most critics complain about in today's American civil-military relationship is precisely the opposite—that the military is too self-limiting, both in the use of force and in its engagement in activities other than war."

11. Christopher P. Gibson and Don M. Snider, "Civil-Military Relations and the Potential to Influence: A Look at the National Security Decision-Making Process," *Armed Forces and Society* 25, no. 2 (Winter, 1999): 195.

12. Avant, "Conflicting Indicators of 'Crisis' in American Civil-Military Relations," 383.

13. Samuel Huntington and Zbigniew Brzezinski, *Political Power, US/USSR* (New Haven: Yale University Press, 1964).

14. Desch, *Civilian Control of the Military.*

15. Desch, "Soldiers, States and Structures," 390.

16. Compare, for example, Desch's discussion of the Russian experience with this writer's *The Kremlin and the High Command* (Lawrence: University Press of Kansas, 2006). The Russian military was far less of an internal threat to political control than Desch's study indicated, in fact, it was in a state bordering on chaos given Yeltsin's lack of leadership and respect for the military.

17. Peter D. Feaver, *Armed Servants: Agency, Oversight, and Civil-Military Relations* (Cambridge, MA: Harvard University Press, 2003).

18. Rebecca Schiff, *The Military and Domestic Politics: A Concordance Theory of Civil-Military Relations* (New York: Routledge, 2009).

19. Ibid.

20. Douglas Bland, "A Unified Theory of Civil-Military Relations," *Armed Forces and Society* 26, no. 1 (Fall 1999): 6, 18, 19, and 20 discussed in text.

21. Ibid., 10.

22. Ibid., 19. Emphasis in the original.

23. Edwin Dorn, Walter F. Ulmer, Joseph J. Collins, and T. O. Jacobs, *American Military Culture in the Twenty-first Century* (Washington, DC: CSIS Press, 2000), 3. See also Edgar Schein, "Organizational Culture," *American Psychologist* (February 1990): 110.

24. Nick Jans with David Schmidtchen, *The Real C-Cubed: Culture, Careers, and Climate and How They Affect Military Capability* (Canberra: Strategic and National Studies Centre, Australian National Defence University, 2002), 39.

25. One may argue that paramilitary forces such as the police also require the individual to put his or her life on the line in carrying out duties, and that is why some of the military's cultural characteristics are shared by police forces. However, the military is more removed from civilian society and is trained to use more complex forms of violence. For a discussion of civilian and military culture, see, Thomas Langston, "The Civilian Side of Military Culture," *Parameters* (Autumn 2000): 21.

26. Sam G. Sarkesian and Robert E. Connor, *The US Military Profession into the 20th Century* (Portland: Frank Capps, 1999), 79.

27. For a more detailed discussion of military culture, see Williamson Murray, "Does Military Culture Matter?" *Orbis* (Winter 1999): 27; John Hillen, "Must U.S. Military Culture Reform?" *Orbis* (Winter 1999): 43; Williamson Murray, "Military Culture Does Mat-

ter," *FPRI Wire* 7, no 2, http://www.fpri.org/fpriwire/0702.199901.murray.militaryculture doesmatter.

28. *German sources:* Detlef Bald, *Die Bundeswehr: Eine kritische Geschichte, 1955–2005* (Munich: Verlag Beck, 2005); Donald Abenheim, *Reforging the Iron Cross: The Search for Tradition in the German Armed Forces* (Princeton: Princeton University Press, 1988); Wayne C. Thompson and Marc D. Peltier, "The Education of Military Officers in the Federal Republic of Germany," *Armed Forces and Society* 16, no. 4 (Summer 1990); Ralf Zoll, "German Civil-Military Relations: The Problem of Legitimacy," *Armed Forces and Society* 4, no. 4 (Summer 1979); Andre Uzulis, *Die Bundeswehr: Eine politische Geschichte von 1955 bis heute* (Hamburg: Mittler, 2005).

Russian sources: In addition to the author's own contacts with Russian military officers, the sources utilized include: Herspring, *The Kremlin and the High Command*; Pavel K. Baev, "The Challenge of Small Wars for the Russian Military," in *Russian Military Reform, 1992–2000*, ed. Anne C. Aldis and Roger N. McDermott (New York: Frank Cass, 2003), 189–202; Alexandr Golts, "The Social and Political Condition of the Russian Military," in *The Russian Military Power and Policy*, ed. Steven F. Miller and Dmitri Trenin (Cambridge, MA: MIT Press, 2004), 80; Anatol Levin, *Chechnya: The Tombstone of Russian Power* (New Haven: Yale University Press, 1998), citing General Vroybev, 293; Christopher C. Losksley, "Concept, Algorithm, Indecision: Why Military Reform Has Failed in Russia since 1992," *Slavic Military Studies* 14, no. 1 (March 2001): 1–26; Michael Orr, *Manpower Problems in the Russian Armed Forces, 1992–1993*, no. D62 (Camberly, Surrey: Conflict Studies Research Centre, Royal Military Academy Sandhurst, February 2002), 8; Idem, "Reform and the Russian Ground Forces, 1992–2002," in Adis and McDermott, *Russian Military Reform*, 136; Brian Taylor, "The Russian Military outside Politics: An Outside Perspective," PONARS *Policy Memo*, no. 2 (October 1997); Robert Barylski, *The Soldier in Russian Politics* (New Brunswick, NJ: Transaction, 1998), 9–12, 57–58.

American sources: In addition to this writer's many discussions with military officers, including his 33-year association with the U.S. Navy, the sources include: Jans and Schmidtchen, *The Real C-Cubed*, 42–53; A. J. Bacevich, "Tradition Abandoned: America's Military in a New Era," *National Interest* 58 (Summer 1997): 3; John Allen Williams, "The Military and Modern Society," *The World and I* (September 1999): 311; Edgar R. Puryear, *American Generalship: Character is Everything; The Art of Command* (Novato, CA: Presidio, 2002), 1–43; Peter Maslowski, "Army Values and American Values," *Military Review* 70, no. 4 (April 1990): 10–23; Richard K. Betts, *Soldiers, Statesman and Cold War Crisis* (New York: Columbia University Press, 1977), 157–58; Richard H. Kohn, "How Democracies Control the Military," *Journal of Democracy* 4, no. 8 (1997): 140; Thomas E. Ricks, "The Widening Gap Between the Military and Society," *Atlantic Monthly*, July 1997, 66–67; "The Cultural Demolition in the Military, *Washington Times*, November 20, 1998; Peter D. Feaver, "The Gap: Soldiers, Civilians and Their Mutual Misunderstanding," *National Interest* 61 (Fall 2000): 29–37; Gregory D. Foster, "Failed Expectations: The Crisis of Civil-Military Relations in America," *Brookings Review* (Fall 1997): 46–48; Elliot Cohen, *Supreme Command: Soldiers, Statesmen, and Leadership in Wartime* (New York: Free Press, 2002). See also the articles in Feaver and Kohn, *Soldiers and Civilians*.

Canadian sources: Allan D. English, *Understanding Military Culture: A Canadian Perspective* (Montreal: McGill-Queen's University Press, 2004); M. D. Chapstick, "Defining the Culture: The Canadian Army in the 21st Century," *Canadian Military Journal* (Spring

2003); David Bercuson, *Significant Incident: Canada's Army, the Airborne, and the Murder in Somalia* (Toronto: McClelland and Steward, 1996); MG D. C. Loomis and LTC D. T. Lightburn, "Taking into Account the Distinctiveness of the Military from the Mainstream of Society," *Canadian Defence Quarterly* 10 (1980).

29. Betts, *Soldiers, Statesmen and Cold War Crisis*, 5, 8.

30. Richard Neutstadt, *Presidential Power and the Modern Presidency: The Politics of Leadership from Roosevelt to Reagan* (New York: Free Press, 1990), 11.

31. There are those who fear that allowing senior officers to speak their mind may well result in them crossing the line into military disobedience. See, for example, Richard H. Kohn, "How Democracies Control the Military," *Journal of Democracy* 8, no. 2 (Winter 1966). If that happened, joint responsibility would cease because it assumes military subordination to civilian authority. It is impossible to determine where the line is between the military and civilians, and this writer would argue that the debate by scholars over this point does little to advance our knowledge of civil-military relations.

32. Dale R. Herspring, *The Pentagon and the Presidency: Civil-Military Relations from FDR to George W. Bush* (Lawrence: University of Kansas Press, 2005).

33. Dale R. Herspring, "Creating Shared Responsibility through Respect for Military Culture: The Russian and American Cases," *Public Administration Review* (July/August 2011).

34. In preparing this book, one of my colleagues asked, "Why Canada? Who cares about it?" My response is that it exemplifies a midsized country that has a very different history than the U.S., Germany, or Russia, and provides additional insights on civilian-military relations.

35. See, for example, Eliot Cohen, *Supreme Command: Soldiers, Statesmen, and Leadership in Wartime* (New York: Free Press, 2002); Peter Feaver, *Armed Servants: Agency, Oversight, and Civil-Military Relations* (Cambridge, MA: Harvard University Press, 2004); Feaver, "The Civil-Military Problematique: Huntington, Janowitz, and the Question of Civilian Control," *Armed Forces and Society* 23, no. 2 (Winter 1996); Richard Kohn, "How Bureaucracies Control the Military," *Journal of Democracy* 8 (October 1997): 140–153; Kohn, "The Constitution and National Security: The Intent of the Framers," in *The United States Military under the Constitution of the United States, 1789–1989*, ed., Richard H. Kohn (New York: New York University Press, 1991); Kohn, "Out of Control: The Crisis in Civil-Military Relations," *National Interest* 25 (Spring 1994).

36. Most work on civil-military relations, including that done on at least two of the countries covered in this book, focus on the democratization process—the transition from authoritarian rule to a democratic form of government. See, for example, Marybeth Ulrich, *Democratizing Communist Militaries: The Cases of the Czech and Russian Armed Forces* (Ann Arbor: University of Michigan Press, 1999).

CHAPTER 2. **From John F. Kennedy through Jimmy Carter**

1. There were problems in civil-military relations prior to President Kennedy's election, but looking at the period from 1940 to the present, none was as negative as the Kennedy/McNamara/Johnson period. See this writer's *The Pentagon and the Presidency: Civil-Military Relations from FDR to George W. Bush* (Lawrence: University of Kansas Press, 2005), 23–117.

2. Maxwell D. Taylor, *Swords and Plowshares* (New York: Da Capo, 1972), 200.

3. Lawrence Freedman, *Kennedy's Wars* (Oxford: Oxford University Press, 2000), 40.

4. Fred I. Greenstein, *The Presidential Difference: Leadership Style from FDR to Clinton* (Princeton: Princeton University Press, 2000), 72.

5. Freedman, *Kennedy's Wars*, 45.

6. Quoted in Russell F. Weigley, *The American Way of War* (Bloomington: Indiana University Press, 1973), 447.

7. Freedman, *Kennedy's Wars*, 45.

8. Quoted in Thomas M. Coffey, *Iron Eagle: The Turbulent Life of General Curtis LeMay* (New York: Crown, 1986), 370, 372.

9. Taylor, *Swords and Plowshares*, 254.

10. Freedman, *Kennedy's Wars*, 126.

11. Lucien Vandenbroucke, "Anatomy of a Failure: The Decision to Land at the Bay of Pigs," *Political Science Quarterly* 99, no. 3 (Autumn 1984): 476.

12. Richard M. Bissell Jr., *Reflections of a Cold Warrior: From Yalta to the Bay of Pigs* (New Haven: Yale University Press, 1996), 177.

13. L. James Binder, *Leminitzer: A Soldier for His Time* (Washington, DC: Brassey's 1997), 202.

14. Peter Wyden, *Bay of Pigs: The Untold Story* (New York: Simon and Schuster, 1979), 100.

15. Trimbull Higgens, *The Perfect Failure: Kennedy, Eisenhower and the CIA at the Bay of Pigs* (New York: W. W. Norton, 1987), 124.

16. Wyden, *Bay of Pigs*, 267.

17. Arthur M. Schlesinger Jr., *A Thousand Days: John F. Kennedy in the White House* (Boston: Houghton Mifflin, 1965), 295.

18. Wyden, *Bay of Pigs*, 317.

19. Robert Smith Thompson, *The Missiles of October* (New York: Simon and Schuster, 1992), 191–92.

20. Freedman, *Kennedy's Wars*, 180.

21. Ibid.

22. Dino A. Brigioni, *Eyeball to Eyeball* (New York: Random House, 1991), 399–400.

23. Elie Abel, *The Missile Crisis* (Philadelphia: Lippencott, 1966), 155. He also reportedly told McNamara that he "felt McNamara's actions were unbecoming the secretary of defense." Brigoni, *Eyeball to Eyeball*, 400.

24. Brigoni, *Eyeball to Eyeball.*

25. Quoted in George Anderson, "The Cuban Blockade: An Admiral's Memoir," *Washington Quarterly* 5, no. 4 (Autumn 1982): 84.

26. Hugh Sidney, *A Very Personal Presidency* (New York: Atheneum, 1968), 203.

27. Freedman, *Kennedy's Wars*, 45.

28. Robert S. McNamara, *In Retrospect: The Tragedy and Lessons of Vietnam* (New York: Vintage, 1995), 238.

29. William Westmoreland, *A Soldier Reports* (New York: Doubleday, 1976), 83.

30. Deborah Shapley, *Promise and Power: The Life and Times of Robert McNamara* (Boston: Little, Brown, 1993), 414.

31. Thomas Moorer, "Lessons Learned from the Air War over Vietnam," *Proceedings of the US Naval Institute* 113, no. 7 (August 6, 1987): 21.

32. H. R. McMaster, *Dereliction of Duty* (New York: Harper, 1998), 163.

33. Ibid., 68.

34. Ibid., 72.

35. Ibid., 70, 76–79.

36. Ibid., 92.

37. Ibid., 175.

38. Sidney, *Very Personal Presidency*, 204.

39. Mark Perry, *Four Stars: The Inside Story of the Forty-Year Battle between the Joint Chiefs of Staff and America's Civilian Leaders* (New York: Houghton Mifflin, 1989), 156.

40. Bruce Palmer, *The 25-Year War: America's Military Role in Vietnam* (Lexington: University Press of Kentucky, 1984), 41.

41. Perry, *Four Stars*, 161–62.

42. Ibid., 164.

43. Ibid., 165. See also Palmer, *25-Year War*, 44.

44. Perry, *Four Stars*, 172.

45. Lyndon Baines Johnson, *The Vantage Point: Perspectives of the Presidency, 1963–1969* (New York: Holt, Rinehart and Winston, 1971), 435.

46. Sidney M. Milkis and Michael Nelson, *The American Presidency: Origins and Development, 1776–1990* (Washington, DC: Congressional Quarterly, 1990), 313.

47. Alexander L. George and Eric Stern, "Presidential Management Styles and Models," in *Presidential Personality and Performance*, ed. Alexander L. George and Juliette George (Boulder: Westview Press, 1998), 213.

48. Milkis and Nelson, *The American Presidency*, 314.

49. Westmoreland, *A Soldier Reports*, 386.

50. Perry, *Four Stars*, 211.

51. Ibid., 217.

52. Elmo R. Zumwalt Jr., *On Watch: A Memoir* (New York: Quadrangle, 1976), 309–10.

53. H. R. Haldeman, *The Ends of Power* (New York: Times, 1978), 82–83.

54. Perry, *Four Stars*, 219.

55. Richard Nixon, *Two Foreign Policy Classics: Real Peace, No More Vietnams* (New York: Touchstone, 1990), 210.

56. Palmer, *The 25-Year War*, 96.

57. Ibid.

58. Perry, *Four Stars*, 221, 222.

59. Nixon, *The Foreign Policy Classics*, 230.

60. Perry, *Four Stars*, 209.

61. Ibid., 236.

62. Jeffrey Kimball, *Nixon's Vietnam War* (Lawrence: University of Kansas Press, 1998), 92–94.

63. President Gerald Ford is not mentioned here because of his limited time in office.

64. George C. Edwards III and Stephen J. Wayne, *Presidential Leadership: Politics and Policy Making*, 3rd ed. (New York: St. Martin's Press, 1994), 443.

65. Phil Williams, "Carter's Defense Policy," in *The Carter Years: The President and Policy Making*, ed. M. Glenn Abernathy, Dilys M. Hall, and Phil Williams (New York: St. Martins Press, 1984), 86.

66. Ibid., 87.

67. John K. Singlaub, *Hazardous Duty: An American Soldier in the Twentieth Century* (New York: Summit, 1991), 425.

68. John A Wickham Jr., *Korea on the Brink: A Memoir of Political Intrigue and Military Crisis* (Washington, DC: Brassey's, 2000), 120.

69. Nick Kotz, *Wild Blue Yonder: Money, Politics and the B-1 Bomber* (New York: Pantheon Books, 1988), 140.

70. Perry, *Four Stars*, 268.

71. Kotz, *Wild Blue Yonder*, 14.

72. Peter Feaver, "The Civil-Military Problematique: Hungtington, Janowitz, and the Question of Civil-Control," *Armed Forces and Society* 23, no. 2 (Winter 1996): 2, 3, 6.

73. Perry, *Four Stars*, 269.

74. "Washington's Naval Battle," *Washington Post*, September 4, 1978.

75. "Shortages of Parts Hamstring Warplanes," *Washington Post*, March 17, 1980.

76. "Sinking the Navy," *Washington Post*, May 21, 1980.

77. "Joint Chiefs Dissent on Carter-Brown Military Budget," *New York Times*, May 30, 1980.

78. Perry, *Four Stars*, 301.

79. "Arms Readiness: Glass Half Empty, Half Full," *Washington Post*, November 1, 1980.

80. Gary Sick, *All Fall Down: America's Tragic Encounter with Iran* (New York: Penguin Books, 1986), 250, 253.

81. Charlie Beckworth, *Delta Force* (New York: Avon, 1983), 249.

82. Ibid., 10.

83. Sick, *All Fall Down*, 349.

84. Beckworth, *Delta Force*, 316–17.

CHAPTER 3. **From Ronald Reagan through Barack Obama**

1. This account is from Mark Perry, *Four Stars: The Inside Story of the Forty-Year Battle between the Joint Chiefs of Staff and America's Civilian Leaders* (New York: Houghton Mifflin, 1989), 279–83.

2. Ronald Reagan, *An American Life* (London: Arrow, 1991), 234–35.

3. Colin Powell, *My American Journey* (New York: Random House, 1995), 258.

4. Perry, *Four Stars*, 288.

5. "Pentagon is Balancing for Two 'Waves': Rising Costs Threaten Weapons, Readiness," *Washington Post*, November 13, 1988.

6. Ibid.

7. Perry, *Four Stars*, 306.

8. Edmund Morris, *Dutch: A Memoir of Ronald Reagan* (New York: Modern Library, 1999), 463–64.

9. Larry Speakes, *Speaking Out: The Reagan Presidency from inside the White House* (New York: Avon, 1988), 189.

10. Perry, *Four Stars*, 312.

11. George Schultz, *Turmoil and Triumph* (New York: Simon and Schuster, 1993), 108–9.

12. Caspar Weinberger, *Fighting for Peace: Seven Crucial Years in the Pentagon* (New York: Warner, 1990), 441–42.

13. Roland H. Cole, *Operation Urgent Fury* (Washington, DC: Joint History Office, Office of the Chairman of the Joint Chiefs of Staff, 1997), 11.

14. Robert C. McFarlane, *Special Trust* (New York: Cadell and Davis, 1994), 263.

15. Cole, *Operation Urgent Fury*, 39–40.

16. Hedrick Smith, *The Power Game: How Washington Works* (New York: Ballantine, 1988), 197.

17. H. Norman Schwarzkopf, *It Doesn't Take a Hero* (New York: Bantam, 1992), 254. Emphasis in the original.

18. John Burke, *The Institutional Presidency: Organizing and Managing the White House from FDR to Clinton*, 2nd ed. (Baltimore: Johns Hopkins University Press, 2000), 170.

19. Ibid., 164.

20. The incident is described in Bob Woodward, *The Commanders* (New York: Pocket Star Books, 1991). Quotes are from pages 44, 46, and 47.

21. Thomas Donnelly, Margaret Roth, and Caleb Baker, *Operation Just Cause: The Storming of Panama* (New York: Lexington, 1991), 7.

22. Ibid., 43.

23. Ibid.

24. Ibid., 52.

25. Ibid., 64, 65.

26. Ibid., 96.

27. "The Conversation of General Powell, Incidents Led JCS Chief to Reverse Opposition to the USE of Force," *Washington Post*, December 21, 1989.

28. Ibid., 29.

29. Woodward, *The Commanders*, 144.

30. James A. Baker III, *The Politics of Diplomacy, Revolution, War and Peace, 1989–1992* (New York: Putnam, 1995), 189.

31. Colin Powell, *My American Journey*, 425.

32. Ibid., 429.

33. Ibid., 432.

34. Michael Gordon and Bernard E. Trainor, *The General's War* (Boston: Little, Brown, 1995), x.

35. Schwarzkopf, *It Doesn't Take a Hero*, 291–92.

36. "Transformed," *Economist*, July 20, 2002, 9.

37. Powell, *My American Journey*, 461.

38. Schwarzkopf, *It Doesn't Take a Hero*, 295.

39. Quoted in Woodward, *The Commanders*, 209.

40. Woodward, *The Commanders*, 220.

41. Powell, *My American Journey*, 464–65. Emphasis in the original.

42. Ibid., 466. Emphasis in the original.

43. Woodward, *The Commanders*, 265.

44. Schwarzkopf, *It Doesn't Take a Hero*, 236.

45. Ibid.

46. Rick Atkinson, *Crusade: The Untold Story of the Persian Gulf* (New York: Houghton Mifflin, 1993), 123.

47. Woodward, *The Commanders*, 289.

48. Atkinson, *Crusade*, 110.

49. Ibid., 111.

50. Woodward, *The Commanders*, 297.

51. Ibid., 305–6.
52. Burke, *The Institutional Presidency*, 180.
53. Robert "Buzz" Paterson, *Dereliction of Duty* (New York: Regency, 2003), 51.
54. George Stephanopoulos, *All Too Human* (Boston: Little, Brown, 1999), 75.
55. Ibid., 132.
56. David H. Hackworth, "Rancor in the Ranks: The Troops vs. the President," *Newsweek*, June 28, 1993.
57. "Feeling Snubbed by Administration, Military Views Clinton with Growing Disgust," *Baltimore Sun*, March 21, 1993.
58. Patterson, *Dereliction of Duty*, 90.
59. Powell, *My American Journey*, 454.
60. Elizabeth Drew, *On the Edge: The Clinton Presidency* (New York: Simon and Schuster, 1994), 87.
61. Stephanopoulos, *All Too Human*, 123, 124.
62. Thomas H. Henriksen, *Clinton's Foreign Policy in Somalia, Bosnia, Haiti and North Korea* (Stanford: Hoover Institution Press, 1996), 9.
63. Bill Clinton, *My Life* (New York: Knopf, 2004), 450.
64. Drew, *On the Edge*, 320.
65. This is taken from Mark Bowden, *Black Hawk Down* (New York: Signet, 2001).
66. David Halberstam, *War in a Time of Peace: Bush, Clinton, and the Generals* (New York: Scribner, 2001), 207, 329.
67. Ibid., 262–63.
68. Clinton, *My Life*, 533.
69. Cited in Drew, *On the Edge*, 358.
70. Warren Christopher, *In the Stream of History* (Stanford: Stanford University Press, 1998), 468.
71. Henriksen, *Clinton's Foreign Policy*, 22–23.
72. Christopher, *In the Steam of History*, 278.
73. Stephanopoulos, *All Too Human*, 305.
74. Powell, *My American Journey*, 576.
75. Halberstam, *War in a Time of Peace*, 315.
76. Richard Holbrooke, *To End a War* (New York: Random House, 1988), 110.
77. Wesley K. Clark, *Waging Modern War* (New York: Public Affairs, 2001), 394.
78. Ibid., 169–70.
79. Benjamin S. Lambeth, *NATO's Air War for Kosovo* (Santa Monica: Rand, 2001), 25.
80. Clark, *Waging Modern War*, 269, 270, 273.
81. Bob Woodward, *Bush at War* (New York: Simon and Schuster, 2002), 256.
82. Dana Priest, *The Mission: Waging War and Keeping Peace with America's Military* (New York: W. W. Norton, 2003), 24.
83. "Rumsfeld on High Wire of Defense Reform: Military Brass, Conservative Lawmakers Are among Secretive Review's Unexpected Critics," *Washington Post*, May 20, 2001.
84. Priest, *The Mission*, 34.
85. Rowan Scarborough, *Rumsfeld's War: The Untold Story of America's Anti-Terrorist Commander* (Washington, DC: Regnery, 2004), 121.
86. Priest, *The Mission*, 38.

87. Woodward, *Bush at War*, 43, 44.

88. Ibid., 62–63.

89. Ibid., 129.

90. Ibid., 189.

91. "Transformed," *The Economist*, July 20, 2002, 3.

92. "Wolfowitz Criticizes 'Suspect' Estimate of Occupation Force," *Washington Times*, February 28, 2003.

93. Bob Woodward, *Plan of Attack* (New York: Simon and Schuster, 2004), 232.

94. James Fallows, *Blind into Baghdad: America's War with Iraq* (New York: Vintage, 2006), 76.

95. Thomas E. Ricks, *Fiasco: The American Military Adventure in Iraq* (New York: Penguin, 2006), 66.

96. "Remarks by Secretary of Defense Donald H. Rumsfeld," Transcript of Meeting at Council on Foreign Relations, New York, May 27, 2003, http://www.cfr.org/publication/5998/remarks_by_secretary_of_defense_donald_h_Rumsfeld.html.

97. Andrew Cockburn, *Rumsfeld, His Rise, Fall, and Catastrophic Legacy* (New York: Scribner, 2007).

98. "Rumsfeld Leaves His Successor in a Difficult Position," GOVEZEC.com, December 18, 2006, http://www.govexec.com/dailyfed/1206/121806nj1.htm.

99. Peter Baker, "As He Touts a 'Way Forward,' Bush Admits Errors of the Past," *Washington Post*, January 11, 2007.

100. Thom Shanker, "Gates Seeks Troop Estimates," *New York Times*, January 18, 2007.

101. Peter Baker, Karen DeYoung, Thomas E. Ricks, Ann Scott Tyson, Jody Warrick, and Robin Wright, "Among Top Officials, 'Surge' Has Spared Dissent, Infighting," *Washington Post*, September 9, 2007.

102. David Cloud, "Gates Offers Blunt Review of Progress in Iraq," *New York Times*, November 3, 2007, accessed November 3, 2008.

103. David Sands and Sharon Behn, "Are We Winning the War?," *Washington Times*, November 14, 2007.

104. "Raising the Bar at the Pentagon," *New York Times*, June 7, 2008.

105. "Gates Says New Arms Must Play Role Now, *New York Times*, May 14, 2008.

106. "Military Budget Reflects a Shift in US Strategy," *New York Times*, April 7, 2009.

107. "Gates and Mullen Disagree," *Politico*, March 1, 2009.

108. Bob Woodward, *Obama's Wars* (New York: Simon and Schuster, 2010).

109. "Marine Commandant: Keep Policy on Gays in Military," *Washington Times*, November 7, 2010; "3 Military Chiefs Oppose 'Don't Ask, Don't Tell' Repeal," *Los Angeles Times*, December 3, 2010.

CHAPTER 4. **From Konrad Adenauer through Willy Brandt**

1. For a discussion of the problems faced in military transition, See Marybeth Ulrich's, *Democratizing Communist Militaries: The Cases of the Czech and Russian Armed Forces* (Ann Arbor: University of Michigan Press, 2000).

2. Donald Abenheim, *Reforging the Iron Cross: The Search for Tradition in the West German Armed Forces* (Princeton: Princeton University Press, 1988), 13. This is by far the best book written in German or English on the search for symbols in the Bundeswehr up to the late 1980s.

3. The Reichswehr refers to the German military up to the end of World War I. The term Wehrmacht refers to the German military prior to and during World War II.

4. Hans von Seekt, *Die Reichswehr* (Leipzig: R. Kittler, 1933), 47.

5. Karl Demeter, *The German Officer Corps in Society and State, 1650–1965* (New York: Praeger, 1965), 54.

6. *Civic Education and Tradition*, The Ministry of Defense, 1982, http://bmvg.de/portal/a/bmvg/kexml/04_Sj9SPykssyoxPLMnM.

7. Abenheim, *Reforging the Iron Cross*, 290.

8. Loretana de Libero, *Tradition in Zeiten der Transformation: Zum Traditionsverständnis der Bundeswehr im frühen 21. Jahrhundert* (Paderborn: Schöningh, 2006), 26. Emphasis in the original.

9. Bernard Fleckenstein, "Federal Republic of Germany," in *The Military: More Than a Job?*, ed. Charles C. Moskos and Frank R. Wood (Washington, DC: Pergamon-Brassey's, 1988), 177.

10. Jürgen Groß, "Einführung," in Detlef Bald, Hans-Günter Fröhling, and Jürgen Groß, *Zurückgestutzt, sinnentleert, unverstanden: Die Innere Führung der Bundeswehr* (Baden-Baden, Nomos, 2008), 7. Emphasis in the original.

11. Abenheim, *Reforging the Iron Cross*, 50ff.

12. Much of this discussion is taken from ibid., 44–52. It is one of the most coherent, clear explanations of the confusing term Innere Führung.

13. Ibid., 89.

14. Heiko Biehl, *Die Neue Bundeswehr* (Strausberg: Sozialwissenschaftliches Institute der Bundeswehr, August 1998), 51–52.

15. Rolf Clement and Paul Elmar Jöris, *50 Jahre Bundeswehr, 1955–2005* (Hamburg: Mittler, 2005), 75.

16. Ulrich de Maiziere, "Der Wehrbeauftragte, die Innere Führung und die Soldaten," *Europeaische Wehrkunde* (May 1984): 291.

17. See, for example, Hans-Christian Beck, "Der Bürger in Uniform, die Konzeption der Innere Führung und die möglichen Konsequenzen eines 'Bruchs' in der wehrstrukturellen Kontinuität," in *Wehrhafte Demokratie 2000: zu Wehrpflicht und Wehrstruktur,*" ed. Armin A. Steinkamm and Dietmar Schössler (Baden-Baden: Nomos, 1999).

18. Klaus Abel, "Foundations and Conditions for Training and Education of the Citizen in Uniform," *South African Defense Review* 3 (1992), http://www.iss.co.za/Pubs/ASF/SADR3/Abel.html.

19. Most German officers believe that Innere Führung was a necessity in the aftermath of Hitler's Germany. See Jörg Bahnemann, *Parlamentsarmee? Bundeswehr braucht Führung* (Aachen: Helios, 2010), 19–22.

20. An argument could be made that Theodor Blank was the first defense minister, although he did not carry the formal title.

21. Abenheim, *Reforging the Iron Cross*, 59.

22. Abenheim, *Reforging the Iron Cross*, 112. For a recent work evaluating von Baudissin's contributions to Germany, see Rudolf J. Schlaffer and Wolfgang Schmidt, eds., *Wolf Graf von Baudissin, 1907–1993* (Potsdam: Oldenbourg, 2010).

23. Andre Uzulis, *Die Bundeswehr: Eine politische Geschichte von 1955 bis heute* (Hamburg: Mittler, 2005), 46.

24. Ibid., 26.

25. General Dieter Farwick reports having run into former SS soldiers. "I met several of them in various units and headquarters." E-mail from General Farwick to the author, February 7, 2012.

26. Uzulis, *Die Bundeswehr,* 28.

27. As quoted in ibid., 47.

28. In 1981 its name was changed to Zentrum Innere Führung.

29. This is based on Abenheim's commentary on the topic; Abenheim, *Reforging the Iron Cross,* 152–55.

30. Ibid., 154.

31. Ibid., 169.

32. Klaus Abel, "Foundations and Conditions for Training and Education of the Citizen in Uniform," *South African Defense Review* 3 (1992), http://www.iss.co.za/Pubs?ASR/SADR3?Abel.html.

33. Ibid., 170.

34. Uzulis, *Die Bundeswehr,* 47.

35. Ibid., 64.

36. Bald, *Die Bundeswehr,* 66–67.

37. Ibid., 67. By technical soldiers Foertsch appears to have had in mind those who were primarily trained in highly technical areas. His point was that they would only be able to serve as competent soldiers once they had the basic military training required of every other soldier.

38. Abenheim, *Reforging the Iron Cross,* 202.

39. Hans Georg Studnitz, *Rettet die Bundeswehr* (Stuttgart: Seewald, 1967), 158.

40. Ibid., 67.

41. Ibid., 94.

42. Ibid., 55.

43. Uzulis, *Die Bundeswehr,* 67.

44. "Seine Kritik provozierte Reformen in der Bundeswehr. Bonn im August," *Die Zeit,* August 14, 1964, no. 33, http://www.zeit.de/1964/33/Heyes-Erfolg.

45. Heiko Biehl and Nina Leonhard, "Militär und Tradition," in *Militärsoizologie: Eine Einführung,* ed. Ed Leonard and I. J. Werker (Wiesbaden, 2005), 227.

46. As cited in Abenheim, *Reforging the Iron Cross,* 211.

47. "Was ist Tradition?" *Die Zeit,* July 23, 1965, no. 30, http://www/zeit.de/1965/30/Was-ist-Tradition.

48. Abenheim, *Reforging the Iron Cross,* 216.

49. Klaus Hornung, "Das politisch-militärische Verhältnis in der Bundesrepublik Deutschland und der Generalinspektur der Bundeswehr," in F. E. Becker, D. Dietrich, E. Lutz, and V. Stahl, *Armee für den Frieden* (Hannover: Fackelträrer-Verlag, 1980), 138.

50. Ibid.

51. Uzulis, *Die Bundeswehr,* 71.

52. Klaus Hornung, "Das politisch-militärische Verhältnis in der Bundesrepublik Deutschland und der Generalinspektur der Bundeswehr," 138.

53. Uzulis, *Die Bundeswehr,* 71.

54. Helmut Fröchling, "Soldatische Vorbilder?" *Journal für Geschichte* 2, no. 3 (1980): 37.

55. Abenheim, *Reforging the Iron Cross,* 237.

56. Hermann Hagena, "Civilian Control of the German Armed Forces," *Air University*

Review (May–June 1967), http://www.airpower.maxwell.af.mil/airchronicles/aureview/1967/may-jun/hagena.html.

57. Abenheim, *Reforging the Iron Cross*, 238.

58. Studnitz, *Rettet die Bundeswehr*, 85.

59. Ibid., 84.

60. Angelika Dörfeler-Dierken, "Die Bedeutung des Jahres 1968 für die Innere Führung," Bald, Fröhling, Groß, and von Rosen, *Zurückgestutzt, sinnentleert, unverstanden*, 70–71.

61. Dörfeler-Dierken, "Die Bedeutung des Jahres 1968."

62. In Abenheim, *Reforging the Iron Cross*, 240. Most of the discussion of Karst is taken from Abenheim, 240–41.

63. Ibid., 242. See also Bahnemann, *Parlamentsarmee?*, 105.

64. Franz Uhle-Wettier, *Rührt Euch!* (Graz: Ares Verlag, 2006), 83.

65. Abenheim, *Reforging the Iron Cross*, 240.

66. Ibid., 243.

67. Ibid., 244.

68. Bald, *Die Bundeswehr*, 56.

69. Ibid., 55.

70. Abenheim, *Reforging the Iron Cross*, 245.

71. Bald, *Die Bundeswehr*, 88.

72. "Der Generalprobe," *Die Zeit*, January 1, 1970.

73. Bald, *Die Bundeswehr*, 88.

74. Abenheim, *Reforging the Iron Cross*, 247.

75. "Besser als ihr: Ruf," *Die Zeit*, March 31, 1972, http://www.zeit.de/1972/13/Besser-als-ihr-Ruf; Abenheim, *Reforging the Iron Cross*, 248.

76. Abenheim, *Reforging the Iron Cross*, 250.

77. Deflef Bald, *Politik der Verantwortung: Das Beispiel Helmut Schmidt* (Hamburg: Aufbau, 2008), 128.

78. "Besser als ihr Ruf."

79. Abenheim, *Reforging the Iron Cross*, 250.

80. Führerbunker refers to Hitler's bunker in Berlin.

81. Abenheim, *Reforging the Iron Cross*, 251.

82. Ibid.

83. *Volkstrum* is the collection of young men and boys who were called upon to reinforce the Wehrmacht during the closing days of World War II.

84. "Besser als ihr Ruf."

85. Ibid.

86. Ibid.

87. For an excellent discussion of the educational changes formulated under Schmidt, see Hans Eberhard Radbruch, "From Scharnhorst to Schmidt: The System of Education and Training in the Bundeswehr," *Armed Forces and Society* 5, no. 4 (Summer, 1979): 606–25.

88. Uzulis, *Die Bundeswehr*, 81.

89. Wayne C. Thompson and Marc D. Peltier, "The Education of Military Officers in the Federal Republic of Germany," *Armed Forces and Society* 16, no. 4 (Summer, 1990): 591.

90. Ibid., 592.

91. Ibid.

92. Ibid., 620.

93. Ibid., 594.

94. Bald, *Die Bundeswehr*, 65.

95. Eckart Opitz, "Geschichte der Inner Führung: Vom 'Igefüge' zur Führungs Philosophie der Bundeswehr," in *50 Jahre Innere Führung: Vom Himmerod (Eifel) nach Pristina (Kosovo)* (Bremen: Edition Temmen, 2001), 21. In his book on Helmut Schmidt, Detlef Bald makes much of Schmidt's willingness to stand up to the German military over the issue of civilian control over the use of nuclear weapons. While there is no question that Schmidt played a key role in this discussion, primarily though his ties to U.S. Secretary of Defense Melvin Laird, the real battle was not with the German military, but in this author's opinion, with generals like Andrew Goodpaster at SACEUR. See Detlef Bald, *Politik der Verantwortung* (Berlin: Verlagsgruppe, 2008).

CHAPTER 5. From Helmut Schmidt through Angela Merkel

1. It is perhaps ironic, that when discussing the issue with an individual who served in the Bundeswehr, he commented, "The Thema tradition was not a major problem among the troops; we did what we considered right. One had to be careful when the press or very senior officers were present." E-mail from General Farwick to the author, February 8, 2012.

2. Donald Abenheim, *Reforging the Iron Cross: The Search for Tradition in the West German Armed Forces* (Princeton: Princeton University Press, 1988), 262; Andre Uzulis, *Die Bundeswehr: Eine politische Geschichte von 1955 bis heute* (Hamburg: Mittler, 2005), 48.

3. Abenheim, *Reforging the Iron Cross*, 263.

4. Ibid., 270.

5. Friedrich Döpner, "Über die Traditionspflege in der Bundeswehr," *Europäishe Wehrkunde*, no. 10 (1978): 524–25.

6. Ibid.

7. Abenheim, *Reforging the Iron Cross*, 274.

8. Helmut Fröchling, "Soldatische Vorbilder," *Journal für Geschichte* 2, no. 3 (1980): 35.

9. Bernard Fleckenstein, "Der gesellschaftliche Wandel und seine Auswirkungen auf das zivil-militärische Verhältnis und die Bundeswehr," in *Innere Führung im Wandel*, ed. A. Prüfer (Baden Baden: Nomos, 1998), 65.

10. Abenheim, *Reforging the Iron Cross*, 277.

11. Ibid., 280.

12. Winfried Heinemann, "Tradition per Erlaß," November 14, 2007, http://www.y-punkt.de'portal/a/ypunkt/archiv/2007.

13. Alfred Paschek, "Die Tradition der Bundeswehr," *Deutsche Geschichte*, November 26, 2008, http://deutsche-geschichte.suite101.de/article.cfm/die_Tradition_der_Bundeswehr.

14. Franz H. U. Borkenhagen, "Unbewältigte Tradition," in *Bundeswehr in Oliv?*, ed. Franz H. U. Borkenhagen (Berlin: Verlag, J. H. W. Dietz Nachf, 1986), 190.

15. M. Newmann, "Zum Traditionsverständnis der Bundeswehrverwaltung," *Bundeswehrverwaltung* 44, no. 6 (2000): 126.

16. One indication of how little the Bundeswehr is valued in Germany is provided by

a recent biography of Schmidt. Most observers would argue that Schmidt and Apel had a tremendous impact on the Bundeswehr, yet there is no mention of it in the book. Apel is mentioned several times, but only as Schmidt's close confidant. Hans-Joachim Noack, *Helmut Schmidt: Die Biographie*, 4th ed. (Berlin: Rowohlt, 2008).

17. Detlef Bald, *Die Bundeswehr: Eine kritische Geschichte 1955–2005* (Munich: C. H. Beck Verlag, 2005), 110–11. Bald also noted that Woerner had attended the funerals of Grand Admiral Doenitz and Colonel Hans Rudel.

18. Detlef Bald, "Militärische Mentalität versus Innere Führung," *Wissenschaft und Frieden* 3 (2000), http://www.iwif.de/wf300-33.htm.

19. The latter view was expressed by General Farwick who served more than four years on the Planning Staff. He considered Wörner "the best defense minister we ever had." E-mail from General Farwick to the author, February 18, 2012.

20. Bald, *Die Bundeswehr*, 114.

21. Jürgen Kuhlmann, "The Bundeswehr and the Challenge of Change," *The Public* 1, no. 4 (1994): 36.

22. See Hans-Joachim Noack and Wolfram Bickerich, *Helmut Kohl: Die Biograpie* (Berlin: Rowohlt, 2010), 169–71.

23. "Der Krieg ist der Ernstfall," *Truppenpraxis* 3 (1991).

24. "Der General und die Verbrechen," *Die Zeit*, May 18, 1990, http://www.zeit.de/1990/21/Der-General-und-die-Verbrechen.

25. Wilfred Penner, "Das Experiment ist gelungen. Die Innere Führung," *Truppenpraxis* 10 (2000): 631.

26. For a discussion of the collapse and unification of the National People's Army with the Bundeswehr see this writer's *Requiem for an Army: The Demise of the East German Military* (Boulder: Roman and Littlefeld, 1995).

27. Eckardt Opitz, "Geschichte der Innere Führung" in *50 Jahre Innere Führung*, ed. Eckardt Optz (Bremen: Edition Temmen, 2001), 24.

28. Heiko Biehl, "Die neue Bundeswehr," *Sozialwissenschaftliches Institut der Bundeswehr*, Strausberg (August 1998), 48.

29. Karl-Heinz Boener, "The Future of German Operations outside NATO," *Parameters* (Spring 1996): 62–72.

30. Heiko Biehl, "Die Neue Bundeswehr," Sozialwissenschaftliches Institut der Bundeswehr, Strausberg (August 1998), 21–22.

31. De Libero, *Tradition in Zeiten der Transformation* (Paderhorn: Ferdinand Schöningh, 2006), 89. See also Manfred Neumann, "Zum Traditionsverständnis der Bundeswehr," *Bundeswehrverwaltung* 44, no. 6 (2000): 126.

32. "Die Wehrmacht ist kein Vorbild," *Die Zeit*, no. 49 (1995), http://www.zeit.de/1995/49/Die_Wehrmacht_ist_kein_Vorbild_.

33. H. Biehl and N. Leonard, "Militär und Tradition in Militärsoziologie," in *Militärsoziologie: Eine Einführung*, N. Leonard and I. J. Werkener (Wiesbaden, 2005), 232. These authors continued that "today the problem is not so much that the young look back to the Nazi period, but that for them the primary symbol is Rambo." Ibid., 232.

34. Elmar Wiesendahl, "Einleitung: Neue Bundeswehr unter die Weiterenwicklung der Innere Führung," in *Neue Bundeswehr, Neue Innere Führung* (Baden-Baden: Nomos, 2005), 9.

35. Winfried Heininemann, "Militär und Tradition," in *Handbuch Militär und Sozialwissenschaften* (Wiesbaden: VS Verlage für Sozialwissens, 2005), 412.

36. "Zuverlässiges Instrument in die Hände Politik," *Frankfurter Allgemeine Zeitung*, October 27, 1995.

37. Paul Schäfer, "Bundeswehr wohin?" *W&F*, no. 4 (1996), http://www.uni-muenster.de/PeaCon'wf-96/96402m.htm.

38. Tom Dyson, *The Politics of German Defence and Security: Policy Leadership and Military Reform in the Post–Cold War Era* (New York: Berghahn Books, 2007), 67.

39. Ibid., 68.

40. Hilmar Linnenkamp, "Neue Aufgaben der Bundeswehr: alte Ausbildung?" *S&F*, no. 3 (1997): 166.

41. Detlef Bald, *Eine überfällige Bildugsreform: Zur Sache der Militärelite der Bundeswehr, Zusammenfassung der Literatur*, in *Vierteljahresschrift für Sicherheit und Frieden* 15, no. 3 (1997): 131.

42. Luke Grossman, *Command and General Staff Officer Education for the 21st Century: Examining the German Model; A Monograph* (Fort Leavenworth, KS: US Army Command and Staff College, School of Advanced Military Studies, 2002), http://bib.cfc.dnd.ca/ipac20/ipac.jsp?session=F2489316667R.661; and "Wir sind eine ganz normale Uni," *Die Zeit*, May 18, 2006, http://images.zeit.de/text/2006/21/CoNIehuss_xml.

43. Tom Dyson, *The Politics of German Defense and Security: Policy Leadership and Military Reform in the Post–Cold War Era* (Oxford: Berghahn Books, 2008), 52.

44. Mary Elise Sarotte, *German Military Reform and European Security*, Adelphi Paper 340 (London: IISS, 2001), 20.

45. Ibid., 88.

46. Ibid., 95.

47. "Nachdenken, dann nachrüsten," *Die Zeit*, no. 39, 1999, http://images.zeit.de/text/1999/39.bundeswehr.xml.

48. As quoted in Christoph Nesshöver, "Preparing Germany's Armed Forces for the Future: The Bundeswehr at a Crossroads," *AICGS Analysis*, June 15, 2001, http://www.aicgs.org/analysis/at-issue/bundeswehr.aspx.

49. "Scharping entläßt Generalinspektuer," *Welt Online*, http://www.welt.de/print-welt/article15564/Scharping_entlaesst_Generalinspekteur.html.

50. Ibid.

51. Dyson, *The Politics of German Defense and Security*, 104.

52. "Scharpings Affront," *Die Zeit 2000*" (n.d.), http://www.zeit.de/2000/13/200013.bundeswehr.xml. For Scharping's defense of his actions, see "Keine Sonderwege," *Die Zeit* (n.d.), http://www.zeit.de/2001/24/200124_bundeswehr.xml.

53. Dyson, *The Politics of German Defense and Security*, 109.

54. Andre Uzulis, *Die Bundeswehr: Eine politische Geschichte von 1955 bis heute*" (Hamburg: Mittler, 2005), 108. Dyson notes correctly that part of the problem was a lack of CDU support because the CDU had cut the Bundeswehr when Rühe was defense minister. Dyson, *The Politics of German Defense and Security*, 97–98.

55. Dyson, *The Politics of German Defense and Security*, 107.

56. "Die Reform-Armee," *Die Zeit 2000*" (n.d.), http://www.zeit.de/2000/20/200020.titel_budeswehr.xml.

57. Dyson, *The Politics of German Defense and Spending*, 112.

58. Nesshoever, "Preparing Germany's Armed Forces for the Future."

59. "Armee, Armee," *Welt Online*, September 12, 2001, http://www/welt/de/print-welt/article475397/Armee_Armee.html.

60. "Experten halten Bundeswehr für kaum noch einsatzfähig," *Welt Online*, November 8, 2001, http://www.welt.de.print-welt/article48931/Experten_halten_Bundeswehr_fuer_kaum_noch_einsatzfaehig.html.

61. "Scharpings Luftnummer," *Die Zeit*, October 2002, http://images.zeit.de/text/2002/10/Scharpings_Luftnummer.

62. "Scharping: Bundeswehrreform braucht Zusammenarbeit mit Wirtschaft," November 9, 2001, http://www.welt.de/print-welt/article486334/Scharping_Bundeswehr reform_braucht_Zusammenarbeit_mit_Wirtschaft.html.

63. "Die arme Armee," March 1, 2002, *Welt Online*, http://www.welt.de/print-welt/article376898/Die_arme_Armee.html.

64. Ibid.

65. "Die Bundeswehrreform nimmt Gestalt an," *Die Zeit*, http://images.zeit.de/text/200216/20016_difinterview_16041.xml.

66. *Bundeswehr 2002: Sachstand und Perspektiven* (Berlin: Bundesministerium der Verteidigung, 2002), 25–27.

67. "Scharping fehlen 4,5 Euros," June 4, 2002, *Welt Online*, http://www.we.t.de/pring-welt/article392584?Scharping_4_5 Millarden_Euro.html.

68. In General Farwick's view, he was one of the worst defense ministers in recent years. E-mail form General Farwick, February 18, 2012.

69. "Schroeder Fires His Defense Minister," *LA Times*, July 19, 2002, http://www.latimes.com/news/nationworld/world/la-fg-rudi19jul19.story?coll=la%2Dheadlines%2Dworld%2Dmanual.

70. Cited in Dyson, *The Politics of German Defense and Security*, 120.

71. The following description is based on Josef Janning and Thomas Bauer, "Into the Great Wide Open: The Transformation of the German Armed Forces after 1990," *Orbis* 51, no. 3 (Summer 2007): 531–36.

72. Elmar Wisendahl, "Die Innere Führung auf dem Prüfstand: Zum Anpassungsbedart eines Leitbildes," in Wisendahl, *Neue Bundeswehr, Neue Innere Führung?* (Baden-Baden: Nomos, 2004), 17.

73. E-mail from General Farwick to the author, February 2, 2012.

74. Bundesministerium der Verteidigung, *Defense Policy Guidelines for the Area of Responsibility of the Federal Ministry of Defense*, Berlin, May 21, 2003, http://www.bmvg.de/sicherheit/vpr.php.

75. Dyson, *The Politics of German Defense and Security*, 123.

76. "Die Bewährungsprobe kommt nach der Wahl," *Die Welt*, June 28, 2003.

77. Dyson, *The Politics of German Defense and Security*, 125.

78. Ibid., 132.

79. "Bundeswehr trennt sich von fast 50.000 Dienstposten," November 3, 2004, *Welt Online*, http://www.welt.de/print-welt/article350154/Bundeswehr_trennt_sich_von_fast_50_000_Dienstposten.html.

80. "Bundeswehr will die Teilstreitkräfte auflösen," *Welt Online*, December 16, 2005,

http://www.welt.de/print-welt/article184700/ Wütende Proteste gegen Radikalreform der Bundeswehr," *Welt Online*, December 17, 2005, http:/www.welt.de/print-welt/article184940/ Wuetende_Proteste_gegen_Radikalreform_der_Bundeswehr.html.

81. "Offiziere stehen vor neuen Herausforderungen," June 30, 2005, *Welt Online*, http:// www.welt.de/print-welt/article679499/Offiziere_stehen_vor_neuen_Herausforderungen .html.

82. "German General Sacked for Praising MP's Anti-Semitism," *The Independent*, November 5, 2003, http://license,icopyright.net/user/viewFreeUse.act?find+MzrMGT.

83. Ibid.

84. Fritz Zwicknagl, "Bundeswehr und Traditionsverbände," Munich, January 18, 2005, http://www.swg-hamburg.de/Archiv?Beitrage_aus_der_Rubrik_-_Mili/Bundeswehr.

85. Werner Baach, "Auslandseinsätze und Innere Führung: Transformation und ihre Risken—Führung und Vertrauen," *Europäische Sidherheit* 54 (February 2005): 78.

86. Uzulis, *Die Bundeswehr*, 116.

87. "Fristlos Enlassen," *Zeit Online*, Reuters, April 4, 2007, http//:images.zeit.de/text/ 2007/16/bundeswehr-nuer-skandal.

88. Jürgen Arose, "Vision, 'Zivilisierung des Militärs,' " in *Zurückgestutzt, sinnentleert, unverstanden: Die Innere Führung der Bundeswehr*, ed. Detlef Bald, Hans-Günter Fröhling, Jürgen Groß, and Claus Freiherr von Rossen (Baden-Baden: Nomos, 2008), 146.

89. Bald, *Die Bundeswehr*, 20–22.

90. Ibid., 188.

91. "Falsche Vorbilder—Die Bundeswehr ehrt Wehmacht Oberst Moelders," *Die Zeit*, April 1, 2004, http://www.rbb-online.de/kontraste/beitrag/2004/falshe_vorbilder_l.

92. "Soldaten mashierten vor Bundestag auf," *Die Zeit*, October 27, 2005, http://images .zeit.de/text/online/2005/43/zapenstreich.

93. *White Paper 2006 on German Security Policy and the Future of the Bundeswehr*, Federal Ministry of Defense, 59.

94. "Struck suspendiert 23 Bundeswehr-Ausbilder," December 4, 2004, *Welt Online*, http://www.welt.de/print-welt/article356438/Struck_suspendiert_23_Bundeswehr_Aus bilder.html.

95. *Der Spiegel Online*, April 9, 2009, http://www.spiegel.de/politik/deutschland/0,15 18,druck-618528,00.html.

96. "Bundeswehr Lehrbuch verkläert die Wehrmacht," *Die Welt*, April 10, 2009, *Welt Online*, http://www.we.de/politik/article3536452/Bundeswehr-Lehrbuch-verklärt die Wehrmacht.html.

97. Hans Christian Beck, "Der Bürger in Uniform, die Konzeption der Innere Führung und the möglichen Konsequenzen eines 'Bruchs' in der wehrstrukturellen, Kontinuität," in *Wehrhafte Demokratie 2000: zu Wehrpflicht und Wehrstruktu*, ed. Armin A. Steinkamm and Dieter Schößler (Baden-Baden: Nomos, 1999), 166–67.

98. "German General Quits over Airstrike," *New York Times*, November 27, 2009.

99. "Jung blamiert Angela Merkel und die Bundeswehr," *Die Welt*, November 26, 2009, http://www.weld.de/politik/deutschland/article5339894/Jung-blamiert-Angela -Merkel-und-die-Bundeswehr.html; "Schneiderhand tritt zurück: Auch Jung in Erklärungsnot," *Frankfurter Allgemeine Zeitung*, http://www.faz.net/s/Rub594835B672714/ A1DB1A121534010EE1.

100. "Guttenberg spricht von angemessenem Luftschlag," *Die Welt*, November 6, 2009, http://www.welt.de/politik/deutschland/article5110882/Guttenberg-spricht-von-angemessenem-Luftschlag.html; "Guttenberg stellt sich vor Oberst Klein," *Die Zeit*, November 11, 2009, http://www.zeit.de/politik/deutschland/2009-11/guttenberg-nato-beri; "Guttenberg rechtfertigy Luftangriff auf Tanklaster," *Spiegel Online*, November 6, 2009, http://spiegel.de/politik/ausland/0,1518,druk-639783,00.html.

101. "Zu Guttenberg beurteilt Angriff neu," *Frankfurter Allgemeine Zeitung*, December 3, 2009, http://www.stuttgarter-zeitung.de/stz/page/230212_afghani. NATO also criticized Col. Klein's actions in ordering the air attack: "NATO-Bericht sieht Fehler der Bundeswehr," *Frankfurter Allgemeine Zeitung*, October 31, 2009, http://www.fax.net/s/RubDDBDABB9457A437BAA85A49C26FB2. Eventually, Ambassador Richard Holbrooke, President Obama's special envoy to Pakistan and Afghanistan, called the attack "a catastrophe." "Im Gespräch: Richard Holbrook—'Kundus was eine Katastrophe,'" *Frankfurter Allgemeine Zeitung*, December 9, 2009.

102. "Oberst übernimmit Verantwortung," *Suttgarter Zeitung*, February 10, 2010, http://www.stuttgarter-zeitung.de/stz/page/2382954_0_5468_.

103. "Soldat mit Afghanistanerfahrung wird neuer Generalinspekteur," *Die Zeit*, December 19, 2009, http://zeit.de/politik/deutschland/2009-12/wieker-generalinspekteur.

104. "Germany Reviews Training after Army Scandal," *Financial Times*, October 27, 2006. See also, "Nach Schädel-Skandal wird Ausbildung der Soldaten überprüft," *Welt Online*, October 25, 2006, http://www.welt.de/politik/article90060/Nach_Schaedel_Skandal_wird_Ausbildung_der_Soldaten_ueberprueft.html.

105. "Generalinspekteur zieht Konsequenzen aus Totenschädel-Affäre," *Welt Online*, http://www.welt.de/politik/article702906/Generalinspekteur_zieht_Konsequenzen_aus_Totenschaedel_Affaere.html.

106. Interview, "Die Bundeswehr ist nicht die Schule der Nation," December 16, 2006, http://www.welt.de/politik/article703025/Interview_Die_Bundeswehr_ist_nicht_die_Schule_der_Nation.html.

107. I am indebted to a retired U.S. officer living in Germany for this observation.

108. "Soldaten mussten rohe Schweineleber essen," *Die Welt*, February 9, 2010; "Demütigung bei der Bundeswehr, Soldaten mussten rohe Schweineleber essen," *Spiegel Online*, February 9, 2010, http://www.spiegel.de/politik/deutschland/0,1518,druck-676897,00.html; "Bundeswehrskandal—'Gesoffen wird doch überall,'" *Die Welt*, February 10, 2010, http:www.welt.de/politik/deutschland'article6336584/Bundeswehrskandal-Gesoffen-wird-doch-ueberall.html; "Staatsanwalt ermittelt gegen Mittenwald-Soldaten," *Die Welt*, February 12, 2010, http://www.welt.de/politik/deutschland/artikle632080/Staatsanwalt-ermittelt-gegen-Mittenwald-Soldaten.html.

109. "Miese Stimmung in der Truppe," *Der Spiegel*, April 26, 2007.

110. "Armee an Grenze der Belastbarkeit," April 12, 2007, *Welt Online*, http://www.welt.de/welt_print/article804856/Armee_an_Grenze_der_Belastbarkeit.html.

111. "General beklagt sich über zu viele jammernde Soldaten," *Die Zeit*, June 19, 2009.

112. "USA halten Rettungshubschrauber am Hindukush," *Der Spiegel*, January 20, 2012.

113. "German General Breaks his Silence on Afghanistan," *New York Times*, November 30, 2008, http://www.nytimes.com/2008/11/30/world/europe/30iht-germany.4.

114. "Ausrüstung der Bundeswehr hält mit Tempo der Einsätze nicht Schritt," *Welt*

Online, http://www.welt.de/welt_print/article1789576?Ausruestung_der_Bundeswehr_haelt_mit_Tempo_Einsaetze_nicht_Schritt.html.

115. "Die überforderte Armee," *Die Welt*, September 17, 2006, http://www.welt.de./print-welt/article153321/Die_ueberforderte_Armee.hmtl.

116. "German Reviews Training after Army Scandal," *Financial Times*, October 27, 2006, http://www.ft.com/cons/s/2call5de-6553-lldb-90id-000079c2340.

117. "Miese Stimmung in der Truppe," *Der Spiegel*, August 26, 2007.

118. The following breakdown shows the change in public opinion of German troops in Afghanistan:

March 2002, 62% stay, only 33% leave
September 2007, 52% leave
September 2008, 58% leave
September 2009, 61% leave, only 33% stay

"SPD kritisiert Jungs Einsatz-Prognose als riskant," *Welt Online*, http://www/welt.de.politik/deutschland/article-4066372/SPD-kritisiert-Jungs-Einsatz-Prognose-als-riskant.html.

119. "Die harte Wahrheit wird nicht ausgesprochen," *Welt Online*, June 20, 2009, http://www.we.t.de/politik/article3970819/Die-harte-Wahrheit-wird-nicht-ausgesprochen.hmtl.

120. "Wehrbeauftrageter fordert mehr Rückhalt für die Truppe," *Zeit Online*, June 24, 2009, http://images.zeit.de/text/online/2009/26/bundeswehr-afghanistan-2.

121. "Angriff auf Bundeswehr war Militärisch geplant," April 30, 2009, *Spiegel Online*, http://www.spiegel.de/politik/ausland/0,1518.druck-622125.00.html.

122. "Bundeswehr in studenlange Gefechte verwickelt," May 8, 2009, *Welt Online*, http://www.welt.de/politik/article3700679/Bundeswehr-in-studenlange-Gefechte-verwickelt.

123. "Angariff auf deutsche Soldaten" (n.d.), *Frankfurter Allgemeine Zeitung*, FAZ.NET, http://www.fax.net/s/RubFC06D389EE76479E9E76425072B196C3.

124. "Mit Panzern gegen die Taliban," *Zeit Online*, June 19, 2009, http://www.zeit.de/online/2009/26/bundeswehr-afghanistan.

125. Ibid. Rather than a explosive shell, the Bundeswehr was supplied with star shells. They emit a white or infrared light and it slowly drift down beneath a heat resistant, parachute illuminating the area below. "Shell," *Wikipedia*, http://en.wikipedia.org/wiki/Shell_(projectile).

126. "AWACS nach Afghanistan," June 12, 2009, FAZ.NET, http://www.faz.net/s./RbuDDBDABB9457A437BAA85A49C26FB2.

127. "Deutsche Soldaten haben strengste Vorschriften für den Einsatz der Waffe," *Frankfurter Allgemeine Zeitung*, Sonntagszeitung, June 22, 2008.

128. "Jung will offensivere Einsatzregeln für Bundeswehr," July 1, 2009, *Welt Online*, http://www.welt.de/politik/deutschland/article4038084/Jung-will-offensivere-Einsatzregeln-fuer-Bundeswehr.html.

129. "Soldaten jammern auf hohem Niveau," *Spiegel Online*, June 16, 2009, http://www.spiegel.de/politik/deutschland/0,1518,druck-630849,00.html.

130. "Merkel will Debatte über den Wandel der Bundeswehr," July 6, 2009, http://www.freenet.de/freenet/nachricten/politik/200907/20090706.

131. "Merkel will Debatte über den Wandel der Bundeswehr," July 7, 2009, *Die Zeit*, http://www.zeit.de/newsticker/2009/7/6/iptc-bdt-20090705-621-21725014xml.

132. Klaus Naumann, *Einsatz ohne Ziel? Die Politikbedürftigkeit des Militärischen* (Hamburg: HIS Verlages, 2008).

133. "No Parade for Hans," *New York Times*, November 15, 2009.

134. "Jung hat Ärger mit dem Generalinspekteur," September 7, 2006, *Welt Online*, http://www.welt.de/print-welt/article150751/Jung_hat_Aerger_mit_dem_Generalinspek teur.html.

135. " 'Die Bundeswehr' eine Generalsabrechnung," *Zeit Online*, January 16, 2008, http://blog.zeit.de/bittner/2208/01/16/die-bundeswehr-eine-generalsabrechnung.

136. Ibid.

137. "Bundeswehr nur bedingt modern," *Zeit Online*, March 26, 2009, http://www .zeit.de/online/2009/14/wehrbereict-robbe.

138. As quoted in Paul Balkin, *German Foreign Security Policy: Trends and Transatlantic Implications* (Washington, DC: Congressional Research Service, 2009), RL34199, 12.

139. Nesshoever, "Preparing Germany's Armed Forces for the Future"; see also Dyson, *The Politics of German Defense and Security*, 122; and Mary Elise Sarotte, *German Military Reform and European Security* (Abingdon, Oxford: Routledge, 2001), 27.

140. "Guttenberg: 'Kriegsnähe Zustände,' " *Frankfurter Allgemeine Zeitung*, November 3, 2009, http://www.faz.net/s/sRub594835B672714A121534F010EE1.

141. "Guttenburg: Militärisch angemessen," *Frankfurter Allgemeine Zeitung*, http:// www.faz.net/s/RubDDBDABB9457A437BAA85A49C26FB2.

142. "Liebling Kundus," May 12, 2009, *Die Zeit*, http://www.zeit.de/2009050/Vertei gungsministerium?page=all&prin.

143. Lest the reader get the impression that military officers always take the side of other military officers, Farwick criticized Schneiderhan, noting, "In eight years he did too little for the troops. He should have created better conditions for the troops. He did not consider the political side of issues as Nauman did. This was much to the displeasure of von Rühe." Farwick e-mail to the author, February 18, 2012.

144. "Soldat mit Afghanistanerfahrung neuer Generalinspekteur," *Die Zeit*, December 18, 2009, http://www.zeit.de/politik/deutschland/2009-12wiecker-generalinspekteur.

145. "Kujat kritisiert Bundesregierung," *Stuttgarter Zeitung*, April 4, 2010, http://www .stuttgarter-zeitung.de/stz/page/2442723_0_9346_nach-d.

146. "Rühe fordert Experiment aus Ex-Militärs," *Der Spiegel*, April 5, 2010, http://www .spiegel.de/politik/ausland/0,1518,druck-687301,00.html.

147. "Es geht nicht nur um Brunnen bohren," *Frankfurter Allgemeine Zeitung*, April 6, 2010, http://www.faz.net/s/Rub0CCA23BC3D3C4C7894F85DED3BED3B54F.

148. "Bundeswehr bestellt eilig 60 neue Panzer-Wagen," *Der Spiegel*, April 15, 2010, http://www.spiegel.de/politik/deutschland/0,1518.druck-689068,00.html.

149. "Ich will wissen, wie es hier aussieht," *Der Spiegel*, May 27, 2010, http://www .spiegel.de/politik/ausland/0,1518,druck-696310,00.html.

150. "Tiefe Einschnitte in die Struktur der Bundeswehr," *Frankfurter Allgemeine Zeitung*, http://www.faz.net/s/Rub594835B672714A1DB1A121534F010EE1.

151. Ulf Gartzke, "The Battle Over German Armed Forces Reform," *Weekly Standard*, September 1, 2010.

152. "Generalinspekteur beklagt Verschwendung bei Bundeswehr," *Die Zeit*, September 2, 2010, http://www.zeit.de/politik/2010-09/bundeswehr-verschwendung-wiek.

153. "Die ganze Dissertation wurde abgeschrieben," *Frankfurter Allgemeine Zeitung*, February 2, 2011, http://www.faz.net/s/Rub594835B672714A1DB1A121534F010EE1/; "Guttenberg kopierte auch aus der Zeit," February 21, 2011, http://www.zeit.de/politik/deutschland/2011-02/guttenberg-plagiat-zeit.

154. "Merkel: Als Minister ist Guttenberg hervorragend," *Frankfurter Allgemeine Zeitung*, February 21, 2011, http://www.faz.net/s/Rub594835B672714A1DB1A121534F010ee1/.

155. "Merkel Announces New Defense Minister," CNN.com, March 3, 2011.

156. "Security: A German Military Overhaul," *Financial Times*, January 31, 2011, http://www.ft.com/cms/cofedfdc-2d6f-11-8153-00144fwB-49A,DW.

157. "Machtkampf im Ministerium, *Die Zeit*, February 2, 2011, http://www.zeit.de/politik/deutschland/2010-11/bundeswehr-reform-ve. See also, "Report of the Commission," October 26, 2010, http://translate.google.com/translate?hl=en&sl=de&u-http//aussen-sic.

158. "Weniger U-Bootes, Weniger Panzer, Weniger Kampfjets," *Der Spiegel*, April 22, 2011, http://www.spiegel.de/politik/deutschland/0,1518,druck-758644,00.html.

159. "Die Nestbauer," *Frankfurter Allgemeine Zeitung*, June 2, 2011, http://www.faz/s/Rub594835B672714AlDBlA121534F010EE1.

160. "Maiziere streicht 31 Bundeswehrstandorte," *Die Zeit*, October 26, 2011, http://www.zeit.de/politik/deutschland/2011-10/bundeswehr-reform-ka.

161. "Kritik an Bundeswehrreform," *Frankfurter Allgemeine Zeitung*, January 9, 2012. As one might expect, there is a lot of criticism from those in uniform.

CHAPTER 6. **From Paul Hellyer through Pierre Trudeau**

1. Roy Rempel, "The Need for a Canadian Security Policy," *Canadian Defence Quarterly* (April 1990): 38.

2. See, for example, Pierre Trudeau, *Memoirs* (Toronto: McClelland and Stewart, 1993); Brian Mulroney, *Memoirs* (Toronto: McClelland and Stewart, 2007); Jean Chrétien, *My Years as Prime Minister* (Toronto: Vintage-Canada, 2008); Paul Martin, *Hell or High Water: My Life in and out of Politics* (Toronto: McClelland and Steward, 2008). There are a few mentions of the Canadian Forces, but with a few exceptions (e.g., the role of the military during the problems in Quebec under Trudeau), the military is scarcely mentioned.

3. When reference is made to quotes from Canadians, or to Canadian institutions, the Canadian spelling will be used. Thus, *defence* versus *defense*.

4. General G. C. E. Theriault, "Reflections on Canadian Defence Policy and Its Underlying Structural Problems," *Canadian Defence Quarterly* (July 1993): 3.

5. Jeff Tasseron, "Facts and Invariants: The Changing Context of Canadian Defence Policy," *Canadian Military Journal* (Summer 2003): 23.

6. Or to quote Tasseron, "This contrasts significantly with the American view, which holds the institution of defence as an infinitely (and some would say artificially) higher level than the majority of other government endeavours." Ibid.

7. Douglas Bland, "Parliament's Duty to Defend Canada," *Canadian Military Journal* (Winter 2000–2001): 37.

8. "Managing Change with Shrinking Resources," in Charles C. Moskos, John Allen Williams, and David R. Segal, *The Post Modern Military* (New York: Oxford, 2000), 158.

9. Douglas J. Murray, "Canada"; Douglas J. Murray and Paul R. Viotti, *The Defense Policies of Nations: A Comparative Study*, 3rd ed. (Baltimore: Johns Hopkins University Press, 1994), 57.

10. Peter Newman, *"True North, Not Strong and Free": Defending the Kingdom in the Nuclear Age* (Toronto: McClelland and Stewart, 1983), 4.

11. Canadian Forces share one commonality with their German, Russian, and American colleagues—the love of abbreviations. They are commonly used throughout almost all documents, official and unofficial.

12. Gerry Thereiault, "Democratic Civil-Military Relations: A Canadian View," in *The Military in Modern Democratic Society*, Jim Hanson and Susan McNish (Toronto: The Canadian Institute of Strategic Studies, 1996), 5.

13. Ibid.

14. Ibid., 6–7.

15. David Bercuson, *Significant Incident: Canada's Army, the Airborne, and the Murder in Somalia* (Toronto: McClelland and Steward, 1996), 27.

16. MG D. C. Loomis and LTC D. T. Lightburn, "Taking into Account the Distinctness of the Military from the Mainstream of Society," *Canadian Defence Quarterly* 10 (1980): 17.

17. Bercuson, *Significant Incident*, 60.

18. Loomis and Lightburn, "Taking into Account the Distinctness of the Military," 19.

19. Ibid., 20. Emphasis added.

20. Allan D. English, *Understanding Military Culture: A Canadian Perspective* (Montreal: McGill-Queen's University Press, 2004), 33.

21. Ibid., 9.

22. M. D. Capstick, "Defining the Culture: The Canadian Army in the 21st Century," *Canadian Military Journal* (Spring 2003): 50.

23. For example, the last CDS (General Walter Natynczyk) served as deputy commander of an American division during the invasion of Iraq, while his predecessor, General Rick Hillier, served with American troops in Afghanistan. Also, most Canadian weapons systems are produced in the U.S. or by American companies working under license in Canada.

24. Bercuson, *Significant Incident*, 7ff, 64.

25. See Douglas Bland, *Transforming National Defence Administration* (Kingston: School of Policy Studies, 2005), v.

26. Douglas Bland, "Hillier and the New Generation of Generals: The CDs, the Policy, and the Troops," *Policy Options* (March 2008): 54.

27. Bercuson, *Significant Incident*, 48–49.

28. Bland, "Hillier and the New Generation of Generals," 54.

29. Desmond Morton, *A Military History of Canada*, 5th ed. (Toronto: McCelland and Stewart, 2007), 238.

30. K. W. Baily, "Integration and Unification Equals Jointness in 21st-Century Canadian Forces," Canadian Forces College, unpublished manuscript, May 6, 2002, 17.

31. Bercuson, *Significant Incident*, 50.

32. Ibid., 51.

33. Ibid., 53.

34. K. W. Bailey, "Integration and Unification Equals Jointness in 21st-Century Canadian Forces."

35. Douglas Bland, *Canada's National Defence*, vol. 2, *Defence Organization* (Kingston: School of Policy Studies, 1997), 70.

36. Morton, *A Military History of Canada*, 180.

37. Ibid.

38. Bercuson, *Significant Incident*, 69.

39. W. Harriet Critchley, "Civilianization and the Canadian Military," *Armed Forces and Society* 16, no. 1 (Fall 1989): 123.

40. Lt. Col. Ross Fetterly, "The Influence of the Environment on the 1964 Defence White Paper," *Canadian Military Journal* (Winter 2004–2005): 50.

41. Ibid.

42. Bercuson, *Significant Incident*, 68.

43. Ibid.

44. Paul Hellyer, *Damn the Torpedoes: My Fight to Unify Canada's Armed Forces* (Toronto: McClelland and Stewart, 1990), 33.

45. Paul T. Hellyer, "Canadian Defence Policy," *Air University Review* 19, no. 1 (November–December 1967): 3.

46. Daniel Gosselin and Craig Stone, "From Minister Hellyer to General Hillier: Understanding the Fundamental Differences between the Unification of the Canadian Forces and Its Present Transformation," http://www.journal.dnd.ca/vo6/no4/trans-eng.asp.

47. Douglas L. Bland, "Transforming Defence Administration," in *Transforming National Defence Administration*, ed. Douglas Bland (Kingston: School of Policy Studies, 2005), 1.

48. Ibid.

49. Bland, *Canada's National Defence*, vol. 1., *Defence Policy* (Kingston: School of Policy Studies 1997), 58.

50. Ibid., 59.

51. Vernon Kronenberg, *All Together Now: The Organization of the Department of National Defence* (Toronto: Canadian Institute of International Affairs, 1973), 13.

52. Douglas Bland, *Canada's National Defence*, vol. 1, 60.

53. Ibid., 20.

54. V. J. Kronenberg, "All Together Now: Canadian Defence Organization," MA thesis, Carleton University; as cited in Douglas Bland, *The Administration of Defence Policy in Canada, 1947 to 1985* (Kingston: Ronald Frye and Company, 1987).

55. Bland, *Canada's National Defence*, vol.1, 95.

56. Ibid., 19.

57. Hellyer, *Damn the Torpedoes*, 147.

58. Jack Lawrence Granatstein, *Who Killed the Canadian Military?* (Toronto: HarperCollins Canada, 2004), 78.

59. Hellyer, *Damn the Torpedoes*, 147.

60. While Hellyer said in his memoirs that he used the term "buttons and badges," Granatstein says he used the term "buttons and bows" (*Who Killed the Canadian Military?*, 78). Regardless of which term was actually used, both would be seen as an insult to the Canadian military. I will use Hellyer's term, button and badges.

61. Granatstein, *Who Killed the Canadian Military?*, 83
62. Hellyer, *Damn the Torpedoes*, 178–79.
63. Granatstein, *Who Killed the Canadian Military?*, 83.
64. For purposes of full disclosure, this writer should note that he wore the uniform of the U.S. Navy for 33 years beginning as an E-1 and retiring O-6, and I am probably a bit more sympathetic to the emotions felt by Canadian sailors.
65. Geoffrey D. T. Shaw, "The Canadian Armed Forces and Unification," *Defense Analysis* 17, no. 2 (2001): 160.
66. Paul Martin, "Forward from the Prime Minister," *Canada's International Policy Statement: A Role of Pride and Influence in the World* (Ottawa: Department of Foreign Affairs, 2005), 243.
67. Morton, *A Military History of Canada*, 252.
68. Bercuson, *Significant Incident*, 76.
69. As cited in Ibid., 72.
70. Morton, *A Military History of Canada*, 241–42.
71. Jean Allard, *The Memoirs of General Jean Allard* (Vancouver: University of British Columbia Press, 1988), 253.
72. Much of the following discussion is taken from, Bland, *The Administration of Defence Policy in Canada*, 39.
73. Hellyer, *Damn the Torpedoes*, 70.
74. Bland, *The Administration of Defence Policy in Canada*, 42.
75. Ibid.
76. Granatstein, *Who Killed the Canadian Military?*, 84.
77. Hellyer, *Damn the Torpedoes*, 88.
78. Bailey, "Integration and Unification," 27.
79. Allard, *The Memoirs of General Jean Allard*, 256.
80. Granatstein, *Who Killed the Canadian Military?*, 79.
81. Hellyer, *Damn the Torpedoes*, 156.
82. Granatstein, *Who Killed the Canadian Military?*, 79.
83. Ibid.
84. Ibid.
85. Hellyer, *Damn the Torpedoes*, 165.
86. Ibid.
87. Allard, *The Memoirs of General Jean Allard*, 255.
88. Granatstein, *Who Killed the Canadian Military?*, 76.
89. Allard, *The Memoirs of General Jean Allard*, 225.
90. Bland, *The Administration of Defence Policy in Canada*, 49.
91. Bailey, "Integration and Unification," 24.
92. Daniel Gosselin and Craig Stone, "From Minister Hellyer to General Hillier: Understanding the Fundamental Differences Between the Unification of the Canadian Forces and its Present Transformation," *Canadian Military Journal* 4 (2006): 11.
93. Allard, *The Memoirs of General Jean Allard*, 267.
94. Morton, *A Military History of Canada*, 254.
95. Hellyer, *Damn the Torpedoes*, 161.
96. Ibid., 127.
97. Allard, *The Memories of General Jean Allard*, 247–48.

98. Ibid., 219.

99. Serge Bernier, "French Canadians and the Canadian Armed Forces: 1966–1994," in *The Military in Modern Democratic Society,* Jim Hanson and Susan McNish (Toronto: Canadian Institute of Strategic Studies, 1966), 76.

100. Allard, *The Memories of General Jean Allard*, 258.

101. Bernier, "French Canadians and the Canadian Armed Forces," 76.

102. Allard, *The Memories of General Jean Allard*, 281.

103. Lawrence Martin, *Iron Man: The Defiant Reign of Jean Chrétien* (Toronto: Viking Canada, 2003), 34.

104. J. L. Granatstein and Robert Bothwell, *Pirouette: Pierre Trudeau and Canadian Foreign Policy* (Toronto: University of Toronto Press, 1990), 7–8.

105. Granatstein, *Who Killed the Canadian Military?*, 115.

106. Granatstein and Bothwell, *Pirouette*, 7.

107. Ibid., 13.

108. Granatstein, *Who Killed the Canadian Military?*, 115.

109. Granatstein and Bothwell, *Pirouette*, 13–14.

110. Ivan Head and Pierre Trudeau, *The Canadian Way: Shaping Canada's Foreign Policy, 1968–1984* (Toronto: McClelland and Stewart, 1995), 76.

111. Ibid.

112. Ibid., 76–77.

113. Ibid., 79.

114. Ibid., 83. Much of the discussion of the foregoing discussion is taken from Head and Trudeau, *The Canadian Way.*

115. John English, *Just Watch Me: The Life of Pierre Elliott Trudeau, 1968–2000*, vol. 2 (Toronto: Alfred A. Knopf Canada, 2009), 62.

116. Head and Trudeau, *The Canadian Way*, 83.

117. Ibid.

118. English, *Just Watch Me*, 63.

119. Granatstein, *Who Killed the Canadian Military?*, 117–18.

120. Granatstein and Bothewell, *Pirouette*, 235.

121. Ibid., 245.

122. Much of the following is taken from Allard, *The Memoirs of General Jean Allard*, 286–88, and Morton, *A Military History of Canada*, 21–22.

123. Granatstein and Bothwell, *Pirouette*, 246.

124. Ibid.

125. Bernier, "French Canadians and the Canadian Armed Forces," 77.

126. Trudeau, *Memoirs*, 137.

127. Ibid., 150.

128. Granatstein and Bothwell, *Pirouette*, 236.

129. Trudeau, *Memoirs*, 142.

130. As quoted in English, *Just Watch Me*, 81–82.

131. See Granatstein and Bothwell, *Pirouette*, 236–37.

132. Ibid.

133. Sean Mahoney, "Better Late than Never: Defence during the Mulroney Years," in *Transforming the Nation: Canada and Brian Mulroney*, ed. Raymond B. Blake (Montreal: McGill-Queen's University Press, 2007), 134.

134. Bland, *Canada's National Defence*, vol. 2, 160.

135. Granatstein and Bothwell, *Pirouette*, 242.

136. Critchly, "Civilianization and the Canadian Military," 128. Emphasis in the original.

137. Colonels J. E. Neelin and L. M. Pederson, "On the Effect of Restructuring of NDHQ on the Profession of Arms in Canada," *Canadian Defence Quarterly* (Summer 1974): 54.

138. As quoted in English, *Understanding Military Culture*, 35.

139. Douglas L. Bland and Sean M. Maloney, *Campaigns for International Security* (Montreal: McGill-Queen's University Press, 2004), 38.

140. Douglas Bland, *Chiefs of Defence* (Toronto: Canadian Institute of Strategic Studies, 1995), 93.

141. Gerald Porter, *In Retreat: The Canadian Forces in the Trudeau Years* (Toronto: Deneau and Green, 1978), 23.

142. Ibid., 24.

143. Ibid., 25.

144. Ibid.

145. Ibid., 12.

146. Grantatstein and Bothwell, *Pirouette*, 254.

147. Much of the discussion of the 1975 Review is taken from ibid., 255. Dextraze's quote is from that source.

148. Porter, *In Retreat*, 13.

149. Ibid., 15.

150. Ibid., 18.

151. Tasseron, "Facts and Invariant," 25.

152. Ibid.

153. Morton, *A Military History of Canada*, 262.

154. Sean M. Maloney, "Better Late than Never: Defence during the Mulroney Years," in *Transforming the Nation: Canada and Brian Mulroney*, ed. Raymond B. Blake (Montreal: McGill-Queen's University Press, 2007), 137.

155. Douglas Bland, "The Government of Canada and the Armed Forces: A Troubled Relationship," in *The Soldier and the Canadian State: A Crisis in Civil-Military Relations?*, ed. David A. Charters and J. Brent Wilson (Conflict Studies Workshop, University of New Brunswick, 1995), 28–29. Emphasis in the original.

156. Ibid.

157. Geoffrey D. T. Shaw, "The Canadian Armed Forces and Unification," 168.

158. Bland, *Canada's National Defence*, vol. 2, 253.

159. Ibid., 253–54.

160. Ibid., 256.

161. "Task Force on Review of Unification of the Canadian Armed Forces: Final Report, March 15, 1980" (Ottawa: Ministry of National Defence, 1980).

162. Bland, *Canada's National Defence*, 256

163. Bland and Maloney, *Campaigns for International Security*, 38.

164. Peter Kasurak, "Civilianization and the Military Ethos," *Canadian Public Administration* 25, no. 1 (Spring 1982): 109.

165. Howie Marsh, "The Gathering Defence Policy Crisis," in *Canada Without Armed Forces?*, Douglas Bland (Montreal: McGill-Queen's University Press, 2004), 85.

166. Granatstein, *Who Killed the Canadian Military?*, 122.

167. Maloney, "Better Late than Never," 122.

CHAPTER 7. **From Brian Mulroney through Stephen Harper**

1. Jack Lawrence Granatstein, *Who Killed the Canadian Military?* (Toronto: HarperCollins Canada, 2004), 128–29.

2. Sean M. Mahoney, "Better Late than Never: Defence during the Mahoney Years," in *Transforming the Nation: Canada and Brian Mahoney*, ed. Raymond R. Blake (Montreal: McGill University Press, 2007), 138–39.

3. Ibid., 138.

4. R. B. Byers, "The 1987 White Paper: An Analysis," *Canadian Defence Quarterly* (Autumn 1987): 16.

5. Mahoney, "Better Late than Never," 140.

6. Donald Neill, "Back to the Basics: Defence Interests and Defence Policy in Canada," *Canadian Defence Quarterly* (December 1991): 41.

7. Brian Mulroney, *Memoirs* (Toronto: McClelland and Stewart, 2007), 332.

8. Ibid.

9. Granatstein, *Who Killed the Canadian Military?*, 127.

10. Ibid., 131.

11. Wilf Lund, "Integration and Unification of the Canadian Forces," CFB Esquimal Naval and Military Museum (n.d.), http://www.navalandmilitarymuseum.org//resource_pages/controversies/unification.html.

12. Perrin Beatty, "A Defence Policy for Canada," *Canadian Defence Quarterly* (July 1987): 12.

13. Douglas Bland, *Canada's National Defence*, vol. 2, *Defence Organization* (Kingston: School of Policy Studies, 1997), 413.

14. Ibid., 415.

15. W. Harriet Critchley, "Does Canada Have a Defence Policy?," *Canadian Defence Policy* (October 1989): 7.

16. Douglas Bland, "The Government of Canada and the Armed Forces: A Troubled Relationship," in *The Soldier and the Canadian State: A Crisis in Civil-Military Relations?*, ed. David A. Charters and J. Brent Wilson (Conflict Studies Workshop, University of New Brunswick, 1995), 32.

17. Granatstein, *Who Killed the Canadian Military?*, 93.

18. Maloney, "Better Late than Never," 150.

19. General G. C. E. Theriault, "Reflections on Canadian Defence Policy and Its Underlying Structural Problems," *Canadian Defence Quarterly* (July 1993): 4.

20. David Bercuson, *Significant Incident: Canada's Army, the Airborne, and the Murder in Somalia* (Toronto: McClelland and Steward, 1996), 219–20.

21. Ibid., 222.

22. Ibid., 224.

23. Granatstein, *Who Killed the Canadian Military?*, 152.

24. Ibid.

25. Douglas Bland, "The Government of Canada and the Armed Forces: A Troubled Relationship," in *The Soldier and the Canadian State: A Crisis in Civil-Military Relations?*,

ed. David A. Charters and J. Brent Wilson (Fredericton, NB: Centre for Conflict Studies, 1996), 31.

26. Bercuson, *Significant Incident*, 31.

27. Ibid., 241–42. Emphasis in the original.

28. Lawrence Martin, *Iron Man: The Defiant Reign of Jean Chrétien* (Toronto: Viking Canada, 2003), 4.

29. Jean Chrétien, *My Years as Prime Minister* (Toronto: Vintage-Canada, 2008), 54.

30. Granatstein, *Who Killed the Canadian Military?*, 166.

31. John Gray and Paul Martin, *In the Balance* (Toronto: Key Porter Books, 2004), 174.

32. Granatstein, *Who Killed the Canadian Military?*, 138, 152.

33. Martin, *Iron Man*, 192.

34. Ibid., 197.

35. Bland, "The Government of Canada and the Armed Forces," 31.

36. Marc Miller, "Defence Policy for New Century: Report of the University of New Brunswick Workshop on the Defence Review," *Canadian Defence Review* (June 1994): 20.

37. Douglas L. Bland and Sean M. Maloney, *Campaigns for International Security* (Montreal: McGill-Queen's University Press, 2004), 130.

38. Rick Hillier, *A Soldier First: Bullets, Bureaucrats and the Politics of War* (Ontario: HarperCollins, 2009), 158. This is one of the most fascinating books this writer has read on military politics in any of the four countries discussed here.

39. Ibid., 158.

40. Ibid., 133.

41. Ibid., 134.

42. Ibid.

43. Colin Galigan, "Canadian Defence Spending," in *The Canadian Strategic Forecast 1996: The Military in Modern Democratic Society*, ed. Jim Hanson and Susan McNich (Toronto: Canadian Institute of Strategic Studies, 1996), 26–27.

44. As cited in Allan D. English, *Understanding Military Culture: A Canadian Perspective* (Montreal: McGill-Queen's University Press, 2004), 57.

45. Martin, *Iron Man*, 136.

46. Ibid.; and "PM Denies Plan to Send Troops into Quebec," *CBC*, October 21, 2003, http://www.cbc.ca/canada/story/2003/10/21/referendum_troops0310.

47. Desmond Morton, *A Military History of Canada*, 5th ed. (Toronto: McCelland and Stewart, 2007), 287.

48. Ibid., 287–88.

49. David Bercuson, "Up from the Ashes: The Re-professionalization of the Canadian Forces after the Somalia Affair," *Canadian Military Journal* 9, no. 3 (2009): 36. Emphasis in the original. Jeffrey's first name is not available.

50. Ibid., 37.

51. English, *Understanding Military Culture*, 60.

52. Bercuson, "Up from the Ashes."

53. Morton, *A Military History of Canada*, 298.

54. "Canadian Soldiers Depart to Balkans Delayed," CBC, June 7, 1999, http://www.cbc.ca/news/story/1999/06/07/canada990607.html.

55. Martin, *Iron Man*, 342.

56. Hillier, *A Soldier First*, 345. Emphasis in the original.

57. D. W. Middlemiss and J. J. Sokolsky, *Canadian Defence: Decisions and Determinants* (Toronto: Harcourt Brace Jovanovich, Canada, 1989), 28–29.

58. "Bidding to Begin for Canada's New Sea Kings," CBC News, November 10, 2000, http://www.cbc.ca/canada/story/2000/08/17/seakings000817.html; "Eggleton Overhauls Military Health Care," CBC News, November 11, 2000, http://www.cbc.ca/canada/story/2000/01/11military000111.html.

59. "Budget Will Have More Money for Defence, CBC News, November 11, 2000, http://www.cbc.ca/money/story/2000/02/22/defence000222.html.

60. "Military Getting Pay Hike, New Equipment," CBC News, March 1, 2001, http://www.cbc.ca/news/story/2001/03/01mb_military 010301.

61. "Making War to Keep the Peace," October 30, 2009, *Globe and Mail*, October 30, 2009, http://www.theglobeandmail.com/books/review-a-soldier-first-by-rick-hillier.

62. "Speaking Notes for General Raymond Henault, Chief of the Defence Staff at the Reserves 2000 Dinner," Speeches Archive, August 22, 2001, http://www.admpa.forces.gc.ca/news-nouvelles/news-nouvelles-eng.

63. Morton, *A Military History of Canada*, 2.

64. "Sovereignty at Stake in Military Budget Crisis, Group Says," September 9, 2002, http://www.cbc.ca/canada/story/2002/09/09defence_020909.html.

65. "McCallum Makes Case for Defence Spending Increase," October 25, 2002, http://www.cbc.ca/canada/story/2002/19/25/defence_021025.html.

66. Ibid.

67. David J. Bercuson, John Ferris, J. L. Granatstein, Rob Huebert, and Jim Keeley, "National Defence, National Interest: Sovereignty, Security and Canadian Military Capability in the Post 9/11 World," *A Report Prepared by the Canadian Defence Council of Chief Executives for the Canadian Council of Chief Executives* (2003), 2.

68. Douglas L. Bland, ed., *Canada without Armed Forces* (Kingston: School of Policy Studies, Queen's University, 2004), x.

69. Ibid., xiii

70. Howie Marsh, "The Gathering Defence Policy Crisis," in *Canada without Armed Forces*, ed. Bland, 85.

71. Chrétien, *My Years as Prime Minister*, 303.

72. Martin Shadwick, "Defence and Conservatives," *Canadian Military Journal* (Spring 2006): 72.

73. "McCallum Expected to Boost Army Spending," CBS News, October 22, 2003, http://www.cbc.ca/canada/story/2003/10/22/army031022.html.

74. "Minister Says Canada's Soldiers are 'Going to Take a Rest,'" CBC News, January 9, 2004, http://www.cbc.ca/canada/story/2004/01/16pratt040116.html.

75. "The 2000 Red Book, Military," 2004, http://www.cbc.ca/canadavotes2004/politicalcanada/redbook/military.

76. "Harper Promises Armed Forces $1.2B a Year Boost," CBC News, May 21, 2004, http://www.cbc.ca/canada/story/2004/05/31/harp040531.html.

77. Janice Gross Stein and Eugene Lang, *The Unexpected War: Canada in Kandahar* (Toronto: Viking Canada, 2007), 157.

78. Christopher Ankersen, "The Personnel Crisis," in *Canada without Armed Forces*, ed. Bland, 61.

79. Paul Martin, *Hell or High Water: My Life in and out of Politics* (Toronto: McClelland and Steward, 2008), 329.

80. Ibid., 151.

81. Stein and Lang, *The Unexpected War*, 181.

82. Hillier, *A Soldier First*, 335.

83. Daniel Gosselin and Craig Stone, "From Minister Hillyer to General Hillier: Understanding the Fundamental Differences between the Unification of Canadian Forces and its Present Transformation," *Canadian Military Journal* 6, no. 4, http://www.journal,dnd ,ca./vo6/no4/trans-eng.as.

84. Martin, *Hell or High Water*, 393.

85. Hillier, *A Soldier First*, 348.

86. Ibid., 349.

87. Ibid.

88. "Q&A: General Rick Hillier on Canada's Mission in Afghanistan," *Globe and Mail*, March 12, 2007.

89. Ibid.

90. William Johnson, *Stephen Harper and the Future of Canada* (Toronto: McClelland and Stewart, 2005), 458.

91. Stein and Lang, *The Unexpected War*, 230.

92. "Attaining the Elusive Higher Loyalty to the CF," http://www.journal.forces.gc .ca/vo9/no3/04-gosselin-eng.asp.

93. Stein and Lang, *The Unexpected War*, 262.

94. Hillier, *A Soldier First*, 403.

95. David T. Jones and David Kilgour, *Uneasy Neighbors* (Mississauga, ON: John Wiley and Sons, 2007), 248.

96. LTG George MacDonald (ret), "Implementing a Canadian Defence Strategy," *Canadian Defence & Foreign Affairs Institute* (Calgary: Canadian Defence & Foreign Affairs Institute, 2007), http://www.cdfai.org/PDF/Implementing%20a%20Canadian%20Defence%20Strategy%20LGen%20(Retd)%20George%20Macdonald.pdf.

97. LTG George MacDonald, (ret), "Great Expectations: A Breakthrough in Major Defence Projects," *Canadian Defence & Foreign Affairs* (June 2006).

98. "Canada's Military Back on World Stage: PM," CBC News, September 19, 2006, http://www.cbc.ca/canada/story/2006/09/19/harper-afghanistan.html.

99. Stein and Lang, *The Unexpected War*, 195–96.

100. Ibid., 242.

101. "Q&A: General Rick Hillier on Canada's Mission in Afghanistan."

102. Ibid., 243.

103. "The Rebirth of Canada's Military," *National Post*, July 5, 2011.

104. Daniel Gosselin, "Hellyer's Ghosts: Unification of the Canadian Forces Is 40 Years Old, Part Two," *Canadian Military Journal* 9, no. 3 (Autumn 2009): 5.

105. Ibid., 8.

106. Ibid.

107. Ibid.

108. Ibid., 9.

109. "Recruiting is Only Part of the Story," *The Torch*, June 29, 2007.

110. "Chat with General Hillier," March 2007, CBC News, http://www.cbc.ca/news/background/cdnmilitary/chat-hillier.html.

111. Ibid.

112. "O'Connor Lacked Hillier's Charm," *Esprit de Corps* (2009), http://www.espritdecorps.ca/index.php?option-com_content&view-a.

113. Macdonald, "Implementing a Canadian Defence Strategy," 1.

114. J. L. Granatstein, Gordon S. Smith, and Denis Stairs, "A Threatened Future: Canada's Future Strategic Environment and its Security Implications," *Canadian Defence & Foreign Affairs Institute* (Fall 2007): 17.

115. "On the Record: Walt Natynczyk," *Globe and Mail*, January 21, 2011.

116. LTG George Macdonald (ret), "The Canada First Strategy—One Year Later," *Canadian Defence and Foreign Affairs Institute* (October 2009): 1.

117. "Hillier Warns against Civil Servants Directing Military Operations," *Globe and Mail*, October 11, 2010.

118. "Our Army Needs Soldiers and Guns—Not more Bureaucrats," *National Post*, May 19, 2011.

119. "General Walter Natynczyk (Interview)," *MacLean's*, July 7, 2008, http://www.thecanadianencyclopedia.com/PrinterFriendly.cfm?Para.

120. Elinor Sloan, "Canada First Defence Strategy," *Canadian Defence and Foreign Affairs Issue Response Paper* 2 (2008), http://www.cdfai.org/PDF/CanadaFirstDefenceStrategy.pdf.

121. "Canadian Military to Get 15 New Copters," UPI.com, August 11, 2009.

122. Ibid.

123. "Military Cuts Costs to Find $80M Savings," *National Post*, December 16, 2009. The money saved would be used to support programs such as training soldiers for international and domestic operations and purchasing new equipment.

124. Brian Steward, "Military Brass Bite the Tongues Over the 'Hollow Army,'" CBC, June 30, 2009.

125. Ibid.

126. "Canadian Navy's Ships Risk Being Banned from Foreign Ports," *Globe and Mail*, August 5, 2010.

127. *The Center for Grassroots Oversight*, March 9, 2009, http://www.historycommons.org/entity.jsp?entity-walter_natynczyk_.

128. "Forces Prepare for Afghan Withdrawal," *Globe and Mail*, November 6, 2009.

129. "If Ottawa Fights a Deficit, the Military Has No Allies," *Globe and Mail*, March 10, 2010.

130. "Military Sees F-35's Stealth as Way to Assert Sovereignty," *Globe and Mail*, August 31, 2010.

131. "Harper, Ignatieff Duel Over Jets," *Globe and Mail*, October 7, 2010.

132. "Multibillion-dollar Jets But 'Best Value for Canada,' Top Soldier Says," *Globe and Mail*, January 21, 2011.

133. "Plan to Replace Aging Sea Kings Hits New Snag," *Globe and Mail*, November 22, 2010.

134. "Taxpayers, Prepare to Run Aground," *National Post*, October 2011.

135. "Slash Staff at Defence Hq: Report," *National Post*, August 2011.

136. " 'Everything's on the Table': Ministry Chief Backs Calls for Cuts," thestar.com, September 1, 2011, http://www.thestar.com/primarticle/1047971.

137. "The Canadian Force Names: A Mark of Respect," August 15, 2011. "The Land Forces will not be called the Royal Canadian Army because Canada follows British Tradition which holds that the navy and the air force are commanded by the Queen but the army is a collection of independent regiments that serve the sovereign but are not part of the Royal Canadian Forces." "Conservatives to Restore 'Royal' Moniker to Canada's Navy, Air Force," *Globe and Mail*, August 15, 2011.

138. Ibid.

CHAPTER 8. **From Boris Yeltsin through Vladimir Putin**

1. In Russia it is common to refer to the Russian or Soviet Army as "the Army" when all services are meant. Normally, when the army is meant, the reference is to the ground forces.

2. Even during the communist period, the Russian military stayed out of politics, even though it was politicized in the sense that the overwhelming majority were Communist Party members. There was what amounted to a division of labor. The political leadership decided the strategic issues and occasionally even became involved in operational matters, but most operational and tactical questions were left to the military. See this writer's *Russian Civil-Military Relations* (Bloomington: Indiana University Press, 1996); *The Soviet High Command, 1967–1989: Personalities and Politics* (Princeton: Princeton University Press, 1990).

3. *Krasnaya zvezda*, November 15, 1986.

4. Ibid., March 6, 1993.

5. "Minister's Position," *Rossiyskiye vesti*, January 4, 1993, in FBIS: SOV, January 6, 1993.

6. "Russian Army Close to Chaos," *Dagens Nyheter*, September 12, 1992, in FBIS: SOV, September 16, 1992.

7. As quoted in Lila Shevtsova, *Yeltsin's Russia: Myths and Reality* (Washington, DC: Carnegie Endowment for International Peace, 2003), 49.

8. Ibid., 74.

9. "General Armii Pavel Grachev: U armii zadacha odna—zashchita otechestva," *Krasnaya zvezda*, September 23, 1993.

10. "Obrashchenie Prezidenta Rossiiskoi Federatsii—Glavnokomanduyuschego Vooruzhennymi Silami Rossii," *Krasnaya zvezda*, September 24, 1993.

11. Robert V. Barylski, *The Soldier in Russian Politics: Duty, Dictatorship, and Democracy under Gorbachev and Yeltsin* (New Brunswick, NJ: Transaction, 1998), 257.

12. Boris Yeltsin, *The Struggle for Russia* (New York: Random House, 1994), 277.

13. Ibid., 278.

14. Ibid.

15. "The Army Is Not a Policeman," *Nezavisimaya gazeta*, October 29, 1993, in FBIS: CEU, November 2, 1993.

16. Barylski, *The Soldier in Russian Politics*, 275.

17. "Moscow's Military Power: Russia's Search for Security in an Age of Transition," in *The Russian Military: Power and Policy*, ed. Steven E. Miller and Dmitri Trenin (Cambridge, MA: MIT Press, 2004), 1–42.

18. "The Sword of Crisis over the Military Budget," *Oriyentir*, no. 2 (February 1999).

19. "Armiya vypolnaet zvoi zadachi, nesmotrya na vse slozhnosti I problemy," *Krasnaya zvezda*, March 17, 1994.

20. "Officers! Russian Federation of Ministry of Defense Information Publishes Data on Armed Forces' Officer Corps," *Rossiiskaya gazeta*, August 26, 1995, in FBIS: CEU August 31, 1995.

21. "Leytanty XXI veka," *Krasnaya zvezda*, July 27, 1994.

22. "The Crisis in the Soviet Union," *Jane's Intelligence Review*, February 1992, 73.

23. Charles Dick, "The Russian Army—Present Plight and Future Prospects," *Jane's Intelligence Review Yearbook, 1994–1995*, 44.

24. Ibid.

25. "Lyudi v pogonakh: kogda Vooruzhennye Sily RF sokrashchayitsya shislennost silogykh struktur rastet," *Krasnaya zvezda*, August 2, 1994.

26. Ibid.

27. Christopher Locksley, "Concept, Algorithm, Indecision: Why Military Reform Has Failed in Russia since 1992," *Journal of Slavic Military Studies* 14, no. 1 (March 2001): 11.

28. "Blitzkrieg of Anatoliy Serdyukov. Part Two." *Voyenno-Promyshlennyy Kuryer Online* (February 19, 2010), in World News Connection (WNC), February 20, 2010.

29. Robert W. Duggleby, "The Disintegration of the Russian Armed Forces," *Journal of Slavic Military Studies* 11, no. 2 (June 9, 1998): 11.

30. Stephen Foye, "Rebuilding the Russian Military: Some Problems and Prospects," *RFE/RL Research Report* (November 6, 1993): 53.

31. Ibid.

32. Rensselaer W. Lee, "The Organized Crime Morass in the Former Soviet Union," *Demokratizatsiya* 2, no. 3 (1994): 396.

33. "Predsezdovskie khlopoty vlastey," *Nezavisimaya gazeta*, November 25, 1992.

34. "Pavel Grachev: 'Armii segodnya trudno, kak I vssmu narodu,'" *Krasnaya zvezda*, February 23, 1993.

35. "Letter to the Editor," *Argumenty i Fakty*, no. 40 (October 1992): 8.

36. "Posle ubiytsva u raketnogo komplesksa," *Izvestiya*, May 14, 1994.

37. Dick, "The Russian Army," 43.

38. Ibid., 44.

39. "The Defense Minister Has It in for Everyone," *Novaya yezhednevaya gazeta*, December 9, 1994, in FBIS: CEU (December 12, 1994).

40. "Minister's Position," *Rossiyskiye vesti*, January 4, 1993, in FBIS: CEU, January 6, 1993.

41. "Grachev Tells the Duma, 'I Am Clean before the Army,'" Moscow Mayak Radio Network, November 18, 1994, in FBIS: CEU, November 21, 1994.

42. Roy Allison, "Russia, Regional Conflict, and the Use of Military Power," in *The Russian Military*, 124.

43. General M. A. Gareyev, "Applying Zhukov's Command Heritage to Military Training and Reform in Today's World," *Journal of Slavic Military Studies* 12, no. 4 (December 1999): 84.

44. As quoted in C. W. Blandy *Chechnya: Two Federal Interventions; An Interim Comparison and Assessment*, no. P23 (Surrey: Conflict Studies Research Centre, Royal Military Academy Sandhurst, January 2000), 13.

45. Olgs Oliker, *Russia's Chechen Wars 1994–2000* (Santa Monica, CA: Rand, 2001), 9–10.

46. Anatol Lieven, *Chechnya: Tombstone of Russian Power* (New Haven: Yale University Press, 1998), 106.

47. Quoted in Barylski, *The Soldier in Russian Politics*, 315. Emphasis in the original.

48. Lieven, *Chechnya: Tombstone of Russian Power*, 105.

49. Vitaly Shlykov, "The War In Chechnya: Implications for Military Reform and Creation of Mobile Forces," Conference Paper, Naval Postgraduate School, Monterey, CA, November 7–8, 1995, 7–8.

50. Cited in Michael J. Orr, *Rodionov and Reform*, no. C92 (Surrey: Conflict Studies Research Centre, Royal Military Academy Sandhurst, January 1997), 4.

51. Ibid., 13.

52. Miller, "Moscow's Military Power," 14.

53. "Army Faces Disruption in Its Food Supply," *Interfax*, August 27, 1996, in FBIS: SOV, August 28, 1996.

54. Timothy L. Thomas, "The Caucasus Conflict and Russian Security: The Russian Armed Forces Confront Chechnya III; The Battle for Grozny, 1–26 January 1995," *Journal of Slavic Military Studies* 10, no. 1 (March 1997): 52.

55. Cited in Michael McFaul, *Russia's Unfinished Revolution: Political Change from Gorbachev to Putin* (Ithaca: Cornell University Press, 2001), 290.

56. Quoted in Barylski, *The Soldier in Russian Politics*, 370.

57. Shevtsova, *Yeltsin's Russia*, 172.

58. Ibid., 416.

59. Cited in David J. Betz, *Civil-Military Relations in Russia and Eastern Europe* (London: Routledge Curzon, 2004), 56.

60. Pavel Felgenhauer, "Russian Military Failure: Ten Years of Failure," Conference Paper, Naval Postgraduate School, Monterey, CA (March 26–27, 1997), 8.

61. Cited in Vitaly V. Shylkov, "Does Russia Need a General Staff?" *European Security* 10, no. 4 (Winter 2001): 64.

62. Makhmut Gareyev, *If War Comes Tomorrow? The Contours of Future Armed Conflict* (London: Frank Cass, 1998), 143.

63. "Federalnyy zakon 'Ob Oboronie,'" http://www.mil.ru/articles/article3863.shtml.

64. Dick, "The Russian Army," 41.

65. Duggleby, "The Disintegration of the Russian Armed Forces," 5.

66. Betz, *Civil Military Relations in Russia and Eastern Europe*, 54.

67. "Yevgeniy Podkolzin: "'I Am Proud of the Airborne Troops,'" *Zavtra*, December 1995, in JPRS, *Russian Military Affairs*, February 7, 1996.

68. Duggleby, "The Disintegration of the Russian Armed Forces," 5.

69. Deborah Yarsike Ball, "The Unreliability of the Russian Officer Corps: Reluctant Domestic Warriors," in *Director's Series on Proliferation*, ed., Kathleen Bailey and M. Elaine Price (Livermore, CA: University of California Radiation Laboratory, Report UCRL-LR-114070-9, 19, November 17, 1995).

70. "Grachev on Effects of Defense Budget Underfunding," ITAR-TASS, July 11, 1994, in FBIS: CEU, July 12, 1994.

71. Cited in Betz, *Civil-Military Relations in Russia and Eastern Europe*, 56.

72. Michael J. Orr, *Manpower Problems in the Russian Armed Forces*, no. D62 (Sur-

rey: Conflict Studies Research Centre, Royal Military Academy Sandhurst, February 2002), 2.

73. Lester W. Grau and Timothy L. Thomas, "The Russian Military and the December 1995 Duma Elections: Dissatisfaction Continues to Grow in the Armed Forces," *Journal of Slavic Military Studies* 9, no. 3 (September 1996): 514.

74. Christopher C. Locksley, "Concept, Algorithm, Indecision: Why Military Reform Has Failed in Russia since 1992," *Journal of Slavic Military Studies* 14, no. 1 (March 2001): 10.

75. Michael J. Orr, *The Russian Armed Forces as a Factor in Regional Stability* (Surrey: Conflict Studies Research Centre, Royal Military Academy Sandhurst, June 1998), 8.

76. Cited in Pavel Baev, *The Russian Army in a Time of Troubles* (London: Sage, 1996), 77.

77. Duggleby, "The Disintegration of the Russian Armed Forces," 8.

78. *Rabochaya tribuna*, March 23, 1996, in FBIS: SOV, April 3, 1996.

79. Duggleby, "The Disintegration of the Russian Armed Forces," 7.

80. Dick, "The Russian Army," 43.

81. "Conversation without Middlemen," Moscow Television, September 14, 1995, in FBIS: CEU, September 18, 1995.

82. "Chinovnichya volokita tormozit povyshenie denezhnogo soderzhaniya voenno-sluzhashchikh," *Krasnaya zvezda*, September 12, 1995.

83. Dick, "The Russian Army," 43.

84. Betz, *Civil-Military Relations in Russia and Eastern Europe*, 52.

85. Graham Turbiville, "Mafia in Uniform: The 'Criminalization' of the Russian Armed Forces," US Army Foreign Military Studies Office, July 1995, 34.

86. Aleksandr Golts, *Armii Rossii: 11 Poteriannykh let* (Moscow: Zakharov, 2004), 172.

87. "Grim Picture of Russian Missile Forces," *RFE/RL Daily Report*, November 3, 1994.

88. "Russia's Red Army Has Lost Its Roar," *Christian Science Monitor,* June 2, 1997.

89. "Russia: Damage and Casualty Effect of Advanced Weapons," *Technika i vooru-zhenniye*, February 2, 1998, in FBIS: CEU, March 7, 1998.

90. Conversation with Middlemen, Moscow TV, September 14, 1993.

91. Cited in Orr, *Rodionov and Reform*, 1.

92. Ibid., 3.

93. Ibid, 4.

94. Golts, *Armii Rossii*, 34.

95. Gustaf Bruinus, "Organizational Evolution within the Russian Federation Armed Forces," in *Russian Military Reform and Russia's New Security Environment*, ed., Yuri Federov and Bertil Nygren (Stockholm: National Defense College, 2003), 70.

96. Ibid.

97. Golts, *Armii Rossii*, 41.

98. "Nada zdelat vse vozmozhnoe, shtoby armiya bystree vyshla iz rizisa," *Krasnaya zvezda*, October 2, 1996.

99. John Moran, *From Garrison State to National-State* (Westport: Praeger, 2002), 94.

100. "Rodionov Thinks Professional Army by 2005 Impossible," *Nezavisimoye voyen-noe obozreniye*, in FBIS: SOV, April 12, 1997.

101. Moran, *From Garrison State to Nation-State*, 94.

102. Shevtsova, *Yeltsin's Russia*, 198.

103. Ibid.

104. Boris Yeltsin, *Midnight Diaries* (New York: Public Affairs, 2000), 4.

105. "Vernem lyudam v pogonakh dostoinstvo I uvazhenie," *Krasnaya zvezda*, August 7, 1996.

106. Michael J. Orr, *The Russian Armed Forces as a Factor in Regional Stability* (Surrey: Conflict Studies Research Centre, Royal Military Academy Sandhurst, June 1998), 5.

107. As quoted in Betz, *Civil-Military Relations in Russia and Eastern Europe*, 57.

108. Barylski, *The Soldier in Russian Politics*, 478.

109. *Voyennaya reforma v Rossii: materially konfrentsii provedennoi v ISK RAN v 9 Dekabra 1996g* (Moscow: Rossiiskaya Nauk, 1997), 50.

110. As cited in Brian D. Taylor, *Politics and the Russian Army: Civil-Military Relations 1689–2000* (New York: Cambridge University Press, 2003), 310.

111. Golts, *Armii Rosii*, 155.

112. Moran, *From Garrison State to Nation-State*, 39.

113. Michael Orr, "Reform and the Russian Ground Forces, 1992–2000," in *Russian Military Reform, 1992–2002*, ed. C. Adlis and Roger N. McDermott (Portland: Frank Class, 2003), 131.

114. Golts, *Armii Rosii*, 44.

115. Brunius, "Organizational Evolution within the Russian Federation Armed Forces, 73.

116. Shevtsova, *Yeltsin's Russia*, 247.

117. Ibid., 252.

118. Victor Esin, "The Military Reform in the Russian Federation: Problems, Decisions and Prospects," in *Russian Military Reform and Russia's New Security Environments*, ed. Yu. Fedorov and B. Nygren (Stockholm: Swedish National Defence College, 2003), 107.

119. Taylor, *Politics and the Russian Army*, 308.

120. "Russian Armed Force Equipment at 100%," ITAR-TASS, September 28, 1999.

121. Taylor, *Politics and the Russian Army*, 308.

122. Cameron Ross, *Russian Politics under Putin* (Manchester: Manchester University Press, 2004), 260.

123. Cited in Paul Murphy, *The Wolves of Islam* (Washington, DC: Brassey's, 2004), 91.

124. Ibid., 63.

125. Aleksandr Golts, "Putin and the Chechen War: Together Forever," *Moscow Times*, February 11, 2004.

126. M. A. Smith, "The Second Chechen War: The All-Russian Context," in *The Second Chechen War*, ed. Anne Aldis (Camberley: Conflict Studies Research Centre, 2000), 8. Emphasis in the original.

127. Ibid.

128. C. W. Blandy, Moscow's Failure to Comprehend, in *The Second Chechen War*, ed. Anne Aldis (Camberley: Conflict Studies Research Centre, 2000), 14. Emphasis in the original.

129. Taylor, *Politics and the Russian Army*, 314. In 1989, the author was part of a U.S. Navy ship visit to Vladivostok. It soon became clear that nothing was happening. It was

also clear to those who spent time at sea that the ships we visited had not been to sea for a long time and that the equipment and weapons were outdated.

CHAPTER 9. From Vladimir Putin through Dmitry Medvedev

1. "Survey of Military Reform in the Russian Federation," *Yadernyy kontrol*, April 19, 2002, in World News Connection (WNC), September 6, 2002.

2. Frank Umbach, *Future Military Reform: Russia's Nuclear and Conventional Forces*, no. D65 (Surrey: Conflict Studies Research Centre, Royal Military Academy Sandhurst, August 2002), 12.

3. Ibid.

4. S. J. Main, "Russia's Military Doctrine," Conflict Studies Research Centre Occasional, Brief no. 77 (April 2000), 5.

5. "Hope Glimmers for Reform," *Moscow Times*, March 29, 2007, in *Johnson's Russian List, Military News*, March 29, 2001.

6. "Development Strategy of the Armed Forces Defined," *Military News Bulletin*, no. 8, August 2000.

7. Steven J. Main, *The Strategic Rocket Forces, 1991–2002*, no. D66 (Surrey: Conflict Studies Research Centre, Royal Military Academy Sandhurst, July 9, 2003), 26.

8. Ibid.

9. Aleksandr Golts, *Armii Rossii: 11 Poteriannykh let* (Moscow: Zakharov, 2004), 80.

10. "Vystuplenie Prezidenta Rossiyskoi Federatsii V. V. Putina na sborakh rukovodyashchego sostava Vorruzhennykh Sil Rossiyskoy Federatsii, 20 noyarbrya 2000 goda," http://president.kremlin.ru/events/102.html.

11. "Russia: Survey of Military Reform in the Russian Federation," *Yadernyy kontrol*, April 19, 2002, in WNC, September 6, 2002.

12. "Decisions on the Reform of the State's Military Organization Have Been Adopted," *Military News Bulletin*, no. 11, November 2000.

13. Steven J. Main, *The Strategic Rocket Forces, 1991–2002*, no. D66 (Surrey: Conflict Studies Research Centre, Royal Military Academy Sandhurst, July 9, 2003), 29.

14. "Russia: Analysts Assess Kremlin Reshuffle," in *Johnson's Russia List*, March 29, 2001.

15. Ibid.

16. Ibid.

17. Patrick E. Tyler, "High Level Shake-up, Putin Replaces Russia's Defense, Interior and Nuclear Energy Chiefs," *New York Times*, March 29, 2001.

18. Vladimir Mukhin, "Reshuffle Brings Putin People to the Top," *Russia Journal*, May 4, 2001.

19. See Roger McDermott, *The Restoration of Russia's Ground Forces High Command: Prepared for Future War?*, no. A103 (Surrey: Conflict Studies Research Centre, Royal Military Academy Sandhurst, March 2002), 2.

20. "Assessing Putin's Meeting with the Military Command," *Monitor*, October 29, 2001.

21. "Survey of Military Reform in the Russian Federation, *Yadernyy kontrol*, April 19, 2002, in WNC, September 2002.

22. "More than Half of Russians Unfit to Serve in the Army," *Agence France-Press*, November 29, 2001.

23. "What Is the Price of a Professional," *Itogi*, January 22, 2002, in *Johnson's Russia List*, January 28, 2002.

24. "Problems, Including Low Pay, in Converting the 76th Airborne Division to Unit of Contract Soldiers," *Rossiiskaya gazeta*, August 16, 2002, in *Johnson's Russia List*, August 21, 2002.

25. Roger McDermott, "Putin's Military Priorities: The Modernization of the Armed Forces," in *Russian Military Reform and Russia's New Security Environment*, ed. Yuri Fedorov and Bertil Nygren (Stockholm: Swedish National Defense College, 2003), 270.

26. "Russia's Army Still Mired in Conscript Crisis," *Russia Journal*, April 24–30, 2000, in *Johnson's Russia List*, April 27, 2000.

27. "Scandal Brews over Military Reform, Pskov Contract Service Experiment," *Moskovskiye novosti*, October 8, 2002, in WNC, October 10, 2002.

28. "Kvashnin Attacks Airborne Forces," *RFE/RL Daily Report*, December 11, 2002.

29. Rod Thornton, "Military Organizations and Change: The Professionalization of the 76th," *Journal of Slavic Military Studies* 17, no. 3 (July–September 2004): 464.

30. "The Military Reform Card," *Moscow Times*, May 22, 2003.

31. "Military Reforms: The First Steps," *Mir novosti*, July 18, 2002, in *Johnson's Russia List*, July 18, 2002.

32. "Russian Defense Minister in Address Government on Military Reform," *ITAR-TASS*, November 20, 2002, in WNC, November 21, 2003.

33. "MOD Ivanov Visits 76th Airborne Division, Satisfied with Experiment," *Trud*, December 4, 2003, in WNC, December 31, 2003.

34. "Federalnyi zakon 'Ob obranne,'" April 24, 2004, http://www/mil.ru/articles/articles3863,shtml.

35. "Defense Minister Says General Staff to Focus on Future Wars," *RFE/RL Daily Report*, July 20, 2004.

36. "Kvashnin Won't be Missed," *Moscow Times*, July 20, 2004, in *Johnson's Russia List*, July 21, 2004.

37. "General Staff Relieved of Superfluous Functions while Defense Minister Is Handed All the Reins of Control over the Army," *Rossiiskaya gazeta*, June 15, 2004, in WNC, June 17, 2004.

38. "First Deputy Defense Minister Aleksandr Belousov: 'In Order to Make It Worth People's Will to Serve, We Should Not Be Afraid to Spend,'" *Izvestiya*, September 22, 2005, in WNC, September 23, 2005.

39. "Soldiers' Pay Seen as 'Main Stumbling Block' to Contract Manning of Russian Army," *Rossiiskaya gazeta*, August 25, 2004, in WNC, August 31, 2004.

40. "Chief of Russia's General Staff Speaks about Current Challenges," *Krasnaya zvezda*, November 6, 2004, in *Johnson's Russia List*, November 13, 2004.

41. "First Deputy Defense Minister Aleksandr Belousov: 'In Order to Make It Worth People's While to Serve, We Should Not Be Afraid to Spend," *Izvestiya*, September 22, 2005, in WNC, September 23, 2005.

42. "Russia's TV Bid to Recruit Troops," BBC, January 9, 2005, in *Johnson's Russia List*, January 11, 2005.

43. "Russian Airborne Division Misses Contract Manning Deadline," *Agenstvo voyennykh novostey*, January 13, 2005, in WNC, January 14, 2006.

44. "All Volunteer Force Program Funding Expect to Increase by 15%," *Agenstvo voyennykh novostey*, September 9, 2005, in WNC, September 10, 2005.

45. "Ivanov's Budget," *Rossiyskiye vesti*, September 8, 2005, in WNC, September 12, 2005.

46. "Russian General Says 2006 Budget Not to Improve Military Combat Potential," *Agentstvo Voyennykh novostey*, December 7, 2005, in WNC, December 8, 2005.

47. Vladimir Mukyhin, "Reshuffle Brings Putin People to the Top," *Russian Journal*, May 4, 2001.

48. "Duma Defense Committee Head Says Military Reform Not Yet under Way," *RFE/RL Daily Report*, March 22, 2002.

49. "State Oks $2.5 Billion Arms Budget," *Moscow Times*, January 18, 2002, in *Johnson's Russia List*, January 18, 2002.

50. "Klebanov Stresses Need for 'Modernization' of Old Army Hardware," *Rossiiskaya gazeta*, August 8, 2002, in WNC, August 9, 2002.

51. "Russia's Ground Troops Not to Get New Weapons Soon," *ITAR-TASS*, December 26, 2001, in WNC, December 21, 2001.

52. "Russia's Military Aviation Said in Crisis," *Interfax*, September 18, 2002, in *Johnson's Russia List*, September 19, 2002.

53. "Russia Military Reform, A Priority on Paper, Continues to Confound Kremlin," *RFE/RL Daily Report*, February 11, 2002, in *Johnson's Russia List*, February 11, 2002.

54. "Russian Air Force to Receive 20 Modernized Planes in 2003," *ITAR-TASS*, August 27, 2003.

55. "Plan to Double Military Procurement in 2004 Not to Be Fulfilled," *Trud*, August 19, 2003, in WNC, March 27, 2003.

56. "Russian Air Force Command Worried by Aging of Aircraft," *ITAR-TASS*, March 26, 2003, in WNC, March 27, 2003.

57. "80% of Russia's Defense Industry Is Obsolete," *Rosblat*, August 18, 2003, in *Johnson's Russia List*, August 20, 2003.

58. "Russia's Army to Acquire 14 T-90S Tanks in 2004," *ITAR-TASS*, July 6, 2004, in WNC, July 10, 2004.

59. "Russia without an Army," *Vedomosti*, November 18, 2004, in *Johnson's Russia List*, November 18, 2004.

60. "Defense Spending Is Growing, Armed Deliveries Are Sliding," *Nezavismoye voyennoye obozreniye*, August 31, 2005, in WNC, September 2, 2005.

61. "Russian Army to Get New Strike Helicopter from 2006," *ITAR-TASS*, October 11, 2004.

62. "Russian General Says 2006 Budget Not to Improve Military Combat Potential," *Agentstvo voyennykh novostey*, December 7, 2005, in WNC, December 8, 2005.

63. "We Need at Least One Million Military Personnel," *Izvestiya*, February 22, 2005, in *Johnson's Russia List*, February 22, 2005.

64. "Is the Army Unhappy with Putin?" *RFE/RL Daily Report*, August 17, 2001.

65. "Army Pay, Same Old Story," *Moscow Times*, March 21, 2002, in *Johnson's Russia List*, March 22, 2002.

66. "Majority of Russian Army Officers Live in Poverty: Official," *Agence France Press*, February 27, 2003, in *Johnson's Russia List*, May 30, 2002.

67. “Roundtable Pushes Legislative Changes to Improve Service in Russian Army,” *Trud*, June 24, 2003, in WNC, June 28, 2003.

68. “Russian General: Housing Situation for Servicemen in Moscow ‘Catastrophic,’ ” *ITAR-TASS*, February 14, 2002, in WNC, February 15, 2002.

69. “House Issue Remains among ‘Most Serious’ Problems for Military,” *ITAR-TASS*, May 31, 2002, in WNC, June 3, 2002.

70. “Russian Army Suffers from Mass Exodus of Officers,” *RFE/RL Daily Report*, February 14, 2002.

71. “Declining Financial Well-Being, Training of Military Officers Alleged,” *Nezavisimoye voyennoye obozreniye*, December 24, 2004, in WNC, January 1, 2005.

72. “No One to Defend the Defenders of the Fatherland: Angry Men in Uniform Have Taken to the Streets,” March 1, 2005, in WNC, March 2, 2005.

73. “Russian Defense Minister Welcomes New Housing Program for the Military,” *ITAR-TASS*, August 8, 2002.

74. “Establishment of House Mortgage System in Russian Armed Forces Enters Final Stage,” *Agenstvo voyennykh novostey*, April 21, 2005, in WNC, April 22, 2005.

75. “Government Plans for Provision of Homeless Soldiers with Housing Not Working,” *Nezavisimoye voyennoye obozreniye*, February 14, 2005, in WNC, February 15, 2005.

76. “Government Plans for Provision of Homeless Soldiers with Housing Not Working.”

77. Michael Orr, “Reform and the Russian Ground Forces, 1992–2002,” in *Russian Military Reform, 1992–2002*, ed. Anne C. Aldis and Roger N. McDermott (London: Frank Cass, 2003), 137.

78. “Former Defense Minister CEO Gets Five Years,” *The Monitor*, July 25, 2003.

79. “Illegal Caviar Seized on Military Plane: Armed Forces Are Involved in Poaching Rackets,” *Izvestiya*, December 26, 2003, in WNC, December 31, 2004.

80. “More than 2,000 Officers Convicted in Russia in 2005,” *Interfax*, February 1, 2006, in WNC, February 2, 2006.

81. “Poll Reveals 11 Percent of Russian Soldiers with Alcoholism,” *Interfax*, December 6, 2001, in WNC, December 7, 2001.

82. Paul Jenkins, “Red Army Blues,” *World Today*, September 5, 2001.

83. “As Desertions Continue, Russia’s Military Drafts Men with Mental Illnesses and Criminal Records,” *Associated Press*, October 6, 2002.

84. Aleksandr Golts, “The Social and Political Condition of the Military,” in *The Russian Military: Power and Policy*, ed. Steven E. Miller and Dmitri Trenin (Cambridge, MA: MIT Press, 2004), 76.

85. “Russian Chief Prosecutor on Bullying, Draft Problems, Bribes, Specific Cases,” *Rossiiskaya gazeta*, June 10, 2003, in WNC, June 13, 2003.

86. “Moscow Raises Spending for Defense, Police, Secret Services,” in *Johnson’s Russia List*, August 24, 2004.

87. “Military-Fiscal Secrets Are Multiplying: The Number of Classified Items in the 2007 Ministry of Defense Budget Has Increased Substantially,” *Nezavisimoye voyennoe obozreniye*, October 27, 2006, in WNC, October 28, 2006.

88. “Defense Ministry Officials Are Firmly Ensconced on the Boards of Directors of

Various Companies," *Nezavisimoye voyennoe obozreniye*, March 9, 2007, in WNC, March 12, 2008.

89. E-mail of April 4, 2008, to the author from a colleague in Moscow who requested anonymity.

90. The same source noted that in 2007, "224 officers were criminally prosecuted, while hundreds of officers were dismissed from their posts and faced administrative proceedings. Of them, 16 generals and 180 colonels were criminally prosecuted. A total of 565 officials were convicted last year." "Russian Official Says 30 Percent of Military Budget Lost through Corruption," *Agenstvo voennykh novostei*, July 2, 2008, in WNC, July 3, 2008.

91. "Defense Ministry Will Shed Excess Equipment," *RFE/RL Daily Report*, April 3, 2008.

92. E-mail of June 9, 2008, to the author from a colleague in Moscow who requested anonymity.

93. "Bloggers Ridicule New Defense Minister Serdyukov," *Russia—OSC Report*, February 16, 2007, in WNC, February 17, 2007.

94. "Russian Radio Pundit Sees Sham Civilian Control of Ground Forces," *Ekho Moskvy*, February 24, 2007, in *Johnson's Russia List*, March 1, 2007.

95. "Russia's Generals Don't Believe that the New Defense Minister Can Help the Military," *Versiy*, no. 8, February 26, 2007, in *Johnson's Russia List*, March 1, 2007.

96. "Nakhimov Naval College Chief Dismissed," *Agentstvo voyennykh novostey*, March 28, 2007, in WNC, March 29, 2007.

97. "Serdyukov Streamlines Defense: Financier and Inspecting General Will Be Main Levers at Current Stage of Russian Army Reform," *Nezavisimaya gazeta*, April 15, 2007.

98. "Targeted Financing: Anatoly Serdyukov Tightens up Financial Monitoring of the Military and Plans to Build Accessible Officer Housing," *Rossiiskaya gazeta*, June 8, 2007, in WNC, June 11, 2007.

99. "In Thrall to a Myth: The Russia Army; Revival or Degradation," *Vremya novostei*, February 22, 2008; "Eight Years of Falling behind and Weakening," *Nezavisimaya gazeta*, February 13, 2008, in *Johnson's Russia List*, February 14, 2008.

100. "Frustrated Baluyevskii Offers His Resignation," *Moscow Times*, March 25, 2008, in *Johnson's Russia List*, March 26, 2008; "Russia Resignation Signals Trouble within Defense Ministry," *Radio Free Europe / Radio Liberty*, March 27, 2008; "Russian Military Chief Quits after Row with Defense Minister," *Times of India*, March 26, 2008.

101. "Military Reform: Professionalism is Highly Valued, but Expensive," *Slovo*, June 11, 2008, in WNC, November 11, 2008.

102. "The Price of Victory: Military Experts on the Mistakes of the Campaign in South Ossetia," *Trud*, August 18, 2008, in WNC, August 19, 2008; Viktor Barents, "Army Sent to Fight in Old Suit of Armor," *Komsomolskaya pravda*, August 26, 2008; "Interview with Anatoliy Nogovitsyn," *Rossiyskaya gazeta*, September 9, 2008.

103. "The Army Needs to Be Protected from Dilettantes," *Utro*, October 22, 2008, in WNC, July 24, 2008; "About 300,000 Officers Will Be Discharged in the Next Few Years," *Interfax*, March 9, 2010. For the increase to 220,00, see, "Doubling the Contract: The Russian Army Will Become 70% Professional Force within Five Years," *Rossyskaya gazeta*, July 8, 2011, in WNC, July 7, 2011; and "Army: Repromised Promises; Russia 'Will Move Calmly in Direction of Professional Army,'" *Nezavisimaya gazeta*, November 28, 2011, in WNC, November 29, 2011.

104. "Russia to Have 1 Million Troops by 2016," *ITAR-TASS*, April 3, 3008; "Russia May Introduce Civilian Posts in Army," *Agenstvo voynnykh novostey*, March 31, 2008, in WNC, April 1, 2008.

105. "No One Needs War, but Russia Is Ready," *Utro*, November 20, 2008, in WNC, November 21, 2008.

106. "Russia to Close 22 Military Hospitals, Cut over 10,000 Medical Officers Post," *Interfax*, May 27, 2009.

107. "Military Reform: 2009–2013," *Nezavisimoye voyennoye obozreniye*, January 1, 2009, in WNC, January 2, 2009; "Defense Ministry to Close Officer Jobs in Military Media," *Interfax-AVN Online*, December 3, 2008, in WNC, December 4, 2008.

108. "Within the Framework of Reform in the RF Armed Forces," *Voyenno-promyshlennyy kurier*, October 29, 2008, in WNC, November 20, 2008.

109. "The Ownerless Nuclear Football," *Nezavisimaya gazeta*, April 4, 2009, in WNC, April 3, 2008; "The President Is Not Being Briefed on the Real Consequences of Reform," *Segodnya.ru*, April 4, 2009, in WNC, April 5, 2009.

110. "Russian Military Battles Overweight Soldiers," *Times*, April 11, 2008; "Russian Defense Ministry Introduces Stricter Fitness Requirements," *Agentstvo voyennykh novostey*, June 24, 2008, in WNC, June 25, 2008.

111. "Professionals Are Necessary for the Army," *Armeyski sbornik*, September 2, 2008, in WNC, September 3, 2008.

112. "NCO No Comrade for the Cadet: Training of the Professional Junior Commanders Has Ground to a Halt," *Gazeta*, March 27, 2009, in WNC, March 28, 2009.

113. "Professionals Are Necessary for the Army."

114. "The Sergeants Road Lead to Ryazan," *Krasnaya zvezda*, September 9, 2009, in WNC, September 10, 2009; "The Russian NCO Will Be Like the American," *Rossiyskiye vesti*, December 24, 2009, in WNC, December 30, 2009.

115. "Not a 'Professional Army' but an Army of Lumpen Individuals: Why Manning of the Armed Forces with Contract Personnel Is Failing," *Nezavisimoye voyennoye obozreniye*, October 27, 2009, in WNC, October 28, 2009.

116. "Modular Army: The New Commander in Chief of Ground Troops Has Acknowledged Failures of the Military Reform," *Vremya novostey online*, March 1, 2010, in WNC, March 2, 2010.

117. "Draft Remission: Defense Ministry Freezes Contract Service until Election of Supreme Commander, Draft-age Youths Will Answer for This," *Russkiy Newsweek*, March 25, 2010, in WNC, March 28, 2010.

118. "Professional Army Spending Slashed by Nearly 90%," *Interfax*, March 6, 2010, in WNC, March 7, 2010.

119. "General Staff Proposes to Increase Term of Service: Task of Building a Professional Army Has Not Been Accomplished," *Voyennoye obozreniye online*, March 6, 2010, in WNC, March 6, 2010.

120. "Draft Remission: Defense Ministry Freezes Contract Service until Election of Supreme Commander."

121. "Russian CGS quizzed about Military Reform," *Interfax-AVN*, June 7, 2009, in WNC, June 8, 2009.

122. "A More Intensive Training Program Is Being Introduced in the RF General Staff Military Academy," *Interfax*, September 1, 2011.

123. "General Reductions," *Rossiyskaya gazeta*, October 18, 2008, in WNC, October 19, 2008.

124. Ibid.

125. Victor Ozerov, "Formation of the New Aspect of the Armed Forces Is a Statewide Objective," *Regions.ru*, April 3, 2009, in WNC, April 4, 2009.

126. Personal communication from a source in Moscow who asked to remain unidentified.

127. "A Criminal Record in the Army," *Vremya novostey*, July 8, 2009.

128. "Russian Defense Minister Explains Plans for Priests in the Army," *Interfax*, July 21, 2009, in WNC, July 22, 2009.

129. "Russian Army Changing Its Image," *Gazeta*, November 19, 2008, in WNC, November 11, 2008.

130. "Armed Forces and Society: The Training and Look of the Armed Forces Will Change," *Kraznaya zvezda*, June 24, 2008.

131. "Kurdin's Dismissal Good for Russia's Defense Capability," *Interfax*, September 27, 2011; "Defense Spending Threatens Social Programs, Kurdin Says," *Moscow Times*, October 11, 2011.

132. "Kremlin Power Struggle Flares with Minister Ousting," *Novosti*, November 6, 2012; "Putins Katastrophen-Manager soll Armee reformne," *Die Welt*, November 6, 2012.

CHAPTER 10. **The Search for Shared Responsibility**

1. With the exception of change (gays and women), U.S. civil-military has not had to deal with other facets of military culture in recent years.

2. Dale R. Herspring, *The Pentagon and the Presidency: Civil-Military Relations from FDR to George W. Bush* (Lawrence: University Press of Kansas, 2005).

3. As this book is written, Panetta has not been in office long enough to say anything authoritative about his leadership style or how he is relating to President Obama.

4. It is impossible to verify this rumor, although this writer saw it first hand in other segments of the USG. I can also attest to hearing complaints from individuals who sat on promotion boards to this effect.

5. "We Have Fallen Short of Our Goal," *Spiegel*, December 27, 2011, http://www.spiegel.de/international/germany/0,1518,druck-805900,00.

Index